100 YEARS AT WARRINGTON

York County, Pennsylvania Quakers
Marriages, Removals, Births and Deaths

NEWBERRY, WARRINGTON, MENALLEN,
HUNTINGTON AND YORK MEETINGS

Compiled by
Margaret B. Walmer

HERITAGE BOOKS
2007

HERITAGE BOOKS
AN IMPRINT OF HERITAGE BOOKS, INC.

Books, CDs, and more—Worldwide

For our listing of thousands of titles see our website
at
www.HeritageBooks.com

Published 2007 by
HERITAGE BOOKS, INC.
Publishing Division
65 East Main Street
Westminster, Maryland 21157-5026

Copyright © 1989 Margaret B. Walmer

Other books by the author:
*Menallen [Pennsylvania] Minutes, Marriages and Miscellany:
Quaker Records, 1780-1890*

All rights reserved. No part of this book may be reproduced or transmitted in any form or by any means, electronic or mechanical, including photocopying, recording or by any information storage and retrieval system without written permission from the author, except for the inclusion of brief quotations in a review.

International Standard Book Number: 978-1-55613-269-8

TABLE OF CONTENTS

Introduction	v
Chronology	vii
Maps	viii
Marriages	1
Removals	163
Appendix A: Births and Deaths	233
Appendix B: Locations of other meetings	287
Appendix C: Sample Certificates	291
Index	295

INTRODUCTION

The Meetings

In 1738, York County, Pennsylvania, was still a part of Lancaster County. At that time, Sadsbury Monthly Meeting of the Religious Society of Friends (Quakers), in the eastern end of Lancaster County, authorized an 'indulged meeting' at Newberrytown across the Susquehanna for some of its members who had moved over the river and were too remotely settled for regular attendance. In the beginning, meeting for worship was held in the homes of individual Friends. The first marriage west of the Susquehanna took place at the home of John Day on May 29, 1740, when Theodate Seal became the wife of Robert Hodgin. This marriage was entered in the records of Sadsbury Monthly Meeting.

In 1745 the Friends at Newberry built a log meeting house and in 1792 replaced it with a stone building beside the little burial ground in Newberrytown. This was used until 1811 when they built a new stone building two miles west of Newberrytown and the older meeting house was sold. Today, it is occupied as a private residence, and only the graveyard remains in Newberrytown. The new building, often referred to as 'Redlands', is still owned by Friends and is used for worship one day a year. Newberry never became a monthly meeting, but continued as a preparative meeting until it was laid down in 1862.

The earliest Quakers in Warrington Township settled there about 1735 and for a few years worshipped with others at Newberry. In 1745 a preparative meeting was formed at Warrington and a log meeting house was built. It was replaced by a stone building in 1769, enlarged in 1782 to double the original size and it is this building which stands today and in recent years has again become an active Monthly Meeting, after having been laid down, along with Newberry, in 1862 when the property was placed under the care of Menallen Monthly Meeting.

Although in its last years there were very few attenders at meeting, in 1779 the congregation had grown so large and had so much business to attend to at Monthly Meeting, they decided to divide Warrington. With the permission of the Quarterly Meeting, the new Menallen Monthly Meeting was formed from Warrington with meetings to alternate with Huntington Preparative Meeting. The first Meeting was held at Menallen 10th mo 7th day 1780.

It appears from deed records that Friends in Huntington Township obtained land for a meeting house as early as 1766, although they did not obtain a Patent Deed from the Commonwealth until 1799. Huntington became a preparative meeting to Menallen Monthly Meeting in 1780. Today the stone meeting house is still maintained in good repair, used once a year for Meeting for Worship, and the burial ground is regularly cared for and overseen by the Trustees of Menallen.

Menallen has been an active Monthly Meeting from the time it was formed until the present. The first meeting house is thought to have been a log structure in what is now Butler Township, Adams County. In 1838 this log building was dismantled and moved to a location directly in front of the present brick structure, built in 1884, in Menallen Township, Adams County. When the other meetings were 'laid down' they were all placed under the care of the Trustees of Menallen Monthly Meeting and continue so to this day, with the exception of Warrington which has been reactivated, and York which was never under the care of Menallen.

York Monthly Meeting was formed from Warrington in 1786. The meeting house is located on Philadelphia St. in the city of York and regular meetings for worship were held there until the property was placed in the care of Trustees in 1854.

The Records

The Quakers had strong religious beliefs, but one of these was that they should have no 'hireling priest'. They also felt it was wrong to take an oath or to take their problems to a court of law, preferring to work out disagreements at Monthly Meeting. For this reason they felt it was important to keep careful records, especially of marriages and transfer of membership. Marriages were performed without a preacher and every guest signed the certificate as witness. The custom, but not necessarily the rule, was for the parents and the immediate family to sign in the right hand column, directly under the signatures of the bridal couple, a fact which is often very helpful to the patient genealogist.

This book consists of abstracts of the original marriage records of Warrington Monthly Meeting from 1748 through 1854, as well as abstracts of the Certificates of Removal issued by or received by York Monthly Meeting for the years 1787-1857. All of the names except for the witnesses are included in the index. The brides are indexed under their maiden name and their married name. A consolidated list of Births and Deaths for Warrington and Menallen is found in Appendix A. These names are not included in the index.

I acknowledge, with gratitude, the help of Ann Higgins for the illustrations, Andrew Walmer for the maps, and Kathy Marinucci for proofreading.

Margaret B. Walmer

CHRONOLOGY

Date	Meeting	Parent Meeting
1739	Newberry Prep. Meeting formed	by Sadsbury MM
1745	Warrington Prep. Meeting formed	by Sadsbury MM
1747	Warrington Monthly Meeting formed	by Concord QM
1748	Menallen Prep. Meeting formed	by Sadsbury MM
1750	Huntington Meeting formed	by Sadsbury MM
1754	York Meeting formed	by Warrington MM
1780	Menallen Monthly Meeting formed still active	by Warrington MM
1786	York Monthly Meeting formed	by Warrington MM
1854	York Monthly Meeting laid down property in care of trustees	by Baltimore YM
1862	Warrington MM laid down membership and care transferred to Menallen Trustees	by Baltimore YM
1862	Newberry Prep. Meeting laid down membership and care transferred to Menallen Trustees.	by Baltimore YM

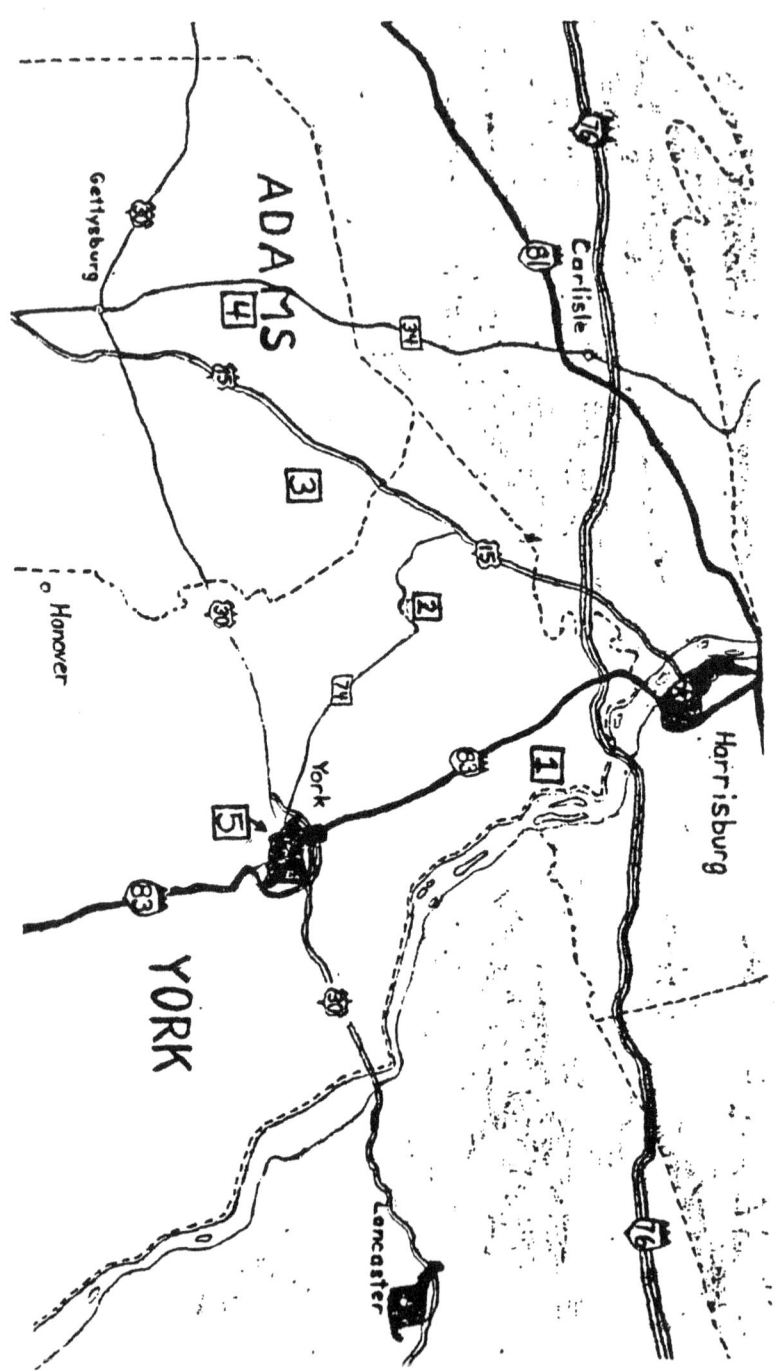

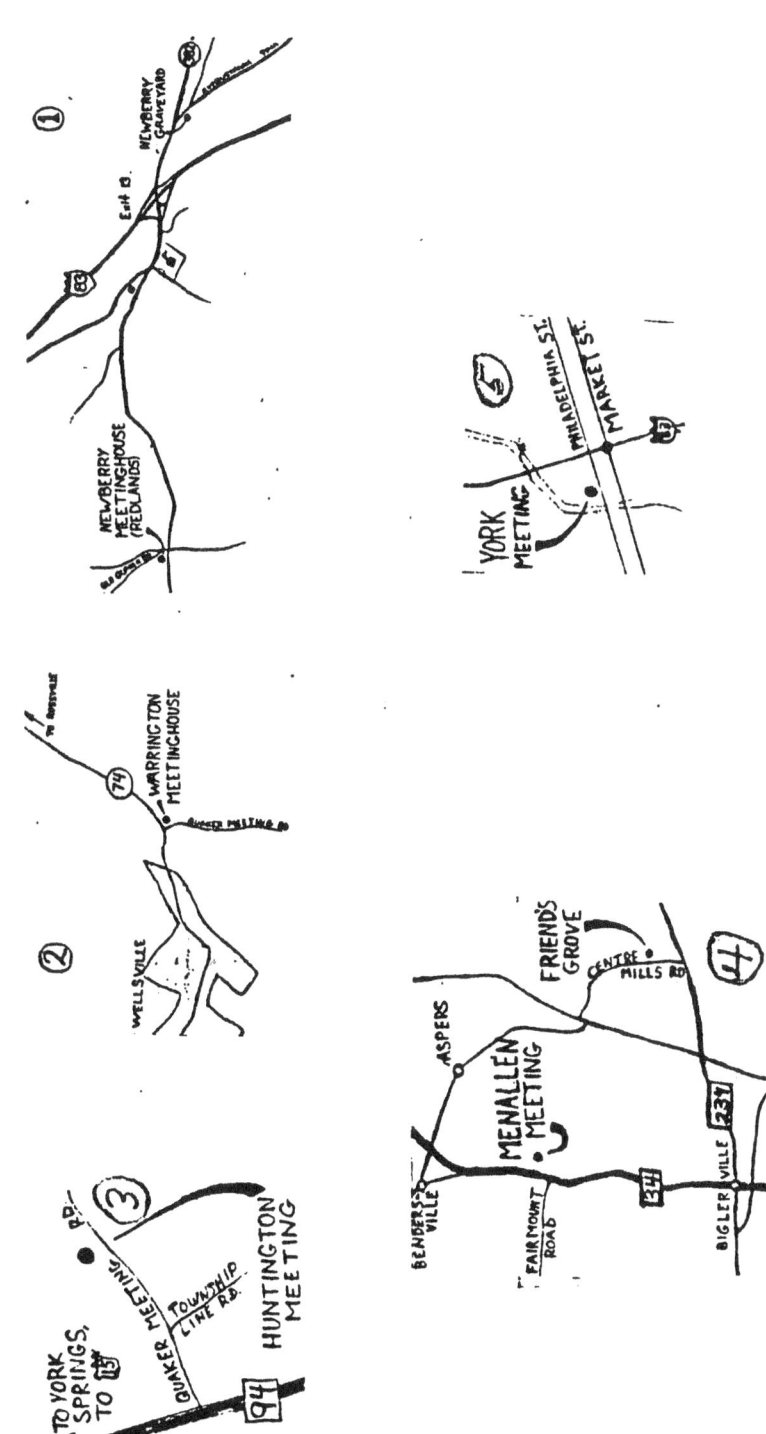

MARRIAGES

#1 1st 10th mo 1748   WILLIAM BEALS-MARY MULLINEUX
William Beals son of Jacob Beal of huntington in the County of Lanchter and province of pencilvania and Mary Mullineux widow of Edward Mullineux, deceased of Newbery in the County and province aforesd,...at newbery the First day of the tenth month in the year of our Lord one thousand seven hundred and fourty Eight

Alexander Underwood	Sarah Underwood	William Beals
William Underwood	Rachel Beals	Mary Beals
Peter Stout	Margaret Stout	Jacob Beals
Nathan Hufsey	Theodate Hodgen	Patrick Carson
James Robenet	Ann Day	Margaret Carson
Benjamin Underwood	Susanna Heald	John Beals
Francis Fincher	Archie Mackey	Jane Carson
Robert Vale	John Garretson	Margret Carson
Joseph Garretson	John Day	Caleb Beals
Mathew Dill juner	Richard Cox	
Thomas Dill	Joseph Bennet	
James Willoby	Archibald McAlister	
Robert Mills juner		

#2 26th 2nd mo 1749   NATHEN HUSSEY-SUSANA HEALD
Nathen Hussey of Newbery in the county of Lanchester and province of pencilvania yeoman and Susana the daughter of Thomas Heald of the same place...twenty sixth day of the second month in the year of our Lord one thousand seven hundred and fortynine...at a public meeting houfe in newbery aforesd
                                                                Nathen Hufsey
                                                                Susana Hufsey

WARRINGTON MONTHLY MEETING

Rebecah Bennet	Alexander Underwood	Thomas Heald
Sarah Underwood	Petter Stout	Joanna Heald
Margret Stout	Joseph Bennet	Christopher Hussey
Hannah Fincher	Patrick Carson	John Day
Mary Mills	William Cox	Ann Day
Margret Carson	Archee Mackey	William Garretson
Sarah Packwood	James Mills	John Garretson
Martha Fincher	John Wright	Robert Hodgen
Mary Hussey	James Frazor	Theodate Hodgen
Jane Carson	John Day juner	Mary Garretson
Sarah Mills	Joseph Day	Mary Garretson
Martha Garretson	William Bennet	Nathen Hussey juner
Olwe Cox	James Heald	
	Syda Heald	
	Susana Hussey juner	

#3 22nd of 6th mo 1749　　　　　　　　JOHN GARRETSON-JANE CARSON

<u>John Garretson</u> of Newbery in the County of Lanchester in the province of pencilvania and <u>Jane Carson</u> daughter of <u>Patrick Carson</u> of Newbery in the County and province aforesaid...at Newbery this twenty second day of the sixth month in the year of our Lord one thousand Seven hundred and Fourty nine...

Abraham Ellot	Thomas Cox	John Garretson
James Mills	Christopher Hufsey	<u>Jane Garretson</u>
William Griffiths	John Day	Margaret Carson
Archey Mackey	Joseph Garretson	Ann Hufsey
Francis Fincher	Samuel Cox	Martha Garretson
Armol Fincher	William Beals	Mary Garretson
Joseph Heald	Benjamin Underwood	Mary Garretson
John Day	William Bennett	Sarah Carson
Robert Mills jur	Alexander	Sarah Farmer
John Cefna	Underwood	Sarah Leach
Jesper Robenet	Petter Stoute	Joanna Heald
Sarah Mills	William Underwood	Ester Foulk
Mary Kinwithey	Samuel Underwood	
Neomie Cox	John Ellot	

#4 14th of 1st mo 1749/50　　　　　　　　ROBERT VALE-SARAH BULLER

<u>Robert Vale</u> of Warrington in the County of York and province of pencilvania and <u>Sarah Buller</u> of the Township and county aforesaid,...at Warrington this fourteenth day of the first month in the year of our Lord one thousand seven hundred and forty nine/fifty

MARRIAGES

Sarah Underwood	John Douglas	Robert Vale
Mary Cox	William Griffith	Sarah Vale
Isabel Ofbun	Mofes Mapping	Thomas Cox
Mary Garretson	Elihu Underwood	Alexander Underwood
Ann Underwood		William Garretson
Mary Mapping		Robert Comer
Sarah Cook		Mathew Ofbun
Hannah Cook		William Underwood
Ruth Underwood		Isaac Cook
Martha Garretson		
Esther Griffith		
Elizabeth Cox		

#5 5th of 10th mo 1750   WILLIAM OZBUN-REBEKAH COX
William Ozbun son of Mathew Ozbun of Warrington in the County of York and province of pencilvania and Rebekah Cox daughter of Richard Cox of the same place...at Richard Coxes in warring[ton]...this fifth day of the tenth month in the year of our Lord one thousand seven hundred and fifty   William Ozbun
                                                                Rebekah Ozbun

(No witnesses appear)

#6 7th 1st mo 1750/51   BENJAMIN UNDERWOOD-SUSANAH GRIEST
Benjamin Underwood, son of Alexander Underwood of Warrington in the County of York and province of pensilvania and Susanah Griest daughter of John Griest deseased of the same place...at Warrington...thifs seventh day of the first month in the year of our Lord one thousand seven hundred and fifty fifty one

Elihu Underwood	Wm Griffith	Benjamin Underwood
George McMolin	Wm McMolin	Susanah Underwood
Ann Hufsey	Robert Vale	Alexander Underwood
Sarah Cook	Joseph Smith	Sarah Underwood
Elizabeth Wickersham	Roger Waters	John Griest
Wm Ozbun	Isaac Cox	Jacob Beals
Abraham Cook	Joseph Garretson	Samuel Underwood
Joseph Cook	Mary Cook	William Garretson
Mary Garretson	Elizabeth Beals	William Underwood
Mary Carr	Olive Cox	
Isaac Cook	Sarah Griest	
Mathew Ozbun	Susanah Griest	
Robert Comer	Rebecca Jones	
Petter Cook	Rebecca Ozbun	
Richd Wikersham	Ann Underwood	

#7 4th of 7th mo 1751   SAMUEL POPE-ELIZABETH STEVENSON
Samuel Pope of Tyrone: County of York and province of pencilvania and Elizabeth Stevenson of menalen: County aforesd and province

WARRINGTON MONTHLY MEETING

aforesd...in their meeting houfe in menalen in County and province aforesaid...upon the fourth day of the Seventh month called September in the year of our Lord one thousand seven hundred and fifty one

Michael Willson	Sarah Underwood	Samuel Pope
John Shepherd	Mary Wood	<u>Elizabeth Pope</u>
Richard Chesnon	Elizabeth McGrew	John Pope
Jacob Hinshaw	Elizabeth Dicks	William Shepherd
William Wright	Mary McGrew	Alexander Underwood
Richard Procter	Rebeca Blackburn	Jno Blackburn
Charles Pidgen	Elizabeth Pope	John Mickle
Daniel Winter	Richmunday Shepherd	William Delap
Walter Carfon	Sarah Rudduck	Finley McGrew
Thomas Hamilton	Jane Shepherd	James McGrew
Richard Sadler	Sarah Shepherd	Jno Wright
William Young	Eamey Cox	Thomas Blackburn
John Wilson	Agnes Carfon	Robert More
Nicholas Bishop	Elen Carfon	John Cox
Antony Blackburn	Jane Young	
Edward Whitehead	Precila Wireman	

#8 25th 7th mo 1751   THOMAS KENDALL-MARGRET RUDDUCK

<u>Thomas Kendall</u> of the township of huntington, county of york and province of pencilvania and <u>Margret Rudduck</u> of menalen township county and province aforesaid...in their publick meeting houfe in menalen in the County and province aforesaid...upon the twenty fifth Day of the seventh month Called September in the year of our Lord one thousand seven hundred and fifty one

Alexander Underwood	Sarah Underwood	Thomas Kendall
Jno Blackburn	Rabecah Blackburn	<u>Margret Kendall</u>
John Mickle	Elizabeth McGrew	John Rudduck
Finley McGrew	Mary Wood	William Rudduck
Jon Wright	Elizabeth Beals	John Grible
William Delap	Mary McGrew	Charles Mafe
William Wright	Jane Shepherd	Anthony Blackburn
James Reay	Rebecah Blackburn	William Dunwide
Jacob Beals	Archibald Douglas	John Pope
William Squibb	James McGrew	
Jonathan Hughs	John Sheppherd	
Samuel Pope		

#9 30th of 4th mo 1752   WILLIAM SQUIBB-SARAH GRIEST

<u>William Squibb</u> son of <u>Robert Squibb</u> of the township of Chester in the County of Chester and province of pencilvania and <u>Mary</u> his wife deceased and <u>Sarah Griest</u> daughter of <u>John Griest</u> of the Township of huntington in County of York and province aforesaid and <u>Martha</u> his wife both Deceased...this thirtyeth day of the fourth month called april in the year of our Lord one thousand seven hundred and fifty two...in a publick meeting of the said people at huntington aforesaid

MARRIAGES

Margaret Kendall	Alexander Underwood	William Squibb
Mary Collins	Robert Comer	Sarah Squibb
Martha Cox	Thomas Kendall	Robert Squibb
	William Garretson	John Griest
	William Beals	Jacob Beals
	Aron Fraizor	Benjamin Underwood
	James Hamel	Mary Cox
		Susanah Underwood
		Susanah Griest
		Mary Garretson
		Sarah Underwood
		Nathaniel Squibb
		Daniel Griest
		Willing Griest

#10 12th of 10th mo 1752   BOATER BEALS-SARAH COOK

Boater Beals of Orange County in North Carolina son of John Beals deceased and Sarah Cook of Warrington in the County of York and province of Pencilvania daughter of Thomas Cook deceased...at warrington in the county aforesd...this twelfth day of the tenth month in the year of our Lord one thousand seven hundred and fifty two

Elihu Underwood	William Beals	Boater Beals
Charls Morthland	Joseph Cook	Sarah Beals
Aron Frazor	Ruth Cook	Alexander Underwood
Ann Hufsey	Ruth Underwood	Sarah Underwood
Mary Garretson	Jacob Beals	Mary Cook
Margret Stout	Hannah Cook	Jacob Beals
Mary Garretson	William Garretson	Mary Beals
Elizabeth Wickersham	Petter Stout	Petter Cook
Ruth Underwood	Joseph Garretson	Isaac Cook
	Richard Wickersham	Abraham Cook
	John Griest	Olive Cox
	Christephor Hufsey	William Underwood
	William Smith	
	Benjamin Underwood	

#11 7th of 12th mo 1752   JOSEPH SMITH-RACHEL BEALS

Joseph Smith of Warrington in the County of York and province of pencilvania son of John Smith deceased and Rachel Beals of huntington in the County and province aforesaid Daughter of Jacob Beals...at huntington this seventh day of the twelfth month in the year of our Lord one thousand seven hundred and fifty two

WARRINGTON MONTHLY MEETING

James Robenet	William Garretson	Joseph Smith
John McElheney	James Nickel	Rachel Smith
Joseph Garretson	Peter Cook	Jacob Beals
Joseph Dodds	John Griest	Mary Beals
John Powel	Thos Kendall	Jacob Beals juner
John Underwood	Thos McMillan	William Beals
Susanah Griest	Thos Phelan	William Smith
Jane Garretson	William McMillan	Jane Smith
Precila Wierman	Joseph Cook	Alexander Underwood
Mary Garretson	James Dill	Sarah Underwood
	Mathew Dill	William Underwood
	John Dill	John Garretson
	William Nevet	Sarah Cook
	William Squibb	Robert Comer
	John Hale	

#12 10th of 5th mo 1753   WILLIAM NEVET-HANNAH COOK

<u>William Nevet</u> of Warrington in the County of York and Province of pencilvania and <u>Hannah Cook</u> Daughter of <u>Peter Cook</u> of Warrington in the County and province aforesaid...at Warrington the tenth day of the fifth month in the year of our Lord one thousand seven hundred and fifty three

Sarah Underwood	Richard Wickersham	William Nevet
Mary Garretson	Alexander Underwood	Hannah Nevet
William Smith	Peter Stout	Peter Cook
Aron Frazer	William Underwood	Sarah Cook
Elizabeth Shepperd	Christopher Hufsey	Isaac Cook
George McMillan	Francis Fincher	Joseph Cook
William Coxson	William Garretson	Thomas Nevet
Margret Stout	Joseph Garretson	Mary Nevet
	Ann Hufsey	Magnees Simonson
	Thomas McMillan	Hannah Fincher
	John Harris	Abraham Cook
	William McMillan	Elenor Simonson
	Samuel Ozbun	Mary Stroude
	John McMillan	Joseph Peck
		Patrick Peck

#13 9th day 5th mo 1753   SAMUEL HUTTON-MARY WRIGHT

<u>Samuel Hutton</u> of minallon in the County of york and Province of Pencilvania son of <u>Joseph Hutton</u> deceased and <u>Mary Wright</u> of the township county and province aforesaid Daughter of <u>John Wright</u> ...this ninth day of the fifth month in the year of our Lord one thousand seven hundred and fifty three...at minallon...

MARRIAGES

Rebecah Blackburn	John Blackburn	Samuel Hutton
Elizabeth Pope	Alexander Underwood	Mary Hutton
Richmunday Sheperd	John Pope	John Hutton
Deborah Hammon	John Mickel	Nehemiah Hutton
Ann Powel	Culbert Mains	William Hutton
Esther Powel	Finley McGrew	Benjamin Hutton
Mary Morton	William Delap	John Wright
	George Willson	Rachel Wright
	John Hamon	
	William Shepherd	
	John Powel	
	John Wierman	
	John Morton	

#14   28th of 6th mo 1753   **WILLIAM WIERMAN-EAMEY COX**

William Wierman son of William Wierman of huntington in the County of york and province of pensilvania and Gartrude his wife and Eamey Cox the daughter of John Cox of the same place as aforesaid and Mary his wife diseased   this twenty Eight Day of the sixth month in the year of our Lord one thousand seven hundred and fifty three...at huntington in the county aforesaid

Richard Cox	William Rudduck	William Wierman
William Pigeon	Gartrude Wierman	Eamey Wierman
Isaac Pigeon	Hannah Cox	William Wierman
Elizabeth Powel	Martha Cox	John Cox
Elizabeth Fickle	Mary Cox	Nicholas Wierman
Mary Garretson	Eamey Cox	John Cox
Mary Cook	Henry Sigfret	Benjamin Cox
Alex Underwood	Ann Sigfret	William Cox
Robert Comer	Ann Hufsey	Henry Wierman
Thos Kendall		
Thos Powel		
Betty Fickes		
Charles Pigeon		
William Beals		

#15   8th of 11th mo 1753   **JAMES HAMEL-MARY CARSON**

James Hamel of the township of warington in the county of york and province of pencilvania and Mary Carson of the township of menallen county and province aforesd...the Eighth day of the eleventh month in the year   of our   Lord   one thousand   seven hundred   and fifty three...meeting house at menallen aforesd

WARRINGTON MONTHLY MEETING

William Bigger	John Blackburn	James Hamel
James Grew	John Pope	<u>Mary Hamel</u>
William Morthland	John Mickle	Rachel Carson
John Smith	Culbert Mains	Jane Shepherd
Aaron Frazor	Nathen Dicks	Richmunday Shepherd
Hance Hamilton	William Beals	Sarah Shepherd
	Jacob Beals	Hanah Winter
	John Wright	Rachel White
	William Shepherd	
	Elihu Underwood	
	John Underwood	
	Finley McGrew	
	John Bell	
	Caleb Beals	
	Charls Morthland	

#16 14th of 5th mo 1754   DAVID JINKINS-ELIZABETH COX
<u>David Jinkins</u> of warrington in the county of york and province of pencilvania and <u>Elizabeth Cox</u> of the township county and province aforesd...at warrington the fourteenth day of the fifth month in the year of our Lord one thousand seven hundred and fifty four
  (No witnesses names appear)   David Jinkins
                                                    <u>Elizabeth Jinkins</u>

#17 13th of 6th mo 1754   WILLIAM MORTHLAND-RUTH UNDERWOOD
<u>William Morthland</u> of warring in the county of york and Province of Pencilvania son of <u>Hugh Morthland</u> and <u>Ruth Underwood</u> of the township county and province aforesd Daughter of <u>Alexander Underwood</u>...at Warrington the thirteenth day of the sixth month in the year of our Lord one thousand seven hundred and fifty four

MARRIAGES

John Collens	Ann Collins	William Morthland
Aaron Frazor	Cathren Traviler	Ruth Morthland
Rebecah Bennett	William Smith	Rebecah Morthland
Wm Boyd	William Ward	Alexander Underwood
James Hamel	Henery Liming	Sarah Underwood
Thomas McMillan	William Coxsun	Wm Underwood
Thomas Kendall	William Nevit	Samuel Underwood
Robert Comer	Hannah Nevit	Benjamin Underwood
Robert Vale	Jacob Beals	John Griest
Joseph Smith	Joseph Bennett	John Pope
Abraham Cook	John Mickle	John Least
John McMillan	John Garretson	Mary Cook
Isaac Cook	William Beals	Elizabeth Beals
Richard Batten	John Beals	Charls Morthland
Thomas James		
Joseph Cook		
Petter Cook		
Sarah Cook		

#18   4th of 9th mo 1754   SAMUEL WRIGHT-GARTRUDE WIERMAN

Samuel Wright son of John Wright of minallen township county of york and province of pencilvania and Gartrude Wierman Daughter of William Wierman of Huntington township County and province aforesd the fourth day of the ninth month in the year of our Lord one thousand seven hundred and fifty four in their meeting house at minallen aforesd

Rachel Blackburn	John Mickle	Samuel Wright
Elizabeth Beals	Joseph Wright	Gartrude Wright
Elizabeth McGrew	Finley McGrew	John Wright
Margreat Loan	Jacob Beals	William Wierman
Ruth Delap	John Least	Henery Wierman
	Benjamin Loan	Nicolas Wierman
	Nathen Dicks	John Blackburn
	William Shepherd	Alexander Underwood
	William Wood	Charls Pidgon
	James Murphy	Isaac Pidgon
		William Delap
		James McGrew
		Richard Proctor

#19   22nd of 4th mo 1756   JOHN DAY-SARAH BENNETT

John Day son of John Day of the County of york and province of Pencilvania and Sarah Bennett Daughter of Joseph Bennett of the County of york and Province aforesd this twenty second day of the fourth month in the year of our Lord one thousand seven hundred and fifty six...at Newbery

WARRINGTON MONTHLY MEETING

Lydia Hufsey
Miriam Harrey
Ruth Cook
Andrew Welch
John Hufsey jur
Joadiah Hufsey
Crisparius Rodgers
Joseph Rodgers
Ann Rodgers
Francis Fincher
Hugh Reding
Cathrine Lane
Mary Lane
Alexander Elliott
Joanna Heald
Margret Stout
Hannah Todd
Bettey Hutton
Miriam Redd
Lydia Heald

Mary Welch
John Hodgen
James Harkins
John Waugh
Thomas Harkins
James Rankin
John Rankin
William Rankin
Rachel Stanton
Abigail Pafmore
Kathrine Brown
Antoney Derimbough
John Derimbough
Alexander Underwood
Petter Stout
Adam Redd
Riccard Hufsey
Thomas Heald
Silas Heald
Armel Fincher
John Garretson jur
William Garretson

John Day
Sarah Day
Joseph Bennett
Rebecah Bennett
Wm Bennett
Phebe Bennett
Lyda Bennett
Theodate Hodgen
John Hufsey
John Garretson
Rebekah Hodgen
Rebekah Rankin
Joseph Day
Abraham Nablet
Joseph Hutton
Rebekah Day
Stephen Day
Joseph Bennett jur
Joshua Bennett
Samuel Stout
Pat Dermond
Humphrey Pafmore
John Mickle
William Way
Elihu Underwood
John Maxfield
Andrew Rodgers
Robert Hodgen

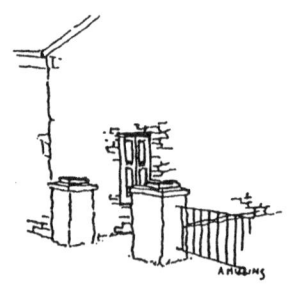

MARRIAGES

#20 9th of 6th mo 1756   RICCORD HUFSEY-MIRIAM HARREY
Riccord Hufsey of newbery in the County of york and Province of
pencilvania and Miriam Harrey of warrington in the County and
province aforesd at warrington the ninth day of the sixth month in
the year of our Lord one thousand seven hundred and fifty six

Hannah Nevet	James Pecket	Riccord Hufsey
Thos Heald	Elizabeth Pecket	Miriam Hufsey
John McMillan	Stephen Hufsey	John Harrey
Deborah McMillan	Alice Loaden	Alexander Underwood
William Ward	Mary Bohanan	Sarah Underwood
Mary McMillan	Elizabeth Beals	Christopher Hufsey
Sarah Vale	Easter Griffith	John Day jur
James Hamel	Rebecah Bennett	Ann Hufsey
Joseph Bennett	Jofhua Speakman	Margret Marsh
John Griest	James Harkins	Sarah Day
Richard Wickersham	Henery Underwood	John Hufsey jur
Petter Cook	John Collins	William Underwood
Char Horfsman	Charls Morthland	Ruth Underwood
Robert Vale	John Beals	William Griffith
Armel Fincher	William Morthland	Benjamin Underwood
Susanah Ward	William Nevett	

#21 22nd of 6th mo 1756   PETTER CLEAVER-MIRIAM FRAZOR
Petter Cleaver junr of the township of warrington in the County of
York and province of pencilvania, son of Peter and Elizabeth Cleaver
of the township of upper dublin in the county of philadelphia and
province aforesaid and Miriam Frazor of the township of warrington in
the county of York and province aforesd Daughter of Alexander and
Sarah Frazer Late of the township of Kennet in the county of Chefter
and province aforesd deceased...this twenty second day of the sixth
month in the year of our Lord one thousand seven hundred and fifty
six they the said Peter Cleaver and Miriam Frazer appeared in a
meeting at Warrington in the county of york

Stephen Hufsey	Christopher Hufsey	Peter Cleaver junr
William Garretson	Mary Garretson	Miriam Cleaver
junr	Ruth Underwood	John Cleaver
Caleb Frazer	Elizabeth Hufsey	Aron Frazer
William Savage	Ruth Cook	Isaac Cleaver
Mary Savage	Rachel Everett	William Garretson
	Amey Hufsey	Alexander Frazer
	Joseph Garretson	Mofes Frazer
	Jacob Beals	John Rich
	Elihu Underwood	Nathen Cleaver
	Joseph Comer	Mary Garretson
	Robert Comer	Sarah Underwood

WARRINGTON MONTHLY MEETING

#22 24th of 11th mo 1756   DAVID COPELAN-RACHEL STANTON

David Copelan son of Richard Copelan of the township of Newbery in the county of York and province of Pencilvania and Rachel Stanton Daughter of John Stanton of the same place...the twenty fourth Day of the 11th month called November 1756 they appeared in a Publick and solemn afsembly of the people and others met together at the meeting house of Newbery aforesd

John Finley	Richard Copelan	David Copelan
Jofeth Hutton	Sufanah Stanton	Rachel Copelan
Joseph Bennett	Sarah Stanton	John Stanton
Liddia Copelan	Petter Stoute	Sarah Stanton
Samuel harris	Margret Stoute	Mary Copelan
	Samuel Stoute	William Copelan
	Phebe Bennett	Thomas Copelan
	James Hill	James Copelan
	Jofiah Moffet	John Copelan
	John Mickle	Henery Willis
	David Hill	Joel Ferree
	Antoney Litle	Philip Ferree
	Charls Stoute	Daniel Stanton
	William Willis	Margret Carson

#23 2nd of 12th mo 1756   ARMEL FINCHER-REBECAH EDMUNDSON

Armel Fincher son of Francis Fincher of warrington in the county of york and province of pencilvania and Rebecah Edmundson daughter of Samuel Edmundson deceased,...this second day of the twelfth month in the year of our Lord one thousand seven hundred and fifty six in a publick meeting at warrington...

Mary Garretfon	William Griffith	Armel Fincher
All Collins	James Traviler	Rebeca Fincher
Elizabeth Wickersham	Joseph Garretfon	Hester Edmundson
Jane Pugh	Richard Wickersham	Thomas Edmundson
Martha Jinkins	John Collins	Rachel Underhill
Susannah Ward	David Jinkins	Hannah Fincher
Mary Cox	William Ward	Jofeph Edmundson
Hannah Cox	Thomas Pugh	John Edmundson
Ann Cook	Thomas Cox juner	Elizabeth Clark
Elizabeth Jinkins		Esther Clark
		Francis Fincher
		Aaron Fincher
		Mofes Fincher

#24 30th of 12th mo 1756   ELIHU UNDERWOOD-MARGRET MARSH

Elihu Underwood of warrington in the county of york and province of pencilvania son of Alexander Underwood and Margret Marsh of the same place Daughter of John Marsh...at a publick meeting of the sd people at warrington the thirtyeth day of the twelfth month in the year of our Lord one thousand seven hundred and fifty six

MARRIAGES

Jane McMillan	Mary Morthland	Elihu Underwood
Rebeca Fincher	John McMillan	Margret Underwood
Elizabeth Hufsey	John Harrey	Alexander Underwood
Richard Wickersham	Ruth Cook	Sarah Underwood
James Peckett	Rebeca Morthland	Wm Underwood
Charls Morthland	Ann Hufsey	John Marsh
James Jones	Mary Garretson	William Marsh
Samuel Morthland	Elizabeth Wickersham	Ruth Marsh
Jonathan Marsh	William Morthland	Ruth Morthland
Susanah Ward	George McMillan	Petter Marsh
	Armel Fincher	Deborah McMillan
	Christopher Hufsey	Mary McMillan
	Joseph Garretson	
	Aaron Frazor	

#25 20th of 1st mo 1757   JOHN UNDERWOOD-MARY MORTHLAND

John Underwood son of Alexander Underwood of Warrington in the county of York and province of pencilvania and Mary Morthland daughter of Hugh Morthland of the same place...at a publick meeting of the aforesd people at warrington the twentyeth day of the first month in the year of our Lord one thousand seven hundred and fifty seven

James Hamel	Mary Garretson	John Underwood
Petter Cook	Sarah Cook	Mary Underwood
William Nevett	Joseph Cook	Alexander Underwood
John Griest	Mary Cook	Sarah Underwood
William Garretson	Nehemiah Dean	William Underwood
John Marsh	Ann Cook	Ruth Underwood
Jonathan Marsh	Margret Rosborough	Agnes Morthland
Ruth Marsh	Ruth Morthland	Margret Morthland
John Smith	Ruth Cook	Elihu Underwood
Abraham Miely		Margret Underwood
Petter Smith		John Harrey
Isaac Rosborough		Charls Morthland
James Jones		Hugh Morthland
		Joshua Speakman
		William Morthland

WARRINGTON MONTHLY MEETING

#26 27th of 4th mo 1757   JOHN WILLIS-PHEBE BENNETT
John Willis of the township of Newbery in the County of york and province of pencilvania son of Henery Willis and Phebe Bennett Daughter of Joseph Bennett...this twenty seventh day of the fourth month in the year of our Lord one thousand seven hundred and fifty seven...in a publick meeting of the sd people at newbery in the county aforesaid

Priscilla Elliott	James Rankin	John Willis
William Higgins	Joshua Hutton	Phebe Willis
Samuel Stout	Mary Fox	Henery Willis
Charls Stout	William Rankin	Mary Willis
Richard Carfon	Jane Garretson	Joseph Bennett
Lydia Heald	Margret Stoute	Rebecca Bennett
Joanna Crage	Joanna Heald	Joseph Hutton
Elizabeth Smith	Hannah Todd	Bettey Hutton
John Garretson	Mary Garretson	William Bennett
Andrew Yeatman	Elizabeth Higgons	Henery Willis juner
Ann Willis	Mary Mickle	Alexander Underwood

#27 9th of 11th mo 1757   EDWARD EVERITT-JANE HODGE
Edward Everitt of Hamiltons bane township in the county of york and province of pencilvania son of John Everitt and Jane Hodge of menalen township county and province aforesd Daughter of Francis Hodge...in their meeting houfe in minallen aforesd upon the ninth day of the eleventh month called November in the year of our Lord one thousand seven hundred and fifty seven

William Delap	John Mickle	Edward Everitt
William Brafsetton	John Pope	Jane Everitt
William Ruddock	John Wright	John Everitt
Sarah Mickle	John Hammond	Isaac Everitt
Rachel Wright	James McGrew	Sarah Hodge
Elizabeth Shepherd	Samuel Hutton	Mary Hodge
Sarah Shepherd	John Mickle	Elizabeth Everitt
Charls Pidgon	William Pidgon	Barbara Everitt
John Wright	John Armstrong	John Willfon
	John Shepherd	John Hodge
	Elijah Mickle	John Blackburn
	Joseph Wright	Jacob Elliott
	Finley McGrew	

#28 5th of 7th mo 1758   JOSEPH BLACKBURN-DEBORAH MCGREW
Joseph Blackburn of menallen township county of york and province of pencilvania son of John Blackburn deceased and Deborah McGrew of the township County and province aforesaid...in their meeting houfe in minallen aforsd upon the fifth day of the seventh month called July in the year of our Lord one thousand seven hundred and fifty eight

MARRIAGES

William Boyd	George Willfon	Joseph Blackburn
Cathren McGrew	John Morten	Deborah Blackburn
Martha McGrew	John Willfon	John Blackburn
Alice Willfon	James Hammond	James McGrew
Sarah Loan	Daniel Winter	Rachel Blackburn
Dinah Cox	Alexander McGrew	Findley McGrew juner
Alice Willfon	William Webb	Rachel Blackburn jr
Esebeal Mackefeild	William McGrew	Abigal Willfon
Margret Blackburn	Alexander McGrew	Ann McGrew
Mary Lackland	Alexander McGrew	Jacob Elliott
Rachel Blackburn	Thomas Willfon	Thomas Kendall
	John Wright	Cuthbert Mains
	James Willfon	John Hammond
	Samuel Hutton	

#29 5th of 10th mo 1758   GEORGE MCMILLAN-ANN HINSHAW

George McMillan of warrington in the County of york and province of pencilvania son of Thomas McMillan deceased and Ann Hinshaw of manahon in the county and province aforesd Daughter of Jacob Hinshaw ...at their meeting houfe at warrington the fifth day of the tenth month in the year of our lord one thousand seven hundred and fifty eight

John Collins	William Griffith	George McMillan
Ann Hufsey	William Nevett	Ann McMillan
Sarah Underwood	Robert Vale	Jacob Hinshaw
Ruth Underwood	John Sharp	Deborah McMillan
Hannah Nevett	Joseph Slofs	John McMillan
Susannah Ward	Petter Cook juner	William McMillan
Elizabeth Slofs	John Hill	Petter Marsh
Ann Collins	Charls Horfman	Jonathan Marsh
Mary Collins	Elizabeth Horfman	Margret Marsh
Ann Cook	Richard Rofs	John Marsh
	William Ward	Jane McMillan
	Abraham Griffith	Thomas Hinshaw
	Eneas Foulk	Alexander Underwood
	Jesse Cook	William Garretson
	John McAdams	Petter Cook
		William Underwood

#30 7th of 12th mo 1758   JOSEPH COMER-ELIZABETH HUSSEY

Joseph Comer son of Robert and Rebecah Comer of Warrington township and county of York in the province of Pencilvania and Elizabeth Hufsey daughter of Christopher and Ann Hufsey of the same place...this seventh day of the twelfth month in the year of our lord one thousand seven hundred and fifty eight...in a publick meeting of the sd people at warrington aforesd

WARRINGTON MONTHLY MEETING

Martha Cox	John Griest	Joseph Comer
Ruth Morthland	Martha Griest	Elizabeth Comer
Jediah Hufsey	Wm Underwood	Robert Comer
Jacob Beals	Jane Rhoads	Christopher Hufsey
Sarah Vale	Abigail Rhoads	William Garretson
Robert Vale	Mary Collins	Ann Hufsey
William Beals	Rachel Leach	Rebecah Comer
Richard Carfon	Mary Underwood	John Garretson
Daniel Griest	John Hodgin	Joseph Garretson
Elizabeth Cox	Elihu Underwood	John Comer
Willing Griest	Wm Morthland	Stephen Hufsey
Charls Morthland	Mary Beals	Robert Comer juner
Henery Clark	John Day	John Marsh
William Ward	Neomy Hufsey	William Griffith
Rebecah Morthland	Alexander Underwood	Wm Garretson
Hannah Nevet	Sarah Underwood	Lydia Heald
	Mary Garretson	Margret Marsh
	Ann Rogers	Agnes Morthland

#31   20th of 12th mo 1758   WILLIAM BRASELTON-SARAH SHIPHERD
William Braselton son of John Braselton of Frederick County in the province of maryland and Sarah Shipherd daughter of Solomon Shipherd late of minallen township county of york and province of pencilvania...in their meeting houfe in minallen aforesd upon the twentyeth day of the twelfth month in the year of our Lord one thousand seven hundred and fifty eight

Sarah Mickle	Thomas Kendall	William Braselton
Barbara Everit	John Pope	Sarah Braselton
James Hamel	Finley McGrew	Jane Shipherd
Samuel Wright	John Mickle juner	Elizabeth Shipherd
Dinah Cox	Allen Farquer juner	Andrew Miller
Gartrude Wright	John Hammond	Andrew Miller juner
Alice Willfon	John Willfon	Joseph Wood
	Rebecca Blackburn	James Nickle
	Rachel Everitt	Alexander Underwood
	Mary Mickle	John Mickle
	Joseph Wright	Isaac Everitt
	Margret Bell	Jacob Elliot
	Rachel Wright	John Blackburn

#32   31st of 5th mo 1759   HARMAN UPDEGRAF-LIDIA HEALD
Harman Updegraf of york town and province of Pencilvania, tanner, and Lidia Heald daughter of Thomas Heald of the same place...this thirty first day of the fifth month in the year of our Lord one thousand seven hundred and fifty nine...at the houfe of Nathen Hufsey in york town aforesd

MARRIAGES

Christian Haner	Susanah Updegraf	Harman Updegraf
John Robison	Samuel Updegraf	Lidia Updegraf
Michael Croll	Abraham Updegraf	Thomas Heald
Ann Harlon	Alexander Underwood	Joanna Heald
Betty Willis	Francis Worley	Nathen Hufsey
Jane Garretson	John Garretson	James Heald
	John Hufsey	Susanah Hufsey
	John Day	Hannah Todd
	William Willis	Joseph Updegraf
	John Hodgin	Derick Updegraf
	David Worley	Ambrus Updegraf
	Siles Heald	William Updegraf
	James Rob	Petter Updegraf
	John Hendricks	John Updegraf
	Jedaah Hufsey	

#33 29th of 8th mo 1759   ANDREW DENEN-RACHEL BLACKBURN
Andrew Dennin and Rachel Blackburn both of minalen township county of york and province of pencilvania...on the twenty ninth day of the eighth month one thousand seven hundred and fifty nine...in their meeting houfe at menallen aforesd

Ann McGrew	Leonard Hatton	Andrew Denen
Ealice Willfon	Nathen McGrew	Rachel Denen
Sarah Hammond	James Hammond	William Denen
Ealice Willfon	William McGrew	Barbarey Denen
Ealice Wright	Joseph Wright	Rachel Blackburn
Margret Blackburn	Thomas Griffith	John Morton
Rachel Blackburn	William Hutton	Jane Willson
	John Mickle juner	Alice Willfon
	Jacob Elliot	Archibald McGrew
	Finley McGrew	James McGrew
	Elizabeth McGrew	Jonathan Hughs
	Jane Mickle	John Blackburn
	Ruth Delap	John Mickle
	Martha McGrew	Finley McGrew
	Margret Hoatin	John Wright
	Margret McGrew	Alexdr McGrew
	Rachel Wright	George Willfon
	Sarah Mickle	Antoney Blackburn
	Elizabeth Wright	John Willfon
	Deborah Blackburn	John Morton

#34 31st of 10th mo 1759   WILLIAM FARQUAR JR-RACHEL WRIGHT
William Farquar Juner of Frederick County in the Province of Maryland and Rachel Wright of minallen township county of york and province of pencilvania...in their meeting houfe in minallen aforesd upon the thirtyfirst day of the tenth month called october in the year of our Lord one thousand seven hundred and fifty nine

WARRINGTON MONTHLY MEETING

William Hutton	Antony Blackburn	William Farquar
Jacob Ellot	John Willson	Rachel Farquar
Jno Blackburn	Daniel Griest	William Farquar
James Hamel	Isaac Rosborough	Jon Wright
John Morten	James Hammond	Agm Farquar
Elizabeth Everit	William Webb	Allen Farquar juner
Ealice Willfon	Jacob Beals	Allen Farquar
Margaret Blackburn	Henery Wierman	Solomon Miller
Ann McGrew	Elizabeth Elot	Mary Garretson
Martha Griest	Joseph Wright	
Rachel Blackburn	John Mickel	
Elenor Rofborough	Sarah Mickel	
Mary Griest	John Mickel juner	
Deborah Hutton	Samuel Wright	
Mary Morton	Sarah Miller	
Rachel Everit	Alice Wright	
Edward Whitecraft	John Wright juner	
Jno Pope	Samuel Spencer	
John Everit	Isaac Everit	
Cuthbert Mains	Mary Hodge	

#35   21st of 12th mo 1759   DANIEL GRIEST-ANN ROGERS

Daniel Griest of warrington in the County of york and province of pencilvania son of John Griest and Ann Rogers of warrington in the county and province aforesaid Daughter of Andrew Rogers...at huntington in the county and province aforesd the twenty first day of the twelfth month in the year of our Lord one thousand seven hundred and fifty nine

Wm Kenworthy	Abraham Bower	Daniel Griest
Petter Bower	Rachel Carfon	Ann Griest
Andrew Bower	Mary Kenworthy	John Griest
Charity Whiteker	Sarah Waters	Susanah Griest
Abel Whiteker	Henery Wierman	Martha Everitt
Caleb Beals	Joseph Rogers	Isaac Everitt
Warrick Miller	Mary Rogers	Jacob Beals juner
Daniel Hains	Jasper Rogers	William Griest
John Mickle	Ann Sigfret	Liddia Beals
John Mickle juner	William Cox	Martha Cox
Rachel Everitt	Mary Griest	Mary Cox
Mary Garretson	Jacob Beals	William Squibb
Mary Beals	Alexander Underwood	Sarah Mickle
Mary Collins	William Underwood	Elizabeth Sheperd
Petter Jones	William Boyd	Neomy Cox
	William Garretson	Sarah Jones
	Thos Kendall	Elizabeth Cox
	James Hamel	
	William Beals	

MARRIAGES

#36 21st of 12th mo 1759   ISAAC EVERITT-MARTHA GRIEST
<u>Isaac Everitt</u> of Frederick County in the province of Maryland son of <u>John Everitt</u> and <u>Martha Griest</u> of warrington in the county of york and province of pencilvania daughter of <u>John Griest</u>...at Huntington in the county and province aforesd the twenty first day of the twelfth month in the year of our Lord one thousand seven hundred and fifty nine

Joseph Rodgers	Mary Kenworthy	Isaac Everitt
Mary Rodgers	William Kenworthy	<u>Martha Everitt</u>
Jasper Rodgers	Ann Sigfret	John Griest
Rachel Carson	Sarah Waters	Susanah Griest
Charity Whitiker	Neomy Cox	John Everitt
Abil Whitiker	William Squibb	Jacob Beals
Caleb Beals	William Cox	Willing Griest
Petter Bower	Mary Griest	Rachel Everitt
John Mickle	Jacob Beals	Lydia Beals
John Mickle juner	Alexander Wierman	Barbary Everitt
Mary Garretson	William Underwood	Martha Cox
Mary Beals	William Boyd	Ann Griest
Mary Collins	William Garretson	Mary Cox
Sarah Jones	Thomas Kendall	Sarah Mickle
Elizabeth Cox	James Hamel	
Petter Jones	William Beals	
Joseph Everitt	Jacob Elliot	
Abraham Bower	Warrick Miller	
Henery Wierman	Daniel Hains	

#37 23rd of 4th mo 1760   JOHN RANKIN-ABIGAIL RODES
<u>John Rankin</u> of the Township of Newbery in the County of york and Province of Pensylvania son of <u>John Rankin</u> deceased and <u>Abigail Rodes</u> daughter of <u>Benjamin Rodes</u> deceased this twenty third day of the fourth month in the year of our Lord one thousand seven hundred and sixty...at Newbery

William Farra	Cathrine Brown	John Rankin
Samuel Stout	Mary Welch	<u>Abigail Rankin</u>
Margarret Stout	Sufanna Miller	Richard Carfon
Rebecka Day	Betty Hutton	William Rankin
Joseph Pharon	Elizabeth Pasmore	James Brown
Alexander Underwood	John Garretson	Mary Rankin
Joshua Bennett	John Day	Margarret Folk
Peter Strong	Abraham Noblet	John Garretson juner
	Alexander Underwood	Ann Garretson
	Charls Stout	Cathrine Treviller
	Robert Wilkinson	Ann Noblet
	Joseph Taylor	Mary Collins
		Ann Willis
		Rebecka Day
		Jane Garretson

WARRINGTON MONTHLY MEETING

#38   29th of 5th mo 1760   **JOSEPH TAYLOR-ANN WILLIS**

Joseph Taylor of the Township of Newbery in the County of york and Province of penfylvania son of Joseph Taylor deceased and Ann Willis daughter of Henry Willis of the township of Newbery & Province aforesaid...this twenty ninth Day of the fifth month in the year of our Lord one Thousand seven hundred and sixty...at Newbery aforesaid

Samuel Stout	Ann Elliot	Joseph Taylor
Benjamin Elliot	John Garretson juner	Ann Taylor
Margreat Stout	Jedaiah Hufsey	Henry Willis
Charls Stout	Ann Garretson	Mary Willis
Jane Garretson	Ruth Lewis	William Banister
William Garretson	Susanah Pafmore	Sarah Banister
Robert Mills juner	Betty Pafmore	John Willis
Isaac Wall	James Brown	Phebe Willis
	Joseph Day	Henry Willis juner
	Susanah Day	Isaih Willis
	Peter Stout	Priscilla Elot
	Abraham Noblet	Margaret Carfon

#39   2nd of 7th mo 1760   **JAMES HAMMOND-ALICE WILSON**

James Hamond son of Daniel Hamond deceased and Alice Wilson daughter of George Wilson both of menalen Township county of york and province of Pensylvania...on the second day of the seventh month in the year of our Lord one thousand seven hundred and sixty in their meeting House at menalen aforesaid

Rachel Blackburn	John Pope	James Hamond
Sarah Wilfon	Anthony Blackburn	Alice Hamond
Jane Hannah	John Morton	George Wilson
Elizabeth Hamond	Joseph Blackburn	John Hamond
Lydia Wilson	William Paterson	Deborah Hamond
Mary Blackburn	John Wright	John Wilfon
Susanna Haley	John Powell	William Cambell
Jane Mickle	John Vance	Daniel Hamond
Rachel Dinin	William Griffith	James Megren
Sarah Mickle	Joseph Wright	Jacob Elliot
Alice Wright	John Mickle juner	John Blackburn
Sarah Hamond	William Pidgeon	John Mickle
Ann Megven	Rebekah Blackburn	
Deborah Hutton		
Elizabeth Sheperd		

#40   4th of 12th mo 1760   **ROBERT TODD-HANNAH WIERMAN**

Robert Todd of Huntington township in york county and Province of Pensylvania son of John Todd of New London in Chester County and Province aforesaid and Hannah Wierman of huntington township & county aforesaid daughter of Henry Wierman & Prifily his wife in the township & county aforesaid...this fourth Day of the twelfth month in

MARRIAGES

the year of our Lord one thousand seven hundred & sixty...at Huntington aforesaid

Mary Beals	Thomas Kenworthy	Robert Todd
Susanna Duffield	Wm Hutton	Hannah Todd
Mary Beals	Henry Sigvret	John Todd
Lydia Beals	Wm Duffield	Henry Wierman
Charity Whiteker	Felty Fickes	James Todd
Mary Griest	Joshua Speakman	William Wierman
William Beals	William Cox	John Morton
Deborah Hutton	Petter Miller	John Wierman
Ann Powell	Daniel Griest	Nicholas Wierman
Mary Morton	John Kenworthy	John Powell
Sarah Warman	Thomas Paty	
Elizabeth Eliot	John Griest	
Ann Young	Susanna Griest	
Rebekah Kenworthy	Jane Jones	
Ann Speakman	Mary Kenworthy	
	Ann Hutton	

#41 18th of 12th mo 1760   JOSHUA LOW-MARY WELSH

Joshua Low of the township of Manchester in the county of York and province of Pencilvania and Mary Welsh of the township of Newbery in the county and Province aforesaid, widow...the Eighteenth day of the twelfth month in the year one thousand seven hundred and sixty in their meeting houfe at newbery

Caleb Low	Peter Stout	Joshua Low
Jedaiah Hufsey	John Garretson	Mary Low
John Garretson juner	William Garretson	Margaret Carson
	William Noblit	Ann Brown
	Thomas Noblit	Elizabeth Welsh
	George Welsh	Margreat Stout juner
	Darby Condrey	Elizabeth Welsh jr
	Jacob Wogan	
	Charles Green	

#42 16th of 6th mo 1761   SAMUEL MORTHLAND-MARGREAT ROSBOROUGH

Samuel Morthland of the township of Warrington in the county of York and Province of Pencilvania son of Hugh Morthland deceased and Rebecca his wife and Margreat Rofborough of allen township in the County of Cumberland and province aforesaid daughter of Robert and Elener Rofborough...at the dwelling houfe of Robert Rofborough in allen township in the County and province aforesd the sixteenth day of the sixth month in the year of our Lord one thoufand seven hundred and sixty one

WARRINGTON MONTHLY MEETING

Mary Garretson	Mary Underwood	Samuel Morthland
William Hunt	Margret Marfh	<u>Margreat Morthland</u>
Wm Underwood	Rebecca Morthland	Robert Rofborough
Samuel Stout	Caterien Rofborough	Elener Rofborough
Charls Stout	Joshua Rofborough	William Morthland
Jacob Hinshaw	Robert Johnston	Alexander Underwood
Thomas Kendall	Thomas Evans	Charls Morthland
Thomas Hinshaw	John Rosbery	John Underwood
Jonathan Marfh	Mary Evans	Ifaac Rutledge
Hugh Morthland	James Rutledge	John Marfh
Elihu Underwood	Sarah Cook	Isaac Lerew
Joseph Garretson		
Petter Cook		

#43   18th of 6th mo 1761   JONATHAN MARSH-REBECCA MORTHLAND
<u>Jonathan Marfh</u> of the township of warrington in the county of york and province of Pencilvania son of <u>John Marfh</u> and <u>Elizabeth</u> his wife deceafed and <u>Rebecca Morthland</u> of the township county and province aforesd Daughter of <u>Hugh Morthland</u> deceased and <u>Rebecca</u> his wife...at Friends meeting houfe in warrington in the county and province aforesd the eighteenth day of the sixth month in the year of our Lord one thoufand seven hundred and sixty one

Hannah Nevet	Joshua Rofborough	Jonathan Marsh
Mary Garretson	Cathrin Rofborough	<u>Rebecca Marsh</u>
Bowater Beals	Margreat Morthland	John Marsh juner
Jacob Hinshaw	Hugh Morthland	William Marsh
William Nevet	John Underwood	Ruth Marsh
William Boyd	Isaac Lerew	Elihu Underwood
John Collins	Joseph Collins	Margreat Underwood
Nicholas Steer	James Rutledge	Ann Collins
James Hamel	Alexander Underwood	William McMillan
Jn Cahoon	William Hunt	George McMillan
Hugh Cook	William Underwood	Ann McMillan
John Miller	Isaac Everit	Samuel Morthland
Peter Cook	William Garretson	Robert Rosborough
John Harrey	William Griffith	

#44   30 of 7th mo 1761   RICHARD CARSON-MARY PASSMORE
<u>Richard Carfon</u> of newbery in the County of York and province of Pencilvania son of <u>Patrick Carfon</u> deceafed and <u>Mergreate</u> his wife and <u>Mary Pafsmore</u> daughter of <u>William and Mary Pafsmore</u> late of Kennet in the County of Chefter and province aforesaid...at friends meeting houfe in warrington the thirtieth day of the seventh month in the year of our Lord one thoufand seven hundred and sixty one

MARRIAGES

Joseph Collins	Joseph Cook	Richard Carson
John Phillips	Wm Ward	Mary Carson
William Farra	Caleb Beals	Susanna Pafsmore
Samuel Cook	James Heald	Abigail Rankin
William Hicklin	John Garretson jr	Jane Rhoads
James Mills	William Garretson	Margaret Carfon
George Marshall	William Rankin	Lydia Bennett
Mary Collins	Michael King	Rebecah Rankin
Abraham Ellot	William Garretson	John Garretson
John Rankin	Jacob Beals	William Beals
Thos Davis	William Wilson	
Alexander Underwood jr	Jesse Beals	
	Margret Stout	
Joseph Hutton	Betty Hutton	
Samuel Stout	Mary Garretson	
Thos Steward		
Thos Pugh		

#45 16th of 3rd mo 1762   WILLIAM UPDEGRAFF-SARAH DAY
William Updegraff son of Harman Updegraff deceased of the town of York in the County of York and Province of Pennfylvania shoomaker and Sarah Day widow of John Day Junier deceased of the same place this sixteenth Day of the third month in the year of our Lord one thousand seven hundred and sixty two...at the house of Nathan Hufsey in the aforesd town

James Smith	Sarah Updegraff	William Updegraff
Jacob Smith	Barbara Updegraff	Sarah Updegraff
John Kay	Ann Harlan	Harman Updegraff
Jacob Worley	Thos Heald	Joseph Bennett
Andrew Denis	Joanna Heald	Joseph Updegraff
Elizabeth Freck	Jane Dunn	Ambros Updegraff
Daniel Ragon	Betty Willis	Harman Updegraff
Nathan Hufsey	Mary Jones	Jacob Updegraff
Jesse Falkner	Ruth Smith	Abraham Updegraff
William Willis	Jane Falkner	William Way
John Morris	Mary Falkner	John Willis
John Jones	James Heald	Susanna Updegraff
Thos Falkner		
William Hodgen		

#46 29th of 4th mo 1762   JOHN COMER-ELIZABETH COX
John Comer son of Robert Comer deceased of warrington in the County of York and Province of Pencilvania and Elizabeth Cox Daughter of Richard Cox of the township and County aforesd...at Huntington in the afforesaid County this twenty ninth day of the fourth month in the year of our Lord one thousand seven hundred and sixty two

WARRINGTON MONTHLY MEETING

Francis Dods
Susana Dods
John Carfon
Daniel Griest
Abraham Coble
Andrew Bower
Rebecah Jones
Martha Jones
Abraham Bower
Willing Grieft
William Garretfon
Mary Grieft
Lydia Beals

Isaac Everit
Thomas Kendall
Jacob Beals senr
Jacob Beals juner
John Everit
Isaac Jones
Aaron Frazor
William Dods
William Squibb
Martha Everit
William Beals
John Jones
Jane Everit
William Kenworthy
William Wierman

John Comer
Elizabeth Comer
Richard Cox
Mary Cox
Mary Cox
Naomi Cox
Richard Cox juner
Robert Comer
Tamer Comer
Peter Bower
Ann Sigfret
Susanah Grieft
William Cox
Ann Collins
Ann Grieft
Esther Jones

#47 19th of 8th mo 1762   ALEXANDER UNDERWOOD-MARY UNDERHILL
Alexander Underwood of the township of warrington county of york and province of Pencilvania son of Samuel Underwood and Ann his wife and Mary Underhill of Warrington in the County and Province aforesd Daughter of Joseph Underhill deceased and Martha his wife surviving...at their meeting houfe at warrington in the county and province aforesaid the nineteenth day of the Eighth month in the year of our Lord one thousand seven hundred and sixty two

Jane Pugh
Charls Morthland
Samuel Morthland
George Anderson
Nathan Philips
Jane Anderson
William Morthland
Ruth Morthland
John Harrey
William Bennet
John Clark
Wm Simsson
William Ward

Job Ward
Thomas Pugh
Cathrin Harrey
Barbara Everit
James Ewing
James Traller
Elihu Underwood
John Underwood
William Griffith
Elizabeth Clark
Joseph Garretson
John Edmundson
William Garretson
William Nevet

Alexander Underwood
Mary Underwood
Alexander Underwood
Henery Clark
Caleb Edmundson
Thomas Edmundson
William Underwood
Ruth Underwood

#48 28th of 10th mo 1762   WILLIAM GARRETSON-LIDDIA BEALS
William Garretson of the township of Newbery in the County of york and Province of Pencilvania son of John Garretson and Liddia Beals Daughter of Jacob Beals junr of huntington township in the County and Province aforsd...this twenty eighth day of the tenth month in the year of our Lord one thousand seven hundred and sixty two...at huntington afforesd

24

MARRIAGES

Michael Fickel	Betty Hutton	William Garretson
Benjamin Underwood	Catharin Brown	Liddia Garretson
William Squibb	John Comer	John Garretson
Rebecah Jones	Elizabeth Comer	Jacob Beals
Jacob Beals	William Garretson jr	Elizabeth Beals
Richard Cox	Ann Collings	John Garretson jr
George Robinett	James Brown	Ann Garretfon
Aaron Frazor	William Hodgen	Jacob Beals sr
John Jones	William Kenworthy	John Grieft
Martha Jones	Hannah Bennett	Sufannah Grieft
Willing Griest	Hannah Grieft	William Garretson
Prifila Wierman	Mary Cox	Rachel Smith
Sarah Bowman	Naomi Cox	Mary Garretfon
John Carfon	Samuel Robinet	William Cox
Thomas Kendall	Jacob Schorh	John Beals
Luke Garret	Sufannah Cox	Daniel Grieft
	Elizabeth Cox	Ann Grieft
		Joseph Smith
		Alexander Underwood
		Martha Everit
		Isaac Everit

#49   4th of 11th mo1762   WILLIAM MILLS-SUSANAH WILKESON
William Mills son of Robert Mills of the township of newbery in the
county of york and province of Pencilvania and Mary his wife and
Susanah Wilkeson daughter of Joseph Wilkefon deceafed and Elizabeth
his wife of the township of paxton and county of Lanchefter and
Province aforesd...this fourth day of the eleventh month in the year
of our Lord one thoufand seven hundred and sixty two   at their
publick meeting Houfe at newbery afforesd

Henery Renick	Phebe Mills	William Mills
John Folwiell	John Mills	Sufanah Mills
Isaac Hancock	Moses Key	Robert Mills
Isaac Wall	Sufannah Mills	Mary Mills
Elizabeth Hufsey	Mary Key	Elizabeth Wilkefon
Betty Hutton	John Garretfon	Robert Mills juner
Rachel Copelin	John Hufsey	Sufanah Warren
Lydia Garretson	William Willfon	Francis Wilkinfon
Elizabeth Welch	Thomas Jennings	Mary Garretfon
Jane Fifher	David Copelin	Sarah Nickle
	William Garretson	James Mills
	Joseph Gregg	Elizabeth Higgins

#50   12th of 10th mo 1762   JAMES SMITH-MARY JONES
James Smith of helm township in the county of york and province of
pensylvania yeoman and Mary Jones of the same place...in their
meeting house at York upon the twelfth day of the Tenth month in the
year one thousand seven hundred sixty & two

WARRINGTON MONTHLY MEETING

Jacob Hinshaw	Faithfull Love	James Smith
John Jones	Mary Garretson	<u>Mary Smith</u>
James Love	Sinfonia Twinlin	Susanna Jones
William Willis	Jane Hendricks	Martha Falkner
Joseph Updegraff	Catherine Brown	Eve Griffith
Joseph Garretson	John Morgan	Jane Dunn
William Updegraff	William Hodgen	Jane Falkner
John Morris	Zofigna Grigg	Mary Falkner
George Moul	John Kay	Eve Morris
George Springett	Daniel Bonine	Joanna Heald
Henry Clayton	Jesse Falkner	Mary Smith
John Griffith	John Jones	Susanna Updegraff
	Thos Falkner	Sarah Updegraff

#51   21st of 10th mo 1762   THOMAS EDMUNDSON-MARY PENROSE

Whereas <u>Thomas Edmundson</u> of the township of warrington county of york and province of pencilvania son of <u>Caleb Edmundson and Esther</u> his wife and <u>Mary Penrose</u> of the township county and province afforesd Daughter of <u>William Penrofe and Ann</u> his wife...at warrington in the county and province aforesd the twenty first day of the tenth month in the year of our Lord one thousand seven hundred and sixty two...

No names in	William Garretson	Thomas Edmundson
this column	William Underwood	<u>Mary Edmundson</u>
	Joseph Garretson	Caleb Edmundson
	William Nevet	John Edmundson
	William McMillan	William Penrofe
	Nicholas Steer	Esther Edmundson
	Enos Ellis	Ann Penrofe
	John Borrey	Mary Garretson
	John Clark	Susanah Underhill
	John Smith	Elizabeth McMillan
	Jonathan Hughs	Patience Berrey
		Ann Steer
		Sarah Reed
		Jane Penrofe

#52   20th of 10th mo 1762   ISAAC OLDHAM-MARY YOUNGER

Whereas <u>Isaac Oldham</u> of menalen township county of york and province of Pencilvania & <u>Mary Younger</u> of the township county & province aforesaid...on the twentieth day of the tenth month called october in the year of our Lord one thousand seven hundred and sixty two...at menalen

MARRIAGES

Alexander Megrew	Hannah Mickle	Isaac Oldham
Samuel Hutton	Mary Lacland	Mary Oldham
Thos Blackburn	Sarah Mackrell	James Megrew
Solomon Shepherd	Ruth Wilson	Mary Megrew
John Wilson	Martha Macknight	John Ingland
Jno Megrew	Mary Broustee	John England
James Megrew	Sarah Hammon	Robert England
John Wright juner	John Blackburn	Benjamin Mackrall
Alexander Megrew juner	John Mickle	Nathan Megrew
	Wm Farquer	Simeon Megrew
Finley Megrew	Benja Loan	Mary Hutton
	Wm Griffith	Margreat Blackburn
		Mary Fleming
		Rachel Blackburn
		Ann Megrew
		Sarah Mickle
		Elizabeth Shepard

#53   22nd of 12th mo 1762   GEORGE PHILIPS-JANE FISHER
Whereas <u>George Philips</u> of the township of warrington in the county of york and province of pencilvania son of <u>John Philips</u> deceased and <u>Jane Fisher</u> of the township of newbery in the county and province aforesd Daughter of <u>James and Alice Fisher</u>...at newbery in the county and province aforesaid the twenty second day of the twelfth month in the year of our Lord one thousand seven hundred and sixty two

John Garretson	Betty Hutton	George Philips
Joseph Hutton	Rachel Leech	Jane Philips
William Wilson	Mary Chrarige	James Fisher
Abraham Elliot	Elizabeth Hufsey	Allice Fisher
James Ewing	Mary Mills	Hannah Phillips
Samuel Cook	Joseph Cook	Edmund Philips
William Penrofe	Prifilla Elliot	Nathen Philips
William Garretson	Robert Lindsey	Samuel Fifher
Lydiah Garretson		Sarah Stanton
		Susanah Willis
		Francis Wilkinfon
		William Mills
		Thomas James
		David Copeland
		John Philips
		Rachel Copeland
		Sarah James

#54   9th of 6th mo 1763   JOHN GARRETSON-MARY GRIEST
Whereas <u>John Garretson</u> of the township of newbery in the county of york and province of pencilvania son of <u>John Garretson</u> and <u>Mary Griest</u> of warrington township in the county and province aforesd daughter of <u>John and Susannah Griest</u>...at huntington in the county

WARRINGTON MONTHLY MEETING

and province afforsd the ninth day of the sixth month in the year of our Lord one thoufand seven hundred and sixty three

Nathaniel Cox	John Griest juner	John Garretson
Elizabeth Everitt	Hannah Griest	Mary Garretson
Patience Berrey	Alexander Underwood	John Garretson
Mary Beals	William Underwood	John Griest
Elizabeth Cox	Benjamin Underwood	Sufanah Griest
Clery Swoap	John Berrey	William Garretson
Elizabeth Beals	Caleb Beals	Ann Garretson
Martha Bower	Petter Bower	Susanah Underwood
Elizabeth Comer	Henery Cayton	Liddia Garretson
Sarah Wierman	William Cox	Isaac Everitt
Neomi Cox	Nicholas Wierman	William Garretson
Mary Dill	William Garretson jr	Jacob Beals Sr
Martha Jones	William Beals	Jacob Beals jr
Mary Low	Conrad Swoap	Henery Marfh
Ann Garretson	David Copelin	Richard Cox
	William Kenworthy	Daniel Griest
	John Comer	Martha Everitt
	John Jones	Willing Griest
	John Beals	
	James Brown	

#55 This is a blank page.

#56 21st of 7th mo 1763   WILLIAM GRIFFITH-JOANNA CRAIGE

Whereas <u>William Griffith</u> of the township of warrington county of york and Province of pencilvania and <u>Joanna Craige</u> of the township, County and province aforesd daughter of <u>William Craige and Mary</u> his wife...at warrington in the county and province aforesd the twenty first day of the seventh month in the year of our Lord one thoufand seven hundred and sixty three

Elizabeth Wickersham	William Underwood	William Griffith
Hannah Nevet	William Garretson	Joanna Griffith
Ann Penrofe	William Nevet	William Craige
Barbara Everit	Joseph Garretson	Ruth Simmons
Susannah Ward	Benjamin Underwood	Bethsheba Craige
Margret Patterson	James Ewing	Mary Craige
	William Penrofe	Abraham Griffith
	Joshua Bennett	Rebecca Dun
	Richard Carson	Jane Ewing
	Nathen Phillips	Elizabeth Clark
	William Ward	Ann Steer
	John Simmons	Mary Carson
	John McMillan	
	William Miles	
	Ann Wright	

MARRIAGES

#57   18th of 8th mo 1763   ROBERT THORNBRUGH-CATHRINE ROSBOROUGH
Whereas <u>Robert Thornbrugh</u> of the township of middletown in the county of Cumberland and Province of Pennsylvania and <u>Cathrine Rosborough</u> daughter of <u>Robert & Elinor Rosborough</u> of the township of allin county & Province aforesaid...eighteenth Day of the eighth month in the year of our Lord one thousand seven hundred and sixty three...at warrington

William Garretson	Martha McIntyre	Robert Thornbrugh
Peter Cleaver juner	Rachel Marshall	<u>Cathrine Thornbrugh</u>
Wm Penrofe	Ruth Underwood	Robert Rosborough
Ann Penrofe	Jane McMillan	Elinor Rosborough
John McMillan	Deborah McMillan	Sarah Thornbrugh
Wm McMillan	Mary McMillan	Susannah Thornbrugh
Mary Hutton	Margreat Conover	Thomas Thornbrugh
John Edmundson	Hannah Nevitt	Joshua Rosborough
	Ann Cook	Samuel Morthland
	Mary Everit	Thos Evans
	William Nevitt	Abigail Wily
	Philip Rigbie	Jane Huges
	William Underwood	Sarah Atkinson

#58 19th of 10th mo 1763   SOLOMON SHEPERD-MARGREAT BLACKBURN
Whereas <u>Solomon Sheperd</u> of menalen township county of york and Province of Pencilvania son of <u>Solomon Sheperd</u> deceased and <u>Jane</u> his wife & <u>Margreat Blackburn</u> of the township county and province aforesaid Daughter of <u>John Blackburn and Rebeckah</u> his wife...on the nineteenth Day of the tenth month in the year of our Lord one thousand seven hundred & sixty three...at their meeting in menalen aforsd

WARRINGTON MONTHLY MEETING

Joseph Bigger
William Pidgeon
Alice Wright
Mary McGrew
Sarah Miller
Sarah Wierman
Hannah Mickle
Alice Blackburn
Sarah Nickel
Mary Blackburn
Ann Blackburn
Agnefs Bigger

Jno Hamond
Nathan Megrew
Jesse Falkner
Samuel Dieson
Charls Pigdeon
William Biger
Nicholas Wierman
Jno Galbreath
Robert Miller
Samuel Hutton
William Braselton
Sarah Braselton
Sarah Mickle
Mary Sheperd
Jno Wright
Andrew Dennin
Elizabeth Mickle
John Hall
Robert McGill

Solomon Sheperd
Margreat Sheperd
Jno Blackburn
Thos Blackburn
Finley McGrew
John Sheperd
Thos Blackburn
Rachel Blackburn
Anthony Blackburn
Joseph Blackburn
Jno Mickle juner
Rachel Blackburn
Elizabeth Sheperd
Rebeckah Blackburn
William Hutton
Henry Marsh
Benjamin Loan

#59 19th of 10th mo 1763   WILLIAM GRIFFITH-SARAH HAMOND
Whereas William Griffith of menallen township in the county of york & province of Pensylvania son of Thomas Griffith & Eve his wife and Sarah Hamond of the township County & Province aforesd Daughter of John Hamond and Deborah his wife...this nineteenth Day of ye tenth month in the year of our Lord one thousand seven hundred & sixty three at menalen

Ann McGrew
Alice Wright
Jane Falkner
Jane Falkner
Elizabeth Hamond
Mary Beals
Mary Glasgow
Mary SMith

Elizabeth Griffith
John Mickle
Robert Miller
William Beals
John Pope
William Pigeon
Henry Marsh
John Morton
James Glasgow
Wm Hutton
Samuel Buyers
Robert Mordough

William Griffith
Sarah Griffith
Thos Griffith
Jno Hamond
Finley Megrew
Jesse Falkner
Nathan McGrew
Isaac Oldham
Finley McGrew
Benjamin Wright
Benjamin Wilson
Samuel Hutton
James McGrew
Eve Griffith
Thos Hinshaw

#60 23rd of 11th mo 1763   THOMAS JENNINGS-SUSANNAH WARREN
Whereas Thomas Jennings of the township of newbery in the county of york and in the Province of pensylvania and Susannah Warren of the same place this twenty third day of the Eleventh month in the year of

MARRIAGES

our Lord one thousand seven hundred & sixty three at a publick meeting house in newbery

William Garretson	Hannah Fisher	Thomas Jennings
Stephen Day	Isabel Whinery	Susannah Jennings
Thomas Whinery	Margaret Welch	Robert Mills
Francis Wilkinson	Joseph Hutton	Robert Mills juner
Philip Gibson	John Hussey	James Mills
John Whinery	John Garretson	Elizabeth Hussey
	John Smith	Elizabeth Wilkinson
	William Wilson	Ann Garretson
		Alice Fisher

#61   14th of 2nd mo 1764   JOHN UPDEGRAFF-ANN HARLAN

Whereas John Updegraff son of Harman Updegraff of york town in the county of york and Province of Pensylvania Deceased & Ann Harlan daughter of James Harlan of Chefter County in the Province aforesaid in York town aforesaid on the fourteenth day of the second month in the year one thousand seven hundred & sixty four

Nathan Husey	Daniel Ragen	John Updegraff
Joseph Garetson	Isaac Everitt	Ann Updegraff
Wm Mathews	Jacob Worley	William Updegraff
Ambrofe Updegraff	Joanna Heald	Harman Updegraff
Wm Leas	Edith Hussey	Abraham Updegraff
Geo Nease	Mary Lon	Betty Willis
John Jones	Hanah Mathews	Sarah Updegraff
James Heald	Hannah Richardson	Lydia Updegraff
	Mary Nease	Joseph Updegraff
	Hannah Webb	Am Willis
	Sarah Webb	Susanna Updegraff
	Cathrine Brown	
	Mary Garretfon	

#62   27th of 3rd mo 1764   JOSEPH GREGG-MARY COLLINS

Whereas Joseph Gregg of newbery Township of york County in the Province of Pensylvania cordwainer and Mary Collins of York Town Daughter of John Collins in the County & Province aforesd...this twenty seventh day of the third month in the year of our Lord one thousand seven hundred and sixty four...at york Town in the county & Province aforesaid

WARRINGTON MONTHLY MEETING

Hannah Matthews
Cathrine Brown
Sarah Updegraff
Hannah Webb
Sarah Webb

John Garretson
John Least
Jesse Falkner
Joseph Garretson
Wm Willis
Joseph Updegraff
Wm Mathews
John Jones
James Brown
Joseph Collins
Nathen Hussey
Wm Leas

Joseph Gregg
Mary Gregg
Elizabeth Hussey
Ann Collins
John Hussey
Ruth Collins
Jeddiah Hufsey
George Welch
Miriam Hussey
Andrew Welch
Susannah Updegraff
Edith Hussey
Betty Willis

#63 3rd of 5th mo 1764   JEDAIAH HUSSEY-JANE PENROSE
Whereas Jedaiah Hufsey of the township of newbery County of york and Province of pensylvania son of John Hufsey & Jane Penrofe of the township of warrington in the County & Province aforesaid daughter of William & Ann Penrofe...at warrington in the County and Province aforesaid the third day of the fifth month in the year of our Lord one thousand seven hundred and sixty four

Elihu Underwood
Jonathan Hughes
John Smith
Mary Garretson
Ruth Underwood
Hannah Nevett
Hannah Penrofe
Margreat Underwood
Caleb Edmondson

Alexander Underwood
Wm Underwood
Thos Atherton
Wm Garretson
Robert Miller
Robert Vale
John Edmondson
Jofhua Bennett
Wm Nevett
James Ewing
Wm Thomas
Peter Cleaver juner

Jedaiah Hufsey
Jane Hufsey
Wm Penrofe
Ann Penrofe
Thos Edmondson
Mary Edmondson
Riccord Hufsey
Jno Hufsey
Ann Smith
Thos Penrofe

#64 23rd of 5th mo 1764   JOSEPH COOK-ELIZABETH WILKINSON
Whereas Joseph Cook of the township of warrington County of York and Province of Pensylvania son of Peter Cook & Sarah his wife and Elizabeth Wilkinson of the township of Paxton County of Lanchester and Province aforesaid widow of Joseph Wilkinson deceased...at newbery in the county of york aforesaid the twenty third day of the fifth month in the year of our Lord one thousand seven hundred and sixty four

MARRIAGES

David Johnson	Wm Mills	Joseph Cook
Robert Mills juner	Mary Wilkinson	Elizabeth Cook
Betty Hutton	Peter Cook juner	Sarah Cook
Ruth Lewis	Ann Cook	Samuel Cook
Rachel Johnson	Sarah Cook juner	Susanna Mills
Ann Taylor	Samuel Fisher	Wm Nevett
	Miriam Fisher	Hannah Nevett
	Wm Underwood	James Fisher
	Wm Garretson	Francis Wilkinson
	Joseph Hutton	
	John Smith	

#65 5th of 9th mo 1764   WILLING GRIEST-ANN GARRETSON

Whereas Willing Griest of the township of manahon [Menallen] in the County of York and Province of Penfylvania son of John Griest deceased and Ann Garretson of the township of newbery in the County & Province aforesd Daughter of John Garretson...at newbery in the County and Province aforesaid the fifth day of the ninth month in the year of our Lord one thousand seven hundred and sixty four

Susannah Jennings	John Hufsey juner	Willing Griest
Ann Smith	Elizabeth Hufsey	Ann Griest
Mary Gregg	Lydia Garretson	John Garretson
Cathrine Noblet	Miriam Hufsey	John Garretson
Ann Whinery	Mary Lone	Wm Garretson
Jane Hussey	Joseph Updegraff	John Garretson juner
Joseph Hutton	Margret Hufsey	Daniel Griest
Wm Willson	Robert Whinery	Susannah Griest
Jno Smith	Betty Hutton	Isaac Everitt
Thos Jennings	Rebeckah Willfon	John Hufsey
Joseph Gregg	Ann Taylor	Ricord Hufsey
David Johnfon	Rachel Johnson	Jedaiah Hufsey
Joshua Hutton	Mary Mills	

#66 5th of 9th mo 1764   SAMUEL COOK-HANNAH FISHER

Whereas Samuel Cook of the township of warrington County of york and Province of Pennsylvania son of Peter and Sarah Cook and Hannah Fisher of the township of Paxton County of Lanchefter and Province aforsd Daughter of William Fisher deceased...at warrington in the County of York & Province aforesd the fifth day of the ninth month in the year of our Lord one thousand seven hundred & sixty four

WARRINGTON MONTHLY MEETING

Joshua Clark	Joanna Griffith	Samuel Cook
Wm Stephenson	Wm McMillan	Hannah Cook
John Horfman	Nathan Lewis	Peter Cook sener
Wm Horfman	Elihu Underwood	Sarah Cook
Bob Everitt	Wm Wickersham	Robert Fisher
Mary Miller	Zepheniah Underwood	Joseph Cook
Richard Wickersham	El Horfman	Susannah Carleton
Wm Underwood	David Horfman	Elizabeth Cook
Frederick Lether	Richard Wickersham	Elice Fifher
Betty Lether	Samuel Fisher	Mary Talbot
Sarah Stevenson	Jno Talbot	Peter Cook juner
Joseph Benett	Isaac Hancock	Joseph Wilkinson
Wm Rankin	Thos Pain	Frances Wilkinson
Ruth Morthland	Jesse Cook	Alexander Underwood
Agnes Sharp	Sarah Cook	Wm Underwood
Wm Garretson	John Cook	Wm Griffith
Peter Cleaver juner		Robert Miller
Ruth Underwood		Sarah Miller

#67 19th of 6th mo 1765   JAMES HAMMOND-MARY BLACKBURN

Whereas James Hammond of menalen township County of york and Province of Pennfylvania son of Daniel Hammond deceased & Mary Blackburn of the township County & Province aforesd...on the nineteenth day of the sixth month in the year of our Lord one thousand seven hundred & sixty five...at menalen

Benjamin Loan	Elizabeth Griffith	James Hammond
Solomon Sheperd	Elizabeth Hammond	her
Charles Pidgeon	Margret Sheperd	Mary x Hammond
William Griffith	Robert Graham	mark
Samuel Buyers	John Morton	Jno Blackburn
Jonathan Wright	William Hutton	Anthony Blackburn
Samuel Wright	William Veulon	Joseph Blackburn
Nathan McGrew	Samuel Hutton	William Camble
James McGrew juner	John Wilson	Jno Hammond
Thomas Blackburn	James Glasgow	George Wilfon
	John Wright	Cornelius Campbel
	Ebenezer Harland	Samuel Morton juner
	Alexander Underwood	James Griffey
	John Least	Benjamin Wilson
	William Delap	Patrick Campbel
	David Potts	Mary McGrew
		Rebecah Blackburn
		Sarah Wilson
		Sarah Griffith
		Ann McGrew

34

MARRIAGES

#68 5th of 9th mo 1765   ISAAC WICKERSHAM-ELIZABETH FRAIZER
Whereas Isaac Wickersham of the township of warrington county of york
and province of Penfylvania son of Richard Wickersham and Elizabeth
Fraizer daughter of James Fraizer deceased of the township of Newbery
in the county and Province aforesaid...at warrington ye fifth day of
the ninth month in the year of our Lord one thousand seven hundred
and sixty five

Ruth Underwood	Jno McMillan	Isaac Wickersham
Mary McMillan	Jane McMillan	Elizabeth Wickersham
Hannah Cook	Deborah McMillan	Richard Wickersham
Ruth Morthland	Caleb Frazor	Alice Lodon
Sarah Vale	Aaron Frazor	Richard Wickersham
Hanah Nevett	John Lee	jr
Robert Vale	Peter Cleaver juner	Wm Garretson
John Harry	Wm Nevett	John Leaft
Richard Cox	Wm Underwood	Aaron Frazor
Wm Marsh	Wm McMillan	
	Jonathan Marsh	

#69 26th of 9th mo 1765   WILLIAM KENWORTHY-MARY EVERIT
Whereas William Kenworthy of huntington Township in the County of
york & province of Pencilvania son of Joshua Kenworthy deceased and
Mary Everit of hunting aforesaid Daughter of John Everit...at
huntington in ye county & province aforesaid ye twentisixth day of ye
ninth month in the year of our Lord one thousand seven hundred &
sixty five

Thos Griest	Susanna Moor	William Kenworthy
Jno Berry	Margret Hunter	Mary Kenworthy
Patience Berry	Elizabeth Hunter	John Everitt
Hannah Jones	Wm Cox	Martha Everitt
Susana Cox	David Kenworthy	Joseph Everitt
Anna Cox	Barbara Everit	Joshua Kenworthy
Jno Griest	Anna Everitt	
Susanna Griest	Wm Wierman	
Hannah Griest	Rebekah Kenworthy	
Ann Griest	Wm Cox juner	
	John Griest juner	
	Jacob Beals	

#70 10th of 12th mo 1765   JOSEPH COLLINS-REBECKAH PHILIPS
Whereas Joseph Collins son of John Collins of York Town in ye county
of york and Province of Pensylvania and Rebeckah Philips Daughter of
John Philips late of baltimore County in ye Province of maryland,
Deceased...this tenth day of ye twelfth month in the year of our Lord
one thousand seven hundred and sixty five

WARRINGTON MONTHLY MEETING

Susana Robison	Shinoh Eting	Joseph Collins
Hannah Webb	Betty Willis	Rebeckah Collins
Sarah Webb	Mary Garretson	John Collins
Betty Jones	Lydia Updegraff	Ann Collins
Ann Smith	Susanna Updegraff	Deborah Philips
Susanna Nails	Mary Low	Mary Gregg
Alice Falkner	Kathrine Leas	Hannah Mathews
Thos Day	Jane Falkner	Jane Philips
Ambrose Updegraff	Mary Key	Deborah Philips
David Falkner	Elinor Linch	Ruth Collins
Nathan Updegraff	Hannah Bennet	Priscilla Philips
Jno Willis	George Philips	Sarah Collins
Wm Welch	Wm Mathews	Harman Updegraff
Samuel Day	Jno Collins	Wm Updegraff
Andrew Welch	Joseph Gregg	
Amos Fisher	Nathan Hussey	
Wm Montgomery	Joseph Updegraff	
Francis Worley	Joseph Garretson	
Joanna Heald	Wm Willis	
Edith Hussey	John Jones	
Margret Matthews	Wm Leas	

#71 29th of 1st mo 1766   SAMUEL HENDRICKS-ALICE WRIGHT
Samuel Hendricks of menalen township County of York and Province of Penfylvania and Alice Wright of the township County and Province aforesaid; Daughter of John Wright & Elizabeth his wife...on ye twenty ninth day of ye first month in the year of our Lord one thousand seven hundred and sixty six at their meeting house in Township of menalen aforesaid

Alexander Ramsey	Mary McGrew	Samuel Hendricks
Thomas Blackburn	Rebeckah Blackburn	Alice Hendricks
James Houlsworth	Sarah Loan	John Wright
Joseph Houlsworth	Sarah Griffith	John Wright juner
	Deborah Hutton	Samuel Hutton
	Eve Griffith	Benja. Wright
	Lydia Wilson	Jonathan Wright
	Rachel Blackburn	Joel Wright
	Frances Beatty	Charls Pidgeon
	James McGrew	Samuel Wright
	Thomas Griffith	Nicholas Wierman
		Benjamin Loan
		William Pidgeon
		William Griffith
		William Hutton

#72 13th of 5th mo 1766   THOMAS LEECH-PHEBE PENROSE
Whereas Thomas Leech of the township of warrington County of york and Province of Pencilvania son of Thomas Leech and Sarah his wife and

MARRIAGES

Phebe Penrose of the same place Daughter of William Penrofe & Ann his wife...at warrington in the county and province aforesaid the thirteenth day of the fifth month in the year of our Lord one thousand seven hundred and sixty six

Hannah Nevett	Jno McMillan	Thomas Leech
Jedaiah Hussey	Jane McMillan	Phebe Leech
Joshua Bennett	Jane Hussey	Thomas Leech
Wm Griffith	Thos Edmondson	Wm Penrofe
Jno Smith	Michael King	Ann Penrofe
Ann Smith	Alexander Underwood	Sarah Leech
Hannah Penrofe	Wm Underwood	Jane Boyd
Joanna Griffith	Wm Garretson	John Boyd
Elizabeth Clerk	Mary Garretson	Sarah L ech
Ruth Underwood	Wm Nevett	Jane Taylor
John Thomas	Mary McMillan	Caleb Edmondson
Rebecah Thomas	Hannah Cook	Jane Marsh
Abraham Griffith		
Zephaniah Underwood		

#73 20th of 5th mo 1766   BENJAMIN WRIGHT-JANE FALKNER

Whereas Benjamin Wright son of John Wright of Menalen Township in the County of york and Province of Pensylvania and Jane Falkner Daughter of Jesse Faulkner of Hellam Township in the County of york aforesaid...this twentieth Day of the fifth month in the year of our Lord one thousand seven hundred and sixty six...at york Town in the county and Province aforesaid

Seth Duncan	Hannah Webb	Benjamin Wright
John Least	Mary Garretson	Jane Wright
Wm Penrofe	Susanna Updegraff	Jesse Faulkner
Wm Mathews	Elizabeth Clayton	Martha Faulkner
John Collins	Ann Smith	Samuel Wright
Joseph Updegraff	Elizabeth Griffith	Thomas Faulkner
James Love	Samuel Griffith	John Wright juner
Wm Willis	Joel Wright	Mary Faulkner
Thos Brown	David Faulkner	Jane Faulkner
Wm Griffith	Charls Pidgeon	
Joseph Collins	Robert Smith	
Joseph Garretson	Robert Smith juner	
Margret Mathews	Faithful Love	
Ann Updegraff	Hannah Bennett	
Ann Collins	Mary Key	
Ann Penrofe		
Mary Hobson		

#74 27th of 11th mo 1766   WILLIAM WICKERSHAM-MARY NEVET

Whereas William Wickersham of the township of warrington in the county of york and Province of Pensylvania son of Richard Wickersham and Mary Nevet of the township county and Province aforesaid daughter

WARRINGTON MONTHLY MEETING

of <u>Thomas Nevet</u> deceafed...at warrington in the county and province aforesd the twenty seventh day of the eleventh month in the year of our Lord one thousand seven hundred and sixty six

Elenor Thomas	Ann Penrofe	William Wickersham
Jehu Thomas	Sarah Vale	<u>Mary Wickersham</u>
Michael Oaker	Jno McMillan	Richard Wickersham
John Woaxth	Jane McMillan	Elizabeth Wickersham
Will Rofs	Aaron Coats	Cathrine Harry
Martha Rofs	Mary Coats	Samuel Wickersham
Sarah Underwood	Wm Nevet	Isaac Wickersham
Jane Underwood	Hannah Nevet	Richard Wickersham
Loy Nelson	Wm Steer	Elizabeth Wickersham
Ann Nelson	Hannah Steer	Elizabeth Nevet
Casper Miller	Jno Harry	
Christian Miller	Charles Muckelwee	
Wm Griffith	Susannah Hint	
Benjamin Underwood	Hannah Muckelwee	
Robert Vale	Wm Underwood	
Jno Thomas	Wm Garretson	
Rebecah Thomas	Mary Garretson	

<u>#75 24th of 2nd mo 1767</u>   SAMUEL UPDEGRAFF-MARY LOW

Whereas <u>Samuel Updegraff</u> son of <u>Harmon Updegraff and Mary</u> his wife deceafed boath of york town in the County of york and province of pencilvania and <u>Mary Low</u> of the same place, widow of <u>Joshua Low</u> late of manchefter township in the county and province aforesd Deceafed...this twenty fourth day of the second month in the year of our Lord one thoufand seven hundred and sixty seven at york town aforesd in the sd province

MARRIAGES

John Willis	Joseph Garretson	Samuel Updegraff
Ludwig Hetig	Wm Leas	Mary Updegraff
John Jones	Francis Jones	John Hufsey
John Hunt juner	Zachariah Northon	Nathan Hufsey
Thos Thompson	John Collins juner	Riccord Hufsey
Thos Day	Thos Worley	Susanah Hufsey
Amos Fisher	Francis Worley	Harmon Updegraff
Andrew Welch	William Welch	William Updegraff
Ann Collins	Nathan Hufsey	John Updegraff
Joannah Heald	Ambros Updegraff	Abraham Updegraff
Mary Garretson	Ambros Updegraff jr	Joseph Updegraff
Ruth Collins	Nathen Updegraff	
Mary Beal	Miriam Hufsey	
Elinor Linch	Jane Hufsey	
Martha Updegraff	Edith Hufsey	
Ann Updegraff	Margaret Hufsey	
Wm Mathews	Sarah Updegraff	
Wm Willis	Lidia Updegraff	
John Collins	Ursila Updegraff	
	Doratha Cromrine	
	Hanah Webb	
	Sarah Webb	
	Mary Updegraff	
	Susan Updegraff	

#76 21st of 5th mo 1767   SAMUEL MORTHLAND-SUSANNAH CREAGE

Whereas Samuel Morthland of the township of warrington in the county of york and province of Pencilvania and Susannah Creage of Middleton township in the County of Cumberland and province aforesd widdow of John Creage deceased...at warrington in the county and Province afforesaid the twenty first day of the fifth month in the year of our Lord one thousand seven hundred and sixty seven

Hannah Nevett	Peter Cleaver	Samuel Morthland
Jane McMillan	William Nevett	Susannah Morthland
Margaret Marsh	John McMillan	Robt Thornbrugh
Hannah Bennett	Robert Vale	William Morthland
	James Cadwallader	Sarah Thornbrugh
	Benjamin Steer	Thomas Thornbrugh
	Joshua Bennett	Joseph Thornbrugh
	Ebenezer Horfman	Eleanar Rofeborough
		William Underwood
		John Underwood
		John Thomas
		William Garretson
		John Marfh juner
		Benjamin Underwood

WARRINGTON MONTHLY MEETING

#77   25th of 6th mo 1767   NATHAN PHILLIPS-MARY MCMILLAN

Whereas <u>Nathan Phillips</u> son of <u>Edmund Phillips</u> of warrington township in the county of york and province of Pencilvania, yeoman, and <u>Mary McMillan</u> daughter of <u>Thomas McMillan</u> of the township County and Province afforesaid Deceafed...this twentyfifth day of the sixth month in the year of our Lord one thoufand seven hundred and sixty seven...at warrington

Lydia Holland	Henery Aterton	Nathan Phillips
William Bartley	Abigail Atherton	<u>Mary Phillips</u>
Hugh Gwinn	William Nevett	Edmond Phillips
Deborah Marfh	Jane Phillips	John McMillan
Peter Cook juner	Mary Garretson	John Phillips
Thomas Holland	Elizabeth Bell	William McMillan
Mary Marfh	Wm Griffith	George McMillan
Hannah Bennett	Johanna Griffith	George Phillips
Deborah McMillan	Jofhua Bennett	Margaret Guinn
Samuel Lewis	John Bell	John Marfh
	Ann McMillan	Henry Holland
	Hannah Nevett	Phebe Philips
	Robert Vale	Richard Atherton
	Sarah Vale	
	Elizabeth McMillan	

#78   8th of 9th mo 1767   WILLIAM KERSEY-HANNAH BENNETT

Whereas <u>William Kerfey</u> of york town in the county of york and province of pencilvania son of <u>William Kersey and Elizabeth</u> his wife (both deceased) and <u>Hannah Bennett</u> of the same place Daughter of <u>Joseph Bennett and Rebecca</u> his wife (both deceased)...this eighth day of the ninth month in the year one thousand seven hundred and sixty seven...in york town

Mary Garretson	William Updegraff	William Kersey
Mary Key	John Jones	<u>Hannah Kersey</u>
Elenor Linch	Ambros Updegraff	Sarah Updegraff
Priscilla Phillips	Wm Montgomery	Bettey Jones
Hannah Webb	Amos Fisher	Joshua Bennett
Ann Coulter	Thomas Day	Joseph Bennett
Lydia Updegraff	Thomas Tomson	Isaac Bennett
Hannah Crookham	Nathen Updegraff	Hannah Richardson
Rebecca Day	Benjamin Deleplain	Margreat Mathews
Hannah Steer	Joanna Heald	Ann Updegraff
	Edith Hussey	Wm Mathews
	Deborah Philips	Nathen Hussey
	Faithfull Love	Joseph Garretson
	Ann Collins	Joseph Updegraff
	Bettey Willis	Wm Leas
	Mary Hayslet	

MARRIAGES

#79 30th of 9th mo 1767   JOHN WRIGHT-ELIZABETH HAMMOND
Whereas <u>John Wright juner</u> of Minalon township county of york and Province of Pencylvania son of <u>John Wright and Elizabeth</u> his wife and <u>Elizabeth Hammond</u> of township county and province afforesd Daughter of <u>John Hammond and Deborah</u> his wife...this thirtieth day of the ninth month in the year of our Lord seven hundred and sixty seven

Isaac Everitt	James Newlan	John Wright
Jesse Faulkner	Martha Faulkner	<u>Elizabeth Wright</u>
Finley McGrew	Elizabeth Farquhar	John Wright
William Newlan	Jane Wright	John Hammond
James McGrew	Deborah Blackburn	Benjamin Wright
Joseph Blackburn	Mary Hammond	Samuel Wright
John Morten	Mary Morten	Joel Wright
William Hutton	Sarah Loan	Alice Hendricks
	George Willson	Samuel Hendricks
	Benjamin Loan	William Wierman

#80 24th of 9th mo 1767   JESSE COOK-MARY WIERMAN
Whereas <u>Jesse Cook</u> son of <u>Peter Cook</u> of warrington in the county of york and province of Pennsylvania and <u>Sarah</u> his wife and <u>Mary Wierman</u> the daughter of <u>Henery Wierman</u> of huntington and County aforesaid and <u>Priscilla</u> his wife...this twenty forth day of the ninth month in the year of our Lord one thousand seven hundred and sixty seven...at huntington in the county aforesaid

John Griest	Jesse Faulkner	Jesse Cook
Susanah Griest	William Wierman	<u>Mary Cook</u>
Isaac Everitt	Phebe Wierman	Peter Cook
Martha Everitt	William Cox	Henry Wierman
Mary Kenworthy	Joshua Kenworthy	Peter Cook jr
Ann Griest	Peter Bower	Sarah Cook
John Berry	Anna Everitt	John Pope
Patience Berry	Martha Faulkner	Hannah Todd
William Kenworthy	Nathaniel Cox	William Nevett
John Pope	Elizabeth Cox	Nicholas Wierman
	John Elliot	Sarah Wierman
	William Delap	Gartrude Wright
		William Pope
		Jean Faulkner

#81 3rd of 11th mo 1767   WILLIAM NEWLAN-MARGARET MORTON
Whereas <u>William Newlan</u> of minallen Township in the County of york and province of pensylvania, son of <u>William Newlan and Hannah</u> his wife and <u>Margaret Morton</u> of the township county and Province aforesaid Daughter of <u>John Morton and Mary</u> his wife...this third day of the Eleventh month in the year of our Lord one thousand seven hundred and sixty seven...at Menallen in the county aforesaid

WARRINGTON MONTHLY MEETING

Mary McGrew
James McGrew
Jane Wright
Susannah Griffith
Elizabeth Wright
Lydia Willson
Ann McGrew
Margaret Hutton
Ann Blackburn
Agnes Blackburn
Jonathan Hughes
Jane Faulkner
Sarah Delap

Finley McGrew
George Wilson
John Blackburn
Leonard Hutton
Robert Fleming
Benjamin Wright
Nathan McGrew
Thomas Mcquown
John McQuown
Jas Glasgow

William Newlan
Margret Newlan
William Newlan
John Morton
James Newlan
Elijah Newlan
William Hutton
Sarah Morton
Debr. Morton
William Delap
Jesse Falkner
Nicholas Wierman

#82 11th of 11th mo 1767   NATHAN MCGREW-RACHEL BLACKBURN
Whereas <u>Nathan McGrew</u> of minallen township county of york and Province of Pensylvania, son of <u>James McGrew and Mary</u> his wife (Deceased) and <u>Rachel Blackburn</u> of the Township County and Province aforesaid, Daughter of <u>John Blackburn and Rebeckah</u> his wife, (both deceased)...this eleventh day of the eleventh month in the year of our Lord one thousand seven hundred and sixty seven...at Monallen in the County aforesd

Mary McGrew
Ann McGrew
Mary McGrew jr
Catheren McGrew
Ruth Willson
Mary Hammond

Benjamin Loan
Wm Mathews
William Delap
Jesse Faulkner
John Wright
John Hammond
Jno Pope
Benjamin Wright

Nathan McGrew
<u>Rachel McGrew</u>
Finley McGrew
James McGrew
Thomas Blackburn
James McGrew jr
Moses Blackburn
Anthony Blackburn jr
Anthony Blackburn
James Hammond
John McGrew
Alexander McGrew

#83 18th of 11th mo 1767   MOSES BLACKBURN-MARY MCGREW
Whereas <u>Moses Blackburn</u> of Monallon Township County of York and Province of Pennfylvania, Son of <u>John Blackburn and Rebeckah</u> his wife both deceased And <u>Mary McGrew</u> of the Township County and Province aforesaid Daughter of <u>James McGrew & Mary</u> his wife Deceased...this eighteenth Day of the Eleventh Month in the year of Our Lord one thousand, seven hundred and sixty seven...at their Meeting house in Monallon aforesaid
                                                        Moses Blackburn
                                                             her
                                                        <u>Mary x Blackburn</u>
                                                             mark

MARRIAGES

Rachel McGrew	Benjamin Loan	James McGrew
Cathern McGrew	John Hammond	Thomas Blackburn
Ann McGrew	John Pope	Anthony Blackburn jr
Mary McGrew	John Sheppard	Anthony Blackburn sr
Elizabeth Buyers	Samuel Buyers	Joseph Blackburn
	Alexander McGrew	Nathan McGrew
	James McGrew	Solomon Sheppard
	Robert Sturgan	John McGrew
	Elizabeth Newlan	

#84 20th of 1st mo 1768   JOHN GARRETSON-PHEBE FRAIZER
Whereas John Garretson of the Township of Newbury in the County of york and Province of Pennsylvania and Phebe Fraizer of Allen Township in the County of Cumberland and Province aforesaid...this Twentieth Day of the first Month in the year of our Lord one thousand seven Hundred and sixty eight...at Newbury

John Rankin	Joseph Hutton	John Garretson
Robt. Miller	Wm Wilson	Phebe Garretson
Susanna Jennings	Thos Jennings	Wm Garretson
Jane Pugh	Henry Clayton	Joseph Garretson
Abigail Rankin	Benjamin Elliot	John Hussey
Margaret Hufsey	Richard Carson	Alexander Eliot
Hannah Webb	Sarah Miller	William Grist
Ann Garretson	Mary Garretson	Mary Garretson
Jane Love	Wm Garretson jr.	Miriam Hussey
Thos Whinnery	Content Garretson	Aaron Fraizer
John Love	Record Hussey	
Moses Fraizer	Wm Garretson	
John Elliot	Samuel Miller	
Sarah Webb	Sylvanus Day	
Hannah Miller	Wm Love	

#85 11th of 10th mo 1768   JOHN GRIFFITH JR-MARY FALKNER
Whereas John Griffith juner son of John Griffith of East Nantmeal Township in the County of Chester and Province of Pennsylvania and Mary Falkner daughter of Jesse Falkner of Menalen township in the County of york and Province aforesaid...this Eleventh Day of the Tenth Month in the year of our Lord one thousand seven Hundred and sixty Eight...in Menalen Meeting House in the County of york and Province aforesaid

WARRINGTON MONTHLY MEETING

Mary John	Wm Hutton	John Griffith
Elizabeth Wright	Henry Wierman jr	Mary Griffith
Samuel Wright	Isaac Everit	John Griffith
George Wilson	Martha Falkner	Jesse Falkner
John Wright	Alice Falkner	Thomas Falkner
Edward Taylor	Mary Smith	David Falkner
	Anna Griffith	James Smith
	Truth John	Wm Griffith
	Mary McGrew	Joel Wright
	Phebe Wierman	Benj. Wright
	Martha Hendricks	Samuel John juner
	Sarah Delap	Jno Wright
	Finley McGrew	John Hammond

#86 20th of 4th mo 1769   JEHU THOMAS-SARAH UNDERWOOD

Whereas <u>Jehu Thomas</u> son of <u>John Thomas</u> of the Township of Warrington in the County of york and Province of Pennsylvania and <u>Sarah Underwood</u> Daughter of <u>Benjamin Underwood</u> of the Township County and Province aforesaid...at Warrington in the County and Province aforesaid the twentieth day of the fourth month in the year of our Lord one thousand seven hundred and sixty nine

Timothy Kirk	Elihu Underwood jr	Jehu Thomas
Elihu Underwood Jr	William John	Sarah Thomas
Saml Cook	Sarah John	John Thomas
Robert Vale	John Underwood	Benjamin Underwood
Abraham Beals	Zephaniah Underwood	Susanna Underwood
Mary Garretson	John Thomas	William Underwood
Jacob Williams	Ann Garretson	Elenor Thomas
Ruth Williams	William Nevett	Martha Underwood
James Cadwallader	Hugh Pugh	Nehemiah Underwood
Wm Garretson	Sarah Vale	Rebekah Thomas
Wm Penrofe		
Ann Penrofe		

#87 15th of 11th mo 1769   JOB PUGH-RUTH JOHN

Whereas <u>Job Pugh</u> son of <u>Jesse and Else Pugh</u> of Fredrick County in Virginey and <u>Ruth John</u> Daughter of <u>Samuel (deceased) and Ann John</u> of Newbery township in the County of york and province of Pensylvania...this fifteenth day of the eleventh month in the year of our Lord one thousand seven hundred and sixty nine...at Newbery

MARRIAGES

John Willson	Ann Taylor	Job Pugh
Joseph Hutton	Elizabeth Lewis	Ruth Pugh
Robert Miller	Rachel Hutton	Ann John
Wm Garretson	Rebecca Willson	Alice Pugh
Riccord Hufsey	Bettey Hutton	Mary John
John Garretson	Susana Jennings	Jane Ruble
Wm Rankin	Ellis Lewis	Isaac John
Wm Lewis	William Willson	Ruth Fisher
	Cad'r Evans	Thos Pugh
		Jacob Jenkin

#88 22nd of 3rd mo 1770   HENERY ATHERTON-ANN HOBSON
Whereas Henery Atherton of Warrington in the county of york and province of Pencilvania, son of Thomas Atherton and Ann Hobson of the township county and province aforesd Daughter of Francis Hobson...at warrington in the County and province aforesd the twenty second day of the third month in the year of our Lord one thousand seven hundred and seventy

Wm Nevet	Mary McClelen	Henery Atherton
Wm Steer	Ann Steer	Ann Atherton
Wm Underwood	Mary Marsh	Thomas Atherton
Wm Griffith	Wm McMillan	Record Atherton
Timothy Kirk	George McMillan	Elizabeth Atherton
Nathen Phillips	Ann McMillan	John Marsh Sr
Jacob Williams	Mary Phillips	John McMillan
John Ellot	Jonathan Marsh	
Abram Griffith	Ann Marsh	
John Phillips	Jonathan Marsh Juner	
Sarah Vale		
Mary Ellot		
Hannah Nevet		
Joanna Griffith		
Lydia Holland		
Lydia Paden		

#89 26th of 4th mo 1770   CADWALLADER EVANS-ELEANOR THOMAS
Whereas Cadwalader Evans son of Cadwalader Evans late of Philadelphia County in the province of pennsylvania (Deceased) and Eleanor Thomas daughter of John Thomas of york county in the province of pennsylvania aforesaid...twenty sixth day of the fourth month in the year of our Lord one thousand seven hundred and seventy at warrington aforesaid

WARRINGTON MONTHLY MEETING

James Cadwalader	Sarah Rees	Cadwalader Evans
Caleb Cadwalader	Rebecca Thomas	Elenor Evans
William Nevet	Timothy Kirk	John Thomas
William Underwood	Mary Cadwalader	Rebeakah Thomas
John Mahlon	Isaac Bennet	William Lewis
Abraham Williams	Amos Fisher	Elizabeth Lewis
William Griffith	Mary Lewis	John Rees
Joanna Griffith	Rebecca Lewis	Catherine Rees
(illegible)	Jacob Williams	Enos Rogers
(illegible)	Sarah Cook	Margaret Rogers
	Ann Penrofe	Jehu Thomas
	Hannah Nevet	Sarah Thomas
	Alice Loaden	Isaac John
	William Lewis	Lydia Johns
		Joshua Dickinson
		Ruth Dickinson

#90 2nd of 5th mo 1770   SAMUEL MILLER-HANNAH RANDLES

Whereas Samuel Miller of the township of Newbery in the county of york and Province of Pencilvania (son of Robert Miller and Sarah Miller) and Hannah Randles Daughter of William and Mary Randles ...this second day of the fifth month in the year of our Lord one thousand seven hundred and seventy...at Newbery in the township afforsd

Joseph Hutton	Bettey Hutton	Samuel Miller
Riccord Hufsey	Miriam Hufsey	Hannah Miller
John Garretson	Jane Hufsey	Robert Miller
Joshua Hutton	Sufanna Jennings	Sarah Miller
William Garretson	Elizabeth Lewis	William Randles
William Lewis	Content Garretson	Mary Randles
Samuel Garretson	Sarah Garretson	Martha Randles
George Boyd	Mary Lewis	Mary Miller
Joseph Taylor	Rebecca Lewis	Sarah Miller jr
Joseph Hutton jr	Ann Taylor	Hannah Miller
William Willson	Rebecca Willson	William Randles jr
(illegible)	(illegible)	Robert Miller jr
		James Miller

#91 11th of 10th mo 1768   THOMAS BLACKBURN-ELIZABETH GRIFFITH

Thomas Blackburn of Manallon Township County of York and Province of Pennsylvania, son of John Blackburn and Rebekhah his wife both deceased, and Elizabeth Griffith Daughter of Thomas Griffith and Eve his wife of the Township County and Province aforesaid...on the Eleventh Day of the Tenth month in the year of Our Lord one thousand seven hundred and sixty eight...at their meeting House in Manallon in the County aforesaid
                                   Thomas Blackburn
                                   Elizabeth (her X mark) Blackburn

MARRIAGES

Benjamin Wilson	William Nevitt	Thomas Blackburn
Elijah Mickle	William Delap	Joseph Blackburn
William Royl	John Griest	Moses Blackburn
Thomas Stockton jr	Benjamin Loan	Solomon Shepherd
David Beatty	John Mickle	Nathan McGrew
Thomas Baldwin	Margaret Shepherd	Jacob Cox
Nathan McGrew	Mary Blackburn	John Morton
John Pope	Sarah Mickle	Rachel Blackburn
Samuel Withers	Martha Everitt	
Isaac Everitt	Mary McGrew	
Frances Lamborn	Susanna Griffith	
	Jane Baldwin	
	Hannah Jones	
	Elizabeth Hammond	

#92 3rd of 5th mo 1770   JOSHUA DAVIES-JANE UNDERWOOD

Whereas <u>Joshua Davies</u> son of <u>John Davies</u> of Pikeland Township in the County of Chester and province of Pensylvania and <u>Jane Underwood</u> daughter of <u>William Underwood</u> of warrington township in the County of York in the Province aforesaid...this third day of the fifth month in the year of our Lord one thousand seven hundred and seventy...in their meeting house in warrington aforesaid Joshua Davies
                                              Jane Davies

Ann Garretson	Jehu Thomas	William Underwood
John Thomas	Sarah Thomas	Ruth Underwood
Jacob Thomas	William Lewis	Benjamin Davies
Robert Vale	Elizabeth Lewis	Elihu Underwood Jr
Mary Lewis	Jane Williams	John Underwood
Rebecca Thomas jr	James Cadwalader	William Underwood jr
Rebecca Cox	William Garretson jr	Jacob Williams
Richard Atherton	John Harrey	Ruth Williams
Saml Lewis	Benjamin Hinshaw	John Davies
William Nevett	Timothy Kirk	William Morthland
Hannah Nevett	Ann Penrofe	Jonathan Worrall
Cadwalader Evans	William Penrofe	Mary Cadwalader
Elenor Evans	Peter Cleaver	Benjamin Worrall
William Lewis Jr	William Garretson	Mordacai Williams
Samuel Underwood jr	Mary Garretson	
Nehemiah Underwood	Sarah Vale	
Samuel Cook	Jane McMillan	

#93 16th of 5th mo 1770   JONATHAN WRIGHT-SUSANNAH GRIFFITH

Whereas <u>Jonathan Wright</u> son of <u>John Wright and Elizabeth</u> his wife of Menallon township...County of york and Province of Pensilvania and <u>Susannah Griffith</u> daughter of <u>Thomas Griffith</u> deceased, and <u>Eve,</u> his wife of...township county and province aforesd...sixteenth day of the fifth month in the year of our Lord one thousand seven hundred and seventy...at menallon meeting houfe in theCounty afforesd

WARRINGTON MONTHLY MEETING

		Jonathan Wright
		Susanna Wright
James McGrew sr	Nicholas Wierman	John Wright
James McGrew	William Waddell	Elizabeth Wright
Francis Hobson	John Hammond	Samuel Wright
Alice Hendricks	William Delap	John Wright Jr
Mary McGrew	Benjamin Willson	William Farquar
Deborah Hammond	John Mickle	Joel Wright
Mary John	Abel John	William Griffith
Sarah Mickle	William Hutton	John Griffith
Elizabeth Wright jr	George Willson	Samuel Hendricks
Sarah Delap	William Wierman	Samuel Hutton
		Thomas Blackburn

#94 4th of 10th mo 1770   ELIHU UNDERWOOD-ANNE GARRETSON

Whereas Elihu Underwood son of William Underwood of the Township of Warrington in the County of York and Province of Pensylvania, and Anne Garretson Daughter of William Garretson of the Township, County and Province aforesaid...at Warrington in the County of York and Province aforesaid, the fourth Day of the Tenth Month in the year of our Lord one thousand Seven hundred and Seventy

		Elihu Underwood
		Anne Underwood
Robert Vale	Anon Griest	William Underwood
William Underwood jr	Elihu Underwood	Ruth Underwood
Hannah Nevet	Samuel Garretson	William Garretson
Sarah Vale	Peter Cleaver	Mary Garretson
Jacob Underwood	Jane Davies	Zephaniah Underwood
John Garretson	Isaac Everit	Sarah Garretson
	William Morthland	Ruth Morthland
	Content Garretson	Jacob Cook
	Sarah Garretson	John Underwood

#95 18th of 10th mo 1770   WILLIAM WIERMAN-HANNAH GRIEST

Whereas William Wierman son of Nicholas Wierman of Huntington in the County of york and province of pencilvania and Hannah Grieft daughter of John Grieft in the township of warrington county and province aforesd...this Eighteenth day of the tenth month in the year of our Lord one thousand seven hundred and seventy...at Huntington

MARRIAGES

John Collings	George McMillan	William Wierman
Mary Collings	Willing Griest	Hannah Wierman
Joseph Pilkinton	Nathaniel Cox	Nicholas Wierman
John Mundorff	Rebekah Pilkinton	Sarah Wierman
Wm Kinworthy	Elizabeth Nickle	John Griest
Mary Kinworthy	William Beals	Susanah Griest
Jacob Coble	Martha Everitt	Isaac Everitt
Neomy Cox	Benjamin Wierman	Daniel Griest
William Cox jr	John Griest jr	Ann Griest
Ann Cox	Joseph Griest	John Garretson
Elizabeth Wierman	Nicholas Wierman jr	Mary Garretson
Prilla Wierman jr	Lydia Griest	Susanah Cox
William Cox	Precilla Wierman	Thomas Griest
William Delap	Henery Wierman	
Joel Wright	Jesse Cook	
Samuel Wright	Mary Cook	
	Phebe Wierman	
	Anna Everitt	

#96   12th of 12th mo 1770   FRANCIS HOBSON-SUSANNA JONES

Whereas <u>Francis Hobson</u> and <u>Susanna Jones</u> both of Monallen Township in the County of York and Province of Pennsylvania...this twelfth day of the twelfth month in the Year of our Lord one thousand seven hundred and seventy...at Monallen in the County and Province aforesaid
                                   Francis Hobson
                                   <u>Susanna(her X mark)Hobson</u>

Jon Wright	Mary Smith	Joseph Hobson
John Hammon	Febe Hobson	Henry Atherton
George Wilson	Anne Atherton	James Smith
Nicholas Wierman	Mary John	John Blackley
Abel John	Mary Scoggin	Francis Hobson
Joseph John	Sarah Pearson	David Falkner
	Elizabeth Blackburn	Jonathan Wright
	Mary McGrew	Benjamin Wright
	Deborah Hammond	James McGrew

#97   23rd of 10th mo 1770   WILLIAM WILLIS-HANNAH RICHARDSON

Whereas <u>William Willis</u> of Manchester township in the County of york and province of pencilvania and <u>Hannah Richardson</u> widow of <u>Samuel Richardson</u> late of Frederick County in the Province of Maryland...this twenty third day of the tenth month in the year one thousand seven hundred and seventy...in york town in the county of york afforesaid   William Willis
                                   <u>Hannah Willis</u>

WARRINGTON MONTHLY MEETING

Nathan Hufsey	Joanna Heald	Wm. Morthland
Joseph Garretson	Edith Hufsey	John Willis
Jos. Updegraff	Mary Webb	Susanna Willis
Nathan Updegraff	Sarah Webb	Susana Pufey
Ambrofe Updegraff	Deborah Crookham	Margreat Matthews
William Norris	Mary Cadwalader	Hannah Matthews
Harman Updegraff	Catharin Woolf	Joel Willis
		George Matthews

#98 20th of 5th mo 1771   JACOB COOK-MARY JOHN

Whereas Jacob Cook of the Township of Warrington in the County of York and Province of Pennsylvania son of Thomas Cook, Deceased and Mary John of the township of Newbury in the County and Province aforesaid Daughter of Samuel John deceased...at Newbury in the County and province aforesaid the twentieth day of the fifth month in the year of our lord one thousand seven hundred and seventy one

                              Jacob Cook
                              Mary Cook

Elizabeth Lewis	Riccord Hussey	William Underwood
Mary Garretson	Henry Worley	John Underwood
Rachel Hutton	Wm Kirk	William Morthland
Rebekah Lewis	Timothy Kirk	Samuel John
Rachel Kirk	Joseph Hutton	Sarah John
John Moore	Sarah Kirk	Mary Underwood
Robert Galbraith	John Garretson	Ruth Worley
Ellinor Maulsby	Ellis Lewis	Zephaniah Underwood
Dorris Galbraith	Joshua Hutton	John Maulsby
	Eli Lewis	Thomas Thornbrugh
	Ebenezer John	Nehemiah Underwood
		William Maulsby

#99 20th of 5th mo 1771   ZEPHANIAH UNDERWOOD-REBEKAH LEWIS

Whereas Zephaniah Underwood son of William Underwood of the township of Warrington in the County of York and province of Pennsylvania and Rebekah Lewis daughter of William Lewis of the township of Newbury in the County and Province aforesaid...at Newbury in the County of York and Province aforesaid the twentieth Day of the fifth month in the year of our Lord one thousand seven hundred and seventy one

                              Zephaniah Underwood
                              Rebekah Underwood

MARRIAGES

Sarah Kirk	Ezekiel Kirk	William Underwood
Jacob Kirk	Timothy Kirk	William Lewis
Hannah Kirk	Rebekah Cox	Ruth Underwood
James Hancock	Rebecca Thomas	Elizabeth Lewis
William Kirk	John Thomas	Elihu Underwood jr
Mary Cadwalader	Sarah Thomas	Mary Lewis
Hannah Cadwalader	David Read	Lydia Read
Rachel Kirk	Sarah Garretson	William Lewis
Miriam Hussey	Content Garretson	Nehemiah Underwood
Riccord Hussey	William Garretson jr	Elihu Underwood
John Garretson	Elizabeth Lewis	Edward Jones
Ellis Lewis	John Garretson	
Robert Whinery	Phebe Garretson	
Robert Millor		
Samuel Garretson		

#100 8th of 5th mo 1771   JOSEPH UPDEGRAFF-MARY WEBB
Whereas <u>Joseph Updegraff</u> of york town in the County of york and province of pencilvania and <u>Mary Webb</u> of the same place daughter of <u>Joseph Webb</u> late of the City of Philadelphia, deceased...this twenty eighth day of the fifth month in the year one thousand seven hundred and seventy one...in yorktown aforesaid

		Joseph Updegraff
		<u>Mary Updegraff</u>
Elihu Kirk	Hannah Matthews	Nathan Hufsey
Caleb Kirk	John Rees	Ambrofe Updegraff
Samuel Eby	John Jones	Jacob Updegraff
John Blackburn	Wm Leas	Jno Morris
Rebecca Day	Geo Gatt	Milford biresci
Margaret Updegraff	Cathrin Leas	Hannah Webb
Rebecca Way	Christina Gerber	Sarah Webb
	George Matthews	Lydia Updegraff
	William Willis	Mary Garretson
	Susanna Willis	Ambrofe Updegraff
	Hannah Willis	Nathan Updegraff
	Lydia Kirk	George Hufsey
	Sarah Reese	Harman Updegraff
	Hannah Kersey	Joseph Garretson
	Hannah Crookham	Deborah Philips

#101 13th of 6th mo 1771   JACOB COX-SARAH LEECH
Whereas <u>Jacob Cox</u> of the township of warrington in the county of york and province of pennsylvania son of <u>Robert Cox</u> deceased, and <u>Sarah Leech</u> Daughter of <u>Thomas Leech</u> of the township county and province afforesd...at warrington in the county of york and province afforesaid the thirteenth Day of the sixth month in the year of our Lord one thousand seven hundred and seventy one

WARRINGTON MONTHLY MEETING

William Underwood
Elihu Underwood jr
Joshua Bennett
Jane Phillips
Thomas Penrofe
Ann Pennrofe
Mary Edmundson
Hannah Cadwallader
Mary Cadwallader
Abigail Cadwallader
Thomas Kirk
Timothy Kirk
Lydia Kirk

Jacob Cox
Sarah Cox
Thomas Leech
Sarah Leech
Jacob Norbery
Aaron Coats
Joseph Taylor
Thomas Leech jr
George Phillips
Rebekah Cox
Joseph Green
Jane Marsh
John McMillon
David Filson

MARRIAGES

#102 15th of 10th mo 1771   JOSEPH ELGAR-MARGARET MATTHEWS
Whereas Joseph Elgar of Frederick County in the Province of Maryland
son of Joseph Elgar late of Chester County in the Province of
Pensilvania Deceased and Margaret Matthews daughter of William
Matthews late of Prince Georges County in the Province of Maryland
also deceased...this fifteenth day of the tenth month in the year one
thousand seven hundred and seventy one...in york town aforesaid

Joanna Heald	James Brown jr	Jos Elgar
Deborah Phillips	Wm Kersey	Margt Elgar
Mary Garretson	Timothy Davis	James Brown
Sarah Whitelook	Benjamin Jones	Elizabeth Brown
Mary Updegraff	Nathen Hussey	Mary Brooke
Mary Updegraff	Isaac Whitelock	Hannah Willis
Sarah Updegraff	Jos Updegraff	Wm. Matthews
Hannah Crookham	Harman Updegraff	Wilm Willis
George Matthews	Joseph Garretson	Hannah Matthews
Nathan Updegraff	Samuel Updegraff	Miriam Hussey
	John Collins	Hannah Kearsey
	Thos. Brooke	
	William Penrose	

#103 17th of 10th mo 1771   TIMOTHY KIRK-MARY CADWALADER
Whereas Timothy Kirk son of Timothy Kirk of Newbery township in the
county of york and province of Pencilvania and Mary Cadwalader of
warrington township in the said county Daughter of David Cadwalader
late of Louden County in the colony of verginia deceased...this
seventeenth day of the tenth month in the year one thousand seven
hundred and seventy one...at warrington aforesaid

Ann Ramsey	Rebecca Thomas	Timothy Kirk
Hannah Penrose	Ann Penrofe	Mary Kirk
Ezekiel Kirk	Ruth Morthland	Timothy Kirk
Caleb Cadwalader	Jane Thomas	Sarah Kirk
Richard Wickersham	Anna Thomas	Hannah Cadwalader
William Penrose jr	John Cadwalader	Jacob Kirk
David Filson	Rachel Kirk	Jacob Williams
Thomas Kirk	Hannah Cadwalader	Ruth Williams
John Edmundson	Abigail Cadwalader	James Cadwalader
William Nevet	Lydia Cadwalader	Mary Cadwalader
William Morthland	Timothy Davis	
Samuel Wickersham	Benjamin Jones	
Isaac Deavs	Wm. Matthews	
Susannah Deavs	William Underwood	
Thomas Penrose	Zephaniah Underwood	
James Wickersham	Mary Lewis	

#104 4th of 12th mo 1771   EDWARD JONES-CONTENT GARRETSON
Whereas Edward Jones son of John Jones late of the county of Chester
in the Province of Pencilvania yeoman deceased and Content Garretson

WARRINGTON MONTHLY MEETING

Daughter of John Garretson of newbery in york county in the sd Province...this fourth day of the twelfth month in the year of our Lord one thousand seven hundred and seventy one...at Newbery aforesaid

Edward Jones
Content Jones

Samuel John	James Hancock	John Garretson
Sarah John	Elizabeth Hancock	Phebe Garretson
Susannah Jennings	Timothy Kirk	Samuel Garretson
Phebe Mills	William Lewis	Levi Jones
Riccord Hussey	Ellis Lewis	John Garretson jr
Zephaniah Underwood	William Willson	Cornelius Garretson
Rebecca Underwood	Ruth Lewis	Sarah Garretson
Mary Lewis	Ann Taylor	Mary Garretson
Rachel Hutton	Thomas Tuckett	
Rachel Kirk	Hannah Miller	
William Kirk	Elizabeth Loudden	
Robert Whinery	Sarah Kirk	
John Moor	Lidia Hussey	
Samuel Miller	Jane Love	
Joshua Hutton		

#105 18th of 12th mo 1771   THOMAS WHINNERY-PHEBE MILLS

Whereas Thomas Whinnery of the Township of Newbery in the County of york in the Province of Pennsylvania and Phebe Mills Daughter of Robert Mills of the same place...this Eighteenth of the Twelfth month in the Year of our Lord one thousand seven hundred and seventy one...in Newbery in the County aforesaid

Thomas Whinnery
Phebe Whinnery

Jacob Kirk	Content Jones	David Wamin
Joseph Taylor	Rebeckah Underwood	Robert Whinery
James Hancock	Elizabeth Hancock	Robert Mills
William Kirk	Betty Hutton	Mary Mills
George Boyd	Rebeckah Wilson	Isobel Whinnery
Ezekiel Kirk	Sarah Garretson	Mary Garretson
John Cook	Katharin Boyd	Robert Mills jr
Joseph Hancock	Robert Dennis	Thomas Mills
John Wilson	Anna Jennings	James Mills
Thomas Jennings	Anna Whinnery	Mary Nickle
William Lewis	James Nickel	Alice Wilkinson
Ellis Lewis	John Mills	Mary Wilkinson
William Randels	James Fisher	Ruth Wilkinson
Robert Miller	Esther Jennings	
William Wilson	John Collins	
Elizabeth Lewis	Joshua Hutton	
Phebe Garretson	Joseph Wilkinson	
Miriam Hussey	Samuel Garretson	
	James Mills	
	William Whinnery	

MARRIAGES

#106 13th of 5th mo 1772   JOSHUA HUTTON-RACHEL KIRK
Whereas Joshua Hutton son of Joseph Hutton late of Newbery Township
in the County of York in the Province of Pennsylvania, Deceased, and
Rachel Kirk, daughter of Timothy Kirk of the Township and County
aforesaid...this thirteenth Day of the fifth month in the year of our
Lord one thousand seven hundred and seventy two...in Newbury

                                                            Joshua Hutton
                                                            Rachel Hutton

Eli Lewis	Jonathan Kirk	Timothy Kirk
William Ranolds	Hannah Cadwalader	Sarah Kirk
Martha Ranolds	Abigail Cadwalader	Betty Hutton
Jane Rankin	William Randel	Joseph Hutton
Ann Rankin	John Garretson	Ann Taylor
Samuel John	Content Jones	Rachel Hutton jr
Hannah John	Zephaniah Underwood	Jacob Kirk
Rebekah Wilson	Rebekah Underwood	Timothy Kirk jr
James Fisher	Mary Lewis	Hannah Kirk
Ruth Lewis	William Lewis Jr	Mary Kirk
Robert Hamothy	Ellis Lewis	Elizabeth Lewis
Mary Hamothy	Isaac Deavs	Wm Kirk
	Susannah Daves	Joseph Taylor
	James Hancock	John Cadwalader
	Elizabeth Hancock	Hannah Cadwalader
	William Wilson	Jacob Williams
		Ruth Williams

#107 21st of 5th mo 1772   THOMAS HOLLAND-MARY WILKINSON
Whereas Thomas Holland son of Henry Holland of the Township of
Warrington in the County of York and Province of Pennsylvania and
Mary Wilkinson of Newbery Township in the County and Province
aforesaid Daughter of Joseph Wilkinson Deceased...at Warrington in
the County of York and Province aforesaid the twenty first Day of the
fifth Month in the Year of our Lord One Thousand seven hundred and
seventy two   Thomas Holland
                                            Mary Holland

WARRINGTON MONTHLY MEETING

Jon Cadwalader
Wm Maulsby
Benard Maulsby
Thomas Mills
Obadiah Pedon
John Horseman
Robert Vale
Sarah Vale
John Cook
Mary Thornburgh
Nathan Philips
William Farmay
Mary Phillips
Ruth Fisher
Peter Cook Jr
Sarah Rees

Ellinor Maulsby
Hannah Cadwalader
Abigail Cadwalader
Ann Steer
Ann John
Saml Cook
Sarah Cook
James Fisher
Samuel Fisher
Isaac Fisher
Rebekah Holland
Joshua Bennett
William Nevett
Thomas Thornbrugh
Rebekah Cox
Ann Cook
Sarah Cook
Ann Vale

Henry Holland
Joseph Cook
Elizabeth Cook
Lydia Holland
Susanna Mills
Joseph Wilkinson
William McMillan
Deborah McMillan
William Mills
Alice Wilkinson
Joseph John
Mary John
Jane Philips

#108 23rd of 4th mo 1772   SAMUEL JOHN-HANNAH PENROSE
Whereas <u>Samuel John</u> son of <u>Samuel John</u> late of newbery township in the county of york and province of pensilvania deceased and <u>Hannah penrose</u> daughter of <u>William Penrose</u> of warrington township in the said County of york...this twenty third day of the fourth month in the year one thousand seven hundred and seventy two...at warrington

Timothy Kirk
Ellis Lewis
Timothy Kirk Jr
Mary Kirk
Joshua Hutton
Rachel Kirk
Mary Garretson
Bettey Hutton
Rebecca Thomas
Sarah Kirk
Ruth Lewis
Rebecca Machlen
Jedaiah Hufsey
Sarah Leech

William Garretson
William Underwood
Benjamin Underwood
Peter Cleaver
Thomas Edmundson
James Cadwalader
Wm Matthews
Wm Maulsby
Zephaniah Underwood
Ebenezer John
Eli Lewis

Samuel John
<u>Hannah John</u>
William Penrose
Ann Penrose
Mary Edmundson
Thomas Penrose
Thomas Leech jr
Sarah John
Pheby Leech
Susanna Penrose
William Penrose

#109 17th of 6th mo 1772   JOHN MICKLE JR-REBEKAH GRIFFITH
Whereas <u>John Mickle junr</u> son of <u>John Mickle senr</u> of Manallin Township in the County of York and Province of Pennsylvania and <u>Rebekah Griffith</u> Daughter of <u>Thomas Griffith</u> late of the Township County and Province aforesaid...this seventeenth Day of the sixth month commonly called July [sic] in the year of our Lord one Thousand seven hundred and seventy two 1772...at Manallin aforesaid John Mickle
<u>Rebekah Mickle</u>

MARRIAGES

William Gilliland	John Hammond	John Mickle
David (illegible)	Finley McGrew	Eve (X) Griffith
John Gilliland	Laurence Cox	Thomas Boyd
William (illegible)	Sarah Rusk	William Griffith
John Pope	Mary McGrew	John Griffith
Jane Wright	Abel John	Elijah Mickle
Deborah Hammond	Mary John	Samuel Mickle
John Morton	Samuel Wright	John Mickle
David Beatty	Mary McGrew	Thomas Blackburn
Joseph John	Nathan Hammond	Anthony Blackburn
John Lingenore	Andrew Logan	Sarah Mickle
		Benjamin Wright

#110 22nd of 12th mo 1772   SAMUEL GARRETSON-JANE LOVE
Whereas Samuel Garretson son of John Garretson (of Newberry Township in the County of York and Province of Pennsylvania) and Jane his wife, deceased, and Jane Love Daughter of James Love (of the same place) and Faithful, his wife...this Twenty second day of the twelfth Month in the year One Thousand seven Hundred and Seventy two...at York in the county aforesaid above written.   Samuel Garretson
                                                                   Jane Garretson

Samuel Miller	Hannah Hersey	John Garretson
Robert Miller	John Collins	James Love
Hannah Miller	Hannah Webb	Faithful Love
John Willis	Sarah Webb	Cornelius Garretson
Ann Whinnery	William Cox	Phebe Garretson
William Whinnery	Sarah Williams	William Love
Mary Ramsey	Hannah Willis	John Love
Martha Ramsey	Margret Elgar	James Love jr
Jane Daniel	Ann Collins	Mary Garretson
Levi Jones	Elizabeth Kirk	Mary Updegraff
Deborah Philips	James Moor	
Willen Grist	Wm Mathews	
William Horsey	Nathan Hufsey	
Joshua Dickinson	Joseph Garretson	
Alexander Ramsey	Joseph Updegraff	
Stephen Foulk	Mordecai Williams	
Margret Foulk	Prisilla Philips	

#111 16th of 12th mo 1772   JAMES MCGRAIL-ELIZABETH BLACKBURN
Whereas James McGrail son of Owen McGrail of Manallin township in York County and Province of Pennsylvania and Elizabeth Blackburn Daughter of Thomas Blackburn of the Township County and Province aforesaid...this sixteenth day of the twelfth month in the year of our Lord one Thousand seven hundred and seventy two...at Monallen
                                                                   James McGrail
                                                                   Elizabeth (X) McGrail

WARRINGTON MONTHLY MEETING

Nathan Hammond
George Wilson
John Morton
Samuel Wright
John Colmen
Sarah Delap
Mary McGrew
Robert Delap
John Delap
William Delap
Nathaniel Glasgow
Deborah Morton
Mary Hammond
Susanna Hutton
William Colmen

John Haman
Abel John
James McGrew
James McGrew
Thos Bracken
Finly McGrew
William Hutton
Jas Glasgow
Benjamin Wright
Mary John
Alice Hindryth
Jane Wright

Owen McGrail
Thomas Blackburn
William McGrail
Anthony Blackburn
Joseph Hewitt
George Hewitt
Mary McGrail
-?- Colmen
Isobel Blackburn
Agnes Glasgow

#112 18th of 3rd mo 1773   JAMES WICKERSHAM-SARAH GARRETSON

Whereas james Wickersham son of James Wickersham of East Malbrough township in the County of Chester and Province of Pennsylvania and Sarah Garretson Daughter of William Garretson of Warrington Township in the County of York and province aforesaid...this eighteenth Day of the third month in the year of [our Lord one thousand] seven hundred and seventy three

                                                                   James Wickersham
                                                                   Sarah Wickersham

William Underwood
Peter Cleaver
William Penrose
William Nevitt
Robert Vale sr
Levi Jones

Samuel Garretson
Jane Garretson
William Cox
Susanna Cox
Cornelius Garretson
Rebekah Cox
Ann Wickersham
Miriam Hufsey
Samuel Cook
Sarah Vale
Hannah Nevitt
Ann Cox
Rebekah Underwood
Anna Vale

William Garretson
Mary Garretson
William Garretson jr
Miriam Garretson
Content Jones
Jesse Wickersham
Richard Wickersham
Elizabeth Wickersham
Alice Loudon
Isaac Wickersham
Amos Griest
Daniel Baily
Richard Wickersham

#113 13th of 5th mo 1773   ABEL WALKER-ANN VALE

Whereas Abel Walker of warrington in the county of york and province of pencilvania son of Isaac Walker, deceased and Ann Vale Daughter of Robert Vale in the township and County afforesaid...at warrington this thirteenth day of the fifth month in the year of our Lord one thousand seven hundred and seventy three   Abel Walker
                                                                                  Ann Walker

MARRIAGES

Mary Thornbery	William Underwood	Robert Vale sr
William Underwood jr	William Nevett	Sarah Vale
Aaron Coats	Peter Cleaver	Sarah Thomas
Joseph Green	Anthony Morris	Benjn Walker
Jacob Cox	Nehemiah Underwood	Ajahel Walker
Robert Cox	John Machlan	Ann Walker
Sarah Cook	Thomas Penrose	Leah Walker
Lydia Holland	William Penrose	Robert Vale
Ruth Cook	Jacob Williams	Benjamin Underwood
Thomas Holland	Ruth Williams	William Garretson
Mary Holland	Henery Boggs	Isaac Morris
Rebekah Machland	George McMillan	Peter Cook jr
Hannah Cadwallader	Ann Cook	William Garretson jr
Abil Cadwalader	William Morthland	William Vale
Ann Davies	Sarah John	Hannah Nevett
Jane Davies		

#114 14th of 10th mo 1773   NEHEMIAH UNDERWOOD-RACHEL YARNEL

Whereas <u>Nehemiah Underwood</u> son of <u>Benjamin Underwood</u> of the township of warrington in the County of york and province of Pensylvania and <u>Rachel Yarnal</u> daughter of <u>John Yarnal</u> of the township of Newbery in the County and province aforesd...at warrington in the county of york and province aforesaid the fourteenth day of the tenth month in the year of our Lord one thousand seven hundred and seventy three

                                              Nehemiah Underwood
                                              Rachel Underwood

Thomas Griest	John Evans	Benjamin Underwood
Leah Morris	Cadr Evans	Susanna Underwood
Jane Underwood	Jane Davies	John Yarnall
Jacob Beals	Mary Beals	Ann Yarnall
James Muckelwe	William Nevett	Jehu Thomas
Sarah Rees	William Underwood	Sarah Thomas
John Griest jr	John Underwood	Martha Underwood
Jonathan Jones	Jane Taylor	Jesse Yarnall
Ann Davies	Rebecca Mahlen	Enoch Underwood
Ellinor Maulsby	Martha Squibb	Sarah Yarnal
Sarah Cox	Robert Squibb	Isaac Morris
Lydia Cox	Joshua Davies	Elizabeth Lewis
Peter Cleaver	Jane Davies	Zepaniah Underwood
Abel Walker	Isaac Everitt	Rebecca Underwood
Thomas Varnum	Martha Everitt	
Asahel Walker	Thomas Thornbrugh	
Jacob Cook	William Maulsby	
Benjamin Walker		

#115 20th of 10th mo 1773   THOMAS DUCKET-MARY MILLER

Whereas <u>Thomas Ducket</u> of Newbery township in the County of york and province of Pencilvania and <u>Mary Miller</u>, daughter of <u>Robert Miller</u> of

WARRINGTON MONTHLY MEETING

the place aforesaid...on the twentieth day of the tenth month in the year one thousand seven hundred and seventy three at newbery meeting house in the county aforesaid

Levi Jones
Sarah Moore
Levy Jennings
Robt Whinery
Eli Lewis
John Mecrery
William Whinery
Mordecai Williams
Sarah Williams
Edward Jones
Thos Whinery
Cornelius Garretson
Ann Noblit
Lidia Updegraff
Samuel Garretson
Jane Garretson

Content Jones
James Rankin
Ruth Lewis
Hannah Whinery
Elisabeth Whinery
Ann Jennings
Ann Whinery
Hugh Randels
Joseph Garritson
John Green
James Hancock
John Garretson
Susannah Jennings
Ellis Lewis
Harman Updegraff

Thomas Ducket
Mary Ducket
Robert Miller
Sarah Miller
Samuel Miller
Sarah Bonine
Hannah Miller
Robert Miller jr
James Miller
Thomas Miller
William Randels
Ann Rankin

#116 21st of 10th mo 1773   THOMAS KIRK-HANNAH CADWALADER

Whereas Thomas Kirk son of Timothy Kirk of Newberry in the county of York and Province of Pennsylvania and Hannah Cadwalader daughter of David Cadwalader late of Louden in the Colony of Virginia Deceased...this twenty first Day of the tenth month in the year of Our Lord one thousand seven hundred and seventy three...at Warrington

Thomas Kirk
Hannah Kirk

MARRIAGES

Sarah Cadwalader	Abel Walker	Timothy Kirk
Hannah Williams	Ann Walker	Sarah Kirk
Sarah Williams	Isaac Griffith	Hannah Cadwalader
Joseph Deaves	Wm Penrose	Jno Cadwalader
Margaret Williams	George Chomlee	Jonathan Kirk
Jediah Hussey	John Machlan	Abigail Cadwalader
Jane Hussey	Jonathan Jones	Mary Kirk
Jane Davies	John Harrey	Ruth Williams
Amos Davies	Rebekah Morthland	Lydia Cadwalader
Jane Davies	Isaac Deavs	Wm Kirk
Rebecca Thomas	Susannah Deavs	Jacob Kirk
Mary Machlan	Miriam Hussey	Timothy Kirk Jr
Amos Williams	William McMillan	Isaac Kirk
John Davies	Richard Wickersham	Ezekiel Kirk
Hannah Davies	Joshua Davies	Cad. Evans
Amos Jones	Riccord Hussey	Elizabeth Kirk
Lydia Hussey	Wm Penrose	Samuel Leves
Susanna Penrose	Jos Elgar	Saml Wickersham
Jacob Williams	William Nevett	Thomas Penrose
Joshua Hutton	Hannah Kirk	Caleb Kirk
Rachel Hutton	Hannah Steer	Richard Wickersham
		Benj. Walker
		Ruth Walker
		Jacob Cook
		Mary Cook

#117   16th of 12th mo 1773   JOSEPH GREEN-LYDIA HOLLAND
Whereas <u>Joseph Green</u> son of <u>Joseph Green</u> deceased of the township of Warrington County of York and Province of Pennsylvania and <u>Lydia Holland</u> Daughter of <u>Henry Holland</u> of Township County and Province aforesaid...this sixteenth of the Twelfth Month in the year of Our Lord one thousand seven hundred and seventy three

William Horsman	Rebekah Holland	Joseph Green
William Farry	Ann Withrow	<u>Lydia Green</u>
William Withrow	Abigail McMillan	Henry Holland
Mary Horsman	Thomas Holland	Lydia Holland
Rebecca Cox	Thos McMillan	John McMillan
Robert Vale	Mary Holland	Sarah Leach
Sarah Vale	Ruth Wilkinson	Sarah Cox
John Machlan	Mary Thornbrugh	
Rebekah Machlan		
Riccord Hussey		
Ebenezer Horsman		
Thomas Thornbrugh		

#118   13th of 1st mo 1774   ISAAC MORRIS-MARTHA UNDERWOOD
Whereas <u>Isaac Morris</u> of the township of warrington County of york and Province of Pennsylvania, son of <u>John Morris</u> of Goshen Monthly

WARRINGTON MONTHLY MEETING

meeting in the County of Chester and Province aforesaid and **Martha Underwood** of the township of warrington County of York and Province aforesd Daughter of **Benjamin Underwood**...at warrington aforesd the thirteenth day of the first month in the year one thousand seven hundred and seventy four.

John Machlan	Miriam Hussey	Isaac Morris
Jediah Hussey	Jane Taylor	**Martha Morris**
William Squibb	Margt Elgar	Benjamin Underwood
Joseph Elgar	Mary Chandley	Susannah Underwood
Jane Hussey	Ann Walker	Benjamin Walker
Mary Cadwalader	Rebecca Underwood	Ruth Walker
James Cadwalader	Jane Morthland	Leah Morris
Ann Yarnall	Jane Ross	William Underwood
Martha Squibb	Alexander Ross	John Underwood
Robert Squibb	Thos Thornbrugh	Nehemiah Underwood
	John Yarnall	Enoch Underwood
		Jehu Thomas
		Sarah Thomas
		Rachel Underwood

#119 14th of 4th mo 1774   ROBERT VALE-SARAH COOK

Whereas **Robert Vale** son of **Robert Vale** of Warrington in the county of york and Province of Penncilvania and **Sarah Cook** Daughter of **Peter Cook** of the township and County aforesd...at warrington this fourteenth day of the fourth month in the year of our Lord one thousand seven hundred and seventy four

John cook	William Underwood	Robert Vale
William Vale	Peter Clever	**Sarah Vale**
Jesse Cook	William Garretson	Robert Vale sr
Mary Cook	Mary Garretson	Sarah Vale
Joshua Vale	Abel Walker	Peter Cook sr
Joshua Davies	William Garretson jr	Sarah Cook
Jane Davies	Cadwalader Evans	Ann Cook
William Underwood jr	Thomas Thornburgh	Henery Wierman jr
	Rebecca Cox	Samuel Cook
	Rebecca Thomas	Peter Cook jr
	John Thomas	Ann Walker
	Thomas Holland	William Nevet
	Mary Holland	Hannah Nevet
	Rebekah McMillan	Susannah Penrose
	Lydia Hussey	Ann Penrose
	Rebecca Hussey	Ruth Wilkinson
	Benjn Walker	Miriam Garretson
	Ruth Walker	
	Rebekah Underwood	
	Prisilla Wierman	

MARRIAGES

#120 20th of 4th mo 1774   FINLEY McGREW-MARY HENDRICKS
Whereas Finley McGrew son of Finley McGrew deceased of Tyrone Township York County and Province of Pennsylvania and Mary Hendricks Daughter of Samuel Hendricks of Monallen Township County and Province aforesaid...this twentieth Day of the fourth month in the year one Thousand seven hundred and seventy four...at Monallen afforesaid.

Joseph Hutchinson	Martha Hendricks	Finley McGrew
Jonathan Riffitt	Dinah McGrew	her
Keziah Hutchinson	Sarah Griffith	Mary M McGrew
William Hutton	John Horsman	mark
Deborah Hutton	Joseph Hewitt	Samuel Hendricks sr
John Gilliland	Jno Pope	James McGrew sr
Jane Cox	John Hammond	Finly McGrew
Finly Dot	George Wilson	Nathan Mcgrew
Rachel (X) Hammond	William Delap	John Mcgrew
	John Delap	Peter Mcgrew
	William Griffith	John Maxwell
		John Maxwell jr
		Nathan Hammond
		Samuel Wright
		Hannah Wright
		Elizabeth McGrew
		Mary McGrew

#121 14th of 12th mo 1774   BENJAMIN WILSON-SARAH BOWEN
Whereas Benjamin Wilson son of George Wilson and Ruth his wife of Monallen Township in the County of York and Province of Pennsylvania and Sarah Bowen Daughter of Thomas Bowen and Jean his wife of the Township County and Province aforesaid...this fourteenth Day of the Twelfth Month (commonly called December) in the year of Our Lord one thousand seven hundred and seventy four 1774...at Manallen aforesaid
                              Benjamin Wilson
                              Sarah Wilson

WARRINGTON MONTHLY MEETING

Thomas Bracken Jr	Sarah Hewit	George wilson
Cyabela Bracken	Alice Hendricks	Ruth Wilson
Martha Griest	John Morton	Thomas Bowen
John Yeager	Samuel Wright	Jonathan Bowen
Nathaniel Glasgow	William Hutton	David Bowen
Robert Eliot	John Colmery	Mary John
Robert John	Abel John	Sarah Kirk
Joseph Blackburn	John Watson	John McCreary
Elisha Gready	Mary McGrew	Finely McGrew
Ann Colmery	Elizabeth McGrew	John Hammond
Nancy Blackburn	-?- Watson	Joseph Hewitt
William Bowen	Thomas McGrew	Joseph Davies
Thomas Bowen	Nicholas -?-	Mary Bowen
Isabell Davies	John Griest	
Susanna Hutton		
Margaret Long		

#122 22nd of 12th mo 1774   WILLIAM GARRETSON-MARY WETHERELD

Whereas <u>William Garretson</u> son of <u>William Garretson</u> of the Township of Warrington in the County of York and Province of Pennsylvania and <u>Mary Wethereld</u> of the Township County and Province aforesaid Daughter of <u>John Wethereld</u> (of the County of Armagh and Province of Ulster in the North of Ireland) Deceased...at Warrington in the County of York and Province aforesaid the twenty second Day of the Twelfth month in the year of our Lord One Thousand seven hundred and Seventy Four

		William Garretson
		Mary Garretson
Rebekah Underwood	Joseph Garretson	William Garretson
Thomas Thornbrugh	John Garretson	Mary Garretson
Rebekah McMillan	Elihu Underwood	Robert Vale sr
Cuff Lippix	Robert Vale Jr	Sarah Vale sr
Abel Walker	Sarah Vale	William Cox jr
Ann Walker	Ruth Cook	Miriam Garretson
Benjamin Underwood	Ann Cook	Anne Cox
Joshua Davies	William Underwood	Ruth Cox
William Griffith	William Penrose	Cornelius Garretson
Abraham Owen	Peter Cleaver	Peter Cook jr
William Morthland	Benjamin Walker	Jesse Cox
Ruth Morthland		
Joshua Vale		
William Vale		
Rebekah Cox		

#123 16th of 11th mo 1774   EZEKIEL FRAIZER-REBEKAH THOMAS

Whereas <u>Ezekiel Fraizer</u> of the Township of Warrington in the County of York and Province of Pennsylvania son of <u>Alexander Frazer</u> Deceased and <u>Rebekah Thomas</u> of the Township County and Province aforesaid Daughter of <u>John Thomas</u> Deceased...at Warrington in the County of

MARRIAGES

York and Province aforesaid the Sixteenth Day of the Eleventh Month in the year of our Lord one thousand seven hundred and seventy four.

                                                                                    Ezekiel Fraizer
                                                                                    Rebekah Fraizer

Cornelius Garretson	James McElwe	Phebe Garretson
Wm Hersey	Martha Everitt	Rebekah Thomas
Hannah Hersey	Sarah Vale	Cadr Evans
Thos Davies	Rebekah Mahlon	Jehu Thomas
Israel Williams	William John	Sarah Thomas
William Underwood	Jonah Thomas	John Thomas
John Yarnal	William Lewis	Mary Fraizer
Hannah Williams	Rebekah Underwood	Sarah Thomas
Rachel (X) Kirk	Elizabeth Lewis	Aaron Fraizer
Mary Kirk	Hannah Cadwalader	
Lydia Cadwalader	Abigail Cadwalader	
Mary Ross	Jon Cadwalader	
Jean Ross	Timothy Kirk	
Alexander Ross		

#124 16th of 11th mo 1774   GEORGE HEWIT-DEBORAH MORTON

Whereas <u>George Hewit</u> son of <u>Joseph Hewit and Sarah</u> his wife of Manallen Township in the County of York and Province of Pennsylvania and <u>Deborah Morton</u> daughter of <u>John Morton and Mary</u> his wife of the Township County and Province aforesaid...this sixteenth day of the Eleventh month in the Year of our Lord one Thousand and seven hundred and Seventy four...at Manallen aforesaid.   George Hewit
                                                                              Deborah M(her mark)Hewit

Leonard Hutton	Elizabeth McGrew	Joseph Hewit
William Delap	Mary McGrew	John Morton
John Delap	Sarah Delap	Mary Morton
Owen McGrail	William McGrail	William Hutton
Thomas Olimson	Henry Wierman	Susanna Hutton
Bert Wilson	John Pope	
James Megrail	Elizabeth Morton	
Nathan Hammond	Dinah McGrew	
John Hammond	John McQuown	
George Wilson	William Thompson	
James Megrew jr	Mary John	

#125 15th of 2nd mo 1775   JAMES FISHER-JANE ATKINSON

Whereas <u>James Fisher</u> son of <u>James Fisher</u> deceased and <u>Alice</u> his wife of the Township Monahan County of York and Province of Pennsylvania and <u>Jane Atkinson</u> Daughter of <u>Cephas Atkinson and Hannah</u> his wife of the Township of Newberry County and Province aforesaid...fifteenth Day of the Second month in the Year of our Lord One thousand seven hundred and seventy five...at Newberry

WARRINGTON MONTHLY MEETING

		James Fisher
		Jane Fisher
Robert Mills	Elizabeth Hutton	Cephas Atkinson
Lydia Updegraff	John Garretson	Hannah Atkinson
Sarah Kirk	William Randals	Alice Fisher
Mary Ducket	William Lewis	Elizabeth Fisher
Jane Rankin	Christopher King	Samuel Fisher
Sarah Baxter	Samuel Heden jr	Isaac Fisher
Mary Randals	Sarah Wickersham	John Atkinson
Isabel Winnery	Jas Kightly	John Rees
Alice Wilkinson	Ellis Lewis	
Timothy Kirk	James Hancock	
Martha Randale	Elizabeth Hancock	
Ellinor Maulsby	Eli Lewis	
William Randals	Sarah Rees	

#126 29th of 3rd mo 1775   **WILLIAM RANDELS-ELIZABETH FISHER**
Whereas William Randels son of William Randels and Mary his wife of Newberry in the County of york and Province of Pennsylvania and Elizabeth Fisher daughter of James Fisher Deceased and Alice his wife of Monohon in the County and Province afforesaid...this twenty ninth day of the third month in the year of our Lord one thousand seven hundred and seventy five...in newberry

Bettey Hutton	Ann John	William Randels
William Kirk	Sarah Bonine	Elizabeth Randels
Jacob Kirk	Hannah Wilkinson	William Randels
Ann Updegraff	Sarah Miller	Mary Randels
Cornelius Garretson	Samuel Miller	Alice Fisher
Joshua Hutton	Thomas Duckett	Samuel Fisher
Wm Rankin	Hugh Randels	Isaac Fisher
Rachel Hutton	Thomas Miller	Martha Randels
Eli Lewis	Hannah Atkinson	Elizabeth Cook
Ezekiel Kirk	Robert Miller	Ruth Wilkinson
Joseph John	Wm Matthews	Alice Wilkinson
Robert Miller	John Garretson	
John Willson	Ellis Lewis	
William Lewis	Harman Updegraff	
Daniel Bonine	Timothy Kirk	
Edward Jones		
William Willson		
Samuel John		
Samuel Garretson		
Jesse Wickersham		
Anna Wickersham		
Ruth Lewis		
Lydia Updegraf		
Jane Rankin		
Sarah Kirk		

MARRIAGES

#127 4th of 5th mo 1775   JOHN WILSON-MARTHA BEALS
Whereas John Wilson son of William Wilson and Rebekah his wife of
Newbery in the County of york and Province of Pensylvania and Martha
Beals daughter of Jacob Beals and Elizabeth his wife of Huntington in
the County and Province aforesaid...this fourth day of the fifth
month in the year of our Lord one thousand seven hundred and seventy
five...in huntington

Ann Yarnall	Isaac Everitt	John Wilson
Susanna Griest	Nehemiah Underwood	Martha Wilson
Martha Everitt	William Beals	William Wilson
MAry Garretson	James Mills	Jacob Beals
Lydia Griest	John Beals	Elizabeth Beals
Rebekah Pilkinton	Michael Miller	Rebecca Willson
John Atkinson	Abraham Cox	Soloman Beals
Elizabeth Cox	Richard Cox	Jacob Beals
Hannah Cox	Thomas Dill	Lydia Garretson
Hannah Beals	Abraham Bower	Mary Beals
Abigail Cox	William Cox	Caleb Beals
Elizabeth Comer	Robert Mills	John Griest
Sarah Thomas	Rebekah Wright	
Rachel Underwood	Patience Berrey	
Thomas Griest		
John Baldwin		
Elizabeth Lewis		
John Griest jr		
William Lewis		
Elizabeth Nickel		
Jesse Glancy		
William Wierman		
Willing Griest		
John Garretson		
Elias Pearson		
John Comer		
Jacob Beals		
James Hancock		

#128 11th of 5th mo 1775   THOMAS PENROSE-ABIGAIL CADWALADER
Whereas Thomas Penrose son of William Penrose and Ann his wife of the
township of warrington in the county of york and Province of
Pencilvania and Abigail Cadwallader of the same place Daughter of
David Cadwallader Late of the County of Louden in the Colony of
Virginia deceased and Hannah his wife...this eleventh day of the
fifth month in the year of our lord one thousand seven hundred and

WARRINGTON MONTHLY MEETING

seventy five...at warrington afforesaid

Rebecca Fraizer	Ann Penrose	Thomas Penrose
Miriam Hussey	Thomas Kirk	Abigail Penrose
Joshua Hutton	Hannah Kirk	William Penrose
Jedaiah Hussey	Mary Chandlee	Ann Penrose
Jane Hussey	Rebecca Thomas	Hannah Cadwalader
Riccord Hussey	James Cadwalader	Lydia Cadwalader
William Underwood	Mary Cadwalader	Susana Penrose
William Nevett	Ezekiel Kirk	Ruth Williams
Benjamin Underwood	Caleb Cadwalader	Timothy Kirk
Peter Cleaver	Jonathan Kirk	John Cadwalader
Abel Walker	Isrel Williams	Mary Kirk
Ann Walker	George Worrel	William Penrose jr
Joseph Elgar	John Thomas	Mary Edmundson
Sarah Leech	Hannah Hussey	
Jane Davies		
John Davies		
Hannah Davies		
Nancey Davies		

#129 11th of 5th mo 1775   THOMAS THORNBRUGH-PHEBE WIERMAN

Whereas <u>Thomas Thornbrugh</u> of the township of Warrington in the County of York and Province of Pennsylvania son of <u>Robert Thornbrugh</u> Deceased and <u>Phebe Wierman</u> Daughter of <u>Nicholas Wierman</u> of the township of Huntington in the County of York aforesaid...at Huntington in the County and Province aforesaid the Eleventh Day of the Fifth Month in the Year of our Lord one thousand seven hundred and seventy five

		Thomas Thornbrugh
		<u>Phebe Thornbrugh</u>
William Hinshaw	Elihu Underwood	Nicholas Wireman
Nathaniel Cox	Cadwalader Evans	Sarah Wireman
Elizabeth Cox	Ebenezer Horseman	Catharine Thornbrugh
Daniel Griest	John Horseman	William Wireman
Ann Griest	Thomas Dill	Hannah Wireman
Jesse Cox	Elias Pearson	Benjamin Wireman
Joseph Griest	John Munding(?)	Nicholas Wireman
William Cox	John Collins	Susanna Morthland
Thomas Griest	Robert Thornbrugh	Mary Thornbrugh
John Griest jr	Mary Garretson	Samuel Morthland
James Wilson	James Speakman	William Cox
Lydia Griest	Susanna Griest	Samuel Wright
Jno Pope	Martha Everitt	Ann Cox
William Hutton	Mary Morton	Susanna Cox
Isaac Everitt	Elizabeth Everitt	Ruth Cox
John Garretson	Elizabeth Blackburn	Willing Griest
John Comer	Ann Griest	Richard Cox
		Hannah Cox

MARRIAGES

#130 18th of 5th mo 1775   RICHARD ATHERTON-PHEBE HOBSON

Whereas Richard Atherton son of Thomas Atherton and Abigail his wife of the Township of Warrington County of York and Province of Pennsylvania and Phebe Hobson Daughter of Francis Hobson and Ann his wife Deceased of Minallen Township York County and Province aforesaid this Eighteenth Day of the fifth month in year of our Lord one Thousand seven hundred and seventy five...at Warrington aforesaid

                                        Richard Atherton
                                        Phebe[her mark]Atherton

Lydia Pedon	Lydia Marsh	Thos Atherton
Robert McClelan	Sarah McMillan	Abigail Atherton
Amos Jones	Thomas McMillan	Elizabeth Atherton
Mary Jones	Ann Atherton	Henry Atherton
Thomas McMillan	Jane Taylor	William McMillan
Sarah Vale sr	Joseph Hobson	John Philips
Nathan Philips	Lydia Wright	Deborah McMillan
Mary Philips	Hannah Griffith	Mary Philips
John McMillan	Edmund Philips	Ann McMillan
John Wright	Hugh Lard	
George McMillan	Robert Vale Sr	
John Harry	William Griffith	

#131 23rd of 11th mo 1775   JOHN GRIEST-SUSANNA COX

Whereas John Griest son of John Griest of the township of warrington in the County of York and Province of Pennsylvania and Susanna Cox Daughter of William Cox of the township County and Province afforesaid...at Huntington afforesaid the twenty third day of the Eleventh month in the year of our Lord one thousand seven hundred seventy five
                                        John Griest
                                        Susanna Griest

Sarah Webb	Nicholas Wierman jr	
Elizabeth Cox	Willing Griest	William Cox
Benjamin Wierman	Henery Wierman jr	John Griest
Elizabeth Wierman	Cornelius Garretson	Susanna Griest
Miriam Garretson	Richard Cox	Ruth Cox
Mary Garretson sr	Nathaniel Cox	Lydia Griest
Ann Pearson	William Wierman	John Garretson
John Wierman	Hannah Wierman	Mary Garretson
Mary Thornbrugh	Ann Griest	Isaac Everitt
Elizabeth Cox jr	Thomas Griest	William Cox jr
Martha Everitt	Ann Griest	Joseph Griest
Ann Griest	Thos Thornbrugh	Jesse Cox
Elizabeth Everitt	Phebe Thornbrugh	Elizabeth Blackburn
Henery Wierman		John Garretson
Elias Pearson		Ambrose Updegraff
Nicholas Wierman		Sarah Webb
Benjamin Wier		

WARRINGTON MONTHLY MEETING

#132   23rd of 11th mo 1775   THOMAS GRIEST-ANN COX
Whereas Thomas Griest son of John Griest of the township of Warrington in the County of york and Province of Pensylvania and Ann Cox daughter of William Cox of the township County and Province aforesaid...at Huntington...the twenty third day of the eleventh month in the year of our Lord one thousand seven hundred and seventy five.

                                                                              Thomas Griest
                                                                              Ann Griest

Miriam Garretson	John Griest jr	John Griest
Mary Garretson sr	Susanna Griest jr	Susanna Griest
Henery Wierman jr	Sarah Webb	William Cox
Thomas Thornbrugh	Martha Everitt	Isaac Everitt
Phebe Thornbrugh	Ann Griest	William Cox jr
Ambrofe Updegraff	Nicholas Wierman	Jesse Cox
Elizabeth Blackburn	Elias Pearson	John Garretson
Benjamin Wierman	Ann Pearson	Mary Garretson
Elizabeth Wierman	Rebecca Pilkinton	Ruth Cox
Mary Thornbrugh	Cornelius Garretson	Lydia Griest
Elizabeth Everitt	Richard Cox	Willing Griest
John Wierman	Nathaniel Cox	Ann Griest
Elizabeth Cox jr	Henery Wierman	William Wierman
	Elizabeth Cox	Hannah Wierman

#133   13th of 3rd mo 1776   JACOB NORBURY-BETTY HUTTON
Whereas Jacob Norbury of Newbury Township in the county of York and Province of Pennsylvania and Betty Hutton widow of Joseph Hutton late of the same Township, Deceased...this thirteenth day of the third month in the year of our Lord one thousand seven hundred and seventy six... in Newberry Township aforesaid

                                                                              Jacob Norbury
                                                                              Betty(her mark)Hutton

Wm Matthews	Rose Maulsby	Joshua Hutton
Jacob Kirk	Mary Duckets	Joseph Hutton
Edward Jones	Lydia Updegraff	Wm Kirk
Harman Updegraff	Anne Updegraff	Rachel Kirk
Ellis Lewis	Content Jones	Joseph Taylor
Timothy Kirk	Margaret Waln	Sarah Kirk
Samuel Garretson	Hannah Crookham	Hannah Matthews
Ezekiel Kirk	Mary Updegraff	Priscilla Philips
Jonathan Kirk	Susanna Willis	Jane Philips
Robert Dennis	George Philips	Sarah Miller

#134   15th of 5th mo 1776   JAMES WATSON-MARY BOWEN
Whereas James Watson of Huntington Township in the County of York and Province of Pennsylvania & Mary Bowen Daughter of Thomas Bowen and Jane his wife of Manallen Township County and Province aforesaid...this fifteenth Day of the fifth Month commonly called May

MARRIAGES

in the Year of Our Lord One thousand seven hundred Seventy six 1776...at Manallen aforesaid

Mary Megrew	William Risk	James Watson
Jane Wright	Mary Morton	Mary Watson
Elizabeth Wright	-?- Hendricks	Thomas Bowen
Susanna Hutton	John Watson	Jonathan Bowen
Ann Blackburn	John Mccreery	Thomas Blackburn Jr
Leah Watson	Finly Megrew	Thomas Bowen Jr
Sarah Risk	Abel John	Jesse Watson
Elizabeth Morton	MAry John	Joseph Hewit
Margaret Long	Benjamin Townsend	Benjamin Wilson
Bettes Hammond	Benjamin Wright	George Wilson
John Morton	John Collins	
James McGrail	Thomas McCreery	
Elizabeth McGrail		
Edith Townsend		

#135 22nd of 5th mo 1776   HENRY WIERMAN-SUSANNA HUTTON

Whereas Henry Wierman of Huntington Township County of York and Province of Pennsylvania son of Henry Wierman and Prifilla his wife and Susanna Hutton Daughter of William Hutton and Deborah his wife of Minnallen Township...this twenty second Day of the fifth Month in the Year of Our Lord one Thousand seven hundred and seventy six at Minnallen aforesaid

Henry Wierman
Susanna Wierman

Alice Blackburn	John Mundorff	William Hutton
Ann Blackburn	William Newlon	Levi Hutton
Isabella Blackburn	George Hewit	Pricilla Wierman
Jane Wright	Mary Megrail	Deborah Hutton
Abel John	Ann John	John Wierman
Mary John	Nicholas Wierman Jr	Deborah Hewitt
Eadith Townsend	Samuel Wright	Nicholas Wierman
William McGrail	Thomas Blackburn	Jno Pope
James Megrail	Joseph Hewitt	
Elizabeth Megrail	John Hutton	
John Wright	George Wilson	
Sarah Hutton	Benjamin Wright	
Mary McGrew	William Pidgeon	
Elizabeth Morton		
Rebekah Blackburn		

#136 29th of 10th mo 1776   SOLOMON BEALS-REBEKAH UNDERWOOD

Whereas Solomon Beals son of Jacob Beals of the Township of Huntington in the County of York and Province of Pennsylvania and Rebekah Underwood of the Township of Warrington in the County and Province aforesaid Daughter of John Underwood deceased...at Warrington in the County of York and Province aforesaid the twenty

WARRINGTON MONTHLY MEETING

ninth Day of the Tenth month in the Year of our Lord one Thousand seven hundred and seventy six

Rebekah Underwood	Rebekah McMillan	Solomon Beals
Jacob Beals	Samuel Underwood	<u>Rebekah Beals</u>
John Beals	Peter Cleaver	Jacob Beals
Isaac Morris	Ann Underwood	Elizabeth Beals
Mary Thornbrugh	Thomas Underwood	William Underwood
Phebe Thornbrugh	Robert Northland	Jacob Beals
Mary Horsman	Nehemiah Underwood	Abraham Beals
Willing Underwood	Jonathan Marsh	Benjamin Underwood
Ann Yarnell	Abraham Cox	Caleb Beals Jr
Jacob Underwood	Isaac Everitt	Caleb Beals Sr
Wm Nevitt	Martha Everitt	John Beals
Wm Garretson	Jonathan Marsh	Elihu Underwood Jr
Martha Morris	John Marsh Jr	Wm Northland
Hannah Beals	John Marsh	Ruth Northland
Jane Northland	Robert Squibb	Mary Beals
Rebekah Northland	Wm Cox	Alexander Underwood
Lydia Cox	Elihu Underwood	Mary Garretson
		Sarah Thomas

#137   10th of 12th mo 1776   WILLIAM WELCH-HANNAH WEBB

Whereas <u>William Welch</u> of york Town in the County of york and Province of Pennsylvania son of <u>Andrew Welch</u> Deceased and <u>Mary</u> his wife and <u>Hannah Webb</u> of the same Place; Daughter of <u>Joseph Webb and Edith</u> his wife both Deceased...this tenth day of the twelfth month in the year of our Lord one thousand seven hundred and seventy six...in york town aforesaid

Thomas Owen	William Kearsey	William Welch
James Todd	Joseph Garretson	<u>Hannah Welch</u>
Joseph Todd	Mary Garretson	Samuel Updegraff
John Patterson	Ann Colins	Mary Updegraff
Faithful Love	Pricilla Phillips	Mary Updegraff
Lydia Willis	Rebekah Way	Sarah Webb
Hannah Willis	Mary Way	Joseph Updegraff
Mary Owen	Phebe Way	Andrew Welch
Ann Springer	Ann Updegraff	Ambrose Updegraff
Ruth Willson	Margaret Updegraff	Nathen Updegraff
Hannah Kearsey	Nancy Irwin	Nathan Hussey
Bettey Jones	Lydia Updegraff	John Love
	Edith Updegraff	Hannah Willis
	Jacob Gartner	William Willis
	James Love	

#138   26th of 12th mo 1776   CORNELIUS GARRETSON-MARGARET ATKINSON

Whereas <u>Cornelius Garretson</u> son of <u>John Garretson</u> of Newbery township in the County of york and Province of Pencilvania and <u>Jane</u> his wife deceased and <u>Margaret Atkinson</u> Daughter of <u>Cephas Atkinson</u> of the

MARRIAGES

same place and <u>Hannah</u> his wife...this twenty sixth day of the twelfth month in the year one thousand seven hundred and seventy six...at the house of <u>William Maulsby</u> in newbery in the County afforesaid

Mary Updegraff	Aaron Frazer	Cornelius Garretson
Lydia Updegraff	George Philips	<u>Margaret Garretson</u>
Ezekiel Kirk	John Rees	John Garretson
Jonathan Kirk	William Maulsby	Cephas Atkinson
Henery Lewis	Jane Phillips	Hannah Atkinson
Solomon Tate	Rose Maulsby	Samuel Garretson
George Hufsey	Jas Heightly	Edward Jones
Isaac Elliot	James Land	Content Jones
	John Cook	Sarah Baxter
	Christopher King	James Fisher
	Alice Wilkinson	Jane Fisher
	Elenor Maulsby	John Baxter
	Sarah Rees	John Atkinson
	Ann Updegraff	

#139 16th of 5th mo 1777   ALEXANDER ELLIOT-ELIZABETH ATHERTON

Whereas <u>Alexander Elliot</u> of Township of Newberry in the County of York and Province of Pennfylvania (son of <u>Isaac Elliot</u> deceased) and <u>Elizabeth Atherton</u> Daughter of <u>Thomas Atherton</u> of the Township of Warrington in the County & Province aforesaid...at Warrington in the County of York and Province aforesaid the sixteenth day of the fifth month in the year of our Lord one thousand Seven hundred and seventy seven

                                                                             Alexander Elliot
                                                                             <u>Elizabeth Elliot</u>

Samuel Morthland	Elihu Underwood	Thos Atherton
Riccord Hufsey	Mary Garretson	Abigail Atherton
Samuel Pedon	Cadr Evans	Richard Atherton
Lydia Pedon	Joseph Elger	Aaron Frazer
Obadiah Pedon	Timothy Kirk	Jane Frazer
Isaac Pedon	Benjn Walker	John Condry
Miriam Hufsey	William Underwood	Sarah Condry
Mise Loudon	Peter Cleaver	
Peter Cook jr	Abel Walker	
Robert Vale Sr	William Nevitt	
Sarah Vale	William Garretson	
William Griffith		
Wm McMillan		

#140 16th of 4th mo 1777   SAMUEL FISHER-SUSANNA WILLIS

Whereas <u>Samuel Fisher</u> of York town in the County of York and Province of Pencilvania son of <u>James Fisher (deceased) and Alice</u> his wife and <u>Susanna Willis</u> of Manchester Township and County aforesaid Daughter of <u>William Willis and Bettey</u> his wife (deceased)...this sixteenth day of the fourth month in the year one thousand seven hundred and

WARRINGTON MONTHLY MEETING

seventy seven...in york town aforesaid

Lydia Updegraff	Joseph Garretson	Samuel Fisher
Mary Garretson	Wm Kersey	Susanna Fisher
Sarah Webb	Saml Updegraff	William Willis
Hannah Kersey	John Jones	Alice Fisher
Mary Worley	Joseph Hutton	Hannah Willis
Mary Owen	Thomas Owen	Hannah Willis jr
Hannah Welch	William Welch	Lydia Willis
Ambrose Updegraff	Sarah Davis	Jane Phillips
Nathan Updegraff	Prisilla Phillips	Elizabeth Randles
Joel Willis	Deborah Phillips	Jane Fisher
George Phillips	Margaret Elger	Isaac Fisher
Wm Matthews	Hannah Matthews	James Fisher
Jo Elgar	Mary Updegraff	John Willis
Jos Updegraff		

#141 15th of 5th mo 1777   NICHOLAS WIERMAN-LYDIA GRIEST

Whereas Nicholas Wierman son of Nicholas Wierman of huntington in the County of york and Province of Pennsylvania and Lydia Griest Daughter of John Griest in the Township of warrington County and province aforesaid...this fifteenth day of the fifth month in the year of our Lord one thousand seven hundred and seventy seven...at huntington

                                                  Nicholas Wierman
                                                  Lydia Wierman

Susanna Griest	John Griest jr	Nicholas Wierman
Elizabeth Cox	Susanna Griest	Sarah Wierman
Daniel Griest	Elizabeth Beals	John Griest
Isaac Garretson	Jesse Cox	Daniel Griest
Samuel Blackburn	Willing Griest	Ann Griest
Ann Pearson	William Garretson	Isaac Everitt
	Elias Pearson	Martha Everitt
	Cathrine Wierman	Joseph Griest
	Elizabeth Everitt	Thomas Thornbrough
	Susanna Everitt	Phebe Thornbrough
	William Cox jr	John Garretson
	William Cox sr	Mary Garretson
	Neomy Cox	Benjamin Wierman
	Nathan Cox	William Wierman
	Elizabeth Cox	Thomas Griest
	Ruth Cox	Ann Griest

#142 17th of 7th mo 1777   RICHARD BLATCHFORD-ELIZABETH HOBSON

Whereas Richard Blatchford of the Township of Monaghan in the County of York and Province of Pennfylvania and Elizabeth Hobson of the Township of Warrington in the County and Province aforesaid Daughter of Francis Hobson Deceased...at Warrington in the County of York and Province aforesaid the seventeenth Day of the seventh Month in the Year of Our Lord one Thousand seven hundred and seventy seven

MARRIAGES

		Richard Blatchford
		Elizabeth Blatchford
Edward Ohail	Margaret Underwood	Henry Atherton
Ann Walker	Sarah Williams	Ann Atherton
Margaret Ohail	William Underwood	Ruth Hobson
Catherine Ohail	Jno Edmundson	
Joanna Griffith	John McMillan	
William Griffith	Peter Cleaver	
Amos Jones	William Garretson	
Rebekah Morthland	Jos Elgar	

#143 12th of 11th mo 1777   JOHN MUSGRAVE-SARAH WEBB

Whereas John Musgrave of the township of Darby in the County of Chester in the Province of Penfylvania son of Abraham Musgrave of the same place and Mary his late wife and Sarah Webb of york town in the County of york in the Province afforesaid Daughter of Joseph Webb and Edith his wife boath formerly of Philadelphia Deceased this twelfth day of the Eleventh month in the year of our Lord one thousand seven hundred and seventy seven...at york afforesaid

Abigail Rankin	Mary Updegraff	John Musgrave
Ann Springer	Hannah Willis	Sarah Musgrave
Ann Updegraff	John Penn	Mary Updegraff
Precilla Phillips	John Willis	Hannah Welch
Faithful Love	Eli Lewis	Joseph Updegraff
Andrew Welch	James Love	Esther Musgrave
Edward Briens	John Jones	William Welch
John Patterson	Wm Love	Thomas Owen
Ean Griffith	John Love	Ambros Updegraff
Wm Cox	Jonathan Kirk	Nathan Updegraff
Ann Owen	Jacob Worley	Samuel Updegraff
Catharine Kirk	Jacob Updegraff	Wm Kersey
Rebecca Way	Joseph Updegraff	Hannah Kersey
Rebecca Day	John Rankin	Hannah Willis Jr
Nancy Irwin	James Henderson	Mary Worley
Phebe Way	Hannah Webster	Lydia Updegraff
Joanna Heald	Mary Owen	Joseph Garretson
Mary Updegraff	Wm Willis	Mary Garretson
Rebecca Griffith	Harman Updegraff	

#144 22nd of 10th mo 1777   NATHAN HENDRICKS-MARY MCGRAIL

Whereas Nathan Hendricks son of Samuel Hendricks of manalen township in the County of york and province of Pennsylvania and Mary McGrail Daughter of Owen McGrail of the township County and Province afforesaid...this twenty second day of the tenth month in the year of our Lord one thousand seven hundred and seventy seven at manalen in the county and province aforesaid

                                                    Nathan Hendricks
                                                    Mary Hendricks

WARRINGTON MONTHLY MEETING

Jacob Worley
Daniel Worley

Sarah Mcgrail
Ann Blackburn
Sarah Hewit
Elizabeth McGrail
Alice Blackburn

Samuel Hendricks
William McGrail
Finley McGrew
Joseph Hewit
Nathan McGrew
John Hammond Jr
Thomas Blackburn
James McGrail
Benjamin Townsend
Benjamin Wright
Nathan Hammond

#145 15th of 1st mo 1778   WILLIAM VALE-ANNA WETHERELD
Whereas <u>William Vale</u> son of <u>Robert Vale</u> of the Township of warrington in the county of york and Province of Pennsylvania and <u>Anna Wethereld</u> of the township Newbery in the County and Province aforesaid Daughter of <u>John Wethereld</u> Deceased...at warrington...the fifteenth day of the first month in the year of our Lord one thousand seven hundred and seventy eight

William Vale
<u>Anna Vale</u>

Jacob Underwood
Elizabeth Lewis
Ebenezer John
Elizabeth Cleaver
Elihu Underwood
John Garretson
Joseph Todd
Mary Whiteker
Stephen Johnson
Sarah Thomas

James Todd
Ruth Walker
William Garretson sr
William Nevitt
Jerman Jordan
Nathan Thomas
Jacob Cook
John Mahlan
Rebekah Mahlan
Mary Mahlan
Joseph Bradley

Robert Vale
Sarah Vale
Robert Vale Jr
William Garretson Jr
Abel Walker
Ann Walker
Joshua Vale
Peter Cook Jr
Mordecai Williams
Sarah Williams
Cadwalader Evans

#146 16th of 5th mo 1770   ANTHONY BLACKBURN-MARY GRIFFITH
Whereas <u>Anthony Blackburn</u> son of <u>John Blackburn and Rebecca</u> his wife deceased of Menallen Township in the County of York and Province of Pennsylvania and <u>Mary Griffith</u> Daughter of <u>Thomas Griffith</u> deceased and <u>Eve</u> his wife of the Township County and Province afforesaid...this sixteenth day of the fifth month One Thousand seven Hundred and seventy...at Menallen Meeting House

Anthony Blackburn
<u>Mary Blackburn</u>

MARRIAGES

Alexander Megrew	William Wierman	Thos Blackburn
William Hutton	Benj Wilson	Moses Blackburn
Samuel Wright	John Mickle	Anthony Blackburn
Joel Wright	John Wright Jr	Joseph Blackburn
James Megrew	John Blackburn	Thomas Blackburn
George Delap	Isabel Blackburn	Rachel Blackburn
John Linganore	Ann Blackburn	Rebekah Blackburn
John McCan	Rebekah Griffith	Elizabeth Blackburn
William McGrail	Alice Griffith	Alice Blackburn
Robert Delap	Mary Megrew	Elinor Blackburn
James McGrail	Debra Hammond	
John Hammond	Catharon Lingenore	
William Farquar Jr	Harry Gofine	
William Delap		
Jon Wright		
Nicholas Wierman		
George Wilson		

#147 11th of 2nd mo 1778   JONATHAN HEWITT-ANN JOHN

Whereas <u>Jonathan Hewitt</u> of the Township of Cumberland County of York and Province of Pennsylvania and <u>Ann John</u> daughter of <u>Abel John</u> of Manalan Township the County and Province afforesaid this eleventh day of second month in the year of our Lord one Thousand seven Hundred and seventy Eight...at the publick Meeting House of Manallen aforesaid

Ann Blackburn	Benjamin Townsend	Jonathan Hewitt
Deborah Hammond	Benj. Wright	<u>Ann Hewitt</u>
Edith Townsend	William Hutton	Joseph Hewitt
Mary McGrew	John Hammond	Sarah Hewitt
Alice Hendricks	George Wilson	Abel John
Mary Hendricks	Finley McGrew	George Hewitt
Mary Morton	William Griffith	Deborah Hewitt
Elizabeth Morton	James McGrew	Joseph John
	Jonathan Wright	Robert John
	John Wright	John Morton
	Samuel Hendricks	Jesse Morton
	John Atkinson	Isaac Fisher
		Thomas Morton

#148 16th of 4th mo 1778   JACOB GRIFFITH-LYDIA HUSSEY

Whereas <u>Jacob Griffith</u> son of <u>William Griffith</u> of the Township of Warrington and County of York and Province of Pennsylvania and <u>Lydia Hussey</u> Daughter of <u>Riccord Hussey</u> of the township county and Province afforesaid...at Warrington in the County of York and Province aforesaid the sixteenth day of the fourth month in the year of our Lord one thousand seven hundred and seventy eight [the rest is illegible]

WARRINGTON MONTHLY MEETING

#149 9th of 3rd mo 1778   ISAAC PEDEN-REBEKAH GARWOOD
Whereas Isaac Peden son of Samuel Peden and Lydia his wife of the
Township of Manohon County of York and Province of Pensylvania and
Rebekah Garwood Daughter of Obed Garwood and Mary his wife of the
Township of Merone County of Cumberland and Province afforesaid
...this ninth day of the third month one thousand seven hundred and
seventy eight...at the House of our friend William Maulsby in Newbury
in the County of York and Province afforesaid

		Isaac Peden
		Rebekah Peden
	Riccord Hussey	Samuel Peden
	William Griffith	Obed Garwood
per{	William Maulsby	Samuel Peden jr
order{	Rose Maulsby	Samuel Garwood
	Elizabeth Cook	Joseph Peden
	Lydia Updegraff	Rachel Garwood
	Ezekiel Fraizer	Joseph Garwood
	Elinor Maulsby	Lydia Peden
	Alice Elliot	Joanna Heald
	Benjamin Maulsby	James Kightly

#150 15th of 4th mo 1778   PETER MCGREW-PATIENCE HENDRICKS
Whereas Peter McGrew of Tyrone Township York County and Province of
Pennsylvania son of Finley McGrew Deceased and Patience Hendricks of
Manallin Township County and Province afforesaid Daughter of Samuel
Hendricks...the fifteenth Day of the fourth month in the year one
Thousand seven hundred and seventy eight... at Manallen afforesaid

		Peter McGrew
		Patience [X] McGrew
Jon Wright	William Hutton	Elizabeth McGrew
Elizabeth Wright	Thos Blackburn	Finley McGrew
Edith Townsend	John McGrew	Mary McGrew
Jonathan Wright	George Hewitt	James McGrew
William Riske	Nathan Hendricks	Nathan McGrew
	James McGrew	Martha McGrew
	Alexr McGrew	Thomas Bowen Jr
	Mary McGrew	Joseph Hewitt
	Sarah Griffith	Sarah Hewitt jr
	Rachel Long	Thomas Blackburn
	George Wilson	John Delap
	Benjn Townsend	Thomas Oldham
		Isbel Blackburn

#151 15th of 4th mo 1778   JONATHAN BOWEN-ANN BLACKBURN
Whereas Jonathan Bowen son of Thomas Bowen and Jean his wife of
Manallen Township in the County of York and Province of Pennsylvania
and Ann Blackburn Daughter of Thomas Blackburn and Alice his wife of
ye Township County & Province afforesd...this fifteenth of ye forth

MARRIAGES

month in the year of our Lord one Thousand seven hundred & seventy Eight 1778...at Manallan aforesaid

		Jonathan Bowen
		Ann Bowen
Levi Hutton	John Morton	Thomas Bowen
William Griffith	William Hutton	Benjamin Townsend
Rachel Blackburn	Finley McGrew	Mary John
Margaret Wilson	Thos Blackburn	Benjamin Wilson
Elizabeth Morton	Rebekah Blackburn	Rachel Long
Edith Townsend	William McGrail	Joseph Hewitt
Isabel Blackburn	Nathan Hammond	Sarah Hewitt
Thomas Bowen Jr	William Newlon	Nathan Hendricks
Deborah Hutton Jr	Alice Blackburn	John Delap
	Hugh King	Thomas Blackburn
	John Colmery	James McGrew
	Wm Colmery	Mary McGrew

#152 6th of 5th mo 1778   AMBROSE UPDEGRAFF-FAITHFULL LOVE

Whereas Ambrose Updegraff of york town in the County of york in Pensylvania son of Joseph Updegraff (and Susanna his wife, deceased) and Faithfull Love of the same place daughter of James Love, deceased and Faithfull his wife...this sixth day of the fifth month in the year one thousand seven hundred and seventy eight...in york town aforesaid

		Ambrose Updegraff
		Faithfull Updegraff
Mary Worley	Lydia Updegraff	Joseph Updegraff
Lydia Worley	Mary Updegraff	Faithfull Love
Ann Dannel	Bettey Jones	Mary Updegraff
Jane Dannel	Hannah Willis	Ann Love
Susanna Leas	Mary Garretson	Edith Updegraff
Abt Harris Sr	Mary Way	John Love
Saml Patton	Mary Owen	James Love
John Dannell	Ann Springer	Nathan Updegraff
James Dannell	Hannah Webster	Joseph Garretson
Joseph Way	Ann Updegraff	Saml Updegraff
Pricilla Phillips	William Welch	Joseph Updegraff
Rebekah Way	Benjamin Thornton	Jos Updegraff Jr
Hannah Kersey	Jacob Gartner	Jacob Updegraff
Ann Bennett	George Toot	Margaret Updegraff
	Thomas Owen	William Willis
	Jacob Worley	John Jones
	Jas Todd	Wm Kersey
	Andrew Welch	
	Sarah Lovett	

WARRINGTON MONTHLY MEETING

#153 11th of 11th mo 1778   ISAAC FISHER-ELIZABETH MORTON
Whereas Isaac Fisher son of James Fisher of Mannahán in the County of york Late Deceased and Elizabeth Morton Daughter of John Morton of Monallin and County of york this eleventh day of the eleventh month in the year of our Lord one thousand seven hundred and seventy eight...at their meeting house in Monallin

                    Isaac Fisher
                    Elizabeth Fisher

John Atkinson	Thomas Blackburn	John Morton
Eve Griffith	John Wright	Alice Fisher
Mary Megrew	Jonathan Wright	James Fisher
Dina Megrew	John Wright	Jane Fisher
Rebekah Blackburn	William Wright	George Hewitt
Alice Blackburn	John Colinery	Deborah Hewitt
Isbel Blackburn	James Moore	William Hutton
Rachel Blackburn	Elisha Icady(?)	John Morton
William Morris	William Colmery	William Newlon
Mary Horsman	Ebn Horfman	Margret Newlon
Ann Bowen	John Glasgow	Sarah Fleming
	Finely Megrew	George Willson
	Samuel Wright	Joseph Hewit
	Jonathan Bowen	Archibald Fleming
	Cephas Atkinson	Finley Megrew
	Deborah Hutton	Thomas Williams

#154 7th of 7th mo 1779   JOHN LOVE-ANN UPDEGRAFF
Whereas John Love of York Town in the County of York in Pennsylvania son of James Love (deceased) and Faithfull his wife and Ann Updegraff Daughter of Harman Updegraff and Lydia his wife...this seventh day of the Seventh Month in the Year one thousand seven hundred and seventy Nine...in York Town aforesaid

                    John Love
                    Ann Love

MARRIAGES

Lydia Willis	Hannah Kersey	Harman Updegraff
Jas Todd	Ann Updegraff	Lydia Updegraff
Joseph Updegraff	Ruth Worley	Faithful Love
Mary Updegraff	Andrew Welch	Mary Updegraff
Lydia Updegraff	Joseph Updegraff	Ann Love
Edith Updegraff	Jacob Updegraff	Faithful Updegraff
Samuel Love	Jonathan Kirk	James Love
Joseph Way	Phebe Way	William Love
Esther Updegraff	Rebekah Way	Ambrose Updegraff
Sarah Jones	Mary Garretson	Saml Updegraff
Elizabeth Willis	Content Jones	Joanna Heald
Margret Maulsby	Jane Garretson	Mary Updegraff
Margaret Updegraff	Samuel Garretson	George Irvin
Ann Bennett	Sarah Dannel	Samuel Fisher
Eli Lewis	John Dannel	Joshua Hutton
Wm Kersey	Rhoda Updegraff	Wm Welch
Enoch Bennett	William Willis	Nathan Updegraff
Hannah Willis	Joseph Updegraff	
Betty Hussey	Benjamin Underwood	
Mary Owen	Joseph Garretson	
Hannah Welch	John Jones	

#155 22nd of 4th mo 1778   JOHN GARRETSON-TAMER HAMMOND

Whereas <u>John Garretson</u> of the Township of Warrington in the County of York and Province of Pennsylvania Son of <u>William Garretson and Mary</u> his wife and <u>Tamer Hammond</u> of the Township of Monallen in the County of York aforesaid Daughter of <u>John Hammond and Deborah</u> his Wife at Manallen in the County of York and Province afforesaid the twenty second Day of the fourth month in the year of our Lord one Thousand seven hundred and seventy eight

                                                                                             John Garretson
                                                                                             Tamar Garretson

Thomas Blackburn	Nathan McGrew	William Garretson
George Wilson	William Cox	Mary Garretson
Jane Wright	John Pope	Aaron Garretson
James McGrew	John McCreary	Peter McGrew
Alice Blackburn	Finley McGrew	William Griffith
John Blackburn	Elihu Underwood	John Wright
Isabel Blackburn	Miriam Garretson	Nathan Hammond
Edith Townsend	Mary Hammond	
Joseph Hewitt	Mary McGrew	
Sarah Hewitt	Joseph Bradley	
Alice Hendricks	Alexander Underwood	
James McGrew		

#156 15th of 9th mo 1779   WILLIAM MCGRAIL-LYDIA HENDRIX

Whereas <u>William McGrail</u> son of <u>Owen McGrail</u> of the Township of Menallen County of York and Province of Pennsylvania and <u>Lydia Hendrix</u> Daughter of <u>Samuel Hendrix</u> of the same place...this fifteenth

WARRINGTON MONTHLY MEETING

Day of the ninth month in the year of our Lord one thousand seven hundred and seventy nine...in Monallen afforesaid

		William McGrail
		Lydia \[her mark]McGrail
Rebekah Blackburn	William Wright	Samuel Hendrix
Alice Blackburn	John Morton	Joseph Hewitt
Elizabeth McGrail	Susanna Wright	James McGrail
Ann Delap	Jonathan Wright	Finley McGrew
Edith Townsend	William Hutton	Nathan Hendrix
Mary McGrew	Thomas Oldham	Peter McGrew
Lydia Richard	Benjamin Townsend	Thomas Blackburn
Rachel Blackburn	Nathan McGrew	Jane Bowen
		Ann Bowen
		Sarah McGrail Jr
		John Hutton

#157 13th of 4th mo 1779   JACOB VORE-MARY MACHLAN

Whereas Jacob Vore of the township of warrington in the county of york and Province of Pennsylvania son of Christian Vore and Mary Machlan of the township county and province aforesaid Daughter of John Machlan...at warrington in the County of york...the thirteenth day of the fourth month in the year of our Lord one thousand seven hundred and seventy nine

		Jacob Vore
		Mary Vore
Elihu Underwood	Jonah Thomas	James Thomas
Ann Underwood	Joshua Davies	Sarah Vore
Rebekah Hussey	Jane Davies	Rebekah Mahlan
Lydia Walker	Rebekah Underwood	William Lewis
Jacob Underwood	Elizabeth Lewis	Elizabeth Lewis
Robert Squibb	Sarah Lewis	John Edmundson
Thomas McMillan	Robert Vale	Peter Vore
Sarah Thomas	Sarah Vale	Isaac Vore
	Jehu Thomas	Jesse Vore
	Sarah Thomas	Henery Tyson
	William Machlan	Sarah Tyson
	Rebekah Fraizer	George Machlan
	James Cadwalader	Nathan Thomas
	Benjamin Walker	Rebekah Thomas
	Mary Thomas	John Thomas
	Sarah Williams	Jane Thomas
		Rebekah Machlan

#158 13th of 10th mo 1779   THOMAS OLDHAM-REBEKAH BLACKBURN

Whereas Thomas Oldham of the Township of Monallin County of York and Province of Pennsylvania Son of William Oldham late of the township of Tyrone County & Province aforesaid Deceased, and Rebekah Blackburn Daughter of Thomas Blackburn of the Township of Monallin County & Province afforesd...this thirteenth Day of the tenth month in the

MARRIAGES

year of our Lord one thousand seven hundred and seventy nine...at Warrington afforesd

Elizabeth Farquahr	George Wilson	Thomas Oldham
Alice Hendrix	William Hutton	Rebekah Oldham
William Garretson	William Griffith	Thomas Blackburn
Elizabeth McGrew	William McGrail	Thomas Blackburn Jr
Lydia McGrew	William Wright	Finley McGrew
Margret Adams	Thomas Bowen	Joseph Hewitt
Jane Bowen	Abel John	James McGrail
Margret Mains	James McGrew	Elizabeth McGrail
Abigail Dinnen	James McGrew Jr	Isabel Blackburn
Sarah McGrail	Jonathan Bowen	William Colmery
		John Colmery
		Alice Blackburn
		Ann Bowen
		Ann Colmery

#159 28th of 10th mo 1779   JOSEPH GARRETSON-REBEKAH MCMILLAN

Whereas Joseph Garretson of the township of Newbery and County of York in Pennsylvania son of John Garretson and Jane his wife and Rebekah McMillan of the township of warrington in the County of York afforesaid Daughter of George McMillan and Ann his wife...at warrington in the county of york afforesaid the twenty Eighth day of the tenth month in the year of our Lord one thousand seven hundred and seventy nine

Joseph Garretson
Rebecca Garretson

Jonathan Kirk	Thomas McMillan	John Garretson
Moses Packer	Elizabeth Garretson	George McMillan
Abel Walker	Aaron Garretson	Ann McMillan
Ebenezer John	Mary Garretson	Margaret Carson
John Marsh	John Garretson	Phebe Garretson
Robert Vale sr	Thomas Griest	Samuel Garretson
Tamer Garretson	Ann Griest	Jane Garretson
John Vale	Joshua Vale	Content Jones
Peter Cleaver	Jonathan Marsh	Jesse Cox
Thomas McMillan	William McMillan	John McMillan
Jonathan Marsh	Miriam Hussey	William Garretson
Alexander Underwood		
Mordecai Williams		
Elihu Underwood		
Sarah Williams		

#160 5th of 1st mo 1780   NATHAN UPDEGRAFF-ANN LOVE

Whereas Nathan Updegraff son of Joseph Updegraff of York Town in the County of York in Pennsylvania and Susanna his wife Deceased and Ann Love daughter of James Love late of the Township of Newberry in said County Deceased and Faithful his wife this fifth day of the first month in the year one thousand seven hundred and eighty in York Town aforesaid.

WARRINGTON MONTHLY MEETING

Enoch Bennett
Joanna Heald
Hannah Willis
Mary Garretson
Betty Jones
Hannah Kersey
Ruth Worley
David Worley
Wm Welch
Samuel Fisher

Joseph Updegraff
Samuel Love
Wm Willis
Joseph Garretson
Wm Kersey
Harman Updegraff
John Jones
Saml Updegraff
Mary Updegraff
Joshua Hutton

Nathan Updegraf
Ann Updegraff
Joseph Updegraff
Faithful Love
Mary Updegraff
Faithful Updegraff
Mary Love
Ann Love
William Love
James Love
Ambrose Updegraff
John Love
Jacob Updegraff
Joseph Updegraff

#161 24th of 2nd mo 1780   WILLIAM SQUIBB-JANE MORTHLAND

Whereas William Squibb of the Township of Warrington and County of York in Pennsylvania son of William Squibb and Sarah his wife and Jane Morthland of the Township and County aforesaid Daughter of William Morthland and Ruth his wife...at Warrington aforesaid the twenty fourth Day of the second Month in the year of our Lord one thousand seven hundred and Eighty

William Squibb
Jane Squibb

Wm Garretson
John Vale
John Godfrey
Sarah Cadwalader
Ruth Underwood
Margaret Underwood
Jonathan Marsh
Willing Underwood
J. Shattelwell
Joshua Vale
Margret Lerew
David Cadwalader
Miriam Hufsey
Sarah Williams

Mary Squibb
Sarah Squibb
Ann Yarnall
Mary Godfrey
Sarah Thomas
Martha Marsh
Jonathan Marsh
Robert Vale
George Newman
Jacob Underwood
Jane Walker
Ruth Walker
Rebecca Cox

Wm Squibb
Wm Morthland
Ruth Morthland
Wm Underwood
Alexander Underwood
Rebekah Morthland
Robert Squibb
Robert Morthland
John Morthland
Joseph Bradley

#162 13th of 10th mo 1779   AARON GARRETSON-MARY HAMMOND

Whereas Aaron Garretson son of William Garretson of the Township of Warrington County of York in Pennsylvania and Mary Hammond of the Township of Manallen in the County of York afforesd Daughter of John Hammond...at Manallen in the County of York afforesd the thirteenth Day of the tenth Month in the year of our Lord one Thousand seven hundred and seventy nine

Aaron Garretson
Mary Garretson

MARRIAGES

William Hutton	George Wilson	William Garretson
Abel John	Joseph Hewitt	Mary Garretson
Finley McGrew	William Griffith	John Hammond
Thomas Blackburn	Eve Griffith	William Garretson jr
Alice Hendrix	Mary McGrew	John Garretson
Jane Wright	William Wright	Elizabeth Wright
		Nathan Hammond

#163 17th of 5th mo 1781   DAVID CADWALADER-SUSANNA PENROSE

Whereas David Cadwalader of the Township of Warrington and County of York in Pennsylvania son of James Cadwalader and Mary his wife and Susanna Penrose of the Township and County aforesaid Daughter of William Penrose and Ann his wife...at Warrington in the county of York afforesaid the seventeenth day of the fifth month in the year of our Lord one thousand seven hundred and eighty one

David Cadwalader
Susanna Cadwalader

Jess Vore	Peter Cleaver	James Cadwalader
Amos Hussey	Joseph Elgar	Mary Cadwalader
Hannah Edmundson	John Edmundson	Wm Penrose
Mary Hussey	Mordecai Williams	Ann Penrose
Mary Cadwalader	Benjmin Williams	Ann Penrose
Margaret Cadwalader	Martha Williams	Phebe Leech
Abel Walker	Miriam Hussey	Sarah Cadwalader
Timothy Kirk jr	Benjamin Walker	Jane Hussey
Samuel John	Benjamin Underwood	Jedaiah Hussey
Thomas Kirk	Rebekah Hussey	Ruth Hewitt
Lydia Griffith	William Garretson	Hannah Cadwalader
John Penrose	Mary Garretson	Mary Kirk
Cadwalader Evans	Elihu Underwood	William Underwood
Lydia Cadwalader		
Joshua Davies		
Jane Davies		
Daniel Davies		
Elizabeth Davies		

#164 17th of 10th mo 1781   JOSEPH JOHN-MARY BONINE

Whereas Joseph John of the township of menallen in the County of York in Pennsylvania, son of Abel & Mary John and Mary Bonine of the township of Derry and County of Lancaster in Pennsylvania aforesaid Daughter of Daniel & Elizabeth Bonine...this seventeenth day of the tenth month in the year of our Lord one thousand seven hundred and eighty one...at Newbery in township of Newbery and County of york aforesaid

Joseph John
Mary John

WARRINGTON MONTHLY MEETING

Elizabeth Hancock Jr
Ann Taylor
Samuel Garretson
James Bond
Jane Garretson
Ruth Bane
Yorcob Felley
George Kneisley

James Wickersham
Robert Miller
Samuel Miller
William Wilson
Cornelius Garretson
James Miller
Thomas Jennings
Elizabeth Lewis
James Hancock jr
Esther Jennings
Elizabeth Stephen

Daniel Bonine
Mary John
Robert John
Elizabeth Bonine
James Bonine
Rachel Copeland
William Lewis
John Garretson
Timothy Kirk Jr
James Hancock
Edward Jones
Timothy Kirk

#165 17th of 11th mo 1779   DANIEL BONINE-MARY COPLAND

Whereas <u>Daniel Bonine</u> of Derry Township in Lancaster County in the Province of Pennsylvania son of <u>James Bonine</u> of Newbury Township in York County in the Province afforesd and <u>Mary Copland</u> Daughter of <u>David Copland</u> of Newbury Township afforesaid...this seventeenth day of the eleventh month in the year of our Lord one Thousand seven hundred and seventy nine at Newbury Meeting House in the County of York afforesaid

Daniel Bonine
Mary [M her mark] Bonine

Rebekah Underwood
Precilla Phillips
Abigail Whinery
Mary Wilson
Ann Taylor
Elizabeth Griffith
William Wilson
Hannah MAtthews
Ruth Bane
Jane Garretson
Margret Garretson
Lydia Garretson

Jehu Hollingsworth
Edward Jones
William Lewis
Samuel Garretson
Robert Miller
Jesse Wickersham
Timothy Kirk Jr
Samuel Miller
Joseph Garretson
Jacob Kirk
Abraham Griffith

Rachel Copland
Sarah Copland
Mary Bonine
Hannah Bonine
Hannah Dain
John Copland
Wm Matthews
William Randles
Timothy Kirk
John Garretson
James Hancock
James Bane

#166 19th of 4th mo 1780   JAMES JOHNSON-ELIZABETH GARRETSON

Whereas <u>James Johnson</u> son of <u>Thomas Johnson</u> late of Newtown Township in Chester County in the Province of Pennsylvania deceased and <u>Elizabeth Garretson</u> daughter of <u>William Garretson</u> of Newbury Township in the County of York in the said Province of Pennsylvania...this nineteenth day of the forth month in the year of our Lord one thousand seven Hundred and eighty...at Newbury

James Johnson
<u>Elizabeth Johnson</u>

MARRIAGES

William Randles	Hannah Matthews	Lydia Garretson
Robert Miller	Ruth Bane	John Garretson
Jacob Norbury	Elizabeth Hancock	Samuel Garretson
Jesse Wickersham	Mary Kirk	Joseph Garretson
Daniel Baily	Hannah Kirk	Cornelius Garretson
Samuel Miller	Priscilla Phillips	Edward Jones
James Bane	Hannah Miller	John Wilson
Daniel Hoopes	Phebe Whinery	Jane Garretson
Caleb Baily	Margaret Miller	Margret Garretson
Nathan Thomas	Abigail Whinery	Rebekah Garretson
Wm Matthews	Timothy Kirk	John Garretson jr
Jesse Lawrence	James Hancock	

#167 20th of 4th mo 1782   JOSEPH BRADLY-RUTH UNDERWOOD

Whereas <u>Joseph Bradly</u> of the Township of Warrington & County of York in Pennsylvania son of <u>Charles Bradly</u> deceased and Mary his wife and <u>Ruth Underwood</u> of the Township & County aforesaid daughter of <u>William Underwood</u> and <u>Ruth</u> his wife...at Warrington in the County of York afforesaid the twentieth Day of the fourth month in the year of our Lord One Thousand seven hundred and Eighty two

		Joseph Bradly
		<u>Ruth Bradly</u>
Ruth Hussey	Peter Cleaver	William Underwood
Amos Hussey	Benjamin Underwood	Mary Thompson
Asahel Walker	Elihu Underwood	John Thompson
Mordecai Williams	Robert Vale	Elihu Underwood jr
Sarah Vole	Benjamin Walker	Jacob Underwood
David Cadwalader	William Garretson	Jesse Underwood
Daniel Davies	William Morthland	Obed Underwood
Mary Underwood	Joshua Vale	Hannah Underwood
Mary Horsman	Elizabeth Vale	William Underwood Jr
Margaret Underwood	Susanna Underwood	Ruth Morthland
Ruth Cook	Mary Cleaver	John Underwood
John Marsh	William Nevitt	Ann Underwood
Robert Morthland	Ann Walker	Mischael Underwood
John Derry	Sarah Williams	Charles Underwood
Enoch Underwood	Margaret Elgar	
Elihu Underwood		
Rebekah Morthland		

#168 25th of 4th mo 1782   JOSHUA VALE-ELIZABETH CLEAVER

Whereas <u>Joshua Vale</u> of the Township of Warrington and County of York in Pennsylvania Son of <u>Robert Vale and Sarah</u> his wife and <u>Elizabeth Cleaver</u> of the Township and County aforesaid Daughter of <u>Peter Cleaver and Miriam</u> his wife...at Warrington in the County of York aforesaid the twenty fifth day of the fourth month in the Year of our Lord One Thousand seven hundred and Eighty two

WARRINGTON MONTHLY MEETING

		Joshua Vale
		Elizabeth Vale
Ezekiel Fraizer	John Cleaver	Robert Vale
Elihu Underwood	Asahel Walker	Sarah Vale
John Thompson	Ann Walker	Ann Walker
Mary Thompson	Jos Elgar	Robert Vale Jr
Margaret Elgar	Joseph Bradley	Sarah Vale Jr
Deborah Thomas	William Garretson	Wm Vale
Ruth Cook	Benjamin Underwood	Peter Cleaver Jr
Hannah Underwood	Wm Nevitt	John Vale
Mordecai Williams	Wm Underwood	Jonathan Potts
Sarah Williams	Susanna Underwood	Ann Potts
Robert Morthland	Mary Cleaver	James Thomas Jr
	Sarah Cleaver	Naomi Garretson
		Peter Cleaver
		Benjamin Walker

#169 27th of 6th mo 1781   SAMUEL STEPHEN-ELIZABETH LEWIS

Whereas <u>Samuel Stephen</u> of the Township of Newbury and County of York in Pennsylvania son of <u>Jonathan Stephen</u> and <u>Mary</u> his wife and <u>Elizabeth Lewis</u> of the Township and County afforesaid Daughter of <u>William Lewis and Elizabeth</u> his wife...at Warrington in the County of York aforesaid the twenty seventh Day of the Sixth Month in the year of our Lord one thousand seven hundred and eighty one

		Samuel Stephen
		Elizabth Lewis
Rebecca Wilson	John Garretson	Jonathan Stephen
Mary Fenslow	William Wilson	Mary Stephen
John Hancock	Samuel Garretson	William Lewis
Lydia Willis	Eli Lewis	Elizabeth Lewis
Sarah Hancock	Jacob Norbury	Sarah Lewis
Abigail Whinnery	Phebe Garretson	Amos Lewis
Ruth Bane	Hannah Miller	Hannah Lewis
Anna Wickersham	Margaret Miller	Rebekah Underwood
Rebekah Thomas	Susanna Mills	Jehu Thomas
Timothy Kirk	Elizabeth Hancock	Elihu Underwood
Mary Kirk	James Miller	
Thomas Jennings	Thomas Miller	
	James Hancock	

#170 22nd of 11th mo 1781   CADWALADER EVANS-SARAH CADWALLADER

Whereas <u>Cadwalader Evans</u> of the Township of Warrington County of York in Pennsylvania (son of <u>Cadwalader Evans</u> Deceased) and <u>Sarah Cadwallader</u> of the Township & County afforesaid Daughter of <u>James Cadwallader and Mary</u> his wife...at Warrington in the County of York aforesaid the twenty second Day of the eleventh Month in the Year of our Lord One Thousand Seven Hundred and eighty one

MARRIAGES

Elihu Underwood
Benjamin Walker
Rebekah Machlan
Ann Atherton
Lydia Machlan
Mary Vore
Ann Walker
Joseph Bradley
John Penrose
Rebekah Underwood
Elinor Evans
William Nevitt
Mordecai Williams
Sarah Williams
John Rogers

Rebekah Morthland
Jehu Thomas
Sarah Thomas
Rebekah Thomas
Hannah Cadwallader
Joshua Dickinson
Ruth Dickinson
Ruth Dickinson
Jedaiah Hussey
Sarah Dickinson
Margret Vernon
Sarah Vernon

Cadwalader Evans
Sarah Evans
James Cadwallader
Mary Cadwallader
David Cadwallader
Susana Cadwallader
John Steuart
Ruth Steuart
John Evans Rees
Joseph Rees
Margret Cadwallader
Mary Cadwallader
"And many more in
the original"

#171 12th of 6th mo 1782   THOMAS TAYLOR-SARAH MUSGRAVE
Whereas <u>Thomas Taylor</u> son of <u>Thomas Taylor</u> of Frederick County in Maryland and <u>Sarah Musgrave</u> widow of <u>John Musgrave</u> late of Darby in Pennsylvania deceased...this twelfth day of the sixth month in the Year of our Lord one thousand seven hundred and eighty two...at York Town in the County afforesaid

Thomas Taylor
Sarah Taylor

Joanna Heald
Ruth Kirk
Hannah Willis
Hannah Matthews
Lydia Updegraff
Elizabeth Kirk
Susanna Hobson
Ann Ball
Mary Garretson
Caleb Kirk
Elizabeth Mills
Nathan Updegraff
Ann Updegraff
Ann Bennett
Ann Love

Wilm Willis
Elisha Kirk
Joseph Garretson
Harman Updegraff
David Ragan
Thomas Matthews
John Jones
Joshua Bennett
Samuel Updegraff
John Love
Wm Kersey
James Love
George Hemal
Edith Updegraff
Mary Ragan

Thomas Taylor
Mary Updegraff
Hannah Welch
Esther Musgrave
Jos Updegraff
Wm Welch
Joel Willis
Elizabeth Smith
Ambrose Updegraff
Mary Updegraff
Thomas Owen

#172 12th of 2nd mo 1783   JAMES SPEAKMAN-HANNAH WILLIS
Whereas <u>James Speakman</u> son of <u>Joshua Speakman and Ann</u> his wife (deceased) of Huntington Township and County of York in Pennsylvania and <u>Hannah Willis</u> Daughter of <u>William Willis and Betty</u> his wife Deceased of Manchester Township in said County...this twelfth day of the Second month in the Year of our Lord one thousand Seven hundred

WARRINGTON MONTHLY MEETING

and Eighty three...at York Town in the County afforesaid

James Speakman
Hannah Speakman

Timothy Kirk Jr	Joseph Garretson	Joshua Speakman
Caleb Kirk	James Bane	William Willis
Nathan Updegraff	Daniel Ragan	Susannah Fisher
Josiah Updegraff	Samuel Updegraff	Edward Jones
Harman Updegraff	Ambrose Updegraff	Lydia Willis
Jacob Whorly	Joshua Bennett	
Sarah Willis	Betty Hussey	
Nathan Worley	Joel Willis	
Caleb Bentley	Ebenezer Cox	
Thomas Pearson	Thomas Speakman	
Lydia Worley	Thomas Shipton	
Lydia Updegraff	Hannah Matthews	
Mary Garretson	Elizabeth Kirk	
Mary Elgar	Lydia Updegraff	
Joseph Elgar	Margaret Elgar	
William Hersey	Hannah Hersey	
Elish Kirk	Mary Updegraff	

#173 18th of 9th mo 1783   JOHN VALE-DEBORAH THOMAS
Whereas John Vale of the Township of Warrington and County of York in Pennsylvania son of Robert Vale and Sarah his wife and Deborah Thomas of the township and County aforesaid Daughter of James Thomas and Deborah his wife...this Eighteenth day of the Ninth month in the Year of our Lord One Thousand seven Hundred and eighty three...at Warrington in the County afforesaid

John Vale
Deborah Vale

Benjamin Walker	Anna Vale	Robert Vale
Benjamin Underwood	Joshua Vale	Sarah Vale
Hannah Nevett	Elizabeth Vale	James Thomas
John Thomas	James Thomas	Deborah Thomas
Sarah Thomas	Lydia Thomas	Abel Walker
Morgan Jones	Sarah Vore	Robert Vale Jr
Jacob Williams	Hiram Hussey	Ann Walker
Joseph Stretch	Elizabeth Cook	William Vale
John Garretson	Elizabeth Loudon	
Hannah Cook		
Ruth Cook		
Elihu Underwood		
Peter Cleaver		
William Nevitt		

#174 12th of 6th mo 1783   SAMUEL JOHN-JANE FRAZER
Whereas Samuel John of the Township of Newberry York County Pennsylvania and Jane Frazer widow of Aron Frazer lately Deceased of Allen Township Cumberland County Pennsylvania aforesaid...this

MARRIAGES

twelfth day of the Sixth Month in the year of our Lord one Thousand Seven Hundred and Eighty Three...at the House of the above said Samuel John in Newberry

Samuel John
Jane John

Mary Freeman	Aaron Vernon	Ebenezer John
Susanna Mills	Samuel Garwood	Ann Penrose
Jane Leech	Samuel Pedon	Thomas Penrose
Sarah Thomas	Solomon Tates	Abigail Penrose
Jane Phillips	Anthony Moore	Benjamin Elot
Mary Updegraff	Ann Moore	Ann Elot
Jane Rankin	Samuel Lewis	George Mansberger
Catherine Davis	John Freeman	Ruth Fraizer
Sarah Veamn	William Miller	Isaac Ellot
Rachel Tates	Jeremiah Tates	James Kightley
Hannah Tates	Alexander Pedon	Ellis Lewis
Elizabeth Lewis	Catherine Lewis	Timothy Kirk
Rachel Varnum	Rose Malsby	George Phillips
Catherine Lewis	Ruth Lewis	Jacob Tate
Ruth Black	Mary Tate	
	Margaret Varnon	
	Feby Vernon	

#175 11th of 5th mo 1784   JOHN MCMILLAN-JOANNA GRIFFITH

Whereas John McMillan of Warrington in the County of York in Pennsylvania and Joanna Griffith of the same...this fifth Day of the Eleventh Month in the year of our Lord One Thousand Seven hundred & Eighty four...at Warrington

John McMillan
Joanna McMillan

James McMillan	William McMillan
Ann McMillan	George McMillan
Sarah McMillan	Mary Philips
Esther Griffith	Abigail Whinnery
Lydia McMillan	Ann Atherton
Benjn Willson	Richard Atherton
Mordecai Williams	William Whinnery
Sarah Williams	Thomas McMillan
Ruth Cook	Daniel -?-
Hannah Hussey	David Griffith
Mary Love	Wm Griffith
Sarah Morthland	Joseph -?-
Mary McMillan	Jas McMillan Jr
Samuel Pedon	
Lydia Pedon	
Esther Pedon	

#176 16th of 12th mo 1784   SAMUEL COOKSON-SARAH EDMUNDSON

Whereas Samuel Cookson of York Town in the County of York and State of Pennsylvania (widower) and Sarah Edmundson of Warrington Township

WARRINGTON MONTHLY MEETING

in the County & State aforesaid (widow)...this sixteenth Day of the twelfth month in the year of our Lord One thousand Seven hundred and eighty four...at Warrington

	Samuel Cookson
	Sarah Cookson
Ruth Walker	Ambrose Updegraff
Mordecai Williams	Elizabeth Updegraff
John McMillan	Joseph Edmundson
Amos Penrose	Samuel Cookson Jr
Miriam Hussey	Mordecai Miller
Benjn Underwood	William Edmundson
Abigail Penrose	Joseph Edmundson
Hannah Edmundson	Rebecca Edmundson
Abigail Edmundson	Edith Updegraff
Mary Canady	Joseph Elgar

#177 17th of 12th mo 1783   DANIEL PRICE-BETTY HUSSEY

Whereas <u>Daniel Price</u> son of <u>Samuel and Ann Price</u> of Baltimore County In Maryland and <u>Betty Hussey</u> Daughter of <u>John Hussey and Betty</u> his wife late of Newberry Township in the County of York in Pennsylvania deceased...this seventeenth day of the twelfth Month in the Year of our Lord one Thousand Seven hundred and Eighty three...at York Town in the County afforesaid

		Daniel Price
		Betty Price
Ruth Worly	Hannah Hersey	Samuel Price
Ann Worly	Sarah Wilbur	Mary Updegraff
Edith Updegraff	Mary Garison	Samuel Price
Mary Coates	Mary Updegraff	Mordecai Matthews
Mary Kirk	Lean M. Colmund	Elizabeth Price
Betty Jones	Rhoda Updegraff	Rachel Price
Ann Love	Isaac Jacobs	Mordecai Miller
Timothy Kirk	Joseph Elgar	Polly Updegraff
Nathan Updegraff	William Willis	Lydia Updegraff
Polly Walker	Edward Jones	Harman Updegraff
Ruth Hussey	Elisha Kirk	Joseph Updegraff
Edith Updegraff	Joseph Garretson	William Welch
Isaiah Welch	Daniel Ragan	Daniel Matthews
Hannah Welch	Samuel Cookson	Mordecai Price
Lydia Updegraff	Jacob Worly	John Cope
	Philip Price Jr	Christopher Hufsey
	Joshua Bennet	Hannah Hufsey
	Michael Garber	Hannah Matthews
	John Jones	Elizabeth Kirk
	John Love	
	Caleb Kirk	

#178 21st of 3rd mo 1852   JOSIAH GRIEST-MARYANN SQUIBB

Whereas <u>Josiah Griest</u> of Warrington Township in the County of York & State of Penna and <u>Maryann Squibb</u> of the Borough of Lewisberry County

MARRIAGES

& State aforesaid...this twenty first day of the third month in the year of our Lord one thousand eight hundred and fifty two...at the house of <u>Susannah Squibb</u>

Sam Aspenfelder
Henry Beamlark
J. E. Palinger
Sue Wickersham

Susanah Squibb
Rebecca Wickersham
Joseph Wickersham
Hannah C Wickersham
Philip Shettle

Josiah Griest
<u>Maryann S. Griest</u>
Jesse Kirk
Maryann Frankelberge

#179 22nd of 6th mo 1785   CALEB KIRK-LYDIA UPDEGRAFF

Whereas <u>Caleb Kirk</u> of York Town in the County of York in Pennsylvania son of <u>Caleb Kirk</u> deceased and <u>Elizabeth</u> his wife and <u>Lydia Updegraff</u> of the same place Daughter of <u>Samuel Updegraff & Mary</u> his wife...this twenty second day of the sixth month in the Year of our Lord one Thousand seven Hundred and Eighty five...at York Town afforesaid

		Caleb Kirk
		Lydia Kirk
Mordecai Miller	Henry Miller	Sam Updegraff
Caleb Bentley	Alexander Russell	Mary Updegraff
Esther Sharpless	Jas Campbell	Elizabeth Kirk
Esther Updegraff	Peter Yarnall	Hannah Welch
Lydia Updegraff	Jos Updegraff	Mary Updegraff
Hannah Yarnall	John Jones	Rhoda Updegraff
Robert Long	Joshua Bennett	Ruth Kirk
Sarah Miller	John Love	Eli Kirk
Hannah Matthews	John Campbell	John Cope
Hannah Miller	Edith Updegraff	Elisha Kirk
Sarah Miller Jr		Christopher Hufsey
Peggy Smith		
Molly Russell		
Ambrose Updegraff		
Elizabeth Updegraff		

#180 21st of 7th mo 1785   JOSEPH GRIEST-REBEKAH HUSSEY

Whereas <u>Joseph Griest</u> of the Township of Warrington and County of York in Pennsylvania Son of <u>John Griest and Susanna</u> his wife both deceased and <u>Rebekah Hussey</u> of the Township and County aforesaid Daughter of <u>Record Hussey</u> Deceased and <u>Miriam</u> his wife ...this twenty first day of the seventh month in the year of our Lord one thousand seven hundred and Eighty five...at Warrington in the County afforesaid   Joseph Griest
                                            Rebekah Griest

WARRINGTON MONTHLY MEETING

Benjamin Underwood	William Nevitt	Miriam Hussey
Enoch Underwood	William Wireman	Hannah Hussey
William Underwood	Nicholas Wireman Jr	Thomas Griest
Thos Penrose	Lydia Wireman	Ann Griest
Abigail Penrose	Jacob Griffith	Isaac Everitt
Sarah Cleaver	Daniel Griest Jr	Martha Everitt
Miriam Cleaver	John Cleaver	Amos Hussey
Sarah Walker	Susanna Cleaver	John Garretson
Benjmn Walker	Isaac Garretson	Mary Garretson
Ruth Walker		
Michael Underwood		
Isaac Pearson		
Elizabeth Pearson		
John Griest		
Susannah Garretson		
Miriam Hussey		
Mary Underwood		
Peter Cleaver		
William Garretson		

#181 24th of 11th mo 1785   JAMES THOMAS-NAOMY GARRETSON
Whereas James Thomas son of James Thomas of Warring Township in the
County of York and State of Pennsylvania and Naomy Garretson Daughter
of William Garretson of the same place...this twenty fourth day of
the eleventh Month in the year of our Lord one Thousand and seven
Hundred and Eighty five...at Warrington in the County afforesaid

                                                James Thomas
                                                Naomy Thomas

Elihu Underwood	Abel Walker	James Thomas
Benjamin Underwood	Peter Bower	Willing Garretson
Willing Underwood	Martha Griest	Deborah Thomas
Samuel Underwood	Erne Cox	William Garretson Jr
Abraham Bower	Michael Underwood	Debrah Vale
John Griest	Ann Walker	Sarah Wickersham
Abraham Lease	Hannah Cook	John Garretson
Benjamin Walker	Mary Fisher	Elizabeth Garretson
Ruth Walker	Deborah McMillan	Vincent Parsons
Deborah Fraizer		

#182 21st of 12th mo 1785   WILLIAM UNDERWOOD-SARAH JONES
Whereas William Underwood of Warrington Township and County of York
in Pennsylvania Son of Benjamin Underwood and Susanna his wife and
Sarah Jones Daughter of John Jones and Betty his wife...this twenty
first day of the twelfth month in the Year one Thousand seven hundred
and Eighty five...at York Town in the County afforesaid
                                                William Underwood
                                                Sarah Underwood

MARRIAGES

Ruth Kirk	Amos Hussey	Benjamin Underwood
Hannah Matthews	Wm Kersey	John Jones
Lydia Updegraff	Hannah Kersey	Elizabeth Jones
Mary Updegraff	William Willis	Nehemiah Underwood
Hanna Willis	Joseph Updegraff	Susanna Hobson
Sarah Miller	Solomon Miller	Samuel Jones
Caleb Kirk	Joseph Garretson	Susanna Jones
Ambrose Updegraff	Elisha Kirk	Mogan Jones
Samuel Updegraff	Daniel Ragan	John Thomas
Mary Updegraff	Jacob Worley	Sarah Thomas
Mordecai Miller	Harman Updegraff	Enoch Underwood
Ann Worley	John Love	Michael Underwood
Pricilla Phillips	Michael Garber	Mary Underwood
Rhoda Updegraff	Timothy Kirk	Joshua Bennett
Lydia Updegraff	Mary Kirk	Mary Bennett
Eliz Louden		Ann Bennett
Mary Garretson		
Ann Green		
Mary Coats		
Lydia Willis		
Esther Cornell		

#183 4th of 1st mo 1786   ELI KIRK-EDITH UPDEGRAFF

Whereas <u>Eli Kirk</u> of York Town in the County of York state of Pennsylvania son of <u>Caleb Kirk</u> and <u>Elizabeth</u> his wife both deceased and <u>Edith Updegraff</u> Daughter of <u>Joseph Updegraff and Susanna</u> his wife deceased...this fourth day of the first month one thousand Seven Hundred and Eighty Six...in the Town of York in the County afforesaid

		Eli Kirk
		Edith Kirk
Jesse Matthews	Cathrine Spangler	Joseph Updegraff
Lydia Miller	Elizabeth Crawford	Elisha Kirk
Pricilla Norbury	Sarah Swope	Caleb Kirk
Susanna Jones	Peter Yarnal	Ruth Kirk
Lydia Worly	Wm Willis	Aaron Coats
George McMunn	Solomon Miller	Mary Coats
Susanna Morris	Hannah Matthews	Lydia Kirk
Ann Worley	Ann Worley Jr	Joseph Garretson
Hannah Welch	Mary Kirk	Wm Welch
John Love	Mary Love	Ambrose Updegraff
Mary Bennett	Harman Updegraff	Lydia Updegraff
Elizabeth Miller	Hannah Willis	Mary Updegraff
Rebekah Miller	Michael Garber	Saml Updegraff
Hannah Kersey	John Jones	Rhoda Updegraff
Joel Willis	Benj. Walker	
Mordecai Miller	Timothy Kirk	
Jesse Milhouse		

WARRINGTON MONTHLY MEETING

#184 16th of 2nd mo 1786   THOMAS FARQUAR-HANNAH EDMUNDSON
Whereas Thomas Farquar of Pipe Creek in Frederick County in the State
of Maryland Son of -?-Farquar and Sarah his wife and Hannah Edmundson
of Warrington Township in York County State of Pennsylvania Daughter
of Thomas Edmundson and Mary his wife...this sixteenth day of the
second month in the year of our Lord one Thousand seven Hundred and
Eighty Six...at Warrington in the County afforesaid
                                              Thomas Farquar
                                              Hannah Farquar

Sarah Williams	Abigail Penrose	Thomas Edmundson
Samuel Cookson	Susanna Cadwallader	Joseph Edmundson
Elizabeth Marsh	David Cadwallader	Mary Edmundson
Margaret Marsh	Mary Hussey	Sarah Farquar
Elizabeth Marsh Jr	Jonathan Marsh	Abigail Edmundson
Mary Cennaday	Joseph Edmundson	Ann Penrose
Peter Cleaver	Benjamin Underwood	William Edmundson
John Marsh	Christopher Hussey	Rebekah Edmundson
Mordecai Williams		John Penrose
Benjamin Walker		
Ruth Walker		
Jesse Hughs		
Edward Jones		

#185 14th of 11th mo 1782   JESSE VORE-LYDIA CADWALLADER
Whereas Jesse Vore of the Township of Warrington and County of York
in Pennsylvania Son of Christian Vore and Sarah his wife and Lydia
Cadwallader of the Township and County afforesaid Daughter of David
Cadwallader and Hannah his wife (Deceased)...this fourteenth day of
the eleventh month in the Year of our Lord one Thousand seven Hundred
& Eighty two...at Warrington   Jesse Vore
                                     Lydia Vore

MARRIAGES

William Levitt	Ruth Walker	Christian Vore
Abrm Griffith	William Underwood	Sarah Vore
Elizabeth Griffith	Benjamin Underwood	Jacob Vore
Miriam Hussey	Abel Walker	Mary Vore
Sarah Williams	Ann Walker	Isaac Vore
Jonathan Marsh	James Cadwallader	Timothy Kirk
Wm Edmundson	Mary Cadwallader	Mary Kirk
Alexander Ross	Jacob Williams	Thomas Kirk
Robert Davis	Ruth Williams	Hannah Kirk
Mordecai Williams	James Thomas	Thomas Penrose
Mary Ross	Deborah Thomas	Abigail Penrose
Rebekah Fraizer	Rebekah Underwood	
Elizabeth Davies	John Thomas	
Griffith John	Jehu Thomas	
Caleb Cadwallader	Sarah Thomas	
Elihu Underwood	Rebekah Thomas	
Ann Underwood	Sarah Walker	

#186 18th of 10th mo 1786   THOMAS KIRK-ELIZABETH JONSTON
"here John Cleaver began to record"
Whereas <u>Thomas Kirk</u> son of <u>Timothy Kirk</u> late of Newbury in the County of york and State of Pennsylvania Deceased and <u>Sarah</u> his wife and <u>Elizabeth Jonston</u> Widdow Daughter of <u>William Garretson and Lydia</u> his wife...this eighteenth day of the tenth month in the year one Thousand Seven Hundred and Eighty Six at Newbury in the County afforesaid

Thomas Kirk
Elizabeth Kirk

Jesse Wickersham	Cornelius Garretson	John Garretson
Anna Wickersham	Ezekiel Kirk	Sarah Kirk
James Bane	Edward Jones	Lydia Garretson
Jane John	Jesse Vore	Timothy Kirk
Lydia Willis	Lydia Vore	Mary Kirk
Phebe Whinnery	John Willis	Martha Garretson
Jane Jones	Hannah Kirk	Samuel Garretson
William Lewis	Jacob Garretson	Alice Garretson
Elizabeth Lewis	John Garretson	Joseph Garretson
Rebecah Underwood		Rebekah Garretson
Samuel Miller		Sarah Baxter
Nathan Thomas		
Isaac Kirk		
Benjamin Walker		

#187 14th of 12th mo 1786   SIMEON HUTTON-MARY UNDERWOOD
Whereas <u>Simeon Hutton</u> of Paxton Township in the County of Dauphin and State of Pennsylvania (son of <u>Joseph Hutton</u> deceased) and <u>Mary Underwood</u> of Warrington Township in the County of York and State afforesaid, Daughter of <u>Benjamin Underwood</u> this fourteenth day of the

WARRINGTON MONTHLY MEETING

Twelfth Month in the year of our Lord One Thousand Seven Hundred and Eighty Six...at Warrington

Mordecai Williams	Hannah Hussey	Simeon Hutton
Miriam Cleaver	Miriam Hussey	Mary Hutton
Cadwallader Evans	Thos McMillan	Benjamin Underwood
Jno McMillan	Esther Griffith	Susanna Underwood
Tho Kirk	Sarah McMillan	Betty Norberry
Elizth Kirk	Susanna Jones	Willing Underwood
Jne Thomas	Peter Cleaver	Enoch Underwood
Benjn Walker	William Nevit	Alexander Underwood
Ruth Walker	Robert Morthland	Jacob Norberry
Samuel Cook	Abel Walker	John Underwood
Ruth Cook	Ann Walker	Margaret Underwood
John Cleaver	Jonah Thomas	Elihu Underwood
	William Underwood	Miriam Hussey
	Amos Hussey	Lydia Griffith
		Edith Hussey

#188 17th of 5th mo 1787   JOHN GRIEST-MIRIAM CLEAVER

Whereas <u>John Griest</u> of Manahan Township in the County of York and State of Pennsylvania son of <u>Daniel Griest and Ann</u> his wife and <u>Miriam Cleaver</u> of Warrington Township in the County and state aforesaid Daughter of <u>Peter Cleaver and Miriam</u> his wife...this seventeenth day of the fifth month in the year of our Lord one thousand Seven hundred and Eighty Seven...at Warrington in the County afforesaid

                                                                  John Griest
                                                                  Miriam Griest

Robert Vale	John Cleaver	Daniel Griest
Isaac Garretson	Susanna Cleaver	Ann Griest
Elihu Underwood	Rebekah Griest	Peter Cleaver
Benjn Walker	Benjamin Underwood	Joseph Griest
Robert Vale Jr	James Thomas Jr	Daniel Griest Jr
Ruth Cook	Wm Garretson	Isaac Griest
Nicholas Wireman	William Nevitt	Joshua Vale
Lydia Wireman	John McMillan	Elizabeth Vale
Sarah Walker	George McMillan	Susanna Griest
Ruth Griffith	Jonathan Marsh	Sarah Cleaver
	Miriam Hussey	Susanna Garretson
	Anne Marsh	Martha Everitt
	John Marsh Jr	Thomas Griest
	Elizabeth Marsh	Ann Griest
	Elizabeth Kirk	Joseph Griest

#189 24th of 10th mo 1787   JOSEPH ATKINSON-SUSANNA WILLIS

Whereas <u>Joseph Atkinson</u> son of <u>Cephas Atkinson</u> of Newbury in the County of york and <u>Susanna Willis</u> Daughter of <u>Robert Willis</u> of the Same place Late Deceased...this twenty fourth day of the tenth month in the year of our Lord one Thousand seven hundred and Eighty

MARRIAGES

seven...at Newbury in the County afforesaid

                                    Joseph (signed his mark) Atkinson
                                    Susanna (signed her mark) Atkinson

Rachel Hutton	John Garretson	Cephas Atkinson
Abigail Whinnery	Jacob Garretson	Cornelius Garretson
James Miller	Jacob Griest	Margaret Garretson
John Garretson	Jeremiah Underwood	Elizabeth Shannare
Benjn Walker	Thomas Miller	Edward Jones
Jacob Tate	Mary McMillan	Robert Miller
Samuel Garretson	Jane John	James Wickersham
Jesse Wickersham	Ruth Bane	James Bane
Anne Wickersham	Sarah Jones	Jas Welch
Alice Garretson	James Love	Jane Phillips
Sarah Baxter		
Joseph Garretson		
Rebekah Garretson		

#190 28th of 11th mo 1787   CEPAS ATKINSON-JANE PHILIPS

Whereas Cepas Atkinson of Newberry in the County of York and Jane Philips of the same Place...this twenty Eighth Day of the Eleventh Month in the Year of our Lord one Thousand Seven Hundred Eighty and Seven...in Newberry

                                    Cepas Atkinson
                                    Jane Atkinson

Mary Kirk	Pannela Landis	Cornelius Garretson
Hannah Kirk	Abigail Whinnery	Margret Garretson
John Garretson	Lydia Garretson	Susanna Atkinson
Sarah Buckley	Hannah Kirk	Joseph Atkinson
Mary Fisher	Isaac Kirk	William Atkinson
Samuel Miller	Martha Kirk	Jas Kightley
Thomas Miller	William Lewis	Edward Jones
Isaac Fisher	John Garretson	Sarah Jones
Jesse Wickersham	Joseph Garretson	Ruth Bane
Jacob Norbury		
Joshua Hutton		
Samuel Garretson		
Sarah Miller		
Rebeccah Garretson		
Alice Garretson		
Timothy Kirk		
Sarah Kirk		
Mary Beals		

#191 28th of 11th mo 1787   ISAAC KIRK-MARTHA GARRETSON

Whereas Isaac Kirk son of Jacob Kirk deceased of Newbury Township in the County of york in Pennsylvania and Hannah his wife and Martha Garretson Daughter of William Garretson of the same place and Lydia his wife...this twenty eighth day of the Eleventh Month in the year

WARRINGTON MONTHLY MEETING

one Thousand Seven hundred and Eighty Seven...at Newbury in the County afforesaid

		Isaac Kirk
		Martha Kirk
William Lewis	John Garretson	John Garretson
Thomas Miller	Cephas Atkinson	Hannah Kirk
Joseph Garretson	Jane Atkinson	Lydia Garretson
Rebekah Garretson	Mary Beals	Edmond Jones
Ruth Bane	Cornelius Garretson	Sarah Jones
Jacob Norbury	Margret Garretson	William Kirk
Faithful Garretson	Samuel Garretson	Sarah Kirk
Mary Miller	Alice Garretson	Timothy Kirk
Jacob Garretson	Abigail Whinnery	Hannah Kirk
Solomon Beals	Susanna Atkinson	Mary Kirk
Martha Griest	Ann Evans	Rachel Kirk
Anna Wickersham	Sarah Buckley	
Samuel Miller	Pamila Lewis	
Ezekiel Kirk	Mary Fisher	
John Griest	Jesse Wickersham	
James Wickersham		
Amos Lewis		
Jacob Griest		
Abraham Topluff		
Sarah Lewis		

#192 15th of 12th mo 1788   MORDECAI MATTHEWS-RUTH HUSSEY

Whereas <u>Mordecai Matthews</u> of Gunpowder in the County of Baltimore and State of Maryland son of <u>Thomas and Rachel Matthews</u> the former deceased and <u>Ruth Hussey</u> of Warrington in the County of York and State of Pennsylvania Daughter of <u>Record and Miriam Hussey</u> the former Deceased...this Fifteenth day of the Twelfth Month in the year of our Lord one thousand Seven hundred and Eighty Eight...at Warrington in the County afforesaid

Mordecai Matthews
<u>Ruth Matthews</u>

MARRIAGES

James Hancock	Benj Walker	Miriam Hussey
William McMillan	Ruth Walker	Hannah Hussey
Sarah Underwood	Mordecai Williams	Amos Hussey
Mary Duckett	Sarah Williams	Elizabeth Matthews
Ann Marsh	John Marsh	John Matthews
James Price	Abigail Penrose	Jesse Matthews
William Edmundson	Daniel Matthews	Ely Matthews
Abigail Edmundson	William Ross	Jedaiah Hussey
Sarah Walker	Samuel Price	Jane Hussey
Elizabeth Ross	Joseph Miller	Joseph Griest
Elizabeth Marsh	Jono Marsh Jr	Lydia Griffith
Esther Edmondson	Mordecai Price	Miriam Hussey
Samuel Cookson	Willing Underwood	Mary Hussey
Peter Yarnall	Enoch Underwood	Rachel Price
	John Bentley	Lydia Kirk
	Susanna Bentley	Rhoda Updegraff

#193 14th of 5th mo 1789   JOHN MARSH-HANNAH HUSSEY

Whereas <u>John Marsh</u> son of <u>Jonathan and Rebecah Marsh</u> of the Township of Warrington and County of york in Pennsylvania and <u>Hannah Hussey</u> Daughter of <u>Record and Miriam Hussey</u> of the Township and County aforesaid...this fourteenth day of the fifth month in the year of our Lord one Thousand Seven Hundred and Eighty nine...at Warrington in the County afforesaid
                                                                    John Marsh
                                                                    <u>Hannah Marsh</u>

Abigail Edmondson		
Esther Edmondson	Sarah McMillan	Jonathan Marsh
Peter Cleaver	Hannah Packer	Ann Marsh
John Cleaver	Philip Packer	Miriam Hussey
Sarah Cleaver	James Marsh	John Marsh
William Fawnstock	Abraham Marsh	Margaret Marsh
Ben Walker	Ann Hussey	Susanna Morthland
William Ross	Miriam Hussey	Jedaiah Hussey
Sarah Walker	Elizabeth Marsh	Hugh Morthland
Charles Underwood	Mary Hussey	Jacob Griffith
Margret Kellowell	Jesse Matthews	Lydia Griffith
William Edmondson	Alexr Underwood	Ruth Matthews
Mordecai Williams	Elizabeth Marsh	Robert Morthland
Sarah Williams	Hannah Yarnall	Thomas McMillan
Enoch Underwood	Ben Underwood	
Mary Marsh	William Nevitt	
Margret Marsh		
Michael Morthland		

#194 17th of 12th mo 1789   JAMES MILLER-MARY McMILLAN

Whereas <u>James Miller</u> of the Township of Newbury and County of york and State of Pennsylvania Son of <u>Robert & Sarah Miller</u> and <u>Mary McMillan</u> Daughter of <u>William & Deborah McMillan</u>...this seventeenth

WARRINGTON MONTHLY MEETING

day of the Twelfth month in the year of our Lord one thousand Seven hundred and Eighty Nine...at Warrington in the County afforesaid

		James Miller
		Mary Miller
John Thomas	Ann McMillan	Robert Miller
Ann Hussey	Deborah McMillan	William McMillan
Peter Cleaver	Sarah McMillan	Deborah McMillan
William Nevitt	Sarah Walker	Samuel Miller
William Lewis	Mary McMillan	Robert Miller jr
Robert Squibb	Thomas Holland	Margret Miller
Benjamin Underwood	George McMillan	John McMillan
Moses Packer	Jno McMillan Jr	Mary Miller
Abel Walker	Samuel Underwood	George McMillan
Ann Walker	Alexander Underwood	Lydia McMillan
	Miriam Hussey	Thomas Miller
	Cornelius Garretson	David McMillan
	Margaret Garretson	Thomas McMillan
	Charles Underwood	Thomas McMillan Jr
	Sarah Williams	Jonathan Marsh
	Mordecai Williams	Jas Kiley
		Wm Griffith

#195 19th of 5th mo 1790   AARON VERNON-MARY DUCKETT

Whereas Aaron Vernon of the Township of Newbury in the County of york and State of Pennsylvania and Mary Duckett...this Nineteenth Day of the Fifth Month in the year of our Lord one Thousand Seven hundred and Ninety...at Newbury in the County afforesaid

	Aaron Vernon
	Mary Vernon
Zephaniah Underwood	Robert Miller
Ezekiel Kirk	Sarah Miller
Daniel Bonine	Tacy Vernon
Samuel Garretson	Rachel Hutton
Alice Garretson	Mary Updegraff
James Bane	Hannah Way
Ruth Bane	Samuel Miller
Hannah Kirk	James Miller
Abigail Whinnery	Thomas Miller
John Garretson	Solomon Hutton
Joseph Garretson	Jesse Miller
Cornelius Garretson	Mary Miller
Hannah Garretson	Sarah Miller
	Sarah Bonine
	Edward Jones
	Rebecah Garretson
	James Hancock
	James Wickersham

MARRIAGES

#196 19th of 8th mo 1790   WILLIAM WIERMAN-SARAH CLEAVER
Whereas William Wierman of Huntington Township York county and State of Pennsylvania Son of William Wierman and Emey his wife and Sarah Cleaver of Warrington Township in the County and State afforesaid Daughter of Peter Cleaver and Miriam his wife...this nineteenth day of the Eighth month in the year of our Lord one Thousand Seven Hundred & Ninety...at Warrington in the County afforesaid

		William Wierman
		Sarah Wierman
James Marsh	Margaret Marsh	William Wierman
Nicholas Wierman	John Vale	Peter Cleaver
-?- Cook	Amos Griest	Mary Wierman
Jonathan Marsh	Sarah Wierman	Emey Cox
Ann Marsh	Joshua Vale	John Cleaver
William Nevitt	John Marsh	Susanna Cleaver
William (X) Underwood	James Thomas Jr	John Griest
Mary Griffith	Miriam Hussey	Miriam Griest
Elihu Underwood	Margaret Marsh	Joshua Cox
Elizabeth Marsh	William Garretson	Benj Underwood
Mary Marsh	William McMillan	Phebe Thornburgh
John Kettelwell	Abel Walker	Thomas Griest
Enoch Underwood	Moses Packer	
Robert Vale		
Benjamin Walker		
Ruth Walker		
William Edmondson		
Susanna Marsh		

#197 23rd of 12th mo 1790   ALEXANDER PEDEN-LYDIA THOMAS
Whereas Alexander Peden of Foffowfield Township Washington County in the State of Pennsylvania son of Samuel Peden and Lydia his wife and Lydia Thomas of Warrington Township york County and State aforesaid Daughter of James Thomas and Deborah his wife... this twenty third day of the Twelfth mo in the year of our Lord one thousand Seven hundred and Ninety at Warrington in the County afforesaid

                                                Alexander Peden
                                                Lydia Peden

WARRINGTON MONTHLY MEETING

Danl Jones	Amos Lewis	James Thomas
Anna Marsh	John Kettlewell	Deborah Thomas
Miriam Hussey	John Elliot	James Thomas Jr
Sarah Williams	Enoch Vanscoyoc	Deborah Vale
Susanna Cleaver	Benj Underwood	John Vale
Jacob Griffiths	John McMillan	William Lewis
Lydia Griffiths	David Ayres	John Thomas
William Edmondson	Willing Underwood	Abel Walker
Anna Vale	Joseph Bradley	Benj Walker
Sarah Vale	William Nevit	Ruth Walker
	Peter Cleaver	Sarah Thomas
	Jonathan Marsh	Hannah Lewis
		Sarah Walker
		Thomas McMillan

#198 19th of 5th mo 1791   WILLIAM GRIFFITH-DEBORAH McMILLAN
Whereas William Griffith son of William Griffith Deceased and Joanna his wife of Warrington Township in the County of York and State of Pennsylvania and Deborah McMillan Daughter of George McMillan and Ann his wife of the Township County and State afforesaid...this nineteenth Day of the fifth month in the year of our Lord one Thousand Seven hundred and Ninety one...at Warrington in the County affores

William Griffith
Deborah Griffith

John Marsh Jr	William McMillan	George McMillan
Hannah Marsh	Benj Walker	Ann McMillan
Enoch Underwood	Ruth Walker	Joanna McMillan
John Cleaver	John Garretson	Joseph Garretson
Susanna Cleaver	William Griffith Jr	Ann McMillan Jr
Jonathan Marsh	Deborah Griffith	Thomas McMillan
Ann Marsh	George McMillan Jr	Joseph Griffith
Peter Cleaver	Miriam Hussey	Ruth Griffith
Wm Edmundson	William Nevit	Mary McMillan
Charles Underwood	Benjamin Underwood	Mary Griffith
Jane Morthland	Mordecai Williams	Thomas McMillan
Alexander Underwood	Sarah Williams	
Ann Boyd	Thomas McMillan	
Esther McMillan	Abraham Underwood	
David McMillan	Wm McMillan	
Lydia McMillan		
Jonathan McMillan		
Deborah Philips		

#199 12th of 1st mo 1792   JOSEPH EDMONDSON-ELIZABETH MARSH
Whereas Joseph Edmondson son of John Edmondson (deceased) and Sarah his wife of the Township of Warrington and County of York in Pennsylvania and Elizabeth Marsh Daughter of Jonathan and Ann Marsh of the Township & County aforesaid...this twelfth day of the First

MARRIAGES

Month in the year of our Lord one thousand seven hundred and ninety two...at Warrington in the County afforesaid

		Joseph Edmondson
		Elizabeth Edmondson
Elizabeth Marsh	Amos Hussey	Jonathan Marsh
Miriam Hussey	Abigail Hussey	Ann Marsh
Mary Edmondson	John Nesbit Jr	Sarah Cookson
Benj Walker	Mary Cook	John Marsh
Abel Walker	Jonathan Marsh	John Marsh Jr
Thos McMillan	Nancy Jackson	Esther Edmondson
John Cleaver	Wm Haines	James Marsh
Wm Lewis	Wm Edmondson	Sarah Edmondson
Enoch Underwood	Michael Morthland	Joseph Edmondson
Joshua Vale	John Marsh Jr	Sarah Morthland
Martha Everitt	Saml Ballinger	Ann Marsh
Deborah Thomas	Nicholas Arnold	
Wm Vale	Robert Morthland	
James McMillan	Susanna Marsh	
Abraham Underwood	Mary Marsh	
Miriam Hussey	Hannah Packer	
Mordecai Matthews		
John Kettlewell		

#200 9th of 4th mo 1792   WILLIAM HAINES-ESTHER EDMUNDSON
Whereas William Haines of Pipe Creek Frederick County and State of Maryland son of Nathan Haines and Sophia his Wife and Esther Edmundson of the township of Warrington County of york and State of Pennsylvania Daughter of John Edmundson Deceased and Sarah his wife...this ninth day of the fourth Month in the year of our Lord one thousand Seven hundred and Ninety two...at Warrington in the County
    afforesaid   William Haines
                                            Esther Haines

WARRINGTON MONTHLY MEETING

Wm Lewis
Wm McMillan
Jonathan Marsh
Miriam Hussey
Benjn Farquar
Rebecah Cook
Mary Way
William Nevit
James Thomas
Enoch Underwood
Jonathan Marsh
Ann Marsh
James Kettlewell
Amos Hussey
Benjn Walker
Abigail Hussey
Hannah Hibbert
Sarah Walker

James Marsh
Thos Edmundson
Jesse Kersey
Joseph Edmundson
Rebecah Edmundson
Thos Edmundson Jr
Daniel Cookson
William Edmundson
Benjamin Underwood
Mordecai Williams
Sarah Williams

Samuel Cookson
Sarah Cookson
Sarah Edmundson
John Edmundson
Joseph Edmundson Jr
Daniel Haines
Rachel Haines
Thos Edmundson
Mary Edmundson

A HIGGINS

MARRIAGES

#201 20th of 9th mo 1793   JOHN EVERITT-SUSANNAH MARSH

Whereas John Everitt son of Isaac and Martha Everitt of Huntington Township York County and State of Pennsylvania and Susannah Marsh Daughter of John and Margaret Marsh of Warrington Township county and State aforesaid...this twentieth day of the Ninth Month anno Domini one Thousand Seven hundred and Ninety three...at Warrington in the County afforesaid

                                                  John Everitt
                                                  Susanna Everitt

Alex Underwood	Peter Cleaver	Isaac Everitt
Sarah Morthland	William Nevitt	Martha Everitt
Jn Underwood	Jno Kettlewell	John Marsh
Robert Morthland	Ann Walker	Margaret Marsh
James Marsh	Joseph Griest	Isaac Pearson
Samuel Morthland	David Griest	Elizabeth Pearson
Alexander Underwood	Jno Garretson	John Cleaver
Nicholas Wierman	Richard Pilkinton	Susanna Cleaver
Wm Edmundson	Michael Morthland	Thos Pearson
Hannah Underwood	Elihu Underwood	Martha Pearson
Wm Marsh	Jane Marsh Jr	Isaac Everitt
Jonathan Marsh	Hannah Everitt	Jno Marsh Jr
Abel Walker	Sarah Wierman	Jon Marsh
Rebekah Marsh	Susanna Griest	Mary Edmundson
Lydia Marsh	Jane Underwood	Miriam Hussey
Elihu Underwood	Ann Marsh	Ruth Walker
Elizabeth Marsh	Mary Hussey	Benjamin Walker
Charles Underwood	Susanna Harlan	
Joseph Edmundson	Sarah Walker	

#202 14th of 11th mo 1793   WILLIAM GRIFFITH-SARAH COOK

Whereas William Griffith son of Abraham Griffith and Elizabeth his wife of the Township of Warrington in the County of york and State of Pennsylvania and Sarah Cook Daughter of Samuel Cook of the Township County and State aforesaid and Ruth his wife deceased...this Fourteenth Day of the Eleventh Month in the year of our Lord one thousand Seven hundred and Ninety three...at Warrington afforesaid

                                                  William Griffith
                                                  Sarah Griffith

WARRINGTON MONTHLY MEETING

Abraham Griffith	Jas McMillan	Abraham Griffith
Mary Cook	Esther McMillan	Samuel Cook
Jedaiah Hussey	Christopher Hussey	Elizabeth Griffith
Hannah Levitt	Saml McMillan	Hannah Cook
Mary Kettlewell	-?- Griffith	Elisha Griffith
Mary Hussey	Rebekah Griffith	Ruth Cook
Ann Hussey	Isaac Cook	Samuel Cook
Mordecai Williams	Elisha Cook	
Sarrah Williams	Wm Cook	
Robert Vale	Wm Griffith	
Saml Cook Jr	Deborah Griffith	
Israel Cook	Ruth Griffith	
	Mary Griffith	

#203 12th of 2nd mo 1794   THOMAS McMILLAN-JANE JONES

Whereas Thomas McMillan son of Wm McMillan and Deborah his wife of the Township of Warrington County of York and Province of Pennsylvania and Jane Jones Daughter of Edward and Content Jones (the latter deceased)...this twelfth day of the second month in the year of our Lord one thousand seven hundred and Ninety four...at Newberry in the County afforesaid
Thomas McMillan
Jane McMillan

James Miller	Joseph Garretson	Wm McMillan
Mary Miller	Rebekah Garretson	Deborah McMillan
Wm McMillan	Saml Garretson	Edward Jones
Henry McMillan	Alice Garretson	Cornelius Garretson
John Hirst		Hannah Garretson
Sarah Farquar		
Elizabeth Kirk		
Lydia Garretson		
Jas McMillan		
Jonathan McMillan		
James Garretson		

#204 16h of 10th mo 1794   THOMAS JAMES-HANNAH COOK

Whereas Thomas James son of Thomas and Sarah James (the former dec'd) of the County of Stafford and State of Virginia and Hannah Cook Daughter of Samuel Cook and Hannah his wife (the latter dec'd) of the township of Warrington County of york and Province of Pennsylvania...this sixteenth day of the tenth Month in the year of our Lord one thousand seven hundred and Ninety four at Warrington in the County afforesaid
Thomas James
Hannah James

MARRIAGES

Sarah Williams	Enoch Underwood	Saml Cook
Jane Hussey	Ruth Cook	Hannah Nevitt
John Griest	Rebekah Griffith	Henry Cook
William Nevitt		Abraham Griffith
Jas McMillan		Elizabeth Griffith
Willing Griest		

#205 15th of 1st mo 1795   DANIEL COOKSON-SARAH EDMUNDSON

Whereas <u>Daniel Cookson</u> of Warrington Township in the County of york and State of Pennsylvania Son of <u>Samuel Cookson and Mary</u> his wife deceased and <u>Sarah Edmundson</u> of the same place Daughter of <u>John Edmundson</u> deceased and <u>Sarah</u> his wife...this fifteenth of the first month in the year of our Lord one thousand Seven hundred and Ninety five...at Warrington in the County afforesaid

                                                      Daniel Cookson
                                                      <u>Sarah Cookson</u>

Thomas Edmundson	Wm Edmundson	Samuel Cookson
Jonathan Marsh	Mary Edmundson	Sarah Cookson
Ann Marsh	Benjamin Underwood	Ambrose Updegraff
Thos McMillan	Peter Cleaver	Elizabeth Updegraff
Saml Garretson	Elizabeth Edmundson	Joseph Edmundson
Wm Lewis	Jonathan Edmundson	
Benjamin Walker	James Thomas	
Ruth Walker	Deborah Thomas	
	Wm Nevitt	

#206 25th of 6th mo 1795   WILLIN GRIEST-ANNE McMILLAN

Whereas <u>Willin Griest</u> son of <u>Willin Griest and Ann</u> his wife of Monallen in the County of york and State of Pennsylvania and <u>Anne McMillan</u> Daughter of <u>George McMillan and Ann</u> his wife of Warrington in the County and State aforesaid...this twenty fifth day of the sixth month in the year of our Lord one thousand and seven hundred and ninety five...at Warrington in the County afforesaid

                                                      Willin Griest
                                                    <u>Anne Griest</u>

WARRINGTON MONTHLY MEETING

Ann Marsh	Mary Phillips	Willin Griest
Sarah Walker	Thomas McMillan	Ann Griest
Benjamin Walker	Wm Griffith	George McMillan
Ruth Walker	Deborah Griffith	Ann McMillan
James McMillan	Mary McMillan	John Griest
Ruth Griffith	George McMillan	William McMillan
Mary Griffith	Rebekah McMillan	Deborah McMillan
Jesse Phillips	Joseph Garretson	William Hinshaw
Rebekah Garretson		Jacob McMillan
Content Griest		
Joseph McMillan		
Benjamin Underwood		
James Thomas		
William Nevitt		
Miriam Hussey		
Deborah Thomas		

#207 24th of 12th mo 1795   NICHOLAS WIERMAN-JANE UNDERWOOD

Whereas Nicholas Wierman son of William Wierman of Huntington Township York County State of Pennsylvania and Hannah his wife and Jane Underwood Daughter of John Underwood late of Warrington Township County and State afforesaid (deceased) and Mary his wife...this twenty fourth day of the twelfth month in the year of our Lord one thousand seven hundred and Ninety five...at Warrington in the County afforesaid

Nicholas Wierman
Jane Wierman

Daniel Griest	Susanna Northland	William Wierman
Thos Thornburgh	Michael Northland	Nicholas Wierman
Phebe Thornburgh	Mary McMillan	Sarah Wierman
Thomas Griest	Content Garretson	Isaac Everitt
Ann Griest	Susanna Griest	Charles Underwood
Robert Vale Jr	John Marsh Jr	Samuel Underwood
Robert Northland	Benjamin Walker	Alexander Underwood
Phebe Northland	Ruth Walker	Benjamin Underwood
Mary Beals	John Kettlewell	Stephen Hendricks
Jane Hussey	Thos Pearson	Sarah Hendricks
David Griest	Joshua Ash	William Nevitt
Jesse Comly	Charles Kettlewell	Susanna Wierman
Samuel Northland	James Marsh	Ann Marsh
John Wierman	Susanna Everitt	Hannah Everitt
Samuel Comly	Robert Northland	Jonathan Marsh
Isaac Wierman	John Packer	John Everitt
Nicholas Wierman	John Garretson	

#208 16th of 8th mo 1796   RICHARD PILKINGTON-SARAH WALKER

Whereas Richard Pilkington son of Vincent Pilkington of Huntington Township york County and State of Pennsylvania and Rebecca his wife and Sarah Walker Daughter of Benjamin Walker of Warrington Township

MARRIAGES

County and State aforesaid and <u>Ruth</u> his wife...this sixteenth day of the Eighth Month in the year of our Lord one thousand Seven hundred and Ninety six...at Warrington in the County afforesaid

		Richard Pilkington
		<u>Sarah Pilkington</u>
Thomas Jennings	Joseph John	Vincent Pilkington
Enoch Underwood	Sarah Walker	Rebekah Pilkington
Mary Underwood	Stephen Speakman	Benjamin Walker
Amos Hussey	Lydia Cook	Ruth Walker
Mary Griffith	John Garretson	Abel Walker
John Vale	Anna Potts	Ann Walker
Deborah Vale	thomas Edmundson Jr	James Thomas
Elias Pearson	Mary Cook	Deborah Thomas
Elizabeth Kirk	Amos Griffith	Isaac Garretson
Miriam Hussey	Mary Edmundson	Edith Hussey
Mordecai Willis	Jas McMillan	John Walker
Sarah Williams	Ruth Griffith	Content Garretson
Ellenor Welsh	Wm Edmundson	
Robert Vale Jr	Sarah Mackland	
Thomas Pearson		

#209 29th of 12th mo 1796   AZARIAH WALL-REBEKAH LEECH

Whereas <u>Azariah Wall</u> son of <u>Absalom Wall</u> of Newbury Township in the County of York and State of Pennsylvania and <u>Margaret</u> his wife and <u>Rebekah Leech</u> Daughter of <u>Thomas Leech</u> of Warrington Township in the County and State aforesaid and <u>Phebe</u> his wife...this twenty ninth day of the twelfth month in the year of our Lord one Thousand Seven hundred and Ninety six...at Warrington in the County afforesaid

		Azariah Wall
		<u>Rebekah Wall</u>
Benjamin Walker	Jas McMillan	Absalom Wall
Ruth Walker	Benjamin Taylor	Thomas Leech
Miriam Hussey	Wm Edmundson	Phebe Leech
Deborah Thomas	Francis Pellet	William Leech
Jno Kettlewell	Tecy Varnon	Jane Hussey
Abel Walker	Sarah Hart	Jedaiah Hussey
John Vale	Jonathan McMillan	Jane Taylor
Isaac Kirk	Edward Griffith	Susanna Leech
James Hoopes	Elizabeth Griffith	Mary Wall
Elizabeth Griffith	Thos Edmundson Jr	John Wall
Jane Taylor	Mary Edmundson	Thomas Leech
Ann Hussey	Anna Boyd	
Edward Jones	Wm Hoops	
Nathan Thomas		
John thomas		
Mary Thomas		
Mary Jones		
Michael Morthland		

WARRINGTON MONTHLY MEETING

#210 16th day of 11th mo 1796   THOMAS MILLER-SARAH KIRK
Whereas Thomas Miller son of Robert Miller of Newbury Township in the
County of york in Pennsylvania and Sarah   his wife and Sarah Kirk
Daughter of Jacob Kirk late of Newbury Township aforesaid Deceased
and Hannah his wife...this sixteenth day of the Eleventh Month one
thousand Seven Hundred and Ninety Six at Newbury in the County afforesaid

                                                         Thomas Miller
                                                         Sarah Miller

Faithful Garretson	Jane Atkinson	Robert Miller
Hannah Long	Rachel Meredith	Sarah Miller
John Mansberger	James Wickersham	Hannah Kirk
John Bentley	Jesse Wickersham	Samuel Miller
Susanna Bentley	Wm Underwood	Isaac Kirk
Danl Mansberger	Elijah Meredith	Ezekiel Kirk
Mary Jones	Edward Jones Jr	Hannah Kirk Jr
Betty Hutton	Hannah Garretson	Margaret Miller
Jane Garretson	Sarah Hutton	Margaret Miller
Cephas Atkinson	Deborah Kirk	Sarah Miller
Joseph Garretson	Ruth Bane	Elizabeth Kirk
Rebecca Garretson	James Bane	Jacob Garretson
Ann Garretson	Saml Garretson	Mary Garretson
William Whinnery	Alice Garretson	Thomas Kirk
Joseph Kirk	Edward Jones	Jacob Kirk
Ruth Miller	Sarah Jones	Rachel Kirk
Anna Wickersham	Cornelius Garretson	Rachel John
Hannah Lightfoot	Hannah Garretson	
Ann Taylor	Ruth Griffith	
Phebe Whinnery	Jesse Miller	
Abigail Whinnery		

#211 13th of 4th mo 1797   DAVID McMILLAN-HANNAH HUSSEY
Whereas David McMillan of Warrington Township york County and State
of Pennsylvania Son of   William McMillan and Deborah his wife of the
same place and Hannah Hussey Daughter of Jediah Hussey and Jane his
wife...this thirteenth day of the fourth Month in the year of our
Lord one thousand Seven hundred & Ninety Seven...at Warrington in the
County afforesaid   David McMillan
                                            Hannah McMillan

MARRIAGES

Samuel Cook	Abigail Hussey	William McMillan
Benjamin Walker	Ruth Griffith	Deborah McMillan
Obed Underwood	Mary Griffith	Jediah Hussey
William Vale	Elizabeth Griffith	Jane Hussey
Enoch Underwood	Mary McMillan	Mary Miller
Thos Edmundson Jr	Rebecca McMillan	Lydia McMillan
Wm Griffith	John Kettlewell	Jonathan McMillan
Thos Leech Jr	Mary Edmundson	Ann Hussey
Joseph John	Amos Griffith	Henry McMillan
William Kirk	Thos McMillan Jr	Sarah Welch
Rachel Kirk	Jesse Phillips	Edith Hussey
Mary Underwood	Rebecca Wall	Jediah Hussey
Jane Phillips	William Leech	Thos McMillan Jr
Margaret Cadwallader	William Cook	Ruth McMillan

#212 14th of 9th mo 1797   JAMES MARSH-EDITH HUSSEY

Whereas <u>James Marsh</u> of the Township of Warrington in the County of York & State of Pennsylvania Son of <u>Jonathan & Ann Marsh</u> decd and <u>edith Hussey</u> of the same place Daughter of <u>Record and Miriam Hussey</u> the former deceased...this fourteenth day of the Ninth Month in the year of our Lord one thousand Seven Hundred & Ninety Seven...at Warrington in the County afforesaid   James Marsh
                                                           Edith Marsh

Elizabeth Marsh	Ann Edmundson	Joseph Edmundson
Margaret Underwood	Jonathan Marsh	Miriam Hussey
Jane Hussey	Sarah Welch	Rebecca Griest
Sarah Updegraff	Amos Hussey	Mary Hussey
	Jedaiah Hussey	Elizabeth Edmundson
		Ann Hussey
		John Edmundson

#213 16th of 11th mo 1797   JONATHAN McMILLAN-ANN HUSSEY

Whereas <u>Jonathan McMillan</u> of Warrington Township york County & State of Pennsylvania son of <u>William McMillan and Deborah</u> his wife of the same place (the latter deceased) and <u>Ann Hussey</u> Daughter of <u>Jedaiah Hussey and Jane</u> his wife of the Township County & State aforesaid this sixteenth day of the Eleventh month one thousand Seven hundred and Ninety Seven...at Warrington in the County afforesaid
                                                           Jonathan McMillan
                                                           <u>Ann McMillan</u>

WARRINGTON MONTHLY MEETING

Samuel Cook	Thomas McMillan	William McMillan
Mary Cadwalader	Ruth McMillan	Jedaiah Hussey
Ruth Griffith	John Cleaver	Jane Hussey
Ann Walker	Susanna Cleaver	per order
Wm Edmundson	Abigail Whinnery	Thomas McMillan
Robert Whinnery	William Griffith	Jane McMillan
Willing Griest	Deborah Griffith	Mary Miller
Joseph Garretson	George McMillan	Lydia McMillan
Benjamin Walker	Rebekah McMillan	Jane Hussey
Ruth Walker	Thos McMillan	per order
James Thoman	Jonathan Marsh	David McMillan
John Kettlewell		Hannah McMillan
		Henry McMillan
		Mary Hussey
		Nathan Hussey
		Thos Leech

#214 14th day of 12th mo 1797   ISAAC GRIEST-MARY COOK

Whereas <u>Isaac Griest</u> son of <u>Willing Griest and Ann</u> his wife of monaghon Township in the County of York and State of Pennsylvania and <u>Mary Cook</u> Daughter of <u>Jacob Cook</u> of Warrington Township in the County and State afforesaid and <u>Mary</u> his wife deceased...this fourteenth day of the twelfth month in the year of our Lord one thousand Seven hundred and Ninety Seven...at Warrington in the County afforesaid

		Isaac Griest
		<u>Mary Griest</u>
John Kettlewell	John Walker	Willing Griest Sr
Charles Underwood	Jonathan Marsh	Jacob Cook
Jane Squibb	Hugh Marsh	Willing Griest Jr
Michael Morthland	Thomas Jennings	Ann Griest
Rebecca Marsh	Margaret Kettlewell	Benjamin Underwood
Mary Griffith	Abel Walker	Content Griest
Salley Machlan	Wm Edmundson	Lydia Cook
Wm Cook	Nicholas Wierman	Elihu Underwood
Susanna Wierman	Elizabeth Griffith	Stephen Speakman
Wm Marsh	Wm Griffith	Elizabeth Speakman
Ann McMillan	Elizabeth Griffith	Robert Vale
	Benjamin Walker	Sarah Vale
	Ruth Walker	Isaac Wierman

#215 13th of 1st mo 1798   ELIJAH MOORE-SARAH ALLEN

Whereas <u>Elijah Moore</u> of Franklin Township in the County of Huntingdon and State of Pennsylvania Son of <u>Andrew Moore and Rebekah</u> his wife and <u>Sarah Allen</u> Daughter of <u>James Allen and Elizabeth</u> his wife (the latter deceased) of London Grove Township in Chester County & State aforesaid...this thirteenth day of the First month in the year of our Lord one thousand Seven hundred and Ninety Eight...at Newberry in the County afforesaid

MARRIAGES

		Elijah Moore
		Sarah Moore
Cornelius Garretson	Hannah Kirk	Andrew Moore
Jacob Garretson	Susanna Cleaver	Sarah Moore
Joseph Garretson	Phebe Whinnery	Samuel Miller
	Benjamin Underwood	Mary Vernon
	Edward Jones	Thomas Miller
	Benjamin Walker	Ruth McMillan
	James Bean	Aaron Vernon
	Robert Vale	George Harris Jr
	Samuel Garretson	Joseph Garretson
	Ezekiel Kirk	Ruth Bane
	Abel Walker	Miriam Hussey
	William McMillan	Anna Wickersham
	James Wickersham	Sarah Jones
	Nathan Thomas	Mary Edmundson
	Isaac Kirk	Elizabeth Griffith

#216 15th of 11th mo 1798   THOMAS McMILLAN-JANE TAYLOR

Whereas <u>Thomas McMillan</u> of Warrington Township york county and State of Pennsylvania Son of <u>George McMillan</u> deceased and <u>Ann</u> his wife and <u>Jane Taylor</u> Daughter of <u>Joseph Taylor and Jane</u> his wife of the same place...this fifteenth day of the Eleventh month in the year of our Lord one thousand Seven hundred and ninety eight...at Warrington in the County afforesaid

                                          Thomas McMillan
                                          Jane McMillan

Henry McMillan	Benjamin Taylor	Joseph Taylor
Jonathan McMillan	Mary McMillan	Jane Taylor
Ann McMillan	Joseph McMillan	Ann McMillan
Thomas Leech Jr	Wm Griffith	Jacob McMillan
Abraham Griffith	George McMillan	Ruth Griffith
Elizabeth Griffith	Rebekah McMillan	Willing Griest Jr
Thomas McMillan	Lydia McMillan	Anne Griest
Mary McMillan	Jane Phillips	Joseph Garretson
	Jesse Phillips	Rebekah Garretson

#217 13th of 12th mo 1798   JACOB McMILLAN-RUTH GRIFFITH

Whereas <u>Jacob McMillan</u> of Warrington Township in the County of york and State of Pennsylvania Son of <u>George McMillan</u> deceased and <u>Ann</u> his wife and <u>Ruth Griffith</u> of the same place Daughter of <u>William Griffith and Joanna</u> his wife both deceased...this thirteenth day of the twelfth month in the year of our Lord one thousand Seven hundred and Ninety eight...at Warrington in the County afforesaid

                                          Jacob McMillan
                                          <u>Ruth McMillan</u>

WARRINGTON MONTHLY MEETING

Abraham Griffith	Willing Griest	Ann McMillan
Abel Walker	Ann Griest	William Griffith
Ann Walker	Deborah Griffith	Deborah McMillan
Sarah Walker	Benjamin Underwood	William McMillan
Henry McMillan	Abigail Whinnery	Jos Garretson
Elihu Underwood	Mordecai Williams	Rebekah Garretson
Samuel Elgar	Sarah Williams	George McMillan
Elisha Cook	David Cadwalader	Joseph McMillan
Robert Whinnery	Susanna Cadwalader	Amos Griffith
William Vale	Wm Griffiths Jr	Mary McMillan
Lydia McMillan	Mary McMillan Jr	Thos McMillan

#218 17th of 1st mo 1799   BENJAMIN TAYLOR-ELIZABETH GRIFFITH

Whereas <u>Benjamin Taylor</u> of Warrington Township son of <u>Joseph Taylor</u> of the same place and <u>Jane</u> his wife and <u>Elizabeth Griffith</u> Daughter of <u>Abraham Griffith</u> of the same place and <u>Elizabeth</u> his wife...this 17th day of the first month 1799...at Warrington in the County afforesaid

                                    Benjamin Taylor
                                    <u>Elizabeth Taylor</u>

Mary McMillan	Thos Leech	Joseph Taylor
Hannah Machlan	Jacob McMillan	Jane Taylor
Willing Griest	Ruth McMillan	Wm Griffith
Mary Hutton	Wm Griffith	Elizabeth Griffith
Charity Robins	Rebekah Griffith	Joseph Taylor
William Leech	John McClelan	Deborah Griffith
Ann Griest	George Machlan	Abraham Griffith Jr
Jos Edmundson	James Thomas	Jennet McClelan
Benjamin Walker	Mordecai Williams	Thos Leech
Ruth Walker	Jas McMillan	Amos Griffith
		Thos McMillan

#219 15th of 5th mo 1799   JAMES WICKERSHAM-ANNA MILLS

Whereas <u>James Wickersham</u> of the township of Newbury in the County of york and State of Pennsylvania and <u>Anna Mills</u> of the same place...this fifteenth day of the fifth month in the year of our Lord one thousand Seven hundred and Ninety nine...at Newbury in the County afforesaid
                                    James Wickersham
                                    <u>Anna Wickersham</u>

MARRIAGES

Thos Miller	Ruth Wickersham	Jesse Wickersham
Jacob Garretson	Sarah Jones	Anna Wickersham
Mary Garretson	Edward Jones	Phebe Whinnery
Hannah Garretson	Robert Hammerly	Mary Mills
Samuel Miller	Thos Kirk	Samuel Jennings
Hannah Miller	James Bane	David Warren
Mary Vernon	Ruth Bane	Wm Wickersham
Samuel Garretson	Aaron Vernon	Thos Whinnery Jr
Alice Garretson	Joseph Garretson	Jas Wickersham
Cornelius Garretson	Joseph Garretson jr	Robert Whinnery
Hannah Garretson	Rebekah Garretson	Enoch Wickersham
		Jesse Wickersham

#220 20th of 3rd mo 1800   WILLIAM UNDERWOOD-DEBORAH KIRK
Whereas William Underwood son of Zephaniah Underwood and Rebeckah his wife of Newbury Township york county and State of Pennsylvania and Deborah Kirk Daughter of Ezekiel Kirk of Warrior Mark Township Huntingdon County and State aforesaid and Hannah his wife...this twentieth day of the third month in the year of our Lord one thousand eight hundred...at Warrior Mark Township Huntingdon County afforesaid known by the name of Centre Meeting

                                              William Underwood
                                              Deborah Underwood

Mary Bye	Hannah Kirk Jr	Ezekiel Kirk
Sarah More	Charity Bye	Hannah Kirk
Esther Wilson	John Penington	Jonathan Kirk
Caleb Kirk		Josiah Kirk
Danl Penington		
Jane McMillan		

#221 14th of 5th mo 1800   JESSE WICKERSHAM-PHEBE JONES
Whereas Jesse Wickersham son of Jesse Wickersham of Newbury Township york County & State of Pennsylvania and Anna his wife and Phebe Jones Daughter of Edward Jones of the same place...this fourteenth day of the fifth month in the year of our Lord one thousand eight hundred...at Newbury in the County afforesaid

                                              Jesse Wickersham
                                              Phebe Wickersham

Samuel Johnson	Hannah Wickersham	Jesse Wickersham
Thos Whinnery	Saml Garretson	Anna Wickersham
Ruth Wickersham	Joseph Garretson	Edward Jones
Abigail Whinnery	Rebekah Garretson	Sarah Jones
Thomas Long	Thos Mills	Enoch Wickersham
Robert Whinnery	John Rankin	Hannah Jones
Thomas Miller	Edward Tyler	James Wickersham

#222 14th of 5th mo 1800   WILLIAM LEECH-JANE GARRETSON
Whereas William Leech son of thomas Leech of Warrington Township york County and State of Pennsylvania & Phebe his wife and Jane Garretson

WARRINGTON MONTHLY MEETING

Daughter of <u>Cornelius Garretson</u> of Manchester Township County & State afforesaid and <u>Margaret</u> his wife deceased...this fourteenth day of the fifth month in the year of our Lord one Thousand Eight hundred...at the Boro of York in the County afforesaid

                                                              William Leech
                                                               <u>Jane Leech</u>

Ann Jessop	John Love	Cornelius Garretson
Sarah Taylor	Caleb Kirk	Hannah Garretson
Mary Coats	Jonathan Jessop	Phebe Leech
Ann Worley	Robert Kenedy	Hannah Garretson
Susanna Jessop	Sarah Welch	Phebe Leech
Edith Kirk	Mary Hussey	Thomas Leech Jr
Rachel Kirk	John Garretson	Susanna Hoopes
Lydia Kirk	Wm Willis	Wm Kirk
Polly Kirk	Abel Walker	James Hoopes
Sarrah Updegraff	Ann Walker	Thos Owen
		Harman Updegraff

#223 14th of 10th mo 1801   ROBERT WHINNERY-PHEBE LEECH

Whereas <u>Robert Whinnery</u> of Newberry Township york County and State of Pennsylvania Son of <u>William Whinnery</u> of the same place & <u>Abigail</u> his wife and <u>Phebe Leech</u> Daughter of <u>Thomas Leech</u> of Warrington Township and County and State Afforesaid and <u>Phebe</u> his wife...this fourteenth day of the tenth Month in the year of our Lord one thousand Eight hundred one...at Newberry in the County afforesaid

                                                              Robert Whinnery
                                                              <u>Phebe Whinnery</u>

Esther McMillan	James McMillan	Thomas Leech
Sarah Jones (p.o)	Mary McMillan	Phebe Leech (p.o)
James Bane	Thomas Whinery	Abigail Whinery
Ruth Bane	Mary Edmundson Jr	Thomas Leech Jr
Nathan Thomas	Phebe Whinery	William Leech
Sarah Thomas	Benjamin Taylor	Jane Leech
Mary Mills	Elizabeth Taylor	John Whinnery
	John McMillan	Thomas Whinnery
		Ruth McMillan

#224 24th of the 3rd mo 1803   DAVID ALLEN-SARAH MOORE

Whereas <u>David Allen</u> of Half Moon Township in the County of Center and State of Pennsylvania son of <u>Thomas Allen and Elizabeth</u> his wife of Little Britain Township in the County of Lancaster and State aforesaid the latter Deceased and <u>Sarah Moore</u> Daughter of <u>Andrew Moore</u> and <u>Rebekah</u> his wife of the said Township of Half Moon the former deceased...this twenty fourth Day of the third month in the year of our Lord one thousand Eight hundred and three...at Centre Meeting house in the Township of Half Moon afforesaid

                                                        David Allen
                                                        <u>Sarah Allen</u>

MARRIAGES

Robert Hutton		
Daniel Pennington	Isaac Miller	Rebekah Moore
Martha Pennington	Emy Moore	James Moore
Wm Pennington	Dinah Moore	Isaac Moore
Ann Hutton	Charity Bye	Thos Moore
Hannah Kirk	Sarah Bye	Elijah Moore
Margaret Whitson	Israel Hollingsworth	Benjamin Fenton
Naomy Way		Rebekah Fenton
John Kirk		Sarah Moore
Jason Kirk		
Elizabeth Kirk		
Thos Kirk		

 # 225   12th of 1st mo 1804   WILLIAM MORSELL-MARY EDMUNDSON

Whereas <u>William Morsell</u> of Frederick County and State of Maryland son of <u>William Morsell</u> of the same place and <u>Mary</u> his wife and <u>Mary Edmundson</u> Daughter of <u>thomas Edmundson</u> of Warrington Township York County and State of Pennsylvania and <u>Mary</u> his wife...this twelfth day of the first month in the year of our Lord one thousand eight hundred and four...at Warrington in the County afforesaid

                    William Morsell
                    <u>Mary Morsell</u>

John Cleaver	John Marsh Jr	Mary Edmundson
Susanna Cleaver	William Vale	Wm Edmundson
Thomas McMillan	James Thomas	Abigail Hussey
Ruth McMillan	Abel Walker	Thos Edmundson
Deborah Vale	Jane Hussey (p.o)	Elizabeth Edmundson
Sarah Walker	Jediah Hussey (p.o)	Ann Edmundson
Hannah Vale	Wm Cadwallader	Amos Garretson
Hannah Walker	Lydia Hussey	Mary Garretson
Eliza Walker	Jediah Hussey	Jane Hussey
Mary Cleaver	Ruth Walker	Hannah Underwood
Mordecai Williams	Hephzebah Walker	

#226 16th of 2nd mo 1804   HENRY FLETCHER-SARAH WALKER

Whereas <u>Henry Fletcher</u> a Member of Centre Monthly Meeting in Pennsylvania Son of <u>John and Sarah Fletcher</u> living in the province of ulster tyrone County kingdom of Ireland and <u>Sarah Walker</u> Daughter of <u>Able Walker and Ann</u> his Wife of Warrington Township in the County & State of Pennsylvania...this sixteenth day of the second month in the year of our Lord Eighteen hundred and four   (1804)...at Warrington in the County afforesaid   Henry Fletcher
                    <u>Sarah Fletcher</u>

WARRINGTON MONTHLY MEETING

Jonathan Marsh	Deborah Griffith	Abel Walker
Abner Walker	William Leech	Ann Walker
James Vale	Jane Leech	Leah Walker
Nathan Vale	Israel Cook	Hannah Walker
Thomas McMillan	Joseph Taylor	Benjamin Walker
Ruth McMillan	Amos Hussey	Ruth Walker
Elizabeth Taylor	Asahel Walker	Joshua Vale
Martha Cleaver	Nehemiah Underwood	William Vale
John Cleaver	Robert Squibb	Robert Vale
Susanna Cleaver		Sarah Vale
Edward Jones		Hannah Vale
James Thomas		Hephzibah Walker
David Cadwalader		Joseph Walker
Susanna Cadwalader		Abel Walker Jr
Jane Hussey Jr		Ann Vale
Wm Edmundson		John Kettlewell
Elizabeth Edmundson		Jehu Thomas
Lydia Hussey		Thomas Leech
Mary Cleaver		

#227 17th of 4th mo 1805   WILLIAM WICKERSHAM-RACHEL MILLS
Whereas William Wickersham son of James Wickersham of Newbury Township york County and State of Pennsylvania and Sarah his wife Deceased and Rachel Mills Daughter of John Mills late of the same place Deceased and Anna his wife...this seventeenth day of the fourth month in the year of our Lord one thousand Eight hundred and five...at Newbury in the County afforesaid

William Wickersham
Rachel Wickersham

MARRIAGES

Margery Hayes	Rachel Jones	James Wickersham
Margaret Updegrave	Eli Waln	Anna Wickersham
Thomas Miller	Miles Hayes	Enoch Wickersham
Sarah Miller	John Frazor	Hannah Wickersham
William Whinnery	Joshua Jones	Anna Wickersham
Elijah Meredith	Martha Kirk	James Wickersham
Jacob Speakman	Hannah Kirk	Ruth Wickersham
Isaac Kirk	Sarah Jones	Jesse Wickersham
Jane Kirk		Joel Wickersham
Jane John		James Wickersham
Nathan Thomas		John Wickersham
Sarah Thomas		Esther Mills
Hannah Bailey		Alenor Wickersham
James Garretson		Mary Wickersham
Hannah Hays		Anne Wickersham
Ruth Miller		Mary Vernon
Ellenor Watts		Faithful Garretson
Rebeckah Garretson		Edward Jones
Alice Garretson		Samuel Garretson
Rebekah Garretson		Alice Garretson

#228 18th of 4th mo 1805   NATHAN HUSSEY-HANNAH VALE
Whereas <u>nathan Hussey</u> of Warrington Township York County and State of Pennsylvania son of <u>Jediah Hussey</u> of the same place and <u>Jane</u> his wife and <u>Hannah Vale</u> Daughter of <u>William Vale</u> of the Township County and State aforesaid and <u>Ann</u> his wife...this Eighteenth day of the fourth month in the year of our Lord one Thousand Eight hundred and five...at Warrington in the County afforesaid

		Nathan Hussey
		Hannah Hussey
Isaac Cleaver	Leah Walker	Jediah Hussey
Willing Griest	Hephsibah Walker	Jane Hussey (p.o)
Anna Griest	Mary Vale	William Vale
C. Morris	Hannah Walker	Ann Vale (p.o)
Robert Vale per order	Ruth Walker	Elisha Vale
John Cleaver	Wm Edmundson	Jediah Hussey
	Jane Leach	Lydia Hussey
	Charles Kettlewell	Ann Vale
	Hannah Nevitt	Jonathan McMillan
	Mary Cleaver	David McMillan
	Jane Hussey	Hannah McMillan
	David Cadwallader	John Vale
	Mary Hussey (p.o)	James Vale
	Joshua Vale	William Cadwallader
	Daniel Jones	Nathan Vale
	Abraham Griffith	Robert Vale
	Jonathan Marsh	Asahel Walker
	Joseph Taylor	Ann Walker

WARRINGTON MONTHLY MEETING

#229 12th of 9th mo 1805   THOMAS WHINNERY-LYDIA HUSSEY

Whereas Thomas Whinnery of Newberry Township york County & State of Pennsylvania Son of William Whinnery and Abigail his wife of the same place & Lydia Hussey daughter of Jediah Hussey & Jane his wife of Warrington Township County & State afforesaid...this twelfth day of the Ninth month in the year of our Lord one thousand Eight hundred & Five at Warrington in the County afforesaid

		Thomas Whinnery
		Lydia Whinnery
John Cleaver	Thomas Leech	William Whinnery
Susanna Cleaver	Thomas McMillan	Abigail Whinnery
Robert Vale	Ruth McMillan	Jediah Hussey
Samuel Cook	Nathan Hussey	Jane Hussey p.o
Elisha Cook	Hannah Hussey	Jediah Hussey p.o
Lydia Cook	Hannah McMillan	Jane Hussey Jr
Deborah Griffith	Mary Edmundson	Miriam Hussey p.o
Jacob Davis	William Edmundson	Christopher Hussey
Ann Pierre	Jane Leech	Lydia Hussey
Martha Cleaver	Thomas Whinnery	James Whinnery
	Amos Hussey	William Whinnery
	Abigail Hussey	William Vale
	Hannah Wickersham	Anna Vale
	Ann Vale	Anne Griest
	Elisha Vale	John Vale
	Mary Hussey (p.o)	Leah Walker
	David Cadwallader	Hannah Walker
	Jonathan McMillan	Joseph Taylor
	David McMillan	

#230 11th of 12th mo 1805   ZEPHANIAH UNDERWOOD-HANNAH BAILY

Whereas Zephaniah Underwood son of Zephaniah Underwood of Centre County in the State of Pennsylvania and Rebecca his wife and Hannah Baily Daughter of Charles Baily of Newbury Township in York County & State afforesaid and Jane his wife Deceased...this Eleventh day of the twelfth month in the year of our Lord one thousand Eight hundred and five...at Newbury in the County afforesaid

Zephaniah Underwood
Hannah Underwood

MARRIAGES

Hannah Wickersham	Sarah Jones	Charles Baily
Ann Pierce	Jane John	James Bane
Ruth Miller	John Whinnery	Charles Baily
Samuel Garretson	Anne Wickersham	Amos Lewis
James Garretson	Joseph Garretson	Jane Owens
Esther Mills	Edward Jones	Nathan Thomas
George Meredith	Jacob Garretson	Sarah Thomas
Mary Gardener	Martha Kirk	John Thomas
Sarah Hutton	Isaac Kirk	John Wickersham
James Hoops	Jane Kirk	Hannah Lewis
Susanna Hoops	Hannah Kirk	Sarah Thomas
Jacob Kirk		John Hutton
James Wickersham Jr		Sarah Miller
Enoch Wickersham		Jesse Wickersham
Elijah Meredith		Phebe Wickersham

#231 13th of 2nd mo 1806   JOHN VALE-DEBORAH GRIFFITH
Whereas John Vale of the Township of Warrington in the County of York and State of Pennsylvania son of Robert Vale & Sarah his wife Deceased and Deborah Griffith of the Township County & State afsd Daughter of George McMillan and Ann his wife, the former deceased...this Thirteenth of the second Month in the year of our Lord one Thousand Eight Hundred & Six...at Warrington in the County affores

John Vale
Deborah Vale

Israel Cook	Susanna Morris	Ann McMillan p.o
Jonathan Marsh	Thomas McMillan	James Thomas p.o
Nathan Vale	Jane McMillan	Robert Vale
Eliza Walker	Willing Griest	Jacob McMillan
Joseph Walker	Anne Griest	Alice Walker
James McElwee	Phebe Leech p.o	William Vale
Elizabeth McElwee	Nathan Hussey	Joshua Vale
Elisha Vale	Hannah Hussey	Elizabeth Vale
Asahel Walker	Isaac Cleaver	Sarah Vale p.o
Mary McMillan	William Ross	George McMillan
Mary Vale	Isaac Walker	George Griffith p.o
William McMillan	John Cleaver	Ann Griffith p.o
Daniel Cookson	Susanna Cleaver	James Vale
	Thomas McMillan	Lydia Vale
	Ruth McMillan	Jonathan McMillan
	Joseph McMillan	Jane Hussey
	Abraham Griffith Jr	Hephzibah Walker
	Wm Edmundson	Abraham Griffith
	Amos Griffith	Leah Walker

#232 12th of 6th mo 1806   DAVID CADWALLADER-ELIZABETH DAVIS
Whereas David Cadwallader of Warrington Township York County & State of Pennsylvania son of James Cadwallader of the same place and Mary

WARRINGTON MONTHLY MEETING

his wife both deceased and <u>Elizabeth Davis</u> Daughter of <u>John Davis</u> of the Township County & State aforesaid and <u>Hannah</u> his wife she being deceased...this twelfth day of the Sixth month in the year of our Lord one thousand Eight hundred and Six...at Warrington in the County afforesaid

		David Cadwallader
		Elizabeth Cadwallader(X)
Abel Walker	Benjamin Walker	William Cadwallader
John Vale	Ruth Walker	Susanna Cadwallader
Eliza Walker	Amos Hussey	Hannah Cadwallader
Sarah Vale	Abigail Hussey	Margaret Cadwalader
Jediah Hussey	Thomas Edmundson	Mary Cadwalader
William Squib	Hephzibah Walker	Benjamin Walker
John Cleaver	Martha Cox	Lydia Walker
Susanna Cleaver	Nathan Hussey	Edward Jones
Ruth McMillan	Hannah Hussey	Sarah Jones
Elizabeth Taylor	Ruth Squib	Ann John
Leah Walker	Hannah Leech	Hannah Garretson
Asahel Walker	William Leech	Mary Edmundson
Hannah Cook	Jane Leech	Wm Edmundson
Joseph John	Henry Cox	James Thomas
	Phebe Morthland	
	Caleb Squib	

#233 15th of 4th mo 1807   GEORGE GARRETSON-LYDIA WICKERSHAM

Whereas <u>George Garretson</u> of Newbury Township in the County of York & State of Pennsylvania Son of <u>Joseph Garretson</u> of the same place & <u>Rebecca</u> his wife and <u>Lydia Wickersham</u> Daughter of <u>Jesse Wickersham</u> late of Newbury Township Deceased and <u>Anna</u> his wife... this fifteenth day of the fourth month in the year of our Lord one Thousand Eight hundred and Seven...at Newbury in the County afforesaid

		George Garretson
		<u>Lydia Garretson</u>
Martha Rankin	Anna Wickersham Jr	Joseph Garretson
Nancy Nebinger	Edward Jones	Rebekah Garretson
Samuel Miller	Sarah Jones	Anna Wickersham
Wm Hoopes	Elizabeth Garretson	John Garretson
John Thomas	John Wickersham	Hannah Wickersham
Hannah Kirk	Ann Peirce	Jacob Garretson
Isaac Kirk	Ruth Wickersham	Wm Wickersham
Jane Kirk	Rachel Wickersham	Samuel Garretson
James Bane	Thomas Garretson	Alice Garretson
Mary Garretson	Rebekah Garretson	Mary Wickersham
Jacob Kirk Jr	Alice Garretson Jr	Rebekah Garretson
John Garretson	Jesse Wickersham	Joseph Garretson
Joshua Jones		Anna Wickersham

MARRIAGES

#234 13th of 5th mo 1807   ELI WALN-SARAH THOMAS
Whereas Eli Waln of Newbury Township in the County of york and State
of Pennsylvania Son of William Waln of West Stratford Township in the
County of Chester and State afforesaid and Alice his Wife deceased
and Sarah Thomas daughter of Nathan Thomas of Newbury Township County
& State afforesaid and Sarah his wife...this thirteenth day of the
fifth month in the year of our Lord one thousand eight hundred and
Seven...at Newbury in the County afforesaid

		Eli Waln
		Sarah Waln
John Laurel	George Garretson	Nathan Thomas
William Randles	John Garretson	Sarah Thomas
Israel Cook	Thomas Garretson	James Bane
Isaac Kirk	Joshua Jones	James Thomas
Jane Kirk	Aaron Frazer	Jane Thomas
Hannah Leech	Elizabeth Collins	John Thomas
Joseph Elliot	Hannah Kirk	Sarah Jones
Elizabeth Elliot	Anna Wickersham	Martha Kirk
Jacob Garretson	Mary Vernon	Hannah Wickersham
Mary Garretson	William Leech	Rebeckah Garretson
Esther Mills	Jane Leech	Elizabeth Garretson
John Hofstat	James Hoops	Lydia Garretson
Mary Hofstat	Susanna Hoops	Ann Peirce
	Joseph Wood	Edward Jones
	Mary Switzer	Samuel Garretson
	Mary Randles	James Wickersham
	John Switzer	Joseph Garretson
		John Wickersham

#235 11th of 11th mo 1807   JACOB KIRK - HANNAH WICKERSHAM
Whereas Jacob Kirk of Newbury Township in the County of york and
State of Pennsylvania Son of Jacob Kirk late of the same place
deceased and Hannah his wife and Hannah Wickersham Daughter of Jesse
Wickersham late of the Township and County afforesaid Deceased and
Anna his wife...this eleventh day of the eleventh Month in the year
of our Lord one thousand Eight hundred and Seven...at Newbury in the
County afforesaid   Jacob Kirk
                                              Hannah Kirk

WARRINGTON MONTHLY MEETING

Rebecca Garretson	Jacob Garretson	Hannah Kirk
Betsy Hutton	Mary Garretson	Anna Wickersham
Esther Mills	Edward Jones	Isaac Kirk
Alice Garretson	Sarah Jones	Jane Kirk
Samuel Garretson	James Bane	James Wickersham
	Samuel Miller	Anna Wickersham
	Joshua Jones	Martha Kirk
	Ann Pierce	Jesse Wickersham
	John Garretson	Phebe Wickersham
	Ann Garretson	Ruth Wickersham
	Thomas Miller	John Wickersham
	William Wickersham	Mary Wickersham
	Rachel Wickersham	Ann Wickersham
	John Garretson	James Wickersham
	Joseph Garretson	Abner Wickersham
	Rebecca Garretson	Jacob Kirk
	Joseph Garretson	George Garretson
	Sarah Hutton	Lydia Garretson

#236 7th of 4th mo 1808   ROBERT VALE-MARTHA CLEAVER
Whereas <u>Robert Vale</u> of Warrington Township in the County of york and State of Pennsylvania Son of <u>John Vale and Deborah</u> his wife of the Same place (the Latter Deceased) and <u>Martha Cleaver</u> daughter of <u>John Cleaver and Susanna</u> his wife of the Township of Washington County and State aforesaid...this seventh day of the fourth month in the year of our Lord one thousand Eight hundred and eight...at Warrington in the County afforesaid   Robert Vale
                                                                  <u>Martha Vale</u>

Elizabeth Taylor	Eli Vale	John Vale
Susanna Morris	William Vale	John Cleaver
Jane Hussey	Hannah Hussey	Susanna Cleaver
Margaret Kettlewell	Charles Underwood	Isaac Cleaver
William Leech	Amos Griest	James Thomas p.o
Wm Edmundson	Robert Vale	Lydia Vale
Benjamin Walker	John Cleaver Jr	Hannah Cleaver
Thomas McMillan	Elizabeth Edmundson	Mary Cleaver
Ruth McMillan		James Vale
Ruth Northland		Nancy Vale

#237 25th of 5th mo 1808   JOHN WICKERSHAM-REBECCA GARRETSON
Whereas <u>JOHN WICKERSHAM</u> of Newbury Township in the County of York and State of Pennsylvania Son of <u>Jesse Wickersham</u> late of the same place deceased and <u>Anna</u> his wife and <u>Rebecca Garretson</u> Daughter of <u>Joseph Garretson</u> of the Township and County aforesaid and <u>Rebecca</u> his wife...this twenty fifth day of the fifth month in the year of our Lord one Thousand Eight hundred and Eight...at Newbury in the County afforesaid   John Wickersham
                                                              <u>Rebeccah Wickersham</u>

MARRIAGES

Ann Peirce	Thomas Garretson	Joseph Garretson
Samuel Garretson	James Garretson	Rebecca Garretson
John Garretson	Samuel Garretson	Anna Wickersham
Rachel Jones	Alice Garretson	James Wickersham
Samuel Garretson	Edward Jones	Joseph Garretson
Cornelius Garretson	Sarah Jones	Elizabeth Garretson
Samuel Miller	Jacob McMillan	Alice Garretson
Zephaniah Underwood	Ruth McMillan	Joseph McMillan
Jacob Kirk Jr	Willing Griest	George Garretson
Wm Hoops	Ann Griest	Lydia Garretson
Phebe Hoops	Sarah GArretson	Ruth Wickersham
Rachel Garretson	Phebe Wickersham	Mary Wickersham
Martha Kirk Jr	Rebekah Garretson	John Garretson
Thomas Baker	Esther Mills	Ann Garretson
Hannah Kirk	Sarah Hutton	Jacob Kirk
	Isaac Kirk	Hannah Kirk
	James Bane	Ann Wickersham

#238 26th of 10th mo 1808   SAMUEL GARRETSON-ANN PIERCE

Whereas <u>Samuel Garretson</u> of Manchester Township in the County of york and State of Pennsylvania Son of <u>Cornelius Garretson</u> of the same place and <u>Margaret</u> his wife now deceased and <u>Ann Pierce</u> Daughter of <u>Moses Pierce</u> late of Goshen Township in the County of Chester and State aforesaid and <u>Elizabeth</u> his wife both deceased ...this twenty sixth day of the tenth month in the year of our Lord one thousand Eight hundred and Eight...at Newbury in the County afforesaid

		Samuel Garretson
		Ann Garretson
James Bane	John Garretson	Cornelius Garretson
Sarah Jones	Joseph Garretson	Hannah Garretson
	Rebecca Garretson	Anna Wickersham
[right column]	Mary Wickersham	John Garretson
Alice Garretson	Sarah Hutton	Thomas Garretson
Samuel Garretson	George Garretson	Sarah Garretson
Alice Garretson	Lydia Garretson	Mary Pierce
Joseph Garretson	John Wickersham	Cornelius Garretson
Wm Kirk Jr	Rebecca Wickersham	James Wickersham
	Hannah Kirk	Thomas Leech Jr
	Mary Vernon	Hannah Leech
	Jacob Kirk	William Leech
	John Felker	Jane Leech
	Joshua Jones	Jesse Wickersham
	Edward Jones	Phebe Wickersham
	Isaac Kirk	Mary Garretson
	Jane Kirk	John Garretson
		Rebecca Garretson

WARRINGTON MONTHLY MEETING

#239 30th of 11th mo 1808   ISAAC CLEAVER-ELIZABETH GARRETSON

Whereas <u>Isaac Cleaver</u> of Washington Town hip in the County of york and the State of Pennsylvania Son of <u>John Cleaver</u> of the same place and <u>Susanna</u> his wife and <u>Elizabeth Garretson</u> Daughter of <u>Samuel Garretson</u> of Newbury Township in the County and State afforesaid and <u>Alice</u> his wife...this thirtieth day of the eleventh month in the year of our Lord one thousand eight hundred and eight...at Newbury in the County afforesaid

                                                                              Isaac Cleaver
                                                                              Elizabeth Cleaver

William Leech	Joseph McMillan	John Cleaver
Jane Leech	Isaac Kirk	Susanna Cleaver
Hannah Leech	Jane Kirk	Samuel Garretson
Joseph Garretson	Edward Jones	Alice Garretson
Mary Pierce	Sarah Jones	Thomas Garretson
Mary Gardner	Hannah Kirk	John Garretson
Cornelius Garretson	Anna Wickersham	Rebecah Garretson
Elizabeth Griest	John Garretson	James Garretson
Joseph Garretson	Ann Garretson	Mary Cleaver
Rebekah Garretson	Samuel Garretson	Robert Vale
Isaac Garretson	Ann Garretson	Martha Vale
Martha Kirk	George Garretson	Hannah Cleaver
Samuel Miller	Lydia Garretson	John Cleaver Jr
John Hancock	John Wickersham	Rachel Garretson
James Bane	Rebekah Wickersham	Nathan Vale
Jesse Wickersham	Ann Wickersham	Amos Griffith
Isaac Kenworthy	Rachel Jones	

#240 29th of 12th mo 1808   AMOS GRIFFITH-MARY CLEAVER

Whereas <u>Amos Griffith</u> of Washington Township york County and State of Pennsylvania Son of <u>William Griffith and Johanna</u> his wife late of Warrington Township -County and State afforesaid (Deceased) and <u>Mary Cleaver</u> Daughter of <u>John Cleaver and Susanna</u> his wife of Washington Township County and State afforesaid ...this twenty ninth day of the twelfth month in the year of our Lord one thousand Eight hundred & Eight...at Warrington in the County afforesaid

                                            Amos Griffith
                                            <u>Mary Griffith</u>

MARRIAGES

Benjamin Walker	Joseph Taylor	John Cleaver
Abel Walker	Thomas Leech p.o	Susanna Cleaver
Elisha Cook	Robert Vale	Joseph Griffith
Thomas McMillan	Wm Edmundson	Joshua Vale
Ruth McMillan	Abram Griffith	William Vale
Jno Cook	Eli Vale	Robert Vale
Hannah Cook	Nathan Vale	Martha Vale
Lydia Cook	Elihu Vale	Jonah Griffith
Hephzebah Walker	James Vale	Hannah Cleaver
Leah Walker		Jacob McMillan
Hannah Hussey		Ruth McMillan
Jane Hussey		
Eliza Walker		
Hannah Hussey		

#241 24th of 5th mo 1809   JOSEPH McMILLAN-REBECCA GARRETSON
Whereas Joseph McMillan of Washington Township in the County of York and State of Pennsylvania Son of George McMillan late of the same place Deceased & Ann his wife & Rebecca Garretson Daughter of Samuel Garretson of Newbury Township in the County & State aforesaid & Alice his wife...this twenty fourth day of the fifth month in the year of our Lord one thousand Eight Hundred and nine...at Newbury in the County afforesaid

                                         Joseph McMillan
                                         Rebecca McMillan
        Aaron Frezer   Samuel Garretson
        James Garretson   Alice Garretson
        Alice Garretson   John Garretson
        Isaac Kirk   Joseph Garretson
        Martha Kirk   Thomas Garretson
        Hannah Leech   Rachel Garretson
        Isaac Cleaver   Anne Griffith
        Sarah Garretson   George Garretson
        Sarah Jones   Lydia Garretson
        Hannah Kirk   John Garretson
        James Bane   Cornelius Garretson
        John Wickersham   Joseph Garretson
        Rebecca Wickersham   George McMillan
                              Rebecca McMillan
                              Willing Griest
                              Anne Griest
                              Phebe Stubbs
                              Anne Wickersham

#242 31st of 1st mo 1810   JAMES BANE-MARGRET KETTLEWELL
Whereas James Bane of Newbury Township in the County of York and State of Pennsylvania and Margret Kettlewell widow of John Kettlewell late of Warrington Township in the County and State aforesaid...this thirty first day of the first month in the year of our Lord one

WARRINGTON MONTHLY MEETING

thousand Eight hundred and ten...at Newbury in the County afforesaid

		James Bane
		Margret Bane
Joel Garretson	Rebekah Garretson	Charles Kettlewell
John Wickersham	Rachel Garretson	Jacob Garretson
Isaac Cleaver	Rachel Jones	Mary Garretson
Elizabeth Cleaver	George Garretson	Wm Hoopes
Martha Rankin	John Garretson	Phebe Hoopes
James Wickersham Jr	Jacob Kirk	James Hoopes
Samuel Pierce	Mary Vernon	Susannah Hoopes
Abner Wickersham	Anna Wickersham Jr	Lydia Walker
Samuel Garretson Jr	Betsy Hutton	Job Hoopes
Jesse Wickersham	Nathan Thomas	Anna Wickersham
Samuel Garretson	Joshua Jones	Hannah Kirk
Alice Garretson	James Wickersham	Rebekah Wickersham
Edward Jones	Alice Garretson	Alice Garretson
Sarah Jones	Sarah Hutton	Martha Kirk Jr
		Joseph Garretson
		Rebecca Garretson

#243 27th of 11th mo 1811   NATHAN VALE-ALICE GARRETSON

Whereas <u>Nathan Vale</u> of Washington Township in the County of york and State of Pennsylvania son of <u>Joshua Vale</u> of the same place and <u>Elizabeth</u> his wife and <u>Alice Garretson</u> Daughter of <u>Samuel Garretson</u> of Newbury Township in the County & State afforesaid and <u>Alice</u> his wife...this Twenty seventh day of the Eleventh Month in the year of our Lord one Thousand Eight hundred & Eleven ...at Newbury in the County afforesaid

		Nathan Vale
		Alice Vale
Isaac Kettlewell	James Wickersham	Samuel Garretson
Ellen Daley	Anna Wickersham	Alice Garretson
	Margaret Speakman	Joshua Vale
	Magdelena Speakman	Thomas Garretson
	Hannah Kirk	Peter Vale
	Isaac Cleaver	Rachel Garretson
	Elizabeth Vale	Isaac Kirk
	Sarah Garretson	Jane Kirk
	James Bane	Jos McMillan
	Margaret Bane	John Garretson
	Martha Kirk Sr	Rebekah Garretson
	Edward Jones	Martha Kirk Jr
	Sarah Jones	Joseph Garretson Jr
	John Wickersham	Asahel Walker
	Rebekah Wickersham	Mary Walker
	Joel Garretson	John Garretson
		Ann Garretson
		George Garretson

MARRIAGES

#244 19th of 3rd mo 1813   ISAAC KENWORTHY-HANNAH CLEAVER
Whereas <u>Isaac Kenworthy</u> of St. Clair Township in the County of Bedford and Commonwealth of Pennsylvania son of <u>William Kenworthy and Mary</u> his wife of the Township and County aforesaid and <u>Hannah Cleaver</u> daughter of <u>John Cleaver and Susanna</u> his wife of Washington Township in the County of York and Commonwealth aforesaid...this 19th day of the third month in the year of our Lord one thousand eight hundred & thirteen...at Warrington in the County afforesaid

                                               Isaac Kenworthy
                                               <u>Hannah Kenworthy</u>
Thos McMillan	Peter Vale	John Cleaver
Joseph McMillan	Hannah Hussey	Susanna Cleaver
Eliza Walker	Willing Griest	Ruth Kenworthy
Stephen Hussey	Ann Griest	Susanna Cleaver
Eli Griest	William Vale	Robert Vale
Anna Griffith	Amos Hussey	Amos Griffith
Thos Garretson	George Garretson	Mary Griffith
Uriah Griest	Hannah Hussey	Isaac Cleaver
Wm Cox		John Cleaver
Nathan Vale		
Alice Vale		
Joel Wierman		
Martha Kirk		
George Hussey		

#245 28th of 4th mo 1813   AARON FRAZER-ALICE GARRETSON
Whereas <u>Aaron Frazer</u> of Newbury Township in the County of York and State of Pennsylvania Son of Aron Frazer late of Allen Township in the County of Cumberland & State aforesaid deceased and <u>Jane</u> his wife and <u>Alice Garretson</u> formerly Alice Oldham Daughter of <u>Thomas Oldham</u> late of the County of Bedford in the State of Pennsylvania aforesaid and <u>Rebecca</u> his wife now both Deceased...this twenty eighth day of the fourth month in the year one thousand Eight hundred and thirteen...at Newbury in the County afforesaid

                                               Aron Frazer
                                               <u>Alice Frazer</u>

WARRINGTON MONTHLY MEETING

Joel Garretson	James Wickersham	Samuel Garretson
James Bane	Robert Garretson	Alice Garretson
Margaret Bane	William Leech	Jane John
	Jane Leech	Isaac Kirk
	Ann Griffith	John Garretson
	Joseph Garretson jr	Thomas Garretson
	Mary Hoopes	Martha Kirk Jr
	George Griffith	Anna Wickersham
	Joshua Jones	Jesse Wickersham
	James Wickersham	Phebe Wickersham
	Wm Hoopes	Mary Vernon
	Wm Cox	George GArretson
	John Wickersham	John T. Garretson
		Edward Jones
		Sarah Jones

#246 24th of 11th mo 1813   ELISHA VALE-MARTHA KIRK

Whereas <u>Elisha Vale</u> of Washington Township in the County of York and State of Pennsylvania Son of <u>William Vale</u> of the same place and <u>Ann</u> his wife and <u>Martha Kirk</u> Daughter of <u>Isaac Kirk</u> of Newbury Township in the County & State afforesaid and <u>Jane</u> his wife deceased...this twenty fourth day of the eleventh month in the year of our Lord one thousand Eight hundred and Thirteen...at Newbury in the County afforesaid

                                                      Elisha Vale
                                                      <u>Martha Vale</u>

William Cox	Edward Jones	William Vale
John Garretson	John Wickersham	Ann Vale
Rebekah Garretson	John T. Garretson	Isaac Kirk
Thos Leech Jr	J. Underwood	Samuel Garretson
Hannah Leech	Jos McMillan	Joseph Garretson
Wm Leech	Rebecca McMillan	Hannah Hussey
Jane Leech	George Garretson	John Vale
James Bane	Aaron Frazer	Sarah Vale
Margaret Bane	Anne Griffith	Sarah Kirk
Joseph Garretson	Joshua Cox	Jacob Kirk Jr
Sarah Garretson	Israel Garretson	Elizabeth Kirk
	George Griffith	
	Mary Gardner	
	Elizabeth Meredith	
	Joel Garretson	
	Wm E. Dorrey	
	Thos Garretson	
	Peter Vale	
	Rachel Garretson	

#247 30th of 11th mo 1814   SAMUEL GARRETSON-ELIZABETH MEREDITH

Whereas <u>Samuel Garretson</u> of Newbury Township in the County of york and State of Pennsylvania Son of <u>John Garretson</u> late of the same

MARRIAGES

place and <u>Jane</u> his wife both deceased and <u>Elizabeth Meredith</u> widow of <u>Israel Meredith</u> late of the Township aforesaid deceased and Daughter of <u>James Scott</u> of the City of Philadelphia and <u>Elizabeth</u> his wife now also Deceased...this thirtieth day of the eleventh month in the year one thousand eight hundred and fourteen...at Newbury in the County afforesaid

		Samuel Garretson
		<u>Elizabeth Garretson</u>
Edward Jones	Samuel Kirk	John Garretson
Sarah Jones	Benjamin Garretson	Rebekah Garretson
Rachel Jones	William Leech	Thomas Garretson
	Jane Leech	Joel Garretson
	James Wickersham	Rachel Garretson
	Mary Wickersham	George Griffith
	John Wickersham	Joseph Garretson
	Rebecca Wickersham	George Garretson
	Ross Meredith	Anne Griffith
	Isaac Cleaver	Mary Herman
		Rebekah Leech
		Zephaniah Underwood
		William Cox
		Oliver Griffith
		Isaac Kirk
		Ann Kirk
		Martha Kirk
		Jacob Kirk
		Hannah Kirk

#248 29th of 3rd mo 1815   GEORGE GRIFFITH-SARAH KIRK

Whereas <u>George Griffith</u> of Newbury Township in the County of York and State of Pennsylvania Son of <u>William Griffith</u> late of Warrington Township in the County and State afforesaid deceased & <u>Deborah</u> his wife and <u>Sarah Kirk</u> Daughter of <u>Isaac Kirk</u> of Newbury Township aforesaid and <u>Jane</u> his late wife...this twenty ninth day of the third month in the year one thousand eight hundred and fifteen...at Newbury in the County afforesaid   George Griffith
                                                                                                       <u>Sarah Griffith</u>

WARRINGTON MONTHLY MEETING

Thomas Leech
Hannah Leech
Zeph. Underwood
Edward Jones
Sarah Jones
John Wickersham
Rebekah Wickersham
William Leech
Jane Leech
Mary Herman
Rachel Garretson
George Garretson
Thomas Garretson

Isaac Kirk
Ann Kirk
Samuel Garretson
Elizabeth Garretson
Anne Griffith
Joel Garretson
Julia Griffith
Oliver Griffith
William Griffith
Jacob Kirk
Samuel Garretson
Joseph Garretson
Joshua Jones
Rachel Jones
Jacob Kirk
John Garretson
Thomas Cox
Jesse Wickersham
Phebe Wickersham

#249 6th of 4th mo 1815   JOHN CLEAVER -ANN VALE
Whereas John Cleaver of Washington Township York County and State of Pennsylvania Son of John Cleaver and Susanna his wife of the same place and Ann Vale Daughter of John Vale of Collumbianna County and State of Ohio and Deborah his wife (the both deceased) ...this sixth day of the fourth month in the year of our Lord one thousand eight hundred and fifteen...at Warrington in the County afforesaid
                                John Cleaver
                                Ann Cleaver

MARRIAGES

Ruth Walker	Susanna Cleaver
Sarah Cook	Robert Vale
Thomas McMillan	Thomas Garretson
Ruth McMillan	Susanna Cleaver
Rebekah McMillan	William Vale
Jacob McMillan	Joshua Vale
Willing Griest	Hannah Hussey
Elisha Cook	Elisha Vale
Lydia Cook	Sarah Vale
Jacob McMillan	John Vale
Amos Griest	Joel Walker
Abraham Cook	Mary Vale
Daniel Cookson	Amos Griffith
Benjamin Walker	Eliza Walker
	Sarah Cook
	Ruth Cutler
	Maria McMillan
	Anne Griest
	Peter Cleaver
	Joseph McMillan Sr

#250 22nd of 6th mo 1815   SAMUEL ENGLAND-HANNAH HUSSEY

Whereas Samuel England of Frederic County and State of Maryland Son of John England and Sarah his wife late of Chester County and State of Pennsylvania (deceased) and Hannah Hussey Daughter of William Vale and Ann his wife of Warrington Township York County and State aforesaid...this twenty second day of the Sixth month in the year of our Lord one thousand eight hundred and fifteen ...at Warrington in the County afforesaid
                                  Samuel England
                                  Hannah England

Amos Griffith	Jane Hussey Jr	William Vale
Edward Jones	Eliza Walker	Ann Vale
Abner Walker	Lea Walker	Jane Hussey p.o
Ruth Cutler	Susanna Cadwallader	John Vale
Maria Griffith	Hannah Cadwallader	Maria Plummer
Anne Griest	Ann Squibb	Joel Walker
Maria McMillan	Sarrah Walker	Sarah Vale
Abraham Cook	Robert Vale	Abel Walker
Elisha Vale	Ruth McMillan	Ann Walker
Martha Vale	Susan McMillan	Joshua Vale
Elisha Cook	Thos McMillan	Isaac Walker
Lydia Cook	Thos Edmundson	Mary Vale
Elizabeth Vale		
Eli McMillan		
Peter Vale		
Ben Walker		
George McMillan		

WARRINGTON MONTHLY MEETING

#251   29th of 6th mo 1815   THOMAS GARRETSON-SUSANNA CLEAVER

Whereas Thomas Garretson of Newbury Township in the County of York and State of Pennsylvania Son of Samuel Garretson and Alice his wife (deceased) and Susanna Cleaver Daughter of John Cleaver of Washington Township in the County and State aforesaid and Susanna his wife...this twenty ninth day of the sixth month in the year of our Lord one Thousand Eight hundred and Fifteen...at Warrington in the County afforesaid

                                                        Thomas Garretson
                                                        Susanna Garretson

Abraham Cook	Thomas McMillan	Samuel Garretson
Joseph McMillan	Ruth McMillan	Susanna Cleaver
Mary McMillan	William Cox	Peter Vale
Jos Taylor	Thomas Edmundson	Rachel Garretson
Joel Walker	Sarah Cook	Joel Garretson
Hannah Cook	Martha Vale	Elizabeth Vale
Joanne Squibb p.o	Leah Walker	Amos Griffith
Jacob McMillan	Rhoda Altemus	Alice Vale
Susanna G. Underwood	Marie Griffith	Rebecca McMillan
Isaac Pearson	Ann Squibb	Isaac Walker
Eli McMillan	Benjamin Walker	Ben Walker p.o
David Cadwallader	Abel Walker	
Peter Cleaver	Ruth Cutler	
	Maria McMillan	
	Mary Cookson	
	Anne Griest	
	Eliza Walker	

#252 28th of 9th mo 1815   RICHARD RUMMELLS-JANE HUSSEY

Whereas Richard Rummells of the Borough of York and State of Pennsylvania Son of James Rummells and May his wife late of the City of Baltimore and State of Maryland Deceased and Jane Hussey Daughter of Jediah Hussey of Warrington Township York County and State of Pennsylvania and Jane his wife...this twenty eighth day of the Ninth month in the year of our Lord one Thousand Eight Hundred and fifteen...at Newbury in the County afforesaid

                                                     Richard Rummells
                                                   Jane Rummells

MARRIAGES

Anna Squibb	Thomas McMillan	Jane Hussey p.o
Ann Squibb	Ruth McMillan	Jediah Hussey
Joel Garretson	Sarah Vale	Ann Hussey
Abraham Cook	Elisha Vale	David Cadwallader
Samuel Cook	Lydia Cook	Mary Edmundson
Jacob McMillan	Willing Griest	Thomas Edmundson
	Anne Griest	Susanna Cadwalader
	Isaac Pearson	Hannah Cadwallader
	Eli Griest	Thomas Leech Jr
	Daniel Cookson	John Elgar
	Benjn Walker	Maria Plummer
	Joel Walker	Joseph McMillan
	Isaac Walker	John Vale
	Maria Griffith	Joseph Walker
		Jos Taylor
		Jacob Bierbower(?)
		Amos Griffith
		Abel Walker
		Susan McMillan
		Rebecca Griffith

#253 29th of 5th mo 1816   JOHN VALE-LYDIA GARRETSON

Whereas <u>John Vale</u> of Warrington Township in the County of York and State of Pennsylvania Son of <u>William Vale</u> of the Township County and State aforesaid and <u>Ann</u> his wife Deceased and <u>Lydia Garretson</u> daughter of <u>Jacob Garretson</u> of the Township of Newbury in the County and State aforesaid and <u>Mary</u> his wife...this Twenty ninth day of the Fifth month in the year of our Lord one Thousand Eight hundred and Sixteen...at Newbury in the County afforesaid

                                              John Vale
                                              <u>Lydia Vale</u>

WARRINGTON MONTHLY MEETING

Thomas Garretson	Jesse Wickersham	William Vale
Samuel Garretson Jr	Nathan Thomas	Jacob Garretson
Thomas Leech Jr	Wm Sharpless	Mary Garretson
Joel Garretson	George Garretson	Samuel GArretson
Elizabeth Garretson	John Baldwin	Elizabeth Garretson
John Garretson	Edward Jones	Sen
Isaac Cleaver	Sarah Jones	Elisha Vale
Elizabeth Cleaver	Rachel Gibbons	Martha Vale
Benjamin Garretson	Sam Gibbons	Samuel England
Ann Garretson	Anna Wickersham jr	Hannah England
Deborah Griffith	Zeph. Underwood	Sarah Vale
Mary Wickersham	Hannah Underwood	Jediah Hussey
Ruth Wickersham	Rebecca Wickersham	Ann Hussey
Julia Griffith	Mary Wierman	Israel Garretson
Lydia Brenton	Ann Kirk	Daniel Garretson
Mary McMillan p.o	Daniel Hoops	Mary Vale
	Sarah Garretson	Peter Vale
		Joseph Garretson
		Isaac Kirk

<u>#254 31st of 10th mo 1816</u>   JOSEPH GARRETSON-MARIA McMILLAN

Whereas <u>Joseph Garretson</u> of Newbury Township in the County of york and State of Pennsylvania son of <u>Joseph Garretson</u> late of the same place and <u>Rebecca</u> his wife both deceased and <u>Maria McMillan</u> Daughter of <u>Thomas McMillan</u> of Warrington Township in the County & State aforesaid and <u>Ruth</u> his wife...this thirty first day of the tenth month in the Year of our Lord one Thousand Eight hundred and Sixteen...at Warrington in the County afforesaid

		Joseph Garretson
		<u>Maria Garretson</u>
Anne Griest Jr	Joseph McMillan	Thomas McMillan
Mary Cookson	Elisha Vale	Ruth McMillan
Jacob McMillan	Martha Vale	Thomas Garretson
Robert Whinnery	Jesse W. Cook	Hannah Cutler
Eliza Garretson	Alice Vale	Joseph McMillan Jr
Amos Griest	Ruth Griffith	George McMillan
	Maria Griffith	Ann Garretson
	Joseph Taylor	John W. Thomas
	Jane Rummels	Sarah Garretson
	William Vale	Zimri Whinnery
	Samuel Cook	William Whinnery
	Abraham Cook	Willing Griest
	John Cleaver	Anne Griest
	Susanna Cleaver	Jacob McMillan
	Maria Plummer	Ruth McMillan
	Susanna McMillan	John J. Garretson
	Thomas Edmundson	Ann Garretson
	Elizabeth Edmundson	Rebecca Wickersham

MARRIAGES

#255 28th of 11th mo 1816   WILLIAM COX-RUTH GRIFFITH
Whereas William Cox of Newbury Township in the County of york & State
of Pennsylvania Son of Joshua Cox of Latimore Township in the County
of Adams and State aforesaid and Emey his wife and Ruth Griffith
Daughter of Joseph Griffith of Warrington Township in the County of
york and State as first written and Rebecca his wife...this Twenty
eighth day of the eleventh month in the year of our Lord on Thousand
Eight hundred and Sixteen...at Warrington in the County afforesaid

                                                William Cox
                                                Ruth G. Cox

Malon McMillan	Abner Wickersham	Rebekah Griffith
John Cookson	Anne Griest	Joshua Cox Jr
John Cleaver	Ruth McMillan	Maria Griffith
Willing Griest	Thomas McMillan	Rebecca Griffith
Elisha Vale	Jacob McMillan	Thomas Cox
Martha Vale	Ruth McMillan	Samuel Cox
Daniel Cookson	Mary Griffith	Levi Griffith
Jeremiah Elder	Benjn Walker	Samuel Cook
George McMillan	Abel Walker	Jos McMillan
	Leah Walker	Gideon Griest
	Rhoda Altimus	Ethan Griffith
	Eliza Walker	
	Mary Cookson	
	Hannah Cutler	
	Maria Plummer	
	Sarah Vale	
	Susanna McMillan	

#256 25TH OF 3RD MO 1817   JOHN THOMAS-SARAH GARRETSON
Whereas John Thomas son of Isaac Thomas Deceased and Elenor his wife
of Monallin Township Adams County in the State of Pennsylvania and
Sarah Garretson Daughter of Joseph Garretson and Rebekah his wife
Deceased of Newbury Township York County in the State
aforesaid...this 25th day of the 3rd month in the year of our Lord
one thousand Eight hundred and Seventeen...at Newbury in the County affores
                                           John Thomas
                                           Sarah Thomas

WARRINGTON MONTHLY MEETING

Abel Thomas	Elijah Garretson	Thomas Garretson
Ann Garretson	Ellin Thomas	Maria Griffith
Jos R. Thomas	Abner Thomas	John J. Garretson
George Griffith	Jesse Wickersham	George Garretson
Sarah Griffith	Isaac Cleaver	John Wickersham
Anna Wickersham p.o	Jacob Kirk	Ann Garretson
Harriet Potts	Thomas Leech Jr	Rebecka Wickersham
Z Underwood	Hannah Leech	Julian Griffith
Nathan Potts	Hannah Kirk	Samuel Garretson
	Joseph Garretson	Joel Garretson
	Maria Garretson	Benjamin Garretson
	Rachel Garretson	Samuel Garretson Jr
	Hiram Starr	Oliver Griffith
		Jacob Garretson
		Israel Garretson

#257 27th of 11th mo 1817   URIAH GRIEST-MARY VALE

Whereas <u>Uriah Griest</u> of Latimore Township Adams County and State of Pennsylvania Son of <u>Joseph Griest and Rebekah</u> his wife of the same place and <u>Mary Vale</u> daughter of <u>William Vale and Ann</u> his wife (the latter Deceased) of Warrington Township York County and State Aforesaid...this twenty seventh day of the eleventh month in the year of our Lord one Thousand Eight hundred and seventeen ...at Warrington in the County aforesaid

Uriah Griest
Mary Griest

Jacob McMillan	Elisha Vale	Joseph Griest
Nancy Jones	Martha Vale	Rebecca Griest
Roxanna Zinn	Joel Walker	William Vale
John Cookson	Malon Griest	Eli Griest
Abraham Cook	Nathan Griest	Sarah Vale
Mary Hutton	Elizabeth Vale	Stephen Hussey
Ann Squibb	Phebe Vale	Ruth Griest
Thomas Edmundson	Benj Walker	Ann Walker
Mary Cookson	Benjamin Bower	Margaret Speakman
John Cleaver	Amos Griffith	John Vale
Susanna Cleaver	Mary Griffith	Gideon Griest
Thomas McMillan	Willing Griest	Jane M. Griest
Ruth McMillan	Anna Griest	Jediah Hussey
	Joseph McMillan	Ann Hussey
	Joanna Squibb	Joshua Vale
	Deborah Griffith	Elizabeth Vale
		Peter Vale

#258 28th of 1st mo 1818   THOMAS GARRETSON-JANE WARNER

Whereas <u>Thomas Garretson</u> of Newbury Township in the County of york and State of Pennsylvania Son of <u>Samuel Garretson</u> of the same place and <u>Alice</u> his wife lately Deceased and <u>Jane Warner</u> of the Township County and State afforesaid Daughter of <u>Elisha Hoops</u> of New Garden

MARRIAGES

Township in the County of Columbiana and State of Ohio and **Mary** his wife...this twenty Eighth day of the first month in the year of our Lord one Thousand Eight hundred and Eighteen...at Newbury in the County afforesaid

		Thomas Garretson
		Jane Garretson
Ellin Thomas	Jesse Wickersham	Samuel Garretson
Juliann Griffith	Phebe Wickersham	Elizabeth Garretson
George Garretson	Joseph Garretson	Isaac Cleaver
Anna Garretson	Maria Garretson	Jonathan Hoops
Geo Griffith	Mary Hoops	John J Garretson
Sarah Griffith	John J. Garretson	Rebekah Garretson
Oliver Griffith	Ann Garretson	Joel Garretson
Abel T. Thomas	Edward Jones	Benjamin Garretson
Elijah Garretson	Sarah Jones	Rachel Garretson
Israel Garretson	William Cox	Joseph McMillan
Aaron Frazer	Thos Leech Jr	Rebeccah McMillan
Z Underwood	Hannah Leech	Samuel Garretson
	Mary Hutton	Ann Garretson
	John W. Thomas	

#259 29th of 1st mo 1818   WILLIAM VALE-MARY MCMILLAN

Whereas **William Vale** of Warrington Township York County and State of Pennsylvania son of **Robert Vale and Sarah** his wife late of the same place (Deceased) and **Mary McMillan** Daughter of **George McMillan and Ann** his wife of Washington Township County and State aforesaid (Deceased)...this Twenty ninth day of the First month in the year of our Lord one Thousand Eight hundred and Eighteen...at Warrington in the County afforesaid

William Vale
Mary Vale

WARRINGTON MONTHLY MEETING

John Cleaver	John Cookson	Willing Griest
Susanna Cleaver	Samuel Cook	Anne Griest
Amos Griffith	Mary Cookson	Elisha Vale
Mary Griffith	Joseph Taylor	Joshua Vale
Joseph McMillan Jr	Margaret McGorgan	Joel Walker
James Ross	Margaret E. Kerr	Anne Griest Jr
Rebecca Griffith	Eliza Ann Bingman	Amos Griest
Isaac Pearson	Nancy Caldwell	Sarah Vale
Cyrus Griest	Margaret Eaving	Joseph McMillan
Susanna McMillan	Mary Cook	Rebeccah McMillan
Sarah Vale	Martha Morris	John Cook
Sarah Cook	Mary Diseman	Hannah Cook
		Leah Walker
		Thomas McMillan
		Ruth McMillan
		Thomas Edmundson
		Elizabeth Edmundson
		David Cadwallader
		Benjn Walker
		Daniel Cookson

#260 25th of 11th mo 1819   JOEL GARRETSON-ELIZABETH VALE

Whereas <u>Joel Garretson</u> of Newbury Township in the County of York and State of Pennsylvania Son of <u>Samuel Garretson</u> of the same place and <u>Alice</u> his wife Deceased and <u>Elizabeth Vale</u> Daughter of <u>Joshua Vale</u> of Washington Township in the County and State afforesaid and <u>Elizabeth</u> his wife...this twenty fifth day of the eleventh month in the year of our Lord one Thousand Eight hundred and nineteen...at Warrington in the County afforesaid

		Joel Garretson
		Elizabeth Garretson
Julia Griffith	Rebecca McMillan	Samuel Garretson
Benjamin Walker	Thomas Garretson	Joshua Vale
Joel Walker	Jane Garretson	Elizabeth Vale
Eli Garretson	Eve Watts	Peter Vale
Mary Hutton	Peter Griest	Rachel Garretson
Ruth McMillan	Willing Griest	Benjamin Garretson
Joanna Squibb	Anne Griest	Sarah Vale
Jacob McMillan	Susanna Cleaver	Nathan Vale
Joseph Taylor	Elijah Garretson	Ann Vale
Nancy Jones	Jo McMillan Jr	Asahel Walker
Mary Cookson	Mahlon McMillan	Mary Walker
	John Cookson	Esther Griest
	Margaret Garretson	William Vale
	Anna Griest Jr	Lydia Wright
		Rebecca Jones
		Isaac Cleaver
		Jos McMillan

MARRIAGES

#261 25th of 5th mo 1820 **PETER VALE-ESTHER GRIEST**
Whereas <u>Peter Vale</u> of Washington Township in the County of york in the State of Pennsylvania son of <u>Joshua Vale and Elizabeth</u> his wife and <u>Esther Griest</u> of Warrington Township County and state aforesaid daughter of <u>Isaac Griest and Mary</u> his wife (the latter deceased)...this twenty fifth day of the fifth month in the year of our Lord one Thousand Eight hundred and Twenty...at Warrington in the County afforesaid

		Peter Vale
		<u>Esther Vale</u>
Thomas McMillan	John Cleaver	Joshua Vale
Daniel Cookson	Susanna Cleaver	Elizabeth Vale
Amos Griffith	Mary Griest	Jacob Griest
Mary Griffith	Mary Griest	Sarah Vale
Geo Harris Jr	Susannah Morthland	Solomon Griest
Amos Griest	Joel Walker	Sarah Vale
Mahlon McMillan	Mary Hutton	William Vale
John Cookson	Robert Vale	Mary Vale
Samuel John	Martha Vale	Anne Griest
George Squibb	Mary Cookson	Anne Griest
Anne Squibb	Nancy Jones	Samuel Cook
Joanna Squibb	Maryann Wells	Sarah Cook
Joseph Taylor	Susanna McMillan	Joel Garretson
Jacob McMillan	George McMillan	Asahel Walker
Maria Griest	Cyrus Griest	Phebe Vale
		Peter Griest

#262 24th of 5th mo 1820 **LEWIS HARRY-MARIA GRIFFITH**
Whereas <u>Lewis Harry</u> of the Borough of york in the County of york and state of Pennsylvania Son of <u>Jesse Harry</u> late of the same place and <u>Mary</u> his wife both Deceased and <u>Maria Griffith</u> daughter of <u>Joseph Griffith</u> of Warrington Township in the County and State aforesaid and <u>Rebecca</u> his wife...this twenty fourth day of the fifth month in the year of our Lord one Thousand eight hundred and Twenty...at Newbury in the County afforesaid

		Lewis Harry
		<u>Maria Harry</u>
Samuel Garretson	Sarah Quigley	Rebecca Griffith
Elizabeth Garretson	Susanna Morthland	Ruth G. Cox
Anna Wickersham	George Garretson	John T. Garretson
Martha Kirk	Hannah Kirk	Ann Garretson
Harriet Potts	Jane McGrew	Sarah G. Thomas
Abigail Potts	Thos Leech Jr	Z. Underwood
Esther C. Stave	Hannah Leech	Hannah Underwood
Thomas Garretson	Rhoda Hoops	Hiram Star
Jane Garretson	Joseph Garretson	Rebecca Star
Mary Speakman	Maria Garretson	Hannah B. Altemus
	Benjamin Garretson	
	Isaac Altemus	

WARRINGTON MONTHLY MEETING

#263 29th of 3rd mo 1821   JEDIAH HUSSEY-MARY COOKSON

Whereas <u>Jediah Hussey</u> of Warrington Township in the County of york and State of Pennsylvania Son of <u>Jediah Hussey</u> of the same place and <u>Jane</u> his wife and <u>Mary Cookson</u> Daughter of <u>Daniel Cookson</u> of the Township County and State aforesaid and <u>Sarah</u> his wife...this Twenty ninth day of the third month in the year of our Lord one Thousand Eight Hundred and Twenty one...at Warrington in the County afforesaid

    Jediah Hussey
    <u>Mary C. Hussey</u>

Joseph Taylor	Amos Griffith	Daniel Cookson
Sarah Vale	Mary Griffith	Sarah Cookson
Mahlon McMillan	Sarah Walker	John Cookson
Jacob McMillan	Benj Walker	Sarah Cookson Jr
Cyrus Griest	John Cleaver	Mary Halapieten
Alex Wierman	Susanna Cleaver	William Vale
Stephen Hussey	Thomas McMillan	Mary Vale
Thos G. Squibb	Ruth McMillan	David Cadwalader
Enos McMillan	Peter Vale	Elizabeth Cadwalader
Amos Griest	Esther Vale	Susanna Squibb
Abraham Wells	Anne Griest Jr	Mary Wierman
	Maria Jane Cook	Mary Hussey
	Sarah Vale Jr	Thomas Edmundson
		Mary M. Walker
		Joel Walker
		Robert Vale
		Willing Griest
		Samuel Cook

#264 26th of 4th mo 1821   ABNER WICKERSHAM-ANNE GRIEST

Whereas <u>Abner Wickersham</u> of Newbury Township york county and State of Pennsylvania Son of <u>James Wickersham</u> of the same place and <u>Sarah</u> his wife deceased and <u>Anne Griest</u> Daughter of <u>Willing Griest</u> of Warrington Township in the County and State aforesaid and <u>Anne</u> his wife...this twenty sixth day of the forth month in the year of our Lord one thousand eight hundred and twenty one ...at Warrington in the County afforesaid

    Abner Wickersham
    <u>Anne Wickersham</u>

MARRIAGES

Jane Cook	Mary Ann Cook	Willing Griest
John Cookson	Jos McMillan Jr	Anne Griest
Jesse Cook	Elizabeth McMillan	Amos Griest
Samuel Cook Jr	Benjn Walker	Thomas McMillan
Hannah Cook	Robert Vale	Ruth McMillan p.o
Daniel Cookson	Amos Griffith	James Wickersham
Joshua Vale	Asahel Walker	Mary Wickersham
Sarah Cookson	Mary Walker	Abner Walker
	Samuel Cook	Sarah Walker
	Joel Walker	Mary Griest
	Mary M. Walker	Jacob McMillan
	Leah Walker	Maria Jane Cook
	Aaron G. Blackford	Elizabeth Garretson
	Jesse W. Cook	Edith Griest
		Cyrus Griest

#265 30th of 5th mo 1821   ISAAC BOONE-ESTHER STAR
Whereas <u>Isaac Boone</u> of Monallen Township in the County of Adams in State of Pennsylvania son of <u>Joshua Boone</u> of Exeter Township Berks County and State afforesaid and <u>Jane</u> his wife and <u>Esther Star</u> of Newbury Township york County and State of Pennsylvania Daughter of <u>John Star</u> late of Frederick County in the State of Maryland and <u>Phebe</u> his wife both now deceased...this thirtieth day of the fifth month in the year of our Lord one thousand Eight hundred and twenty one...at Newbury in the County afforesaid

		Isaac Boone
		<u>Esther Boone</u>
John Garretson	Mary Reaser	Reuben Star
Ann Garretson	Hannah Kirk	Isaac Thomas
Job Hoops	Thomas Garretson	Hannah Thomas
Rhoda Hoops	Jane Garretson	Rebecca Star
Isaac Altemus	Benjamin Garretson	John G. Garretson
Hannah B. Altemus	Joseph Garretson	Rebekah Garretson
Joseph Leech	Maria Garretson	Hannah Meredith
		John Thomas
		Sarah G. Thomas
		Martha Kirk

NOTE: the following numbered weddings are omitted in the photocopy of the original: 266, 267, 268, 269, 270, 271, 272, 273, 274, 275.

#276 27th of 3rd mo 1823   JACOB MCMILLAN-SARAH VALE
Whereas <u>Jacob McMillan</u> of Warrington Township York County and State of Pennsylvania Son of <u>Thos and Ruth McMillan</u> in the Township Afforesaid and <u>Sarah Vale</u> Daughter of <u>Joshua and Elizabeth Vale</u> of Washington Township County and State aforesaid...this twenty seventh day of the third month in the year of our Lord one thousand Eight

WARRINGTON MONTHLY MEETING

hundred and twenty three...at Warrington in the County afforesaid

		Jacob McMillan
		Sarah McMillan
Willing Griest	Edith Griest	Thomas McMillan
Anne Griest	Miriam Griest	Ruth McMillan
Maria Jane Cook	Jesse Cook Jr	Joshua Vale
Sarah Cook	Cyrus Griest	Elizabeth Vale
Mary Ann Cook	John Cookson	Mahlon McMillan
Mary Griest	Allen Griffith	Susanna McMillan
Samuel Cook	Geo McMillan Jr	Jos McMillan Jr
Nathan Vale	Wm Taylor	Elizabeth McMillan
Rachel Vale	Charles Underwood	Peter Griest
Asahel Walker	Jacob Frome	Anne McMillan
Mary Walker	Joel Walker	Eli McMillan
Martha Vale	Mary M. Walker	Joseph Garretson
Peter Vale jr	Mary Cook	Mariah Garretson
Joseph McMillan	Jacob McMillan	Enos McMillan
	Joel Garretson	Amos Griest
	Elizabeth Garretson	

#277 29th of 4th mo 1824   JOSEPH KENT-MARIA JANE COOK

Whereas <u>Joseph Kent</u> of Deer Creek in the County of Harford in the State of Maryland Son of <u>Daniel and Esther Kent</u> (the latter Deceased) of Chester County Pennsylvania and <u>Maria Jane Cook</u> daughter of <u>Samuel and Jane Cook</u> of York County Pennsylvania...this 29th day of the fourth month in the year of our Lord one Thousand Eight Hundred and twenty four...at Warrington in the County afforesaid

                                              Joseph Kent
                                              <u>Maria Jane Kent</u>

MARRIAGES

Jesse W. Cook MD	Jacob McMillan	Samuel Cook
John Cook	Sarah McMillan	Jane Cook
Hannah Cook	Peter Vale	Mary Ann Cook
Henry Cook	Eli Cookson	Elizabeth T. Cook
Mary Cook	Ruth McMillan	Jesse Cook Jr
Amos Griffith	Lavinia Garretson	Eliza Cook
Mary Griffith	Anne McMillan	Mary Cook
Samuel Cook	Joel Wireman	Daniel Kent Jr
Mathew Black	Edward Wickersham	Jesse Cook
Mary Walker	George W. Cook	George P. Cook
Joel Walker	Edith Griest	Elizabeth Kent
Daniel Cookson	Nathan Cleaver	Samuel P. Cook
Sarah Cookson	Amos Griest	Anne Cook
George Squibb	Cyrus Griest	Sarah Cook
James Welk	Willing Griest	
John Livelsberger	Anne Griest	
Susanna McMillan		
Jane Leech		
Sarah Cookson Jr		
Mary Ann Wells		

#278 10th of 3rd mo 1825   ISRAEL GARRETSON-RUTH WALKER

Whereas <u>Israel Garretson</u> son of <u>Jacob and Mary Garretson</u> of Newbury Township in the County of York and State of Pennsylvania and <u>Ruth Walker</u> Daughter of <u>John and Lydia Walker</u> of Warrington Township County and State afforesaid...this tenth day of the third month in the year of our Lord one thousand Eight hundred and twenty five...at Warrington in the County afforesaid   Israel Garretson
                                              <u>Ruth Garretson</u>

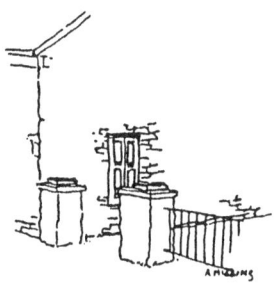

WARRINGTON MONTHLY MEETING

Eli McMillan
Susanna McMillan
Ann McMillan
Ruth Cookson
Elizabeth Bell
Mary Ann Cook
Edith Griest
Mary Griest
Jos Taylor
Jesse McMillan
Daniel Cookson
Sarah Cookson
Benjamin M. Walker
John Leech
Nancy Jones
Willing Griest
Anne Griest
Leah Walker
Abner Walker
Sarah Walker
Amos McMillan

Wm Cadwallader
Sarah Cadwallader
Deborah Griffith
Cyrus McMillan
James Wells
Sarah Cookson
Susannah Walker
Eli Cookson
Hannah Armitage
John Cook
Hannah Cook
Samuel F. Cook
Nathan Hussey
Edwin Cook
Peter Vannert
Jos McMillan
Thos McMillan
Ruth McMillan

Jacob Garretson
Mary Garretson
John Walker
Lydia Walker
Jesse Walker
Daniel Garretson
Rebecca Walker Sr
Ruthanna Walker
Margaret Walker
Sarah Walker
Sally Haywood

#279 22nd of 12th mo 1825   THOMAS SMITH-LEAH WALKER

Whereas Thomas Smith of Sincler Township Bedford County and State of Pennsylvania son of James and Mary Smith of the same place (the former dec'd) and Leah Walker Daughter of Abel and Ann Walker Dec'd late of Warrington Township york County and state aforesaid...this twenty second day of the twelfth month in the year of our lord one thousand Eight hundred and twentyfive...at warrington in the County afforesaid

Thomas Smith
Leah Smith

Peter Cleaver
Samuel Morthland
Thos McMillan
Samuel Cook
Sarah Cook
Nathan Cleaver
Tamil Cookson
Cyrus McMillan
Susan Smith
Enos McMillan
Wm Cadwalader
David Cadwalader
Jacob McMillan
Sarah McMillan
Maryann Cook

Mary Vale
Lydia Walker
Benjamin Walker
Malinda Everitt
Peter Vanegt
Wm Penrose
Isaac Kirk

Joel Walker
Ann Cook
John Cook
Hannah Cook
Abel Walker
Maryanne Walker
Joshua Vale
Wm Vale

MARRIAGES

#280 2nd of 3rd mo 1826   CYRUS GRIEST-MARY ANN COOK

Whereas <u>Cyrus Griest</u> of Warrington Township york County and State of Pennsylvania son of <u>Willing and Anne Griest</u> and <u>Mary Ann Cook</u> daughter of <u>Samuel and Jane Cook</u> all of the Township County and State aforesaid...this second day of the third month in the year of our lord one thousand Eight hundred & twenty six...at Warrington in the County afforesaid

           Cyrus Griest
           <u>Mary Ann Griest</u>

Peter Vale	Cyrus McMillan	Willing Griest
Asahel Walker	Anne Cook	Anne Griest
Samuel John	Amos Griest	Samuel Cook
Sarah John	George W. Cook	Jane Cook
Wm Vale	Jacob McMillan	Jesse W. Cook
John Walker	Ruth McMillan	Elizabeth S. Cook
Jacob McMillan	Malinda Everitt	John Everitt Jr
Sarah McMillan	Sarah Cook	Edith Griest
Ruth McMillan	Joel Walker	Eli Cookson
Peter Cleaver	Mary M. Walker	Mary Griest
Benjamin Walker	E. M. Cook	Jesse Walker
Isaac Kirk Sr	Cornelius G. Cook	Ruth Griest
M. Griffith	Daniel Cookson	
Peter Sackenfelter	Sarah Cookson	
James Griffith	Josiah Griest	
	Thomas McMillan	
	Ruth McMillan	

#281 1st of 3rd mo 1826   THOMAS WICKERSHAM-SARAH MEREDITH

Whereas <u>Thomas Wickersham</u> son of <u>Jesse Wickersham and Phebe Wickersham</u> all of Newberry Township York County in the State of Pennsylvania and <u>Sarah Meredith</u> Daughter of <u>Israel & Elizabeth Meredith</u> of the place above mentioned...this 1st day of the 3rd mo 1826...at Newberry in the County afforesaid

           Thomas Wickersham
           <u>Sarah Wickersham</u>

WARRINGTON MONTHLY MEETING

Hannah Bell	James Hoopes	Elizabeth Garretson
Jane Hoopes	Z. Underwood	Phebe Wickersham
John J. Garretson	Elijah Garretson	Jesse Wickersham
Ann Garretson	Lewis Harry	Abigail Potts
Mary Ann Wells	Aaron Fraizer	Jesse Meredith
Phebe Griffith	Thomas Garretson	Sidney Wickersham
Jane Potts	Isaac Kirk	Joseph Potts
Rebecca Underwood	Ann Kirk	Jane Leech
Benjamin Garretson	John G. Garretson	Joseph Leech
Daniel Garretson	Rebecah Garretson	Eliza Meredith
	Joel Garretson	Ross Meredith
	Thos Leech	Jacob Kirk
	Hannah Leech	Hannah Kirk
		James Wickersham
		Mary Wickersham
		Abner Wickersham
		Josiah Wickersham

#282 28th of 6th mo 1826   JOHN ATKINSON-JANE LEECH

Whereas <u>John Atkinson</u> of Union Township in the County of Clinton and State of Ohio son of <u>Thomas & Alice Atkinson</u> Late of the same place deceased & <u>Jane Leech</u> of Warrington Township york County and State of Pennsylvania Daughter of <u>Thomas & Hannah Leech</u> of the same place this twenty eighth day of the sixth month one thousand eight hundred & twenty six...at Newberry in the County afforesaid

                                                          John Atkinson
                                                          <u>Jane Atkinson</u>

John J. Garretson	Lewis Harry	Thomas Leech
Ann Garretson	Sidney Wickersham	Hannah Leech
Z. Underwood	John Leech	E. J. Wickersham
Hannah Underwood	Thos Wickersham	Susanna McMillan
Benjamin Garretson	Sarah Wickersham	Joseph Leech
Orpah Garretson	Jesse Wickersham	Rebecah Underwood
Joseph Potts	Hannah Bell	Eli McMillan
Abigail Potts	Elizabeth Bell	Margaret Garretson
Mary Ann Odells	Mary Stuker	Jesse Garretson
Jane Garretson	Mary W. Weisman	Rebecca Garretson
Elizabeth Brooks	Anne Wickersham	Edith Griffith

#283 26th of 10th mo 1826   JOSEPH LEECH-ANNE MCMILLAN

Whereas <u>Joseph Leech</u> of Warrington Township in the County of York & State of Pennsylvania son of <u>Thomas & Hannah Leech</u> of the same place and <u>Anne McMillan</u> Daughter of <u>Jacob & Ruth McMillan</u> of Washington Township county & State aforesaid...this twenty sixth day of the tenth month in the year of our Lord one thousand Eight hundred & twenty six...at Warrington in the County afforesaid

                                                          Joseph Leech
                                                          <u>Anne Leech</u>

MARRIAGES

Ruth Griest
Guilelme Griffith
William Vale
Mary Vale
Cornelius Cook
Edwin W. Cook
Enos McMillan
Abraham Griffith
Andrew Griffith
Anne Griffith
Jesse Walker
Eli Cookson
Deborah Griffith
Mary Hutten
Sarah John
John Walker
Lydia Walker
Jane Cook
Peter Vale
Esther Vale

Peter Cleaver
Jane Cook
Sarah Cook
Susanna Griffith
George McMillan
Mary Griest
John Leech
Willing Griest
Anne Griest
Amos McMillan
Susanna McMillan
Jacob McMillan
Sarah McMillan
Joel Walker
Mary M. Walker
Samuel Cook
Sarah Cook

Thomas Leech
Hannah Leech
Jacob McMillan
Ruth McMillan
Cyrus McMillan
Margaret Garretson
Ruth McMillan
Joseph Garretson
Malinda Everitt
Amos Griest
Edith Griest
Nathan Cleaver

#284 29th of 3rd mo 1827   EDWARD WICKERSHAM-SUSANNA MCMILLAN

Whereas Edward Wickersham of Newberry Township in the County of york & State of Pennsylvania son of Jesse and Phebe Wickersham of the same place & Susanna McMillan daughter of George & Rebeckah McMillan of Warrington Township the county & State aforesaid...this twenty ninth day of the third month in the year of our lord one thousand eight hundred & twenty seven...at Warrington in the County afforesaid

Edward Wickersham
Susanna Wickersham

George W. Cook
Amos Griest
Elijah Garretson
Nathan Cleaver
Jesse Walker
Eli Cookson
Edith Griest
Mary Griest
Jacob McMillan
Daniel Cookson
Thos McMillan
Rebecca Underwood
Ruth McMillan
Ann Griest
Willing Griest
George McMillan

Lydia Walker
Sidney Wickersham
Elizabeth Bell
Cyrus McMillan
Thos Wickersham
John Wickersham
George McMillan Jr
Ruth McMillan

George McMillan
Phebe Wickersham
Lavinia Garretson
Eli McMillan
Rebecca R. Garretson
Jesse Wickersham
Hannah Armitage
Amos McMillan

WARRINGTON MONTHLY MEETING

#285 27th of 3rd mo 1828   **AMOS GRIEST-MARTHA MORRIS**

Whereas <u>Amos Griest</u> of Warrington Township york County State of Penna son of <u>Willing & Ann Griest</u> & <u>Martha Morris</u> daughter of <u>Isaac & Martha Morris</u> Deceased all of the township County & State afsd...this twentiseventh Day of the third month in the year of Lord one thousand Eight hundred & twentieight...at Warrington in the County afforesaid

                                                                                             Amos Griest
                                                                                            <u>Martha Griest</u>

Amos Griffith	Nehemiah Morris	Willing Griest
Peter Vale	Abner Wickersham	Anna Griest
Elisha Mcmillan	Anne Wickersham	Jesse Cook
Henry Wireman	Asahel Walker	Edith Griest
Latitia Diseman	Jacob McMillan	Cyrus McMillan
Eli Cookson	Ruth McMillan	Mary Griest
Samuel Cook	George W. Cook	Jesse Walker
Sarah Cook	Ruth McMillan	Ruth Griest
John Walker	Sarah Walker	Jonathan Griest
Lydia Walker	Mary M. Walker	Mary Griest
Josiah Cook	Mary Griest	Cyrus Griest
Edwin W. Cook	Jesse Wickersham	Maryanne Griest
Phebe Vale	Susanna Griffith	Josiah Griest
Ruth Cookson		
Mary Hutton		
Jane Cook		
Julia Griffith		
Daniel Walgemuth		

#286 28th of 5th mo 1829   **DANIEL GARRETSON-ANNE COOK**

Whereas <u>Daniel Garretson</u> of newbury Township in the County of york in the state of Pennsylvania son of <u>Jacob and Mary Garretson</u> the latter Deceased of newbury township and County aforesaid and <u>Anne Cook</u> daughter of <u>John and Hannah Cook</u> of Warrington township County of York and State of Pennsylvania...this twenty eighth day of the fifth month in the year of our Lord one thousand eight hundred and twenty nine...at Warrington in the County afforesaid

                                                                    Daniel Garretson
                                                                    <u>Anne Garretson</u>

MARRIAGES

George W. Cook	Peter Vale	Jacob Garretson
Edwin M. Cook	Esther Vale	John Cook
Susanna Vale	Hezekiah Cook	Hannah Cook
Jane Cook	Mary Cook	Jesse Cook
Jane Cook Jr	Walker Cook	Mary Cook
Julia E. Griffith	Lydia Vale	
Joseph Garretson	Ruth Garretson	
Mariah Garretson	Cyrus Garretson	
Ruth McMillan	Jesse Walker	
Sarah McMillan		
John Walker		
Thomas McMillan		
Ruth McMillan		
Joel Walker		
Pierce Garretson		
Joseph Kent		
Maria J. Kent		
William Hoopes		
Asahel Walker		

#287 29th of 9th mo 1831   JESSE COOK-RUTH MCMILLAN

Whereas <u>Jesse Cook</u> son of <u>Henry and Mary Cook</u> of Warrington Township in the county of York and state of Pennsylvania and <u>Ruth McMillan</u> daughter of <u>Jacob and Ruth McMillan</u> (the latter deceased) of Washington Township the county and State aforesaid...this twenty ninth day of the ninth month in the year of our Lord one Thousand eight hundred & thirty one...at Warrington in the County afforesaid

| | | Jesse Cook |
		Ruth Cook
Edith Griest	Jane Cook	Henry Cook
Sarah Walker	Cornelius G. Cook	Mary Cook
Maria Garretson	Esther Cookson	Jacob McMillan
Sarah McMillan	Jesse W. Cook Jr	Mary Cook
Mary M. Walker	Elizabeth T. Cook	Josiah Cook
Abraham Cook	Willing Griest	Elizabeth Griffith
Eli Cookson	Anne Griest	George W. Cook
Mary Hutton	Ruth McMillan	
Samuel Cook		
Cyrus Griest		
Jacob McMillan		
Sarah McMillan		
Samuel H. Cook		
Ruth Cookson		
Mary Cook		
Joseph Garretson		
Hesekiah Cook		

WARRINGTON MONTHLY MEETING

#288 30th of 8th mo 1832   GEORGE W. COOK-ELIZABETH WALKER
Whereas George W. Cook of Warrington township in the county of york and state of Pennsylvania son of Samuel and Jane Cook and Elizabeth Walker daughter of Asahel and Mary Walker (the latter deceased) of Washington Township County and State aforesaid...this thirtieth day of the eighth month in the year of our Lord one thousand eight hundred thirty two...at Warrington in the County afforesaid

		George W. Cook
		Elizabeth Cook
Isaac G. Vale	Samuel Cook	Nathan Hussey
Elisha Cook	Jane Cook	Ruth Cookson
Abraham Cook	Asahel Walker	Jesse Walker
Amos McMillan	William Hoopes	Edith Griest
William H. Armitage	Priscilla Hoopes	Achilles Whinnery
Elisha McMillan	Cyrus Griest	Jane Cook Jr
Jacob Byers	Mary Ann Griest	Josiah Cook
Mary C. Hussey	Jesse Cook	Louisa Walker
Hannah Wells	Mary Walker	Cornelius Cook
Esther Griest	Hannah Cook	Mary Ann Walker
Jacob McMillan	Jane Beachford	Ruth McMillan
William Underwood	Mary Cook	William Hussey
Abraham Wells	Mary Griest	Mary Vale
Joseph Garretson	Ruth Griest	
Maria Garretson	Eli Cookson	
Sarah Cook	Josiah Griest	
Mary Ann Garretson	Martha Griest	

#289 24th of 10th mo 1835   WILLIAM H. ARMITAGE-RACHEL COOKSON
Whereas William H. Armitage of Warrington Township in the county of york and state of Pennsylvania son of John and Sarah Armitage of Baltimore City State of Maryland (Dec) and Rachel Cookson Daughter of Daniel Cookson (dec) of Warrington township county of york in the state of Pennsylvania and Sarah his wife...this twenty fourth day of the tenth month in the year of one thousand eight hundred and thirty Five...at Warrington in the County afforesaid

		William H. Armitage
		Rachel Armitage
Saml John	Sarah Cookson	C. Armitage
Sarah John	Ruth Griest	Hannah Cookson
Isaac P. Garretson	Edith Griest	Jacob Pike
Elisha Cook	Eli Cookson	Sarah Brinton
Abraham Cook	Phebe Cookson	Samuel Brinton
Peter Vale	John Cookson	Sarah Myers
Amos McMillan		
Hannah McMillan		
Jos Garretson		
Maria Garretson		
Ruth McMillan		

MARRIAGES

#290 6th of 11th mo 1833   JOSHUA F. BENNETT-SARAH WALN
Whereas Joshua F. Bennett of warrington Township in the county of York and state of Pennsylvania son of Joshua and Mary Bennett of east caln township Chester county and state aforesaid (the former decd) and Sarah Waln Daughter of Nathan and Sarah Thomas of the Township of Newbury in the county of york and state aforesaid (the former decd)...this sixth day of the eleventh month in the year of our lord one thousand eight hundred and thirty three...at Newbury in the County afforesaid

                                                  Joshua F. Bennett
                                                  Sarah Bennett

Barzillan Garretson	John Waln	Hannah Thomas
Rebecca Wickersham	Joel Garretson	Nathan Waln
Jane Underwood	Waln Hoopes	Hannah H. Waln
Rebecca Underwood	Phillip Sipe	Thos Leech
Jesse Underwood	John Reeser	John Leech
Isaac T. Garretson	Thos Garretson	Charles Underwood
Z. Underwood		Samuel Garretson
Hannah Underwood		

#291 20th of 12th mo 1833   SAMUEL GARRETSON-HANNAH CADWALLADER
Whereas Samuel Garretson of Ann Arundle County State of Maryland Son of Cornelius and Margaret Garretson(dec) and Hannah Cadwallader Daughter of David and Susannah Cadwallader (the latter decd) of Warrington Township County of york and State of Pennsylvania...this twentieth day of the twelfth month in the year of our Lord one thousand eight hundred and thirty three...at Warrington in the County afforesaid

                                                  Saml Garretson
                                                 Hannah C. Garretson

Hannah Cook	Maryanne Squibb	David Cadwallader
Cyrus Griest	Hannah Leech	John Cadwallader
Mary Ann Griest	Samuel M. Cook	Eliza Garretson
Mary Griest	Sarah Cook	John Leech
Susanna Vale	Joseph Cook	Cornelius G. Cook
Jane Smith	Joseph Leech	
Ruthanna Cook		
Sarah A. Leech		
Eli Leech		
Jesse Walker		
Isaac Vale		
Eli Cookson		

#292 20th of 10th mo 1859   ISRAEL GARRETSON JR-RACHEL GARRETSON
Whereas Israel Garretson Jr of Newberry Township in the County of York and State of Pennsylvania Son of Israel Garretson and Ruth Garretson his wife and Rachel Garretson Daughter of Thomas Garretson and Jane Garretson(deceased) of the Township County and State afforesaid...this twentieth day of the tenth month in the year Eighteen hundred and fifty nine

WARRINGTON MONTHLY MEETING

Asenathe H. Garretson	Israel Garretson Jr
	Rachel Garretson
	Israel Garretson
Jesse B. Garretson	Ruth Garretson
Josiah T. Garretson	Thomas Garretson
	Jacob Garretson
	Samuel Gunkel
	Ruth Anna Gunkel
	Martha Garretson
	Maria Garretson
	Israel Garretson
	Mary Ann Garretson

#293 25th of 9th mo 1834   JOSIAH COOK-MARY VALE

Whereas Josiah Cook of Warrington township in the county of york and state of Pennsylvania son of Henry and Mary Cook and Mary Vale daughter of John and Lydia Vale (the former decd) of Washington Township county and state aforesaid...this twenty fifth day of the ninth month in the year of our Lord one thousand eight hundred and thirty four...at Warrington in the County afforesaid

		Josiah Cook
		Mary Cook
Henry Cook	Ruth McMillan	William W. Cook
Mary Cook	Anne Griest	Susanna Vale
Asahel Walker	Daniel Garretson	Isaac Vale
Lydia Walker	William Vale	Mary Ann Walker
William Vale	Jacob G. Vale	Sarah Vale
Jesse Cook	Uriah Griest	Jos Garretson
Ruth Cook	Morris Walker	Maria Garretson

#294 26th of 4th mo 1837   WALN HOOPES-SARAH ANN LEECH

Whereas Waln Hoopes of Newbury Township County of york and state of Pennsylvania son of William Hoopes of the same place and Phebe his wife and Sarah Ann Leech Daughter of Thomas Leech of Warrington Township County and state aforesaid and Hannah his wife...this twenty sixth day of the fourth month in the year of our lord one thousand eight hundred and thirty seven...at Newbury in the County afforesaid

		Waln Hoopes
		Sarah Ann Hoopes
Elisha G. Cook	Joseph Leech	Wm Hoopes
Mary Ann Squibb	John Leech	Phebe Hoopes
Sarah Hoopes	Isaac T. Garretson	Thos Leech
John Mills	Eliza Garretson	Hannah Leech
Lydia Mills	Cornelius G. Cook	Job Hoopes
Eli Leech	Hannah Maria Garretson	Rhoda Hoopes

MARRIAGES

#295 27th of 7th mo 1837   WILLIAM W. COOK-RUTH GRIEST
Whereas William W. Cook of Monallin Township in the County of Adams and State of Pennsylvania Son of Samuel and Sidney Cook his wife (decd) formerly of Warrington township in the County of York and State aforesaid and Ruth Griest daughter of Willing and Anne Griest (the former decd) of Warrington Township in the county of york and State of Pennsylvania...this twenty seventh day of the seventh month in the year of our Lord one thousand eight hundred and thirty seven...at Warrington in the County afforesaid

                                                  William W. Cook
                                                  Ruth G. Cook

Jane Griest	Jesse Cook	Anne Griest
Jesse Cook	Rebecca Cook	Joseph Griest
Ruth Cook	Abner Wickersham	George G. McMillan
Samuel M. Cook	Anna Wickersham	Eliza Garretson
Sarah Cook	Mary Griest	Jonah Cook
Hiram Griest	Cyrus Griest	Edith Griest
George Griest	Mary Ann Griest	Sarah G. Cook
Amos Griest	Samuel Cook Jr	George W. Reed
Marguret Griest	Jean Cook	Mary Ann Walker

#296 26th of 10th mo 1837   ISAAC VALE-MARY ANN WALKER
Whereas Isaac Vale of Warrington Township in York County and State of Pennsylvania son of Robert and Martha Vale (the former decd) and Mary Ann Walker of Washington township County and state aforesaid Daughter of Asahel and Mary Walker (the latter decd)...this twenty sixth day of the tenth month in the year of our lord one thousand eight hundred and thirty seven...at Warrington in the County afforesaid

                                                  Isaac Vale
                                                Mary Ann Vale

Sarah Vale Jr	John Cookson	Asahel Walker
Hannah Jane Cook	Hannah Cook	Martha Vale
Jesse Walker	Mary M. Walker	Cornelius G. Cook
Joseph Elcock	John Cook Jr	Edith Griest
Joseph H. Cook	Wm Vale	Josiah Griest
Isaac Walker	Abraham Cook	Ruth Anna Cook
David C. Squibb	Jacob McMillan	Wm Hoopes Jr
Belinda Griest	Mahlon McMillan	Priscilla Hoopes
Susanna Squibb	Sarah G. Cook	Morris Walker
Margaret Ross	Hannah C. Squibb	Jacob Garretson Vale

#297 30th of 5th mo 1838   DAVID RICHARDS-PHEBE WICKERSHAM
Whereas David Richards of Patton Township in the county of Centre and state of Pennsylvania son of John and Catharine Richards late of Halfmoon township in the county and state aforesaid and Phebe Wickersham daughter of Edward and Content Jones late of Newberry Township in the county of york and state aforesaid...this thirtieth day of the fifth month in the year of our lord one thousand eight

WARRINGTON MONTHLY MEETING

hundred and thirty eight...at Newbury in the County afforesaid

		David Richards
		Phebe Richards
Jane Garretson	Hannah Kirk	Thos Wickersham
Susanna Squibb	Rachel Marks	Sarah Wickersham
Waln Hoopes	Joseph Wickersham	John Wickersham
Rebecca Garretson	Thos Garretson	Jacob Kirk

#298 31st of 5th mo 1838   JOSIAH COOK-MARY GRIEST

Whereas Josiah Cook of Monallin Township in the county of Adams and state of Pennsylvania son of Henry and Mary Cook (decd) and Mary Griest daughter of Willing and Anna Griest (the former decd) of Warrington Township county of York and State afforesaid...this thirty first day of the fifth month in the year of our lord one thousand eight hundred and thirty eight...at Warrington in the County afforesaid

		Josiah Cook
		Mary Cook
Joel Garretson	Irene Wickersham	Anne Griest
Elizabeth G.	Jesse Cook	Jos Wickersham
Garretson	Cyrus Griest	Edith Griest
Samuel M. Cook	Mary Ann Griest	Josiah Griest
Sarah Cook	Amos Griest	Martha Wright
Eli Cookson	Margaret Griest	William W. Cook
Allen Griffith	Samuel Cook	Ruth G. Cook
Henry C. Griffith	Jane Cook	Abner Wickersham
Thomas Leech		

#299 25th of 12th mo 1839   MAHLON GARRETSON-ELIZA WICKERSHAM

Whereas Mahlon Garretson of Newbury township york county and state of Pennsylvania son of John and Rebecca Garretson of the same place (the former decd) and Eliza Wickersham daughter of james and Mary Wickersham of the township county and state aforesaid...this twenty fifth day of the twelfth month in the year of our Lord one thousand eight hundred and thirty nine...at Newbury in the County afforesaid

		Mahlon Garretson
		Eliza Garretson
Israel Garretson	Thomas Garretson	Rebecca Garretson
Ruth Garretson	Jane Garretson	Mary Wickersham
Jacob Kirk	Thos Wickersham	Samuel Garretson
Hannah Kirk	Sarah Wickersham	Abner Wickersham
		Anne Wickersham

#300 30th of 3rd mo 1842   ELIJAH WRIGHT-MARY A. HOOPES

Whereas Elijah Wright of Monallin Township in the County of Adams state of Pennsylvania Son of Nathan and Elizabeth Wright of the place aforesaid (the latter decd) and Mary A. Hoopes Daughter of Job and Rhoda Hoopes of Newbury Township york county state aforesaid...this thirtieth day of the third month in the year of our lord one thousand

MARRIAGES

eight hundred and forty two...at Newbury in the County afforesaid

		Elijah Wright
		Mary A. Wright
Jane Garretson	Lewis Hoopes	Job Hoopes
Rebecca Garretson	Sarah Hoopes	Rhoda Hoopes
Elizabeth V.	Joel Garretson	Nathan Wright
Garretson	Barzillan Garretson	Isaac J. Wright
Mahlon Garretson	Marlinda Garretson	Sarah A. Garretson
Eliza Ann Garretson	Thomas Garretson	John Wright

#301 25th of 1st mo 1843   ISAAC J. WRIGHT-SARAH GARRETSON

Whereas Isaac J. Wright of monallin Township County of Adams and state of Pennsylvania son of William and Rachel Wright (the latter decd) of the same place and Sarah Garretson of Newbury Township york County and state aforesaid Daughter of Thomas and Jane Garretson...this twenty fifth day of the first month in the year of our lord one thousand eight hundred forty three...at Newbury in the County afforesaid

		Isaac J. Wright
		Sarah G. Wright
Mary Garretson	Alice Garretson	Wm Wright
Eli Garretson	Ann W. Garretson	Thomas Garretson
Benjamin Garretson	Eliza Jane Garretson	Jane Garretson
Elizabeth V.	Rachel Garretson	Hiram Wright
Garretson		

#302 24th of 5th mo 1843   HIRAM WRIGHT-ALICE GARRETSON

Whereas Hiram Wright of Monallin Township County of Adams and State of Pennsylvania Son of Nathan and Elizabeth Wright (the latter decd) and Alice Garretson daughter of Joel and Elizabeth Garretson (the former decd) of Newbury Township County of york and state aforesaid...this twenty fourth day of the fifth month in the year of our lord one thousand eight hundred and forty three...at Newbury in the County afforesaid

		Hiram G. Wright
		Alice G. Wright
Elizabeth Garretson	Jane Garretson	Nathan Wright
Rachel Garretson	Louisa Garretson	Elizabeth V.
Rebecca Garretson	Mary Garretson	Garretson
Israel Garretson	Ann H. Garretson	Joel Wright
Edith Griest	Benjamin Garretson	Julia Kirk
Isaac J. Wright		Thomas Garretson
Sarah G. Wright		

#303 10th of 10th mo 1843   LEWIS MEREDITH-ANN S. TAUGHINBAUGH

Whereas Lewis Meredith of the Borough of Harrisburgh in the county of Dauphin in the State of Pennsylvania son of George and Ann Meredith of the borough of york in the State of Pennsylvania and Ann S. Taughinbaugh late of Carlisle cumberland county in the state of Pennsylvania Widow of George Taughinbaugh late of Carlisle cumberland county state of Pennsylvania Daughter of <u>John and Elizabeth Nebinger</u>(?) of the borough of Harrisburgh Dauphin County in the state of Pennsylvania...this tenth day of the tenth month in the year of our Lord one thousand eight hundred and forty three...at Newbury in the County afforesaid

		Lewis Meredith
		Ann S. Meredith
Israel Garretson	Sarah Wickersham	George Meredith
Rebecca Wickersham	Ross Meredith	R. Nebinger
Mary Ann Squibb	G. R. Nebinger	Elizabeth Nebinger
Thomas Garretson	Benjamin Garretson	Thos Wickersham

#304 23rd of 3rd mo 1848   JOHN G. BROWN-SARAH WALKER

Whereas <u>John G. Brown</u> of Hopewell in the County of Frederick and state of Virginia son of <u>Thomas & Susanna Brown</u> of Washington Township in the County of York & State of Pennsylvania and <u>Sarah Walker</u> of Washington Township in the County of York & state of Pa daughter of <u>Asahel and Mary Walker</u> (latter decd)...this twenty third day of the third month in the year of our Lord one thousand Eight hundred and Forty Eight...at the house of the young womans parents in the County afforesaid

John G. Brown
Sarah W. Brown

Asahel Walker	Morris Walker
Lydia G. Walker	Priscilla Walker
John Cook	George W. Cook

#305 23rd of 8th mo 1849   BENJAMIN GARRETSON-RHODA HOOPES

Whereas <u>Benjamin Garretson</u> of Newberry Township County of York and State of Pennsylvania son of <u>Samuel and Alice Garretson</u> (decd) and <u>Rhoda Hoopes</u> of the Township County and State afforesaid daughter of <u>Leonard and Sarah Altemus</u> (decd)...this twenty third day of the eighth month in the Year of our Lord one Thousand Eight hundred and Forty Nine...at Newberry in the County afforesaid

		Benjamin Garretson
		Rhoda Garretson
Susanna Reeser	Thomas Garretson	Joel G. Hoopes
Jesse Kirk	Waln Hoopes	Ann H. Garretson
Rebecca Starr	Baz Garretson	Almira Altemus
Josiah Wickersham	Jacob Kirk	Rhoda Ann Hoopes
	Hannah Kirk	Phebe Jane Hoopes
	John Reeser	Asanath Garretson

#306 26th of 9th mo 1849   SAMUEL H. HARRIS-JULIA KIRK

Whereas <u>Samuel H. Harris</u> of Monallin Township County of Adams and State of Pennsylvania Son of <u>Benjamin and Jane Harris</u> and <u>Julia Kirk</u> of Newberry Township County of York and State aforesaid daughter of <u>Jacob and Hannah Kirk</u> the latter decd...this twenty sixth day of the ninth month in the year of our Lord one Thousand Eight hundred and

MARRIAGES

forty nine...at Newberry in the County afforesaid

Orpah Jane Garretson	Susan Garretson	Samuel H. Harris
Joel Garretson	John Wickersham	Julia Harris
Elizabeth E.	Jane Garretson	Benjamin Harris
Garretson	John Garretson	Jane Harris
Phebe Jane Hoopes	Israel Garretson	Jacob Kirk
Caroline L. Kirk	Ruth Garretson	Hannah Kirk
Mary A. Morris	Benjamin Garretson	Abel T. Wright
Rachel Garretson	Rhoda Garretson	Mary Ann Squibb
Jacob Garretson	Rebecca T. Garretson	Jesse Kirk
Jane C. Griest	Lewis Hoopes	Hiram L. Harris
Israel Garretson Jr	Waln Hoopes	Thos Wickersham
Eli B. Garretson	J. B. Wright	Sarah Wickersham
Samuel Garretson	Lydia Garretson	Barzillan Garretson
Maria Wickersham	Eliza Hoopes	Malinda Garretson
Elizabeth V.	Mary Ann Ellis	Charles Kirk
Garretson	Elizabeth D Shettle	Ann Grove
George M. Griest		Elmira Foster
Jane Watts		Jesse Meredith

#307 24th of 10th mo 1849   JOSIAH WICKERSHAM-LYDIA GARRETSON

Whereas <u>Josiah Wickersham</u> of Newberry Township York County and State of Pennsylvania son of <u>Abner and Anne Wickersham</u> of Newberry Township York County and State aforesaid and <u>Lydia Garretson</u> daughter of <u>Israel and Ruth Garretson</u> of the same place...this twenty fourth day of the tenth month in the year of our Lord one Thousand Eight hundred and forty nine...at Newberry in the County afforesaid

		Josiah Wickersham
		Lydia Wickersham
Thomas Garretson	Joel G. Hoopes	Abner Wickersham
Benjamin Garretson	Maria Wickersham	Anne Wickersham
Rhoda Garretson	Josiah Griest	Israel Garretson
Barzillan Garretson	Mary Ann Squibb	Ruth Garretson
Malinda Garretson	Israel Garretson Jr	John Walker
Elizabeth Garretson	Ruth Anna Garretson	Lydia Walker
Eli B. Garretson	Edith Griest	Jacob Garretson
Julia Harris	Mary Ann Wickersham	Rachel Garretson
Rebecca J. Garretson	Edith Wickersham	
Susan Garretson	Daniel Hoopes	
Orpah Jane Garretson	Lydia Hoopes	

#308 26th of 10th mo 1854   ASAHEL W. COOK-HANNAH CAROLINE GARRETSON

Whereas <u>Asahel W. Cook</u> of Warrington Township in the County of York and State of Pennsylvania son of <u>George W. and Elizabeth Cook</u> and <u>Caroline Garretson</u> Daughter of <u>Daniel and Anne Garretson</u> of Warrington Township county and state aforesaid...this twenty sixth

WARRINGTON MONTHLY MEETING

day of the tenth month in the year of our Lord one Thousand eight hundred and fifty four...at Warrington in the County afforesaid

		Asahel W. Cook
		<u>Hannah Caroline Cook</u>
Samuel Cook	Joshua Vale	George W. Cook
Israel Garretson	Mary Ellen Garretson	Elizabeth Cook
Jacob Garretson	John M. Underwood	Daniel Garretson
Garretson Walker	Mariah Jane Cook	Anna Garretson
Annie Cook	John Cook 2nd	John C. Garretson
Mary Cook	Hannah Cook	Matilda Jane Ritter
Louisa Griest	Samuel Cook	
Elizabeth Garretson	Walker Cook	
Joel Garretson	Martha Cook	
Lydia G. Walker	Asahel Walker	
John Cook Jr		
Lydia M. Cook		
Priscilla W. Hoopes		
Mary W. Squibb		
Ruth Anna Walker		
Lydia Jane Walker		
Phebe Angelina Walker		
Sarah Ann Cook		
Anna Eliza Cook		

Certificates

of

Removal

Abstracts of all certificates of removal issued to or received by York Monthly Meeting during the years 1787 through 1851

REMOVALS

#1 10th of 10th mo 1787   **LYDIA MILLER**
To Crooked Run Monthly Meeting...Lydia Miller being lately removed to settle within the compass of your Meeting...Clear of Marriage Engagement...behalf of our Monthly Meeting held at York, the 10th of the 10th mo 1787   by Elisha Kirk, Cleark
                                                Hannah Yarnal, Cleark

#2 7th of 11th mo 1787   **CHRISTOPHER HUSSEY**
To the Monthly Meeting of Friends at Fairfax...Christopher Hussey ...to be joined to your Meeting he being removed within the Verge thereof...and is Clear of Debt and Marriage Engagements
by order of ye our Monthly Meeting at York heald the 7th of the 11th mo 1787 by   Elisha Kirk Cleark

#3 9th of 1st mo 1788   **GEORGE MCMUN**
To Crooked run Monthly Meeting
George McMun...in order to be joined to your meeting...and is clear of Marriage engagements as far as appears...signed in and on behalf of York Monthly Meeting, heald the 9th of 1st mo 1788
                                            by Elisha Kirk Clerk

#4 12th of 5th mo 1787   **JACOB NORBURY**
From Warrington Monthly Meeting held ye 12th of ye 5th mo 1787
To York Monthly Meeting
Jacob Norbury requested our Certificate to be joined to your meeting...we recommend him...
Signed in and on Behalf of sd Meeting by Peter Cleaver, clerk.

WARRINGTON MONTHLY MEETING

#5 9th of 1st mo 1788   **JACOB NORBURY**
To Warrington Monthly Meeting
Jacob Norbury produced the within Certificate to our Monthly Meeting in the 6th mo last which we read and accepted and he being returned to settle amongst you...we therefore recommend him
Signed by order of York Monthly Meeting heald the 9th of 1st mo 1788 by
                                                         Elisha Kirk Clerk

#6 11th of 2nd mo 1786   **JESSE AND LYDIA VORE**
From Warrington Monthly Meeting heald the 11th of ye 2nd mo 1786
To Menallen Monthly Meeting
Jesse Vore and Lydia his wife hath requested our Certificate in order to be joined to your meeting...as members we recommend them with their son Gidion...
Signed in and on behalf of our Meeting aforesaid by
                                                         Elisha Kirk Clerk
                                                       Hannah Matthews Clerk

#7 12th of 2nd mo 1787   **JESSE AND LYDIA VORE**
To York Monthly Meeting
The within Certificate for Jesse Vore and Lidia his wife and their son Gidion, was produced to our last Monthly Meeting it having been lost or mislaid for some time Which prevented it being produced to this Meeting in proper season and they having Removed to reside within the verge or your meeting...we Recommend them with their Daughter Hannah who was born since their Removal to you
Signed on behalf of Monallen Monthly Meeting held the 12th of the 2nd mo 1787   by Isaac Pearson Clerk
                                                        Martha Everit Clerk

#8 23rd of 4th mo 1788   **PETER YARNALL**
From our Monthly Meeting heald in York Town Pennsylvania by Adjournment on the 23rd of the 4th mo 1788
To our Friends and Brethren in Maryland:
Our esteemed Friend Peter Yarnall having informed us that he felt an engagement to pay a Religious visit to the meetings in your Governmente and attend your next yearly meeting we hereby Certifie he has our full unity Being a Minifter well approved amongst us.

Saml Fisher	Saml Updegraff	Wm Willis
Edward Stabler	Jacob Worley	Wm Matthews
Jonathan Jessop	Ambrose Updegraff	Joseph Updegraff
Enoch Underwood	John Love	Solomon Miller
Joel Willis	Timothy Kirk	Joseph Garretson
	Aron Coats	Wm Kersey
	Elisha Kirk	John Jones
	Wm Welch	

REMOVALS

#9 23rd of 4th mo 1788   **ANN JESSOP**

From York Monthly Meeting in York County Pennsylvania heald by adjournment the 23rd of the 4th mo 1788---
To New Garden monthly meeting in North Carolina
Our esteemed Friend Ann Jessop on her return from her Religious visit to Friends in Europe having been occasionally detained amongst us about six months past and now proposing to return to you we are free to inform that her service in the Ministry has been truly acceptable, Signed in and on behalf of our Meeting aforesaid.

Hannah Willis	Timothy Kirk	Wm Willis
Ruth Kirk	Aaron Coats	Wm Matthews
Hannah Matthews	Elisha Kirk	Joseph Updegraff
Lydia Updegraff	Wm Welch	Peter Yarnall
Mary Updegraff	Saml Fisher	Joseph Garretson
Mary Updegraff	Edward Stebler	Solomon Miller
Mary Kirk	Jonathan Jessop	Wm Kersey
Hannah Welch	Jesse Mathews	John Jones
Hannah Yarnal	Enoch Underwood	Herman Updegraff
Ann Worley	Joel Willis	Saml Updegraff
Ann Love		Jacob Worley
Sara Owen	Betty Jones	Ambrose Updegraff
Mary Thomas	Ruth Ragen	John Love

#10 19th of 4th mo 1788   **NATHAN PUSEY**

To Friends of York Monthly Meeting
Certificate for Nathan Pusey who by the Direction of his parents is an apprentice within the Verge of your meeting these may Certify on his behalf that he hath a birth Right amongst us: he being in his Minority as such we Recommend him to your care...Signed in and on behalf of Pipe Creek Mo. Meeting held at Bush Creek the 19th of 4th mo 1788   by Thomas Fargher Clerk

#11 2nd of 7th mo 1787   **MARY LOVE**

York Monthly Meeting held ye 2nd of 7th mo 1787
To Menallen Monthly Meeting
Request...by Mary Love...Frequently attended our religious Meetings, has settled her affairs and clear of Marriage engagements as far as appears as a Member we recommend her to your Christian Care...
by   Elisha Kirk Clerk
                                                                Hannah Garretson Clerk

#12 10th of 9th mo 1788   **THOMAS SPEAKMAN**

To Monallen Monthly Meeting
Thomas Speakman who some time past came Recommended to us by certificate from you, having requested our Certificate to be joined to your meeting again he being removed within the verge thereof...as far as we know left us clear of Marriage Engagements as such we recommend him...

WARRINGTON MONTHLY MEETING

Signed in and on behalf of York Monthly Meeting held the 10th of the 9th mo 1788 by Peter Yarnall Clerk at this time

#13 10th of 9th mo 1788   **JESSE & LYDIA VORE**
To the Monthly Meeting of Friends at Deer Creek.
Application hath been made for our certificate by Jesse Vore & Lydia his wife with their Daughter Hannah...we therefore Recommend them to your Christian care. Signed by order of York Monthly Meeting heald 10th of the 9th mo 1788   Peter Yarnall Clerk at this time

#14 27th of 10th mo 1786   **HANNAH JESSOP**
To the Monthly Meeting of Friends in York, York County.
Application was made at our laft Meeting for our certificate, for Hannah Jessop, Daughter of our Friend Ann Jessop, who is removed to reside within the compas of your meeting...as far as we know is clear of Marriage Engagements we recommend her...
Signed in and on behalf of our Monthly Meeting of Philadelphia the 27th of 10th mo 1786   John Field Clerk
     Magaret Haines

#15 15th of 10th mo 1787   **AN PENROSE JR**
To York Monthly Meeting
An Penrose Jr hath Requested our certificate to be joined in Membership with yours...is clear of debt and Marriage engagements as far as appears...we recommend her...Signed on behalf of Monallen Monthly Meeting heald the 15th of 10th mo 1787 by Isaac Pearson Cleark
     Martha Everitt Clerk

#16 30th of 9th mo 1786   **ENOCH UNDERWOOD**
To York Monthly Meeting in Pennsylvania
Enoch Underwood...requested our Certificate...to be joined to your meeting...clear of marriage Engagements as far as appears, as a member we Recommend him...Signed in and on behalf of Gunpowder Monthly Meeting held the 30th of ye 9th mo 1786
     by Joseph Townsend Clerk

#17 10th of 1st mo 1787   **RUTH KIRK**
Our Friend Ruth Kirk in a weighty manner spread before us a concern which has for some time rested on her mind to pay a Religious Visit to Friends of Pipe Creek Monthly Meeting and to their Families...she is left to her Liberty to proceed therein...she is a Minister in good Unity among us and Jacob Worley and Hannah Willis expressing a freedom to accompany her, they have the full approbation of this Meeting
Extracted from the Minutes of York Monthly Meeting held the 10th day of the 1st mo 1787.   Peter Yarnall.

REMOVALS

#18 17th of the 2nd mo 1787   **RUTH KIRK**
Copy of a Minute of Pipe Creek Monthly Meeting heald at Bush Creek the 17th of the 2nd mo 1787
Our esteemed Friend Ruth Kirk with her companions Jacob Worley and Hannah Willis, attended our last Monthly Meeting and Visited the Families of Friends at each particular Meeting, whose company and Labour of Love amongst us was exceptable and Satisfactory. The Clerke is directed to transmit a copy of this minute to York Monthly Meeting. Signed on behalf of this Meeting---
Extracted from the Minutes   Thomas Forker clerke
                                                                  Sarah Pusey clerk

#19 7th of 3rd mo 1787   **PETER YARNALL**
Peter Yarnall proposed to attend the spring Meeting of Ministers & Elders at Philadelphia, informed that he has likewise in prospect to attend the General Meeting at Wilmington, with which this Meeting concurs, leaving him at Liberty to attend to that or any other service on his way, as Truth may point out, he being a Minister in good esteem amongst us, the Clerk is directed to furnish him with a copy of this Minute---
Extracted from the Minutes of York Monthly Meeting held the 7th of ye 3rd mo 1787 by   Elisha Kirk clerk

#20 29th Day of 9th mo 1787   **AMOS SCOTT**
To York Monthly Meeting, Pennsylvania
Amos Scott being Removed within the Verge of your Meeting requests our Certificate...Clear of Marriage Engagements as far as appears, we therefore recommend him...
signed in and by order of our Monthly Meeting of Gunpowder heald this 29th Day of 9th mo 1787 by   Joseph Townsend clerk

#21 15th of 10th mo 1788   **SAMUEL JONES**
To the Monthly Meeting of Gunpowder
Samuel Jones having removed to Baltimore within the limmets of your Meeting and Requesting our Certificate to be joined to you...is clear of Debt and Marriage Engagements as far as appears, as a Member of our Religious society, we Recommend him...Signed by order of York Monthly Meeting held by adjournment the 15th of 10th mo 1788. Elisha Kirk Clerk

#22 15th of 10th mo 1788   **GEORGE PIERCE**
To Sadsbury Monthly Meeting
George Pierce who came recommended from your Meeting hath requested our Certificate in order to be joined to you again...is as far as we know clear of Debt and Marriage engagements as such we Recommend him Signed in and on behalf of York Monthly Meeting heald by Adjournment the 15th of 10th mo 1788. Elisha Kirk Clerk

WARRINGTON MONTHLY MEETING

#23 7th of 1st mo 1789   SUSANNA BENTLEY
To the Monthly Meeting of Warrington
Susanna Bentley having removed within the limmits of your Meeting, and requesting our certificate to you...we recommend...Signed by Order of York Monthly Meeting heald the 7th of 1st mo 1789.
by Elisha Kirk Clerk
        Hannah Yarnall Clerk

#24 6th of 5th mo 1789   WILLIAM MATTHEWS
To Friends of the Governments of New Jersey, New York and elsewhere to the Eastward:
Our Beloved Friend William Matthews having solidly spread before us a Concern he has felt for some time past to pay a Religious Visit to the Meetings in your Parts...he has our Concurrence to proceed therein as best wisdom may direct he being a Minister in good Unity with us...when his Service is over that he may be favourable to Return again to his Family and Friends with Peace in his own Mind --
Signed in and on behalf of York Monthly Meeting in Pennsylvania held the 6th day of the 5th Month 1789 by

Enoch Underwood	Saml Updegraff	Joseph Updegraff
Josiah Jordan	Jacob Norbury	Wm Willis
Eli Kirk	John Love	Solomon Miller
Saml Ballinger	Aaron Coats	Joseph Garretson
Jonathan Jessop	Ambrose Updegraff	Wm Kersey
Jodiah Hussey	Caleb Kirk	Jacob Worley
Joseph Kersey	Wm. McMunn	John Jones
	Saml Fisher	Harman Updegraff

#25 6th of 5th mo 1789   PETER YARNALL
To our Friends and Brethren in Maryland, the lower Counties on Delaware, New Jersey and elsewhere within the verge of our Yearly Meeting--
Our Beloved Friend Peter Yarnall having in a solid manner spread before us...to pay a religious visit; we were brought into a simpathy with him...he being a Minister well approved of amongst us and of an innocent life and conversation...we Recommend him to Divine protection, and your tender regard, and remain your loving Friends.
Signed in and on behalf of York Monthly Meeting in Pennsylvania held the 6th day of the 5th month 1789 by

Josiah Jordan	Jacob Norbury	Joseph Updegraff
Wm McMunn	Saml Updegraff	Wm Willis
Saml Ballinger	Aaron Coats	Solomon Miller
Jodiah Hussey	Saml Fisher	Joseph Garretson
Ambrose Updegraff	Eli Kirk	John Jones
Joseph Kersey	Caleb Kirk	Jacob Worley
	John Love	Wm Kersey
	Enoch Underwood	Herman Updegraff

REMOVALS

#26 6th of 5th mo 1789   WILLIAM MCMILLAN
To Warrington Monthly Meeting:
Request being made for a Certificate for William McMillan who served
as apprentiship with a Member of this Meeting & is returned to you
again...is Clear of Debt and Marriage Engagements as far as we know,
we therefore Recommend him...
Signed in and by Order of York Monthly Meeting held the 6th day of
the 5th mo 1789   by Wm Kersey.

#27 10th of 6th mo 1789   ENOCH UNDERWOOD
To the Monthly Meeting of Warrington
Enoch Underwood hath Requested Our Certificate to be joined to your
Meeting...clear of Debt and Marriage Engagements as far as appears as
a member of our Religious Society we recommend him...
Aproved by and Signed in York Monthly Meeting this 10th of the 6th
month 1789 by Elisha Kirk Clerk

#28 29th of 11th mo 1788   JOSIAH JORDAN
To the Monthly Meeting of Friends heald at York in Pennsylvania.
Dear Friends the occation of our wrighting to you at this time is on
account of Josiah Jordan who requested our Certificate to be joined
to your Meeting...clear of Marriage Engagements known to us, as such
we recommend him
Signed in and on Behalf of Crooked run Monthly Meeting held the 29th
Day of the 11th month 1788   by Goldsmith Chandler Clerk

#29 3rd of 4th mo 1789   LYDIA MILLER
To York Monthly Meeting in Pennsylvania
Lydia Miller hath requested a Certificate in order to be joined to
your Meeting...clear of marriage Engagements known to us, we
Recommend her to your Christian care...Signed in and on behalf of
Crooked Run Monthly Meeting held at Center the 3rd Day of the 4th mo
1789   by Goldsmith Chandler Clerk
                                          Eunice Allen Clerk

#30 27th of 5th mo 1789   PETER YARNALL
Our Esteemed friend Peter Yarnall attended Our Last Quarterly Meeting
and Produced a few lines from York Monthly Meeting in Pennsylvania,
Setting forth friends unity with his Draft of Visiting Some meetings
hereaway and he having attended several Meetings with the Verge of
this Quarter his Company & Religious Labours of love hath been
Acceptable, the Clerk is directed to forward a copy of this minute to
that Monthly Meeting. Extracted from the Minutes of Fairfax
Quarterly Meeting held the 27th of the 5th mo 1789.
     James Mendenhall Clerk

WARRINGTON MONTHLY MEETING

#31 18th of 10th mo 1789   **ASA PLUMER**
To the Monthly Meeting of Friends at York
Whereas Asa Plumer is plased an apprentice to Eli Kirk a member of your meeting thefe may inform you he has a birthright amongst us, he being in his minority, as a member we Recommend him...signed in and on behalf of Pipe Creek Monthly Meeting held at Bush Creek the 18th Day of 10th month 1788   by Thomas Farquar clerk

#32 14th of 2nd mo 1789   **SAMUEL BALLINGER**
To York Monthly Meeting in Pennsylvania
Request being made to us for a few lines by way of Certificate for Samuel Ballinger who is placed an apprentice to John Love a member of your meeting after the needfull Enquiry we don't find anny thing to obstruct, he being a member in his minority we recommend him to your care desiring his welfare from Pipe Creek Monthly Meeting held the 14th of yr 2nd mo 1789.
Signed in and by order of said meeting by Thomas Farquar Clerk.

#33 5th of 8th mo 1789   **JESSE MILHOUS**
To Philadelphia Monthly Meeting--
    Jesse Milhous who some time past went to Reside in Philadelphia hath Requested our certificate to be joined to you...he is clear of Marriage Engagements amongst us, we recommend him...
Signed in and on Behalf of our Monthly Meeting of York held the 5th Day of 8th mo 1789   by Elisha Kirk Clerk

#34 5th of 8th mo 1789   **JOSIAH & LYDIA JORDAN**
To the Monthly Meeting of Kennet
Josiah Jordan and Lydia his wife Requested our certificate to be joined to your Meeting...we therefore recommend them as Members Signed by Order of York Monthly Meeting held the 5th of the 8th mo 1789.   by Elisha Kirk Clerk
            Hannah Yarnall Clerk

#35 19th of 8th mo 1789   **PETER YARNALL**
To Friends in the Southern Governments
Our beloved friend Peter Yarnall having spread before us a prospect which has attended his mind of paying a Religious visit to Friends in some parts of North Carolina and likewise to the Inhabitants in some places on his journeys thither, and particularly in the western parts of this Government--which after solid deliberation we unite with and leave him at liberty to attend to...he being a minister well approved amongst us...we recommend him to Divine protection and your tender regard and subscribe ourselves your loving Friends
                Signed in and on behalf of York Monthly Meeting in Pennsylvania held by adjournment the 19th of 8th mo 1789 by

REMOVALS

Caleb Kirk	John Jones	Wm Willis
Wm McMunn	Saml Updegraff	Wm Matthews
Eli Kirk	Aaron Coats	Joseph Updegraff
Jonathan Jessop	Elisha Kirk	Solomon Miller
Saml Ballinger	John Love	Joseph Garretson
Jos Edmundson	Ambrose Updegraff	Jacob Worley

#36 18th of 3rd mo 1789   WILLIAM MATTHEWS
To Friends of Maryland and Virginia
Our esteemed friend William Matthews having informed this Meeting that he hath for many months past felt a draft of Love to pay a Religious Visit to some of the Inhabitants of the western parts of your governments and requested our Certificate for that purpose...we therefore Recommend him to your brotherly sympathy and regard desiring his return to us when his Service is accomplished with the Reward of Peace
Signed in and on Behalf of York Monthly Meeting of Friends held by adjournment the 18th day of the 3rd mo 1789 by

Elisha Kirk	Daniel Ragen	Wm Willis
Eli Kirk	Wm Welch	Joseph Garretson
Aaron Coats	Ambrose Updegraff	Solomon Miller
Jonathan Jessop	Caleb Kirk	Joseph Updegraff
	Jacob Worley	John Jones

#37 9th of 8th mo 1788   THOMAS EDMUNDSON
To York Monthly Meeting
Thomas Edmundson hath Requested our Certificate in order to be joined to your Meeting within the verge whereof he is placed an apprentice these may inform that he hath a birthright amongst Friends, he being young we need not Say much Concerning him, but Recommend him...
Signed in and on Behalf of Warrington monthly Meeting heald ye 9th day of 8th mo 1788 -by Peter Clever Clerk

#38 9th of 12th mo 1789   JESSE MATTHEWS
To the Monthly Meeting of Gunpowder
Jesse Matthews having Requested our Certificate to be joined to your Meeting...clear of marriage Engagements as far as appears, as a member of our Religious Society we recommend him
Signed in and by order of York Monthly Meeting heald the 9th of the 12th mo 1789. by Elisha Kirk clerk

#39 30th of 5th mo 1789   RACHEL MASON
To the Monthly Meeting of Friends at York in Pennsylvania
These may certify that Rachel Mason has been for some time with her husband settled within the compass of your meeting having requested our certificate in order to be joined thereto...as a member in unity with us we recommend her with Elizabeth her daughter in her minority

WARRINGTON MONTHLY MEETING

Signed by order of Gunpowder Monthly Meeting held 30th of 5th mo 1789 by Joseph Townsend clerk
                              Rachel Price Clerk

#40 11th of 1st mo 1789   JACOB NORBURY
From Warrington Monthly Meeting held the 11th 1st mo 1789 to York Monthly Meeting
Jacob Norbury Requested our Certificate in order to be joined to your Meeting...we recommend him...by Peter Cleaver clerk

#41 7th of 10th mo 1789   SARAH MILLER
To the Monthly Meeting of Horsham
Sarah Miller having lately Removed within the compass of your meeting, and Requests our certificate to you on that account...She frequently attended our Religious Meetings, clear of Marriage Engagements...we Recommend her...Signed by Order of York Monthly Meeting held the 7th of the 10th mo 1789
        by John Love clerk at this time
        Lydia Updegraff clerk at this time

#42 10th of 10th mo 1789   RACHEL HUTTON
From our Monthly Meeting of Warrington held this 10th Day of the 10th mo 1789 to Friends of York Monthly Meeting
Rachel Hutton Requested our Certificate for her self and children in order to be joined to your meeting...as a member we recommend her and her four children, Sarah, Isaiah, Elijah, and Betty...
Signed by Order of our aff'd Meeting by Peter Cleaver Clerk
                            Susanna Cleaver Clerk

#43 31st of 10th mo 1789   SAMUEL JONES
To York Monthly Meeting in Pennsylvania
Samuel Jones having returned to reside within the verge of your meeting, hath requested our Certificate to be joined thereto...is clear of marriage engagements known to us...we recommend him...Signed on behalf of Gunpowder Monthly Meeting, held the 31st of 10th month 1789
                By-- David Brown Clerk

#44 18th of 12th mo 1789   SIDNY COATS
To York Monthly Meeting
The ocasion of our wrighting to you at this time is on account of Sidny Coats, a miner who is returned to Live with her Parents within the verge of your Meeting, she being young we think it needless to say much but recommend her to your care and oversight Signed in and on behalf of Bradford Monthly Meeting held the 18th Day of the 12th mo 1789   by Isaac Coats Clerk
        Magaret Mendinghall Clerk at this time.

REMOVALS

#45 6th of 5th mo 1789   PETER YARNALL
[Duplicate of No. 25]

#46 15th of 1st mo 1790   SAMUEL COATS
To York Monthly Meeting
Saml Coats a member of our Meeting having returned to live amongst you Requested our Certificate. We therefore inform that he hath served out his apprentiship and it dont appear but that he hath conducted in a good Degree orderly, hath attended our religious Meetings, hath left no affairs unsettled, and is clear of Marriage engagements amongst us, We recommend him...
Signed at Bradford Monthly Meeting held the 15th of 1st mo 1790
On behalf thereof by   Isaac Coats Clerk

#47 10th of 3rd mo 1790   BEAULAH STANDLY
To Gwyned Monthly Meeting
Request hath been made for our certificate for Beaulah Standly who is Removed within the compass of your Meeting...is clear of marriage engagements...we recommend her...
Signed in and on behalf of York Monthly Meeting held the 10th of the 3rd mo 1790 by   John Love clerk at this time
                    Mary Updegraff clerk at this time

#48 4th of 8th mo 1790   JOSEPH EDMUNDSON
To Warrington Monthly Meeting
Joseph Edmundson Junior Requested our Certificate in order to be joined to your meeting...is clear of Debt and Marriage engagements...we recommend him...
Signed in and by order of our Monthly Meeting held at York this 4th day of the eighth month 1790 by Ambrose Updegraff clerk

#49 4th of 8th mo 1790   RACHEL MASON
To the Monthly Meeting of Friends at Gunpowder
Rachel Mason having removed with her husband within the compass of your meeting, and requested our certificate to be joined thereto...we recommend her with her Daughter Elizabeth (in her minority)...
Signed in and by order of our Monthly Meeting at York held the 4th of ye 8th mo 1790 by   Ambrose Updegraff clerk

#50 14th of 6th mo 1790   JONATHAN WRIGHT
To York Monthly Meeting
Jonathan Wright having placed his son Thomas an apprentice within the verge of your meeting, requests our certificate for him...we recommend him to your care...
Signed in and on behalf of Monallen Monthly Meeting held the 14th of the 6th mo 1790   by Joseph Grist

WARRINGTON MONTHLY MEETING

#51 16th of 7th mo 1790   JESSE & ELIZA KERSEY
To York Monthly Meeting
Application being made by Jesse & Eliza Kersey members of our Meeting for a certificate in order to join to yours, they being removed within the verge thereof...we therefore Recommend them to your Christian care...Signed in and on behalf of Bradford Monthly Meeting held the 16th of 7th mo 1790   Isaac Coats clerk
                                            Margaret Marshall clerk

#52 7th of 9th mo 1790   SAMUEL COATS
To Bradford Monthly Meeting
Request hath been made for a certificate for Samuel Coats who is Removed within the compass of your meeting...is clear of Debt and Marriage engagements as far as appears, as a member we Recommend him...
Signed by order of York Monthly Meeting held the 7th of the 9th mo 1790   by Ambrose Updegraff clerk

#53 8th of 12th mo 1790   JAMES MCMULLIN
To Warrington Monthly Meeting.
James McMullin a member of our Meeting, hath Removed within the verge of yours and hath Requested our Certificate to be joined to you...clear of Debt and Marriage Engagements known to us--we Recommend him
Signed in and on Behalf of York Monthly Meeting held the Eight Day of the twelfth mo 1790

#54 4th of 5th mo 1791   SAMUEL BALLENGER
To Warrington Monthly Meeting
Samuel Ballenger a Member of our Meeting, requested our Certificate in order to be joined to yours, he being removed within the Verge thereof...free of Debt and Marriage engagements as far as appears. We recommend him to your religious care.
Signed in and on behalf of York Monthly Meeting held the 4th of the 5th mo 1791   by Ambrose Updegraff clerk

#55 26th of 2nd mo 1791   JAMES JANNEY
To York Monthly Meeting
Application being made to us for a Certificate for James Janney, a young lad, who put an apprentice to a friend of your Meeting these may certify that he is of a sober life, conversation and was frequently seen at our Meeting, he being young we recommend him...
Signed in and on behalf of Nottingham Monthly Meeting the 26th of the 2nd mo 1791.   by Jeremiah Brown clerk.

#56 18th of 2nd mo 1791   HANNAH COATES
From Bradford Monthly Meeting held the 18th Day of the 2nd month 1791 To York Monthly Meeting

REMOVALS

Hannah Coates Who is a member of our Meeting and now Residing within the verge of yours Requested a certificate in order to become a member thereof...is clear of Debt and Marriage engagements for ought appears, We recommend her...
Signed in and on behalf of our afforesaid Meeting
      by Isaac Coats Clerk
       Margaret Marshall clerk

#57 10th of 8th mo 1791   PETER & HANNAH YARNALL
To Horsham Monthly Meeting
Peter Yarnall and Hannah his wife members of our Meeting Requested our Certificate for themselves & children in order to be joined to yours...he being a Minister well approved amongst us...We recommend them and their four children Namely Mordecai, Rebeccah, Isaac and Peter...
Signed in and by order of York Monthly Meeting Held the 10th of the 8th mo 1791 by Ambrose Updegraff clerk
      Mary Updegraff clerk at this time

#58 9th of 10th mo 1791   SOLOMON MILLER
To Abington Monthly Meeting
Solomon Miller a Member of our Meeting, hath Requested a Certificate in order for Marriage with Hannah Jenkins, a member of yours... We recommend him to your Christian Care in the accomplishment of his Weighty undertaking and are your Friends.
Signed in and by order of York Monthly Meeting held 9th of 10th mo 1791 by Ambrose Updegraff clerk

#59 7th of 9th mo 1791   JOHN WORLEY
To Westland Monthly Meeting
John Worley having Requested our Certificate in order to be joined to your Meeting...is clear of Debt and Marriage Engagements so far as appears, he being a member of Our Religious Society we Recommend him...
    Signed in and by order of York Monthly Meeting held the 7th of the 9th mo 1791
     by Ambrose Updegraff clerk

#60 8th of 1st mo 1790   JOEL AND HANNAH WILLIS
To Newgarden Monthly Meeting, North Carolina
Joel Willis and Hannah his wife members of our Monthly Meeting who obtained a minute dated _____ in order to accompany their Mother on her Return home and is since settled within the compass of your meeting...we therefore Recommend them with their two Children viz Lydia and Jonathan to your Christian Care...
Signed in and by Order of York Monthly Meeting held the 8th Day of the 1st mo 1790   by Ambrose Updegraff
          Hannah Yarnall   clerks

WARRINGTON MONTHLY MEETING

#61 4th of 1st mo 1792   ANN UPDEGRAFF
To the Monthly Meeting of Westland
Ann Updegraff hath Requested our Certificate for her self and three
Children Namely Eli, Edith and Ann to be Directed to your Meeting,
she Living within the Verge thereof...clear of Debt and Marriage
Engagements known to us, we therefore Recommend her with her children
          Signed in and by order of York Monthly Meeting held the 4th
of the 1st mo 1792   by Ambrose Updegraff clerk
                      Mary Updegraff clerk at this time

#62 9th of 11th mo 1791   BETTY UPDEGRAFF
To Westland Monthly Meeting
Betty Updegraff Requests our Certificate to be joined to your meeting
...Often attended our Religious Meetings considering the Distance she
lived from us. Is clear of Debt and Marriage engagements known to us.
We therefor Recommend her...
Signed in and by Order of York Monthly Meeting held the 9th of 11th
mo 1791   by Ambrose Updegraff clerk
                 Mary Updegraff clerk at this time

#63 7th of 3rd mo 1790   SOLOMON MILLER
To Abington Monthly Meeting
Solomon Miller a member of our Meeting having requested our
certificate in order to be joined to yours...we recommend him...
Signed in and by order of York Mo. Meeting held the 7th of 3rd mo
1790   By Ambrose Updegraff clerk

#64 8th of 8th mo 1792   JAMES JANNEY
To Nottingham Monthly Meeting
Request having been made for a certification for James Janney a
member of our meeting who has returned to live within the limits of
yours...Being young We think it unnecessary to add further but
recommend him to your Christian Care...
Signed in and on behalf of York Monthly Meeting held the 8th of the
8th mo 1792   by Ambrose Updegraff

#65 20th of 7th mo 1792   AMOS GRIFFITH
To Warrington Monthly Meeting
Amos Griffith a member of our Meeting having requested our
certificate in order to be joined to yours...he being young we think
it Unnecessary to add further but Recommend him to your Religious
Care...
Signed in and on behalf of York Monthly Meeting held the 20th of 7th
mo 1792   by Ambrose Updegraff Clerk

REMOVALS

#66 10th of 10th mo 1792   THOMAS WRIGHT
To Monallen Monthly Meeting
Thomas Wright having Requested our Certificate in order to be joined
to your Meeting...is clear of debt and Marriage Engagements known to
us. He being a member of our Religious society We recommend him...
Signed in and on behalf of York Monthly Meeting held the 10th of the
10th month 1792   by Ambrose Updegraff

#67 19th of 9th mo 1792   JAMES AND ELIZABETH WRIGHT
From Sadsbury Monthly Meeting held the 19th Day of the 9th month 1792
--To the Monthly Meeting of York
James Wright and Elizabeth his Wife having Requested our Certificate
for themselves and their child Rhoda Wright in order to be joined to
your meeting they living within the Verge thereof...they have been
frequenters of the Meeting held at Susquehanna We have no reason to
believe but his outward affairs are well circumstanced The child
being young we recommend it with its parents to your Christian care
            Signed in and on behalf of our said Meeting
            by James Cooper Jr. Clerk
            Mary Smith clerk

#68 9th of 1st mo 1793   MARY THOMAS
To Monalin Monthly Meeting
Mary Thomas Requested our Certificate to be joined to your
Meeting...clear of Marriage Engagements as far as appears as a member
in Unity we recommend her...
      Signed in and on behalf of York Monthly Meeting held the 9th of
the 1st mo 1793   by Ambrose Updegraff clerk
                             Ann Love Clerk

#69 19th of 9th mo 1792   JAMES AND LYDIA MOORE
From Sadsbury Monthly Meeting held the 19th day of the 9th mo 1792
To the Monthly Meeting of York
James Moore and Lydia his Wife have requested our certificate for
themselves and their four children to wit Abraham, Hesther, Lydia,
and Anna Moore, in order to be joined to your Meeting they being
removed within the verge thereof...the children being young we
recommend them with their parents to your Christian Care
Signed in and on behalf of our said Meeting
            by James Cooper Jr clerk
            Mary Smith clerk

#70 13th of 10th mo 1792   THOMAS HOLLAND
From Worington Monthly Meeting held the 13th of the 10th mo 1792
To York Monthly Meeting
Request being made for a few lines by way of certificate for Thomas
Holland (a minor) who is placed an apprentice with the verge of your
Meeting he being young we don't think it Needful to say much

WARRINGTON MONTHLY MEETING

concerning him but recommend him as a member of our Society to your Christian Care and oversight...
Signed in and on behalf of our Meeting by
John Cleaver clerk at this time

#71 26th of 2nd mo 1791   WILLIAM MOORE
From Gunpowder Monthly Meeting in Maryland held the 26th of the 2nd month 1791
To York Monthly Meeting in Pennsylvania
The occation of our Wrighting to you is on behalf of William Moore (son of John) he being placed as an apprentice to a member of your meeting and he being in his minority we cannot say much but as a member we recommend him to your Christian Care...
Signed on behalf of Said Meeting   by   David Brown clerk

#72 17th of 2nd mo 1791   LYDIA JORDAN
To York Monthly Meeting
Lydia the wife of Josiah Jordan being returned to you again hath Requested our Certificate in order to be joined to your Meeting...We Recommend her to your Christian Care...Signed in and on behalf of Kennet Monthly Meeting held the 17th of the 2nd mo 1791
        by Reberd Lamborn Jr clerk
        Ruth Nichols clerk at this time

#73 10th of 8th mo 1791   HANNAH COATS
From Bradford Monthly Meeting held the 10th day of 8th month 1791
To York Monthly Meeting
Hannah Coats, who is a member of our Meeting and is residing within the verge of yours Requested a certificate In order to become a Member thereof...is clear of Debt and Marriage Engagements for ought appears we commend her...
Signed in and on Behalf of our afforesaid Meeting by
        Isaac Coats   Clerk
        Margaret Marshall   clerk

#74 1st of 9th mo 1792   REBECCA SHARPLESS
To York Monthly Meeting
Rebecca Sharpless, having settled within the verge of your meeting, requested a certificate in order to be joined thereto...she left us clear of Debt and Marriage Engagements; we Recommend her...
Signed in and on behalf of New Garden Monthly Meeting the 1st of the 9th month 1792   by David Wilson clerk
        Hannah Lindley   clerk

#75 25th of 6th mo 1791   ISAAC GARRETSON
To York Monthly Meeting
Isaac Garretson having removed from hence and settled within the verge of your Meeting and having made application to us for our

REMOVALS

Certificate in order to be joined thereto...is clear of Marriage contracts...We therefore recommend him to your care and oversight... Signed in and by order of Fairfax Monthly Meeting held the 25th of the 6th month 1791   Wm Stabler clerk

#76 27th of 7th mo 1790   ISAAC STRAHL
From Robeson Monthly Meeting held the 27th of ye 7th mo 1790
To the Monthly Meeting of friends in little York
Application having been Made to this Meeting for a Certificate for Isaac Strahl to your Meeting...Clear of debt and Mariage Engagements as far as appears as Such we recommend him...
Signed in and on behalf of the Monthly Meeting afforesaid
          by Isaac Bansall clerk

#77 18th of 2nd mo 1791   JONATHAN MENDENHALL
To York Monthly Meeting
Request being made by Moses Mendenhall for a certificate for his son Jonathan who is placed an apprentice within your verge...we therefore Recommend him to your Christian Care...Signed in and by order of Bradford Monthly Meeting held the 18th of the 2nd month 1791   by Isaac Coats clerk

#78 10th of 9th mo 1790   AMOUS GRIFFITH
From Warrington Monthly Meeting held the 10th of ye 9th mo 1790
to York Monthly Meeting
Application was made for a certificate to your meeting for Amous Griffith a minor he being put an apprentice to John Bentley who is a member we Recommend him to your Notice and care...
                        by Peter Cleaver clerk

#79 8th of 9th mo 1792   REBECCA BLAIR
From our Monthly Meeting of Warrington held the 8th of 9th mo 1792
To the Monthly Meeting of friends at York
Rebecca Blair requested our Certificate in order to be joined to your Meeting. She, being settled within the verge thereof now...we recommend her to your Christian Care...
Signed in and on behalf of ye meeting by Peter Cleaver clerk
                                      Susanna Cleaver clerk

#80 6th of 6th mo 1792   ANN BENNET
To Kennet Monthly Meeting
Ann Bennet a Member of our Meeting having requested our Certificate in order to be joined to yours...is clear of Debt and Marriage Engagements
Signed in and on behalf of York Monthly Meeting held the 6th of the 6th month 1792   by Ambrose Updegraff clerk
                  Hannah Welch clerk at this time

WARRINGTON MONTHLY MEETING

#81 14th of 4th mo 1792   BENJAMIN BENSON
To York Monthly Meeting Pennsylvania
Benjamin Benson requested our Certificate for himself Hannah his wife and their following named children (viz) Abraham; Reuben; Elizabeth; Amos; Levi; Benjamin; Hannah; and Jesse to be joined to your Meeting...we Recommend them...
Signed in and on behalf of Pipe Creek Mo Meeting held at Bush Creek the 14th of 4th mo 1792   Wm Kenworthy Jr
                              Mary Ballinger clerk

#82 21st of 7th mo 1790   MARY COPE
From Sadsbury Monthly Meeting held the 21st of the 7th mo 1790 to the Monthly Meeting of York
Mary Cope wife of John Cope requested our certificate for herself and two children to wit, Lydia and Harman Cope to be joined to your meeting she being removed within the verge thereof.
...The Children being young we Recommend them with their Mother...
Signed in and on behalf of our said meeting.
             by Wm Brinton clerk
                Deborah Gest clerk

#83 12th of 5th mo 1792   AARON FRAZOR
To york Monthly Meeting
The occation of our Writing to you at this time is on account of Aaron Frazor a Minor he being placed an apprentice within the verge of your Meeting...he hath right amongst us as such we recommend him...Giving forth at our Monthly Meeting held at Warrington the 12th Day of the 5th mo 1792 and
signed in and on behalf of the same
               by Peter Cleaver clerk

#84 11th of 9th mo 1790   JOHN BENTLEY
From Warrington Monthly Meeting held the 11th of the 9th mo 1790
To York Monthly Meeting
John Bentley and Susanna his wife requested our Certificate to yours...we recommend them...
Directed to be signed   by   Peter Cleaver clerk
                           Susanna Cleaver clerk

#85 21st of 4th mo 1790   PETER YARNALL
To our friends and Brethren in Pennsylvania and New Jersey
Our esteemed friend Peter Yarnall informed us that he has for some time had a prospect of paying a religious visit to some parts of this Government and New Jersey more espetially in and about the City of Philadelphia and the families of friends of Darby Meeting which being Solidly Considered by us is united with he being a Minister well approved of amongst us Examplary in his Life and conversation...

REMOVALS

Signed in and on behalf of York Monthly Meeting held by adjournment the 21st of the 4th mo 1790
by John Love clerk at this time

#86 6th of 2nd mo 1793   JEDIAH HUSSEY
To Newgarden Monthly Meeting North Carolina
Jediah Hussey hath requested our Certificate in order to be joined to your Meeting...is clear of marriage engagements known to us, as a member of our Religious Society we recommend him
signed in and on behalf of York Monthly Meeting held the 6th of the 2nd mo 1793   by Ambrose Updegraff clerk

#87 6th of 2nd mo 1793   MARY MILLER
To Abington Monthly Meeting
Mary Miller having settled within the verge of your meeting requests a certificate in order to be joined thereto...she is clear of Debt and Marriage engagements as a member we recommend her
Signed in and by order of York Monthly Meeting held the 6th of the 2nd mo 1793   by Ambrose Updegraff   clerk
                            Ann Love clerk

#88 10th of 7th mo 1793   JOHN STRALL
To Exeter Monthly Meeting
John Strall and Ann his Wife members of our Meeting having removed and settled within the limits of your meeting...we recommend them with their two children Mary and Rebekah
Signed in and on behalf of York Monthly Meeting held the 10th of the 7th mo 1793   By   Eli Kirk clerk
                            Ann Love   clerk

#89 10th of 4th mo 1793   THOMAS EDMUNDSON
To Warrington Monthly Meeting
Thomas Edmundson having removed within the compass of your Meeting, requests our Certificate to be joined thereto...clear of debt and marriage engagements as far as appears as a Member of our religious society we recommend him...
Signed in and on behalf of York Monthly Meeting held the 10th of the fourth mo 1793   By Ambrose Updegraff clerk at this time

#90 7th of 8th mo 1793   JOHN BENTLEY
To Warrington Monthly Meeting
John Bentley and Susanna his wife Members of our Meeting hath requested our Certificate in order to be joined to yours...we recommend them...
Signed in and on behalf of York Monthly Meeting held the 7th of the 8th mo 1793   By   Eli Kirk   clerk
                            Ann Love   clerk

WARRINGTON MONTHLY MEETING

#91 1st mo 30th 1793   ANN STRALL
To York Monthly Meeting in Pennsylvania
Application made to us by our friend Ann Strall who is settled within
the limits of your said meeting for a certificate to join you...we
recommend her to you as a member in society
Signed in and by order of our monthly meeting held in Guynedd the 1st
mo 30th 1793   By Jesse' Foulk and
                                         Pricilla Foulk clerks

#92 12th of 6th mo 1793   HANNAH PHILLIPS
To the monthly meeting of Friends little York Pennsylvania
Request having been made for a certificate for Hannah Phillips to
unite her to your meeting...is clear of any engagements on account of
marriage known to us--as such we recommend
Signed in and on behalf of Wilmington Monthly Meeting held the 12th
of the 6th mo 1793   by Samuel Canby clerk at this time
                                    Rebecca Wood clerk

#93 21st of 2nd mo 1793   JOHN WOLLAS HOPKINS
To the Monthly Meeting of Friends at York Town
Application having been made for a certificate for John Wollas
Hopkins a minor who is placed an apprentice to a friend within the
compass of your meeting...we find nothing to obstruct he having right
of membership amongst friends we recommend him...
Signed in and on behalf of Deer Creek Monthly Meeting in Maryland the
21st of 2nd mo 1793
            by   John Wilson clerk at this time

#94 11th of 3rd mo 1793   CALEB BRACHAN
To York Monthly Meeting
Application being made by Caleb Brachen for our certificate to your
meeting...clear of marriage engagements as far as appears as a member
we recommend him
Signed in and on behalf of Monalon Monthly Meeting the 11th of 3rd mo
1793   by Jonathan - ? -   clerk

#95 10th of 4th mo 1793   ISAAC STRALL
To Exeter Monthly Meeting
Isaac Strall requested our certificate to be joined to your Meeting,
he having removed within the compass thereof...clear of Marriage
engagements as far as appears as a member of our religious society we
recommend him...
Signed in and on behalf of York Monthly Meeting held the 10th of 4th
mo 1793   by   Ambrose Updegraff clerk at this time

#96 5th of 6th mo 1793   DAVID HURST
To Goose Creek Monthly Meeting

REMOVALS

David Hurst a member of our Meeting requested our Certificate to be joined to yours he being removed within the verge thereof...clear of debt and Marriage engagements as far as appears. We recommend him to your religious care
Signed in and on behalf of York Monthly Meeting Held the 5th of 6th mo 1793   by   Eli Kirk   clerk

#97 12th of 6th mo 1793   DEBORAH PHILLIPS
To the Monthly Meeting of Friends of Little York Pennsylvania
A certificate having been requested to join your meeting--Deborah Phillips--this may inform you that she hath a right of membership amongst us but being in her minority think it unnecessary to say further then to recommend her to your religious care
signed in and on behalf of Wilmington Monthly Meeting held the 12th of 6th mo 1793   by Samuel Canby clerk at this time
                         Rebekah Wood   clerk

#98 27th of 10th mo 1793   ANN JESSOP
From our Monthly Meeting of Newgarden in North Carolina Guilford County held the 27th of the 10th mo 1793
To the Monthly Meeting of York Town Pennsylvania
Our friend Ann Jessop informs us that she had a mind to travel into your parts about business and to see her friends and relations and requested our certificate...she is a member of our Meeting and is a Member in Unity as such we recommend her...signed in and on behalf of the aforesaid Meeting
          By   Enoch Masy clerk
               Mary Harbuch clerk

#99 4th of 9th mo 1793   ANN JESSOP
(the above Certificate was endorsed as follows viz)
To Newgarden Monthly Meeting
Our Esteemed friend Ann Jessop produced the within certificate to this meeting the 9th of the first month last and now proposes to return to you again--these may inform that whilst amongst us she was a diligent attender of our Religious Meetings Her life and conversation orderly and her Ministry lively and edifying and on enquiry it appears that her outward affairs are settled to sattisfaction.
Signed in and on behalf of York Monthly Meeting held the 4th of 9th mo 1793   By   Eli Kirk   clerk
                       Ann Love   clerk

#100 5th of 2nd mo 1794   JAMES UPDEGRAFF
To Redstone Monthly Meeting
James Updegraff a member of our Meeting having requested a Certificate in order to be joined to yours...pretty frequently attended our religious meetings considering his remote situation from

them, has settled his outward affairs to satisfaction, is clear of debt and marriage engagements known to us--as such we recommend him...
Signed in and on behalf of York Monthly Meeting held the 5th day of 2nd mo 1792   by Eli Kirk clerk

#101 4th of 12th mo 1793   ASA PLUMMER
To South River Monthly Meeting in Virginia
Asa Plummer a member of our Meeting requests a certificate in order to be joined to yours...clear of Debt and marriage engagements as far as appears--We recommend him
Signed in and on behalf of york Monthly Meeting (in Pennsylvania) held the fourth day of the twelfth month 1793
            By Eli Kirk

#102 9th of 4th mo 1794   JESSE KERSEY
To Bradford Monthly Meeting
Jesse Kersey and Elizabeth his wife having removed in order to settle within the Verge of your Meeting requested our Certificate to be joined theirto...He being an approved minster in good esteem amongst us, as such we recommend them with their two Children to wit Hannah and Lydia Kersey   Signed in and on behalf of York M Meeting held the 9th day of the fourth Month 1794
                by Eli Kirk clerk
                Ann Love

#103 9th of 4th mo 1794   HANNAH COATS
To Bradford Monthly Meeting
Hannah Coats a member of our meeting, having requested our certificate in order to be joined to yours...is clear of Debt and Marriage engagements known to us and as such we recommend her
Signed in and on behalf of York M Meeting held the 9th day of the fourth month 1794   by Eli Kirk
                Ann Love

#104 9th of 1st mo 1794   AARON FRAZIER
To Bradford Monthly Meeting
Aaron Frazier having removed with his Master Jesse Kersey to settle within the verge of your Meeting request was made for a certificate in order for him to be joined theirto...he has a right of Membership amongst us--he being in his Minority we recommend him   Signed in and on behalf of York Monthly Meeting held the 9th Day of the 1st mo 1794
            by Eli Kirk clerk

#105 9th of the 4th mo 1794   JONATHAN MENDENHALL
To Bradford Monthly Meeting

REMOVALS

Jonathan Mendenhall having removed with his Master Jesse Kersey to settle within the verge of your Meeting request was made for a certificate in order for him to be joined theirto...he has a right of Membership amongst us--he being in his Minority, we recommend him
Signed in and on behalf of York Monthly Meeting held the 9th day of the 4th mo 1794
By Eli Kirk clerk

#106 6th of 8th mo 1794   RUTH WALMSLEY
To Horsham Monthly Meeting
...Ruth Walmsley a member of our meeting having removed with her husband and settled within the verge of your meeting hath requested our Certificate...is a Minister in good esteem amongst us and hath settled her outward affairs to satisfaction as far as appears, we recommend her with her Daughter, Priscilla Kirk as members...
Signed in and on behalf of York Monthly Meeting held the 6th of the 8th mo 1794   By   Eli Kirk clerk
                                Ann Love clerk

#107 6th of 8th mo 1794   ANN PENROSE
To Horsham Monthly Meeting
Ann Penrose a member of our Meeting hath removed and settled within the verge of yours, hath requested our Certificate...is clear of Debt or Marriage engagements known to us, as such we recommend her...
Signed in and by order of York Monthly Meeting held the 6th of the 8th Mo 1794   By   Eli Kirk clerk
                                Ann Love   clerk

#108 26th of 9th mo 1794   BENJAMIN UNDERWOOD
To York Monthly Meeting
Request being made on behalf of Benjamin Underwood a minor placed an apprentice with a member of your Meeting...he is a member amongst us --as such we recommend him
Signed in and by direction of our Monthly Meeting held the 26th of the 9th mo 1794   By   John Cox clerk

#109 8th of 10th mo 1794   BENJAMIN UNDERWOOD
To Redstone Monthly Meeting
The within Certificate for Benjamin Underwood was produced to our last Monthly Meeting but he being removed with his Master Abner Updegraff to settle within the verge of your Meeting we recommend him to your Christian care and oversight
Signed in and on behalf of York Monthly Meeting held the 8th of the 10th mo 1794   By   Eli Kirk

#110 6th of 8th mo 1794   JAMES WRIGHT
To Sadsbury Monthly Meeting

WARRINGTON MONTHLY MEETING

James Wright and Elizabeth his wife having removed to settle within the verge of your meeting requested our certificate in order to be joined theirto...they attended our Religious meeting at times...his outward affairs are settled to satisfaction--we therefore recommend them with their Daughter Rhoda to your Christian Care...
Signed in and on behalf of York Monthly Meeting held the 6th of the 8th mo 1794   By   Eli Kirk clerk
                                         Ann Love   clerk

#111 14th of 11th mo 1793   THOMAS MOORE
To York Monthly Meeting
Thomas Moore and Dinah his wife being about to settle within the limits of your meeting require our certificate to be joined theirto... we recommend them...
Signed in and on behalf of Kennet Mo Meeting held 14th of 11th mo 1793   by Robert Lamborn Jr clerk
              Martha Lamborn   clerk

#112 22nd of 1st mo 1794   SAMUEL MOORE
To the Monthly Meeting of York
Samuel Moore has requested our Certificate in order to be joined to your Meeting he being removed within the verge thereof...We recommend him...
Signed in and on behalf of Sadsbury M. Meeting held the 22nd Day of 1st mo 1794   by   James Cooper clerk

#113 12th of 12th mo 1793   LYDIA MOORE
From our Monthly Meeting of Kennet held the 12th of the 12th mo 1793
To York Monthly Meeting
Lydia the wife of Saml Moore, requested our certificate in order to be joined to your meeting she being removed to life within the verge thereof...we recommend her...
Signed in and by order of sd Meeting by
              Robt Lamborn clerk
              Martha Lamborn clerk

#114 26th of 6th mo 1794   MOSES WEBB
To York Monthly Meeting
Request being made on behalf of Moses Webb a minor placed an apprentice with a member of your meeting...he is a member amongst us, as such we recommend him
Signed in and by Direction of our Monthly Meeting held at Deer Creek the 26th Day of 6th mo 1794
                     John Cox clerk

#115 7th of 6th mo 1794   SUSANNAH MILLS
From Warrington Monthly Meeting held the 7th of the 6th mo 1794 to York Monthly Meeting

REMOVALS

Susanna Mills requested our certificate in order to be joined to your meeting...clear of Marriage Engagements known to us as a member. We recommend her
And signed by order of the same by Peter Cleaver clerk
Susanna Cleaver clerk

#116 23rd of 5th mo 1794   JOHN WORLEY
To York Monthly Meeting
John Worley being about to return to you hath requested our Certificate in order to join him to your meeting...clear of Marriage engagements as far as appears--therefore we recommend him...
Signed in and on behalf of Redstone Monthly Meeting the 23rd of 5th mo 1794 by   Saml Jackson clerk

#117 23rd of 5th mo 1794   MARY HOLLAND
From our Monthly Meeting of Warrington held the 9th of the 8th mo 1794 to the Monthly Meeting of friends at York
Mary Holland having lately removed from us within the verge of your meeting hath requested our certificate...is clear of marriage engagements as far as we know so we recommend her
Signed on behalf of sd meeting
by Peter Cleaver clerk
Susanna Cleaver clerk

#118 18th of 6th mo 1794   ANN BENNET
To York Monthly Meeting
Ann Bennet requested our certificate to be joined to your meeting she being removed within the verge thereof...clear of Marriage engagements known to us. We recommend her...
Signed in and by order of Sadsbury Monthly Meeting held the 18th Day of 6th mo 1794   By   James Cooper clerk
Mary Smith clerk

#119 26th of 2nd mo 17944   BARZILLA GARDNER
From our Monthly Meeting held at Newgarden North Carolina the 26th of the 2nd mo 1794 to the Monthly Meeting held at York Town Pennsylvania
Barzilla Gardner who resides within the verge of your Meeting as an apprentice...he is a member of our society and as such we recommend him   Signed in and by order of sd meeting
By Richard Williams clerk

#120 9th of 7th mo 1794   ABNER UPDEGRAFF
To Redstone Monthly Meeting
Abner Updegraff a member of our Meeting having removed to settle within the verge of yours--requested our Certificate to be joined to you...he is clear of Debt and Marriage engagements amongst us...We recommend him...

WARRINGTON MONTHLY MEETING

Signed in and on behalf of York Meeting Held the 9th of the 7th mo 1794   By   Eli Kirk clerk

#121 10th of 12th mo 1794   HANNAH PHILLIPS
To Manallin Monthly Meeting
Hannah Phillips who produced the within Certificate recommending her to the care of Friends here hath now requested our Certificate to your Meeting...we therefore Recommend her...
Signed in and on behalf of York Monthly Meeting held the 10th of the 12th mo 1794 by   Eli Kirk clerk
                                                                Ann Love clerk

#122 6th of 5th mo 1795   LYDIA JORDAN
To Horsham Monthly Meeting
Lydia Jordan a member of our meeting who hath removed and settled within the compas of yours hath requested our certificate...clear of marriage engagements known to us we recommend her...
Signed in and on behalf of York Monthly Meeting held the 6th of the 5th mo 1795   By   Eli Kirk clerk

#123 18th of 3rd mo 1795   THOMAS CONARD
To York Monthly Meeting
Thomas Conard by a friend requested our certificate to your Meeting he going to remove within the verge thereof...he is clear of debt and marriage engagements. We recommend him
Signed in and on behalf of Sadsbury Monthly Meeting Held the 18th Day of the 3rd mo 1795   By   James Cooper Jr clerk

#124 10th of 6th mo 1795   SAMUEL JONES
To West Land Monthly Meeting
Samuel Jones a member of our Meeting having removed and settled within the verge of yours Requested our Certificate to be joined thereto...We recommend him...
Signed in and on behalf of York Monthly Meeting held the 10th of the 6th mo 1795   by   Eli Kirk clerk

#125 10th of 6th mo 1795   BETTY JONES
To Westland Monthly Meeting
Betty Jones a member of our meeting having removed to settle within the verge of yours, requests our Certificate to be joined thereto...is clear of Debt and Marriage engagements as far as appears...we recommend her...
Signed in and on behalf of York Monthly Meeting held the 10th Day of the 6th mo 1795   by Eli Kirk Clerk
                                 Ann Love clerk

#126 6th of 1st mo 1796   JOHN WORLEY
To Westland Monthly Meeting

REMOVALS

John Worley a member of our Meeting requested our certificate to be joined to yours he being removed within the boundary thereof...is clear of Marriage engagements as far as appears We recommend him Signed in and on behalf of York Monthly Meeting held the 6th of the 1st mo 1796 by   Eli Kirk clerk

#127 20th of 5th mo 1795   ANDREW MOORE
To York Monthly Meeting
Andrew Moore hath requested our Certificate for himself and Rebecca his Wife in order to be joined to your Meeting...we recommend them
Signed in and on behalf of Sadsbury Monthly Meeting held the 20th Day of the 5th mo 1795   by James Cooper clerk
                               Mary Smith clerk

#128 29th of 10th mo 1794   ELIZABETH COOK
To York Monthly Meeting
Elizabeth Cook being removed from us and settled in your verge, Requested our certificate to you...clear of debt and Marriage engagements. We recommend her...
Signed in and on behalf of London Grove Monthly Meeting in Chester County the 29th of 10th mo 1794   By   Joseph Smith (?)
                               Margaret Janney (?) clerks

#129 20th of 5th mo 1795   JAMES COOPER
From Sadsbury Monthly Meeting held the 20th of the 5th month 1795 To York Monthly Meeting
James Cooper and Rachel his wife requested our Certificate for themselves and seven children (to wit: Hannah; Mary; Catrine; Andrew; Rebecca; James; and Thomas) in order to be joined to your Meeting...Hannah and Mary the two eldest children are of a sober behavior and clear of Marriage engagements known to us, the others being young we think it not needfull to say much about them, but recommend them together with their parents...
Signed in and on behalf of our afforesaid meeting
      By   James Cooper clerk
            Mary Smith clerk

#130 22nd of 4th mo 1795   ISAAC MOORE
To York Monthly Meeting
Isaac Moore by a friend has requested our certificate for himself his wife Lydia and two daughters Dinah and Amy Moore in order to be joined to your Meeting they having removed within the verge thereof...We recommend them with their children who are young
Signed in and on behalf of Sadsbury Monthly Meeting held the 22nd of 4th mo 1795   By James Cooper Jr clerk
                     Deborah -?- clerk at this time

#131 20th of 5th mo 1795   SARAH MOORE

WARRINGTON MONTHLY MEETING

To York Monthly Meeting
Our certificate has been requested for Sarah Moore (Daughter of Andrew and Rebecca Moore) in order to be joined to your Meeting she having removed with her Parents within the verge thereof...is clear of Debt and Marriage engagements known to us...we recommend her
Signed in and on behalf of Sadsbury Monthly Meeting
held the 20th of the 5th mo 1795   by Mary Smith clerk

#132 20th of 5th mo 1795   ANDREW MOORE
To York Monthly Meeting
Andrew Moore has requested our certificate for his son [sic] Eliza Moore in order to be joined to your Meeting he having removed within the verge thereof...is clear of Debt and marriage engagements known to us--we recommend him...
Signed in and on behalf of Sadsbury Monthly Meeting held the 20th Day of the 5th mo 1794   By James Cooper clerk

#133 25th of 12th mo 1794   LEVEN HOPKINS
To York Monthly Meeting
Application being made for a few lines by way of a Certificate for Leven Hopkins a Minor who is placed an apprentice to a member of your Meetings we therefore certify that he hath a right of membership And as such we recommend him
Signed in and by order of Deer Creek Monthly Meeting held the 25th of the 12th Mo 1794   By John Cox clerk

#134 4th of 5th mo 1796   ANN BOWEN
To ?
Ann Bowen having removed with her husband and settled within the verge of your meeting requested our certificate to be joined thereto...she hath right of membership with us and was a frequent attender of our Religious Meetings as such we recommend her
Signed in and on behalf of york Monthly Meeting held the 4th day of the 5th mo 1796   By Eli Kirk clerk
            Lydia Kirk clerk at this time

#135 10th of 8th mo 1796   THOMAS MOORE
To Warrington Monthly Meeting
Thomas Moore and Dinah his wife members of our Meeting having removed and settled up the Susquehanna in Huntingdon County requested our Certificate to be joined to you...their lives and Conversation hath been in a good degree orderly notwithstanding their remote situation frequently attended our Meetings on first Days and those for Discipline at times--have settled their outward affairs to satisfaction as far as appears--as such we recommend them...
Signed in and on behalf of York Monthly Meeting
Held the 10th day of the 8th mo 1796
           by Eli Kirk clerk

REMOVALS

Ann Love   clerk

#136 10th of 8th mo 1796   JAMES MOORE
To Warrington Monthly Meeting
James Moore and Lydia his Wife Members of our Meeting having removed
up Susquehannah in Huntington County and Requested our Certificate
for themselves and their five children to wit Abraham; Esther; Lydia;
Anna and Jeremiah Moore to be joined to you...their lives and
conversation has been in a good degree orderly--Notwithstanding their
remote situation frequently attended our Meetings on first days and
those on weekdays and for discipline at times--their outward affairs
settled to satisfaction as far as appears as such we recommend
them...
Signed in and on behalf of York Monthly Meeting held the 10th Day of
the 8th mo 1796   By   Eli Kirk clerk
                           Ann Love   clerk

#137 7th of 9th mo 1796   ELIJAH MOORE
To Warrington Monthly Meeting
Elijah Moore a Member of our Meeting having removed and settled up
the Susquehannah River in Huntingdon County requested our Certificate
to be joined to you...his life and conversation hath been in a good
Degree orderly Considering he living some what remote, frequently
attended our Religious Meetings is clear of Debt and Marriage
engagements known to us--as such we recommend him
Signed in and on behalf of York Monthly Meeting held the 7th of the
9th mo 1796   By Eli Kirk clerk

#138 9th of 9th mo 1796   RACHEL HUTTON
To Warrington Monthly Meeting
Rachel Hutton who has removed with her Husband and settled within the
verge of your Meeting hath requested our Certificate for herself and
her Daughter Betty to be joined to you...we recommend her with her
Daughter...
Signed in and on behalf of York Monthly Meeting held the 9th day of
the 9th mo 1796   By   Eli Kirk clerk
                           Ann Love   clerk

#139 7th of 9th mo 1796   JOHN WALLIS HOPKINS
To Baltimore Monthly Meeting
John Wallis Hopkins having removed within the verge of your meeting
requested our certificate to be joined thereto...clear of Debt or
Marriage engagements known to us--as a member of our society we
recommend him
Signed in and on behalf of York Monthly Meeting
held the 7th day of 9th mo 1796   By Eli Kirk clerk

WARRINGTON MONTHLY MEETING

#140 12th of 6th mo 1795   SAMUEL COATES
To York Monthly Meeting
Request being made for a certificate for Samuel Coates who is removed
and resides with you this may inform you he hath a right of
membership and conducted in some good Degree of sobriety and attended
Meetings frequently--Clear of Debt or any other engagements known to
us--Therefore we recommend him...
Given from Bradford Monthly Meeting 12th of 6th mo 1795 and signed on
behalf of the same   By John Barnard clerk

#141 13th of 2nd mo 1796   ALEXANDER UNDERWOOD
To York Monthly Meeting
Alexander Underwood requested our certificate to be joined to your
meeting he being removed within the verge thereof...as a member we
recommend him...
from Warrington Monthly Meeting held the thirteenth Day of the second
Mo 1796 Signed in and by order of said meeting
          By Benjamin Walker clerk

#142 7th of 12th mo 1796   NATHAN PUSEY
To Pipe Creek Monthly Meeting
Nathan Pusey having returned to live with his Father within the verge
of your Meeting requested our Certificate...we recommend him
Signed in and on behalf of York Monthly Meeting Held the 7th of the
12th mo 1796   By Eli Kirk clerk

#143 8th of 3rd mo 1797   LYDIA FARQUHAR
To Pipe Creek Monthly Meeting
Lydia Farquhar a member of our Meeting having removed and settled
with her husband within the compass of yours hath Requested our
Certificate...we therefore Recommend her...
Signed in and on behalf of York Monthly Meeting held the 8th day of
3rd mo 1797   By Caleb Kirk clerk at this time
                            Ann Love clerk

#144 10th of 5th mo 1797   JOHN JONES
To Redstone Monthly Meeting
John Jones and Betty his Wife having requested our Certificate for
themselves and two children to your Meeting...we recommend them with
their two children viz Rachel and John...
Signed on behalf of York Monthly Meeting held the 10th of the 5th mo
1797 By Caleb Kirk clerk at this time;   Ann Love clerk

#145 10th of 5th mo 1797   MARY JONES
To Redstone Monthly Meeting
Mary Jones a member of our Meeting hath Requested our Certificate to
your Meeting...is clear of Debt and Marriage engagements known to us
we recommend...

REMOVALS

Signed on behalf of York Monthly Meeting Held the 10th Day of the 5th
mo 1797   By Caleb Kirk clerk at this time
                        Ann Love clerk

#146 4th of 10th mo 1797   JAMES EMBREE
To Bradford Monthly Meeting
James Embree a member of our meeting Requested our Certificate in
order to be joined to yours...is clear of Debt or Marriage
engagements known to us. As such we recommend him
Signed in and on behalf of York Monthly Meeting
Held the 4th Day of the 10th Mo 1797   Jonathan Jessop clerk

#147 6th of 12th mo 1797   JOSEPH GARRETSON
To Warrington Monthly Meeting
Joseph Garretson a member of our Meeting who hath removed and settled
within the verge of yours having requested our Certificate...clear of
Marriage engagements as far as appears.
Signed on behalf of York Monthly Meeting held the 6th of the 12th mo
1797   by Jonathan Jessop clerk

#148 29th of 7th mo 1797   RACHEL SCOTT
To York Monthly Meeting
Rachel Scott requests our certificate in order to be joined to your
meeting...she hath a right of membership with friends but being
sometime removed from us we can say but little about her only to
recommend her
Given forth from Gunpowder Monthly Meeting held at the little falls
the 29th of 7th mo 1797 And signed on behalf of the Meeting
        By Danl Price
            Ruth Matthews clerks

#149 6th of 6th mo 1798   MOSES MORE
To Sadsbury Monthly Meeting
Moses More a member of our meeting having removed within the verge of
yours applyed for our certification in order to be joined
thereto...clear of Marriage engagements known to us. We recommend
him
Signed in and on behalf of York Monthly Meeting
held the 6th day of 6 mo 1798   By Jonathan Jessop clerk

#150 9th of 4th mo 1800   JOSHUA KERSEY
To Ewchlan Monthly Meeting
Joshua Kersey having requested our Certificate having removed within
the Verge of your meeting in order to be joined thereto ...he was in
his minority when he removed with his Father from among us We
therefore recommend him...

WARRINGTON MONTHLY MEETING

Signed in and on behalf of York Monthly Meeting held the 9th of 4th mo 1800   By Jonathan Jessop clerk

#151 10th of 5th mo 1800   HANNAH KIRK
From Warrington Monthly Meeting held the 10th day of fifth month 1800
To York Monthly Meeting
Hannah Kirk requests our Certificate to be joined to your Meeting She being removed within the verge thereof...is clear of debt or marriage engagements known to us as a member we recommend her
Signed by order of the same   by Benjamin Walker clerk
                                 Susanna Cleaver clerk

#152 8th of 8th mo 1798   MOSES WEBB
To Deer Creek Monthly Meeting
Moses Webb a member of our meeting having removed and settled within the verge of yours requested our certificate in order to be joined thereto...is clear of debt or marriage engagements known to us we recommend him
Signed in and on behalf of York Monthly Meeting held the 8th of the 8th mo 1798   by Jonathan Jessop clerk

#153 7th of 11th mo 1798   JAMES FISHER
To Baltimore Monthly Meeting
James Fisher a member of our meeting having removed within the verge of yours requested our Certificate...is clear of Debt and Marriage engagements as far as we know we recommend him...
Signed in and by order of York Monthly Meeting held the 7th of 11th mo 1798   By Jonathan Jessop

#154 20th of 10th mo 1798   THOMAS TAYLOR
To York Monthly Meeting
Application being for a certificate for Thomas Taylor and Sarah his wife who being removed within the limits of your meeting...we recommend them to your care with their five children viz Thomas; Joseph; Caleb; Nicholas; and William...
Signed in and on behalf of Pipe Creek Monthly Meeting held at Bush Creek the 20th of 10th mo 1798
          by Wm ballinger clerk at this time
              Mary Ballinger clerk at this time

#155 25th of 8th mo 1801   THOMAS CONARD
To the Monthly Meeting of Friends at York
Thomas Conard applyed for our Certificate in order to proceed in Marriage with one of your members...it doth not appear that there are any obstructions in his way   We therefore recommend him to your Christian Care in his weighty undertaking...

REMOVALS

From our Monthly Meeting of Philadelphia Held for the Northern District 8th mo 25th 1801   Thos Norris clerk

#156 5th of 12th mo 1798   DEBORAH PHILLIPS
To Indian Springs Monthly Meeting
Deborah Phillips a member of our Meeting requested our certificate in order to be joined to yours... clear of debt or marriage engagements known to us - as such we recommend her
Signed in and by order of york Monthly Meeting held the 5th of 12th mo 1798   By Jonathan Jessop clerk
                    Ann Love clerk

#157 8th of 5th mo 1799   THOMAS CONARD
To the Northern District Monthly Meeting of Philadelphia
Thomas Conard a member of our meeting requested our certificate to be joined to yours...is clear of marriage engagements and settled his outward affairs to satisfaction as far as appears as such we recommend him
Signed in and on behalf of York Monthly Meeting held the 8th day of the 5th mo 1799   by Caleb Kirk clerk at this time

#158 5th of 6th mo 1799   ANDREW MORE
To Sadsbury Monthly Meeting
Our Friends Andrew More and Wife Rebecca having requested our certificate in order to be joined to your Meeting...they were examplary in life and conversation diligent attenders of our religious meetings (considering their remote situation) We recommend them...
Signed on behalf of York Monthly Meeting held the 5th of 6th mo 1799 by John Love clerk at this time
                    Lydia Kirk clerk at this time

#159 5th of 6th mo 1799   SARAH MORE
To Sadsbury Monthly Meeting
Sarah More having requested our certificate in order to be joined to your Meeting...her life and conversation hath been in a good degree orderly careful in the attendance of our religious meetings considering her remote situation and clear of debt and marriage engagements known to us we recommend her...
Signed by order of York Monthly Meetings held the 5th of 6th mo 1799   By John Love clerk at this time
                    Lydia Kirk clerk at this time

#160 5th of 6th mo 1799   CALEB BRACKEN
To Gunpowder Monthly Meeting
Caleb Bracken having removed with his family and settled within the verge of your meeting requested our certificate for himself his wife,

WARRINGTON MONTHLY MEETING

Rebecca, and their three children viz Rachel; Solomon; Elisha in order to be joined thereto...as members we recommend...
Signed in and on behalf of York Monthly Meeting held the 5th of 6th mo 1799   By John Love Clerk at this time
                    Lydia Kirk clerk at this time

#161 4th of 9th mo 1799   SARAH HUTTON
To Warrington Monthly Meeting
Sarah Hutton a member of our meeting having removed and settled within the verge of yours requested our Certificate in order to be joined thereto...is clear of debt or marriage engagements known to us We recommend her...
Signed in and on behalf of York Monthly Meeting held the 4th of 9th mo 1799   By Jonathan Jessop clerk
                    Lydia Kirk clerk

#162 4th of 12th mo 1799   JACOB NORBURY
To Baltimore Monthly Meeting
Jacob Norbury a member of our Meeting having removed and settled within the verge of your requested our certificate in order to be joined thereto...is clear of Marriage engagements known to us We recommend him...
Signed in and on behalf of York Monthly Meeting held the 4th day of 12th mo 1799   By Jonathan Jessop clerk

#163 2nd of 11th mo 1799   ANN JESSOP
To the monthly meeting of York Town Pennsylvania
Our Esteemed friend Ann Jessop informed us that she had a mind to move to your town and requested our Certificate...she is a member and minister in Unity is clear of Marriage engagements for ought we know as such we recommend her...from our monthly meetings in new garden in Guilford County North Carolina held by adjournment the 2nd of 11th mo 1799
Signed in and on behalf of thereof
            By   --?--
            Phebe Stanley clerk

#164 5th of 2nd mo 1800   RICHARD MENDENHALL
To the monthly meeting of Friends held at Deep River in Guilford County Caroline
Richard Mendenhall a member of our meeting having removed and settled within the verge of yours requested our certificate to be joined thereto...is clear of Debt or marriage engagements known to us as such we recommend him
Signed in and on behalf of York Monthly Meeting held the 5th of the 2nd mo 1800   by Jonathan Jessop clerk

#165 5th of 3rd mo 1800   THOMAS FISHER
To Baltimore Monthly Meeting

REMOVALS

Application being made for a certificate for Thomas Fisher who we are informed is placed an apprentice within the Verge of your Meeting...he is a member in his minority as such we recommend him
Signed in and on behalf of York Monthly Meeting held the 5th of the 3rd mo 1800   By   Jonathan Jessop clerk

#166 7th of 5th mo 1800   HANNAH MCKISSON
To Warrington Monthly Meeting
Hannah McKisson a member of our Meeting being about to remove with her husband and settle within the verge of yours Requested our Certificate in order to be joined thereto...she attended our meetings at times...We recommend her...
Signed in and on behalf of York Monthly Meeting held the 7th of 5th mo 1800   By   Jonathan Jessop
                                 Lydia Kirk clerks

#167 7th of 5th mo 1800   ISAAC MORE
To Warrington Monthly Meeting
Isaac More and Lydia his wife members of our meeting requested our Certificate for themselves and their four children in order to be joined to yours they having removed and settled within the Verge thereof...they are of orderly life and conversation they having lived somewhat remote attended our meeting for Worship and discipline at times and have settled their outward affairs to satisfaction as far as appears as such we recommend them with their four children (namely) Dinah, Amy, Sarah and Samuel More
Signed in and on behalf of York Monthly Meeting held the 7th of 5th mo 1800   By   Jonathan Jessop clerk
                                 Lydia Kirk   clerk

#168 1st of 6th mo 1800   NEOMY WAY
To Warrington Monthly Meeting
Neomy Way a member of our Meeting requested our Certificate in order to be joined to yours...is clear of Debt or Marriage engagements known to us. As such we recommend her
Signed in and on behalf of York Monthly Meeting held the 1st day of the 6th mo 1800   By   Jonathan Jessop clerk
                                 Lydia Kirk   clerk

#169 1st of 6th mo 1800   LYDIA MORE
To Warrington Monthly Meeting
Lydia More a member of our Meeting requested our certificate in order to be joined to yours...is clear of debt or Marriage engagements known to us as such we recommend her...
Signed in and on behalf of York Monthly Meeting held the 1st of 6th mo 1800   By Jonathan Jessop clerk
                                 Lydia Kirk   clerk

WARRINGTON MONTHLY MEETING

#170 1st of 6th mo 1800   REBECCA COX
To Gunpowder Monthly Meeting
Rebecca Cox a member of our meeting requested our Certificate in order to be joined to yours she having removed and settled within the verge thereof...is clear of Debt or Marriage engagements known to us as such we recommend her...
Signed in and on behalf of York Monthly Meeting held the 1st of 6th mo 1800   By Jonathan Jessop   clerk
                                            Lydia Kirk   clerk

#171 30th of 11th mo 1799   SARAH HUSSEY
From the Monthly Meeting of New Garden North Carolina held the 30th of 11th mo 1799
To the Monthly Meeting of York Town Pennsylvania
Sarah Hussey having a mind to move to your parts and requests our Certificate...is Clear of Marriage engagements as far as appears As such we recommend her
Signed in and on behalf of said Meeting
       By Hezekiah Harbuck
            Phebe Stanley   clerks

#172 6th of 6th mo 1800   ALEXANDER UNDERWOOD
To Warrington Monthly Meeting
Alexander Underwood and Rhoda his wife members of our meeting requested our certificate for themselves and three children viz: Harman Samuel and Alexander in order to be joined to yours...we recommend
Signed in and on behalf of York Monthly Meeting held the 6th of 6th mo 1800.   By Jonathan Jessop
                                    Lydia Kirk   clerks

#173 12th of 7th mo 1800   HANNAH LEWIS
To York Monthly Meeting
Hannah Lewis a member of our meeting requested our certificate in order to be joined to yours...clear of debt or Marriage engagements...we recommend her
Signed in and on behalf of Warrington Monthly Meeting held the 12th of 7th mo 1800   By Benjamin Walker clerk
                              Susanna Cleaver   clerk

#174 12th of 7th mo 1800   SARAH LEWIS
To York Monthly Meeting
Sarah Lewis a member of our meeting requested our certificate in order to be joined to yours...Clear of Debt and marriage engagements...we recommend her
Signed in and on behalf of Warrington Monthly Meeting held ye 12th of 7th mo 1800   By   Benjamin Walker Clerk
                                    Susanna Cleaver   clerk

REMOVALS

#175 12th of 7th mo 1800   HANNAH GARRETSON
From Warrington Monthly Meeting held the 12th of 7th mo 1800
To York Monthly Meeting
Hannah Garretson Jr a member of our meeting requested our Certificate in order to be joined to yours...clear of Debt or Marriage engagements...we recommend her...Signed in and on behalf of the same By Benjamin Walker clerk
                  Susanna Cleaver clerk

#176 10th of 9th mo 1800   LEAVEN HOPKINS
To Baltimore Monthly Meeting
Leaven Hopkins a Member of our meeting having removed and settled within the limits of yours Requested our Certificate to be joined thereto...is clear of debt or marriage engagements...we recommend him...
Signed in and on behalf of York Monthly Meeting held the 10th of 9th mo 1800   By Jonathan Jessop   clerk

#177 10th of 9th mo 1800   REBECCA BLAIR
To Redstone Monthly Meeting
Rebecca Blair having removed with her husband and settled within the limits of your meeting we thought best to forward a certificate on her behalf in order that she might be joined thereto...we recommend her
Signed in and by order of York Monthly Meeting held the 10th of 9th mo 1800   By Jonathan Jessop clerk
                  Lydia Kirk clerk

#178 5th of 11th mo 1800   JOSIAH UPDEGRAFF
To Pipe Creek Monthly Meeting
Josiah Updegraff a member of this Meeting requested our Certificate in order to accomplish his Marriage with Hannah Farquhar a member of yours...he appears to be clear of all others on that account We therefore Recommend
Signed in and on behalf of York Monthly Meeting held the 5th of 11th mo 1800   By Jonathan Jessop clerk

#179 8th of 4th mo 1801   JAMES COOPER
To Sadsbury Monthly Meeting
James Cooper having requested our Certificate for himself and Children in order to be joined to your meeting...he attended our meetings at times (having lived remote therefrom) and is clear of Marriage engagements known to us As members we recommend him with his four children namely Andrew, Rebecca, James and Thomas
Signed in and on behalf of York Monthly Meeting held the 8th of 4th mo 1801   By Jonathan Jessop clerk

WARRINGTON MONTHLY MEETING

#180 8th of 6th mo 1799   ISAAC KIRK
To York Monthly Meeting
Isaac Kirk and Jane his wife requested our Certificate for themselves and their five children namely Jacob; Martha; Sarah; and Samuel [sic] in order to be joined to your meeting they being settled within the verge thereof...we recommend them...Given forth from Warrington Monthly Meeting held the 8th of 6th mo 1799
Signed by   Benjamin Walker clerk
                    Susanna Cadwalader clerk at this time

#181 14th of 3rd mo 1801   HANNAH UPDEGRAFF
To York Monthly Meeting
Hannah Updegraff having requested our Certificate to your meeting ...we recommend her
Signed in and on behalf of Pipe Creek Monthly Meeting held the 14th of 3rd mo 1801   By Joel Wright clerk
                                      Jane Hibberd clerk

#182 5th of 3rd mo 1801   BENJAMIN WRIGHT
To Fairfax Monthly Meeting
Benjamin Wright having requested our Certificate on account of his son Benjamin Wright a minor who he has placed with a friend within the verge of your meeting as an apprentice ...We recommend him
Signed in and on behalf of York Monthly Meeting
held the 5th of 3rd mo 1801   By Jonathan Jessop clerk

#183 9th of 9th mo 1801   JEREMIAH MORE
To Warrington Monthly Meeting
Jeremiah More requested our Certificate in order to be joined to your Meeting...living remote from us he attended our religious meetings at times...we recommend him...
From York Monthly Meeting held 9th of 9th mo 1801
                    Jonathan Jessop clerk

#184 11th of 4th mo 1801   HANNAH GARRETSON
From Warrington Monthly Meeting held at Newbury the 11th of 4th mo 1801 to York Monthly Meeting
Request having been made for a Certificate for Hannah the wife of Cornelius Garretson and their seven children namely John; Samuel; Sarah; Cornelius; Isaac; Eli; and Margaret In order to be joined to your meeting...we recommend them...
Signed by order of the same   Samuel Garretson
                                  Susanna Clever clerks

#185 6th of 5th mo 1801   ISAAC KIRK
To Warrington Monthly Meeting
Isaac Kirk and Jane his Wife requested our Certificate for themselves

REMOVALS

and their four children to your meeting...we recommend them with their four children viz Jacob; Martha; Sarah; and Samuel
Signed in and on behalf of York Monthly Meeting held the 6th of 5th mo 1801   By   Jonathan Jessop
                     Sarah Naylor   clerks

#186 25th of 8th mo 1801   THOMAS CONARD

To the Monthly Meeting of Friends at York
Thomas Conard applied for our certificate in order to procede in Marriage with one of your members on making the necessary enquiry concerning him we find no obstruction in his way we therefore recommend him to your Christian care in his Weighty Undertaking...
From our Monthly Meeting of Phila held for the Northern District 8th mo 25th 1801   Thos Norris clerk

#187 8th of 7th mo 1801   AMOS SCOTT

To Gunpowder Monthly Meeting
Amos Scott a member of our meeting requested our certificate for himself and his four children to wit, Levi; Esther; William; and Rachel in order to be joined to yours...having lived considerably remote...is clear of Marriage engagements known to us as a member we recommend him with his four Children
Signed in and on behalf of York Monthly Meeting held the 8th of the seventh month 1801   By Caleb Kirk Clerk at this time

#188 4th of 11th mo 1801   SARAH HUSSEY

To Gunpowder Monthly Meeting
Sarah Hussey a member of our meeting having removed and settled within the verge of yours requested our Certificate in order to be joined thereto...clear of debt or Marriage engagements We recommend her
Signed in and on behalf of York Monthly Meeting held 4th of 11th mo 1801   By   Jonathan Jessop
                    Lydia Kirk   clerks

#189 4th of 11th mo 1801   SARAH CONARD

To the Northern District Monthly Meeting Philadelphia
Sarah Conard a member of our Meeting having removed and settled with her husband within the verge of yours requested our Certificate to be joined thereto...We recommend her
Signed in and on behalf of York Monthly Meeting held the 4th of 11th mo 1801   By   Jonathan Jessop
                    Lydia Kirk   clerks

#190 12th of 9th mo 1801   CORNELIUS GARRETSON

To York Monthly Meeting
Cornelius Garretson requested our certificate in order to be joined to your meeting...we recommend him

WARRINGTON MONTHLY MEETING

Given at Warrington Monthly Meeting and signed the 12th of 9th mo 1801 on behalf of the same by Saml Garretson clerk at this time

#191 9th of 12th mo 1801   SAMUEL CLARK
To Redstone Monthly Meeting
Samuel Clark and Ruth his wife members of our Meeting having removed to settle within your limits requested our Certificate to be joined to you...We recommend them
Signed in and on behalf of York Monthly Meeting held the 9th of 12th mo 1801   By   Jonathan Jessop
                                    Lydia Kirk   clerks

#192 9th of 12th mo 1801   SARAH FARQUHAR
To Pipe Creek Monthly Meeting
Sarah Farquhar (Wife of Wm Farquhar) a member of our Meeting requested our certificate to be joined to yours...we recommend her
Signed in and on behalf of York Monthly Meeting held the 9th of 12th mo 1801   By   Jonathan Jessop
                                    Lydia Kirk   clerks

#193 12th of 12th mo 1801   ALEXANDER UNDERWOOD
To York Monthly Meeting
Alexander Underwood and Rhoda (his wife) requests our certificate for themselves and four minor children namely Harman; Samuel; Alexander and Thomas in order to be joined to your meeting...we recommend them...
Warrington Monthly Meeting held the 12th of 12th mo 1801 signed on behalf.   Benjamin Walker
                      Susanna Clever   clerks

#194 10th of 2nd mo 1802   SARAH UPDEGRAFF
To Baltimore Monthly Meeting
Sarah Updegraff a member of our meeting having removed and settled within the verge of yours requested our certificate in order to be joined there to...is clear of Marriage engagements known to us we recommend her...
Signed in and on behalf of York Mo Meeting held the 10th of 2nd mo 1802   by Jonathan Jessop   Ann Love   clerks

#195 10th of 4th mo 1802   HANNAH UPDEGRAFF
To Baltimore Monthly Meeting
Hannah Updegraff a member of our meeting having removed and settled within the verge of yours requested our certificate in order to be joined thereto...is clear of Marriage engagements known to us we recommend her...
Signed on behalf of York Mo Meeting held 10th of 4th mo 1802
                    By   Jonathan Jessop
                         Ann Love   clerks

REMOVALS

#196 13th of 2nd mo 1802   RACHAL JOHN
To York Monthly Meeting
Rachal John requested our Certificate in order to be joined to your
Meetings she being settled within the limits thereof...a frequent
attender of our Meeting when of ability of Body and is Clear of Debt
and Marriage engagements known to us. As a member in good esteem we
recommend her
Signed in and on behalf of Warrington Monthly Meeting held the 13th
of 2nd mo 1802   By   Benjamin Walker
                  Susanna Cadwalader   clerks

#197 13th of 2nd mo 1802   CORNELIUS GARRETSON
To York Monthly Meeting
Cornelius Garretson requested our Certificate to your meeting for his
son Joseph (an Infant born in the interval between the date and the
reception of a certificate from our Meeting to yours for his Wife and
other children) We therefore recommend him a member Signed in and by
order of Warrington Monthly Meeting held the 13th of 2nd mo 1802 By
Benjamin Walker clerk

#198 5th of 5th mo 1802   HANNAH LEACH
To Warrington Monthly Meeting
Hannah Leach (lately intermarried with Thomas Leach Jr) a member of
our meeting   requests our   Certificate in order to be joined
thereto...we Recommend her
Signed in and on behalf of York Monthly Meeting held the 5th of 5th
mo 1802   By   Jonathan Jessop
                  Ann Love   clerks

#199 13th of 2nd mo 1802   ANN JOHN
To York Monthly Meeting
Ann John requested our certificate in order to be joined to your
Meeting she being settled within the verge thereof...is clear of Debt
and Marriage engagements known to us. As a member in good esteem we
recommend her
Signed in and on behalf of Warrington Monthly Meeting held the 13th
of 2nd mo 1802   By Benj Walker   clerk
                  Susannah Cadwalader clerk at this time

#200 4th of 8th mo 1802   ANN JESSOP
To New Garden Monthly Meeting N. Carolina
Our esteemed friend Ann Jessop who has removed and settled within
your limits hath requested our certificate...a Minister well approved
amongst us hath settled her outward affairs to satisfaction and is
clear of Marriage engagements...we affectionately recommend her...

WARRINGTON MONTHLY MEETING

Signed in and on behalf of York Monthly Meeting held the 4th of 8th mo 1802   By Jonathan Jessop   Ann Love   clerks

#201 2nd of 4th mo 1802   JOHN WORLEY
To York Monthly Meeting
John Worley having removed to settle within the verge of your meeting requested our Certificate to join him thereto...clear of Marriage engagements known to us. We therefore recommend him
Signed on behalf of Redstone Mo meeting 2nd of 4th mo 1802
            By   Henry Froth   clerk

#202 11th of 9th mo 1802   AMOS LEWIS
To York Monthly Meeting
Amos Lewis requested our Certificate in order to be joined to your Meeting he being settled within the limits thereof...is clear of Marriage engagements known to us...we recommend him
Signed on behalf of Warrington Mo Meeting
the 11th of 9th mo 1802   By Benj Walker clerk

#203 8th of 12th mo 1802   NATHAN KIRK
To Nottingham Monthly Meeting
Request being for a Certificate for Nathan Kirk a Minor placed with a Member of your Meeting we inform you that he is a minor and as such we request your Christian care and oversight on his behalf & remain your friends
Signed in and on behalf of York Mo Meeting held the 8th of 12th mo 1802   By Jonathan Jessop   clerk

#204 6th of 11th mo 1802   FRANCIS SWAYNE
To York Monthly Meeting
The bearer Francis Swayne hath requested our Certificate to join him to your Meeting We hereby recommend him to your friendly care ...his life and conversation of latter time being best known to you we think it needless to add further than our sincere desire for his welfare...
Signed in and on behalf of New Garden Mo. Meeting the 6th of 11th mo 1802   By Joseph L. Hutton Jr   clerk

#205 9th of 3rd mo 1803   DANIEL RAGEN
To Monallen Monthly Meeting   Beloved Friends
Daniel Ragen and Ruth his wife members of our meeting having settled within your limits request our Certificate...We affectionately recommend them
Signed in and on behalf of York Mo Meeting the 9th of 3rd mo 1803
        by   Jonathan Jessop
             Ann Love   clerks

REMOVALS

#206 4th of 3rd mo 1803   ELY SWAYNE
To York Monthly Meeting
Ely Swayne being about to remove and settle within the limits of your meeting hath requested our certificate in order to join in Membership with you...we recommend him to your friendly notice
Signed in and on behalf of New Garden Mo Meeting the
5th of 3rd mo 1803   By Halliday Jackson Clerk at this time

#207 4th of 5th mo 1803   THOMAS OWEN
To Pine Street Monthly Meeting Philadelphia
Thomas Owen a member of this Meeting requested our certificate he being placed within your limits...We recommend him...
Signed in and on behalf of York Monthly Meeting held the 4th of 5th mo 1803.   Jonathan Jessop clerk

#208 5th of 10th mo 1803   BENJAMIN BENSON
To Gunpowder Monthly Meeting
Benjamin Benson & Hannah his wife having requested our Certificate for themselves and four children (viz Levi; Hannah; Benjamin; Jesse) to your meeting...frequently attended our religious meetings considering their remote situation...we recommend them...
Signed in and on behalf of York Monthly Meeting held the 5th of 10th mo 1803   By Jonathan Jessop
                                Ann Love   clerks

#209 7th of 12th mo 1803   ABRAHAM BENSON
To Gunpowder Monthly Meeting
Abraham Benson a member of our meeting having removed within the limits of yours requests our Certificate...attended our religious meetings at times he living remote from us...we therefore recommend him...
Signed in and on behalf of York Mo Meeting held the 7th of 12th mo 1803   By Jonathan Jessop   clerk

#210 5th of 11th mo 1803   ORPAH SWAYNE
To York Monthly Meeting
Orpah Swayne having removed from amongst us to settle within the verge of yours requests our certificate...she attended our meetings at times and being young We think it needless to say further than recommend her as one who hath a right to membership...
Signed in and on behalf of Newgarden Monthly Meeting held the 5th of 11th mo 1803

Ruth Anna Lindley		Jacob Lindley
Hannah Jackson		Enoch Gray
Lydia Phillips	By	Samuel Spencer
Sarah Jackson		David Wilson
Mary Thompson		Joseph Hutton Jr
Mabel Hadly		Isaac Jackson Jr

WARRINGTON MONTHLY MEETING

#211 6th of 6th mo 1804   **AMOS BENSON**
To Gunpowder Monthly Meeting
Amos Benson a member of our meeting Requested our Certificate to yours...frequented our meetings at times his situation being remote from us...we therefore recommend him
Signed in and on behalf of York Monthly Meeting
held the 6th of 6th mo 1804   By Jonathan Jessop   clerk

#212 8th of 6th mo 1804   **TIMOTHY KIRK**
To Gunpowder Monthly Meeting
Timothy Kirk and Mary his wife members of our meeting requested our Certificate for themselves and their minor children viz Mahlon and Mary to be joined to you...We therefore recommend them Signed in and on behalf of York Monthly Meeting
held the 8th of 6th mo 1804   By Jonathan Jessop clerk
                               Ann Love   clerk

#213 6th of 6th mo 1804   **RACHEL KIRK**
To Gunpowder Monthly Meeting
Rachel Kirk a member of our Meeting requests our Certificate to be joined to yours...clear of debt or Marriage engagements known to us We therefore recommend her...
Signed in and on behalf of York Mo Meeting
held the 6th of 6th mo 1804   By   Jonathan Jessop
                               Ann Love   clerks

#214 9th of 5th mo 1804   **SAMUEL FISHER**
To Gunpowder Mo Meeting
Samuel Fisher and Susanna his wife members of our meeting requested our Certificate in order to be joined to yours for themselves and minor children viz Betty; Ruth; Lydia; Elihu; Joel & Seth...We therefore recommend them
Signed in and on behalf of York Monthly Meeting
held the 9th of 5th mo 1804   By Jonathan Jessop
                               Ann Love   clerks

#215 26th of 10th mo 1804   **DEBORAH PHILLIPS**
To York Monthly Meeting Pennsylvania
Deborah Phillips having removed from amongst us and settled within the verge of your Meeting has requested our Certificate to join her thereto...is clear of Marriage engagements known to us we therefore recommend her
Signed in and on behalf of Indian Spring Mo Meeting
held the 26th of 10th mo 1804   By Caleb Bentley   clerk
                     Hannah G. Lukens clerk at this time

#216 9th of 8th mo 1805   **WILLIAM KIRK**
To Gunpowder Monthly Meeting

REMOVALS

William Kirk a member of our Meeting has removed and settled within your Limits requests a Certificate to be joined to you...is clear of Debt or Marriage engagements known to us
We therefore recommend
Signed in and on behalf of York Mo Meeting
held the 9th of 8th mo 1805   By Jonathan Jessop   clerk

#217 6th of 2nd mo 1805   SAMUEL KERSEY
To Philadelphia Monthly Meeting
Samuel Kersey having requested our Certificate to your meeting these may inform that he removed from us with his parents when young out of the reach of this meeting as his Right remained here we Recommend him to yours...
Signed in and by order of York Monthly Meeting held the
6th of 2nd mo 1805   By Josiah updegraff Clerk at this time

#218 10th of 4th mo 1805   WILLIAM KERSEY
To Uwchlan Monthly Meeting
William Kersey and Hannah his wife members of our Meeting have requested our Certificate to be joined in Membership with you...some years ago they notified this meeting of their prospect of removal to the Gennesee Country which was concurred with, but there being no meeting of discipline there, did not then request a Certificate. Whilst amongst us they were frequent attenders of our religious meetings for Worship and discipline We therefore recommend them to your Christian care...
Signed in and on behalf of York Monthly Meeting
held the 10th of the 4th month 1804
           By   Jonathan Jessop
                 Ann Love   clerks

#219 4th of 12th mo-1805   DEBORAH FRENCH
To Pipe Creek Monthly Meeting
Deborah French (Wife of Iseral French) A member of our Meeting Requested our Certificate to be joined to yours...We recommend her...
Signed in & on behalf of York Monthly Meeting held the 4th
Day of the 12th month 1805   By Jonathan Jessop clerk

#220 7th of 1st mo 1806   HARMAN LOVE
To Philadelphia Monthly Meeting
Request was made for a certificate for Harman Love a Minor placed with Thomas Owen residing within the verge of your Meeting...we Recommend him
Signed in and by order of York Monthly Meeting held the 7th of 1st month 1806   By Jonathan Jessop clerk

#221 10th of 9th mo 1806   ELI SWAYNE
To Londongrove Monthly Meeting

WARRINGTON MONTHLY MEETING

Eli Swayne a member of our meeting having removed and settled within the verge of yours requested our certificate...is clear of debt or marriage engagements known to us.
Signed in and on behalf of York Monthly Meeting held the 10th day of the 9th month 1806   By   Jonathan Jessop clerk

#222 14th of 8th mo 1806   RACHEL UPDEGRAFF
To York Monthly Meeting Pennsylvania
Rachel Updegraff having removed to reside with her Husband, within the Limits of your Meeting requested our Certificate in order to be joined thereto...We recommend her
Signed in and on behalf of Baltimore Monthly Meeting held the 14th of the 8th month 1806   By George Ellicott
                                      Elizabeth Ellicott   clerks

#223 10th of 12th mo 1806   WILLIAM TAYLOR
To Philadelphia Monthly Meeting for North District
Application being made to us for a Certificate for William Taylor a minor, Placed an apprentice with a member of your Meeting...We therefor Recommend him...
Signed in and on behalf of York Monthly Meeting held the 10th day of the 12th mo 1806   By Jonathan Jessop clerk

#224 8th of 7th mo 1807   RACHEL HAINS
To Pipe Creek Monthly Meeting
Rachel Hains a member of our meeting having removed and settled with her husband within the limits of yours Requested our Certificate in order to be joined thereto...We recommend her...
Signed in & on behalf of York Monthly Meeting Held the 8th day of 7th mo 1807   By Jonathan Jessop clerk
                                      Susanna Jessop clerk

#225 8th of 7th mo 1807   SARAH LEWIS
To Robinson Monthly Meeting
Sarah Lewis having removed within the Limits of your meeting...clear of debt and Marriage Engagements known to us...we recommend her
Signed in and on behalf of York Monthly Meeting held the 8th of the 7th mo 1807   By Jonathan Jessop   clerk
                                      Susanna Jessop   clerk

#226 18th of 7th mo 1807   JOSEPH ELGAR
To York Monthly Meeting
Joseph Elgar having requested our Certificate for himself and Margaret his wife to be joined to your meeting...Both are recommended Ministers...we recommend them...
Signed in and on behalf of Pipe Creek Monthly Meeting held the 18th day of the 7th mo 1807   By Thos Russell   clerk
                                      Jane Hibberd   clerk

REMOVALS

#227 7th of 10th mo 1807   HANNAH LEWIS
To Gunpowder Monthly Meeting
Hannah Lewis a member of our Meeting having removed within the limits
of yours, requests our Certificate in order to be joined
thereto...Clear of Marriage engagements known to us, we recommend her
Signed in and on behalf of York Monthly Meeting held the 7th Day of
the 10th mo 1807   By Jonathan Jessop clerk
                             Ann Love clerk

#228 7th of 2nd mo 1807   ELIZA HAMMERSLY
To York Monthly Meeting
Eliza Hammersly requested our Certificate in order to be joined to
your meeting she being removed with her husband within the verge
thereof...we therefor recommend her
Signed in and on behalf of Warrington Monthly Meeting held the 7th of
the 2nd mo 1807   Thos McMillan clerk at this time
                             Susanna Cleaver clerk

#229 17th of 10th mo 1807   JOHN ELGAR
To York Monthly Meeting
John Elgar having requested our Certificate in order to be joined to
your meeting...is clear of marriage engagements so far as we know as
a young man in membership we recommend him
Signed on behalf and by direction of Pipe Creek monthly Meeting held
at Bush Creek the 17th of the 10th mo 1807
                By Thomas Russell clerk

#230 9th of 3rd mo 1808   ORPHA SWAIN
To Philadelphia Monthly Meeting for the Southern District
Orpha Swain having requested our Certificate in order to be joined to
your meeting...is clear of debt and marriage engagements known to
us...we recommend her
Signed in and on behalf of York Monthly Meeting held the 9th day of
the 3rd mo 1808   By Jonathan Jessop clerk
             Susanna Jessop clerk at this time

#231 6th of 4th mo 1808   THOS TAYLOR
To Philadelphia Monthly Meeting
Thos Taylor requested a certificate for his son Caleb Taylor a minor
placed an apprentice to a member of your meeting we...desire his
preservation and your Christian care toward him
Signed in & on behalf of York Monthly Meeting held the 6th day of the
4th mo 1808   By Jonathan Jessop clerk

#232 19th of 4th mo 1808   HARMAN U. COPE
To Baltimore Monthly Meeting
Request being made to us for a certificate for Harman U. Cope a minor

WARRINGTON MONTHLY MEETING

placed with a member of your meeting...we desire his preservation and your Christian care toward him
Signed in and on behalf of York Monthly Meeting held by adjournment the 19th day of the 4th mo 1808.
By Jonathan Jessop clerk

#233 4th of 5th mo 1808   ZEPHANIAH UNDERWOOD
To Warrington Monthly Meeting
Zephaniah Underwood & Hannah his wife Members of our meeting have requested our Certificate for themselves and their two minor children (viz Charles and Rebeckah) to be joined to yours...we therefore recommend them...
Signed in and on behalf of York Monthly Meeting held the 4th day of the 5th mo 1808   By Jonathan Jessop clerk
                              Susannah Jessop clerk

#234 5th of 4th mo 1808   AMOS GILBERT
York Monthly Meeting
Amos Gilbert hath requested our Certificate to your Meeting...no obstruction appears to his being recommended as a member of our Religious society   Signed in and on behalf of Sadsbury Monthly Meeting held the 5th day of the 4th mo 1808
By John Williams clerk

#235 9th of 8th mo 1809   HANNAH MATTHEWS
To Baltimore Monthly Meeting
Our esteemed friend Hannah Matthews having removed and settled within the limits of your Meeting requests our Certificate to be joined thereto...as a member in Unity with us, we affectionately recommend her   Signed in and on behalf of York Monthly Meeting held the 9th day of the 8th mo 1809
           By Jonathan Jessop clerk
              Susanna Jessop clerk

#236 4th of 10th mo 1809   JOSEPH KIRK
To Baltimore Monthly Meeting held for the Western District
Joseph Kirk having requested our Certificate to your meeting he having removed and settled within the verge thereof...we recommend him...
Signed in and on behalf of York Monthly Meeting held the 4th day of the 10th mo 1809   By Jonathan Jessop clerk

#237 8th of 11th mo 1809   LYDIA JEFFRIES
To Baltimore Monthly Meeting for the Western District
Lydia Jeffries a member of our Meeting having removed to reside with her husband within the limits of yours, requests our Certificate in order to be joined thereto...we recommend her...

REMOVALS

Signed in and on behalf of York Monthly Meeting held the 8th day of
the 11th mo 1809   Caleb Kirk clerk at this time
                        Susanna Jessop clerk

#238 10th of 1st mo 1810   ISRAEL UPDEGRAFF
To Concord Monthly Meeting in the State of Ohio
Application...for Israel Updegraff a member of our meeting in order
to be joined to yours...we recommend him...
Signed in and on behalf of York Monthly Meeting in Pennsylvania held
the 10th day of the 1st month 1810
                By Jonathan Jessop clerk

#239 10th of 1st mo 1810   THOS CONARD
To Concord Monthly Meeting in the State of Ohio
Application...for Thos Conard and Sarah his wife members of our
meeting in order to be joined to yours...we recommend them with their
three children (viz) William; Mary and Hannah...
Signed in and on behalf of York Monthly Meeting (In Pennsylvania)
held the 10th day of the first month 1810
                By Jonathan Jessop clerk
                    Mary Updegraff clerk at this time

#240 10th of 1st mo 1810   AMOS GRIST
To Monallen Monthly Meeting
Application being made by Amos Grist and Pheby his wife Members of
our meeting for a Certificate in order to be joined to yours, they
being removed within the verge thereof...we therefore recommend
them...Signed in and on behalf of York Monthly Meeting held the 10th
day of the first Month 1810
                By Jonathan Jessop clerk
                    Mary Updegraff clerk at this time

#241 13th of 1st mo 1810   NATHAN ELGAR
York Monthly Meeting
We are informed Nathan Elgar is now living with his father we
therefore think it best to send a Certificate for him to your Meeting
and as he has been for a long time from among us we can say nothing
about his life and conduct but as a member of our Society we
recommend him... signed in and by order of Pipe Creek Monthly Meeting
held the 13th of the 1st mo 1810
                By Israel Howell clerk

#242 9th of 5th mo 1810   MARY WILLIAMS
To Warrington Monthly Meeting
Mary Williams a member of our meeting having removed and settled with
her husband within the limits of yours, requested our Certificate in
order to be joined thereto...we therefore recommend her...

WARRINGTON MONTHLY MEETING

Signed in and on behalf of York Monthly Meeting held the ninth day of the fifth month 1810   By Jonathan Jessop   clerk
Susanna Jessop   clerk

#243 18th of 1st mo 1810   ELI LEWIS
To York Monthly Meeting
Eli Lewis a minor having resided for some time past within the limits of your meeting we therefore certify you that he has a right of membership with us and as such recommend him...
Signed in and on behalf of Warrington Monthly Meeting held the 18th day of the 1st mo 1810   Thomas McMillan clerk

#244 6th of 6th mo 1810   JESSE HARRY
To York Monthly Meeting
Jesse Harry requested our Certificate for himself, Mary his wife and their Son Lewis Harry (a minor) to be joined to your Meeting...We therefore recommend them
Signed in & by Direction of London Grove Monthly meeting held the 6th of 6th mo 1810
Hannah Pusay   By   Isaac Broomel
Joseph Pennock   Hannah Pennock   clerks
John Pennock   Mary Swayne
Jehu Lord   Lydia Man
Benjamin Walton   Margaret Brookes
                              Naomi Pusey

#245 8th of 8th mo 1810   ANN BENNET
To London Grove Monthly Meeting
Ann Bennet having removed from us in 1796 and being now settled within the limits of your meeting...we therefore recommend her...
signed in and on behalf of York Monthly Meeting held the 8th of the 8th mo 1810   By Jonathan Jessop clerk
Susannah Jessop   clerk

#246 9th of 5th mo 1810   MARY HARRY JR
To York Monthly Meeting
Mary Harry Junr requested our Certificate in order to be joined to your meeting...there is not any thing appears to obstruct her being recommended as a member to your Friendly Care
Signed in and on behalf of London Grove Monthly Meeting held 5th mo 9th 1810
Joseph Smith   By   Hannah Pennock
John Pennock   Elizabeth Pennock clerks
Caleb Pusey   Margaret Brooks
Joseph Pennock   Mary Swayne
                              Neomy Pusey

REMOVALS

#247 9th of 5th mo 1810   **ORPHA HARRY**
To York Monthly Meeting
Orpha Harry requested our Certificate in order to be joined to your Meeting...there is not any thing appears to obstruct her being recommended as a member to your Friendly Care.
Signed in and on behalf of London Grove Monthly Meeting held 5th mo 9th 1810   By Isaac Broomel   clerk

Joseph Smith   Hannah Pennock   clerk
John Pennock   Rebecca Pusey
Caleb Pusey   Margaret Brookes
Joseph Pennock   Elizabeth Penock
                               Naomi Pusey

#248 6th of 3rd mo 1811   **SAMUEL UPDEGRAFF**
To Baltimore Monthly Meeting for the Western District
Samuel Updegraff a member of our Meeting requested our certificate in order to be joined to yours...clear of debt and marriage engagements known to us We recommend him...
Signed in and on behalf of York Monthly Meeting held the 6th day of the 3rd mo 1811   (unsigned)

#249 6th of 3rd mo 1811   **AMBROSE UPDEGRAFF**
To Baltimore monthly Meeting for the Western District
Ambrose Updegraff and Rachel his Wife having Requested our Certificate for themselves and three of their Children to your Meeting...we recommend them with their three children (viz) Cyrus; Edith & Sarah...
Signed in and on behalf of York Monthly Meeting held the 6th day of the 3rd month 1811   Jonathan Jessop   clerk
                                Susanna Jessop   clerk

#250 10th of 4th mo 1811   **SUSANNAH UPDEGRAFF**
To Pipe Creek Monthly Meeting
Susannah Updegraff a member of our meeting requested our certificate in order to be joined to yours...is clear of debt and marriage engagements known to us, we therefore recommend her...
Signed in and on behalf of York Monthly Meeting held the 10th of the 4th mo 1811   By Jonathan Jessop   clerk
                                Susanna Jessop   clerk

#251 10th of 4th mo 1811   **CORNELIUS GARRETSON**
To Baltimore Monthly Meeting for the Western District
Cornelius Garretson (a member of our meeting) when about to remove and settle within the Verge of yours requested our Certificate for himself and Hannah his wife and their six children in order to be Joined thereto...We recommend them with their six children (viz) Isaac; Eli; Joseph; Jesse; Margaret; and Rachel

WARRINGTON MONTHLY MEETING

Signed in and on behalf of York Monthly Meeting held the 10th day of the 4th mo 1811   By Jonathan Jessop   clerk
                                        Susanna Jessop   clerk

#252 7th of 5th mo 1811   SAMUEL SMITH
To Friends of York Monthly Meeting
Samuel Smith requested our Certificate for himself, Ruth his wife and four Children Namely Orpha; Eliza; Lewis and Samuel Smith to be joined to your Meeting they being Removed within the limits thereof...we recommend them with their four minor children...
Signed in and by order of Sadsbury Monthly Meeting held the 7th of 5th mo 1811   By   John Williams   Clerk
                                        Rachel Daniel   clerk
Wm Brinton   Hannah Whitson
Jeremiah Cooper   Susanna Brinton   Mary More
James Cooper   Wm. Gibbons   Deborah Gibbons

#253 22nd of 5th mo 1811   ABNER THOMAS
To Friends of York Monthly Meeting
Abner and Esther Thomas have requested our Certificate to your Meeting for themselves and their four minor children namely Elen Thomas; George Worret Thomas; Charles A. Thomas and Rachel Thomas...we recommend them with their children...
Signed in and on behalf of Menallen Monthly Meeting held the 22nd of the 5th month 1811   By Joseph Griest Jr   clerk
                                        Rebekah Garretson   clerk

#254 8th of 5th mo 1811   AMOS JAMES
To York Monthly Meeting Pennsylvania
Amos James having applyed for our certificate in order to enable him to accomplish his Marriage with Mary Cope a member of your Meeting... as a member we recommend him in his weighty undertaking...
Signed by order of Baltimore Monthly Meeting for the Western District the 8th of the 5th month 1811
                By   Isak Procter clerk

#255 10th of 7th mo 1811   SARAH COOK
To Warrington Monthly Meeting
Sarah Cook a member of our meeting having removed with her husband within the limits of yours...we recommend her...Signed in and on behalf of York Monthly Meeting held the 10th day of the 7th mo 1811
                By Jonathan Jessop   clerk
                   Susanna Jessop clerk

#256 23rd of 5th mo 1811   MARY WILLIAMS
To York Monthly Meeting
Mary Williams Requested our Certificate in order to be joined to your meeting she being removed and settled in the verge thereof ...We

REMOVALS

recommend her...given forth at Warrington Monthly Meeting held the 23rd day of the 5th mo 1811 and signed in and by order of the same By Daniel Cookson   clerk at this time
                                Ann Garretson   clerk at this time

#257 7th of 8th mo 1811   MARY JAMES
To Baltimore Monthly Meeting for the western district
Mary James a member of our meeting having removed with her husband within the limits of yours requested our certificate to be joined thereto...we recommend her...
Signed by order of York monthly Meeting held the 8th mo 7th 1811
                    By   Jonathan Jessop   clerk
                         Susanna Jessop   clerk

#258 6th of 11th mo 1811   RACHEL JOHN
To Baltimore Monthly Meeting for the Western District
Rachel John a member of our meeting has requested our certificate in order to be joined to yours...clear of debt or marriage engagements known to us we recommend her...
Signed in and on behalf of York Monthly Meeting held the 6th of the 11th mo 1811   By Jonathan Jessop clerk
                             Susannah Jessop   clerk

#259 6th of 11th mo 1811   ANN JOHN
To Baltimore Monthly Meeting for the Western District
Ann John a member of our Meeting has requested our certificate in order to be joined to yours...clear of debt or marriage engagements known to us. We recommend her
Signed in and on behalf of york monthly Meeting held the 6th of the 11th mo 1811   By Jonathan Jessop clerk
                             Susannah Jessop   clerk

#260 4th of 3rd mo 1812   SAMUEL GARRETSON
To Baltimore Monthly Meeting held for the western district
Request was made for a certificate for Samuel Garretson and Ann his wife with their two minor Children Isaac and James...we recommend them...
Signed in and by order of York Monthly Meeting held 4th of the 3rd mo 1812   By Jonathan Jessop   clerk
                            Susanna Jessop   clerk

#261 8th of 4th mo 1812   THOMAS TAYLOR
To Baltimore Monthly Meeting held for the Western District
Thomas Taylor requested a Certificate for his son Nicholas Way Taylor a minor placed an apprentice with a friend of your Meeting...we recommend him
Signed in and on behalf of York Monthly Meeting held the 8th day of the 4th month 1812   Jonathan Jessop clerk

WARRINGTON MONTHLY MEETING

#262 8th of 12th mo 1812   WILLIAM HILL
To York Monthly Meeting Pennsylvania
William Hill having removed within the limits of your meeting...We
therefore recommend him as a member...
Signed in and on behalf of Baltimore Monthly Meeting for the western
District 4th mo 8th 1812   Samuel C. Jones clerk

#263 8th of 4th mo 1812   NATHAN KIRK
To Plainfield Monthly Meeting in the State of Ohio
Nathan Kirk having removed for some time past within the limits of
your meeting requested Certificate to be joined thereto...we
recommend him...
Signed in and by order of York Monthly Meeting held the 8th Day of
the 4th mo 1812   Jonathan Jessop clerk

#264 10th of 3rd mo 1813   HENRY COX
To Londongrove Monthly Meeting
Henry Cox (a member of our meeting) being about to remove with his
family and settle within the verge of yours, requested our
certificate for himself and his nine minor children (viz) Mary;
Sackville Hamilton; Elenora Leticia; Henry Washington; Catherine Ann;
Alexander James; William John; and Jane Eliza [and Arabella Dorothy]
In order to be joined thereto...We recommend them...
Signed in and on behalf of York Monthly Meeting held the 10th day of
the 3rd month 1813   By John Elgar clerk
                           Susanna Jessop clerk

#265 10th of 3rd mo 1813   MARTHA COX
To London Grove Monthly Meeting
Martha Cox a member of our meeting being about to remove with her
parents within the limits of yours requests our Certificate in order
to be joined thereto...clear of Marriage engagements known to us, we
therefore recommend her...
Signed in and on behalf of York Monthly Meeting held the 10th of 3rd
mo 1813   By John Elgar clerk
                    Susanna Jessop clerk

#266 10th of 3rd mo 1813   RICHARD COX
To Londongrove Monthly Meeting
Richard Cox a member of our meeting being about to remove (with his
mother) and settle within the Verge of yours...is clear of debt or
Marriage engagements known to us--we recommend him...
Signed in and on behalf of York Monthly Meeting held the 10th day of
the 3rd mo 1813   By John Elgar clerk

#267 10th of 3rd mo 1813   DAVID HUTCHISON COX
To Londongrove Monthly Meeting

REMOVALS

David Hutchison Cox a member of our meeting being about to remove (with his father) and settle within the Verge of yours Requested our certificate in order to be joined thereto...is clear of debt or Marriage engagements known to us--We recommend him...
Signed in and on behalf of York Monthly Meeting held the 10th day of the 3rd mo 1813   By John Elgar clerk

#268 10th of 3rd mo 1813   JOSHUA HAMILTON COX
To Londongrove Monthly Meeting
Joshua Hamilton Cox a member of our meeting being about to remove (with his father) and settle within the Verge of yours, requested our certificate in order to be joined thereto...is clear of debt or marriage engagements known to us--We recommend him...
Signed in and on behalf of York Monthly Meeting held the 10th day of the 3rd month 1813   By John Elgar clerk

#269 5th of 5th mo 1813   JOHN LOVE
To Baltimore Monthly Meeting for the Western District.
Request hath been made for a certificate for John Love a minor who is placed with a friend of your meeting...We therefore recommend him
Signed on behalf of York Monthly Meeting held the 5th Day of the 5th mo 1813   By John Elgar clerk

#270 10th of 3rd mo 1813   JOSEPH KIRK
To York Monthly Meeting
Joseph Kirk having requested our certificate to you...he is clear of debt, and marriage engagements...we recommend him...
Signed in and on behalf of the Monthly Meeting of Baltimore for the Western District held the 10th of the 3rd mo 1813
                          By Samuel G. Jones clerk

#271 7th of 7th mo 1813   SUSANNA UPDEGRAFF
To Redstone Monthly Meeting
Susanna Updegraff a member of our Meeting having requested our Certificate...We therefore recommend her...
Signed in and on behalf of York Monthly Meeting held the 7th of 7th mo 1813   By John Elgar clerk
              Susanna Jessop   clerk

#272 8th of 6th mo 1814   ANN WORLEY
To Redstone Monthly Meeting
Ann Worley a member of our Meeting having requested a Certificate We recommend her...
Signed in and on behalf of York Monthly Meeting held the 8th Day of the 6th month 1814   By Amos Farquhar
                    Mary Updegraff   clerks

WARRINGTON MONTHLY MEETING

#273 8th if 6th mo 1814   **WILLIAM KIRK**
To Baltimore Monthly Meeting held for the Western District
William Kirk a member of our Meeting who has resided remote from us, for some years past has requested our Certificate on his behalf...is clear of Marriage engagements known to us we recommend him
Signed in and on behalf of York Monthly Meeting held the 8th day of the 6th mo 1814   By Amos Farquhar clerk

#274 19th of 6th mo 1813   **AMOS FARQUHAR**
To York Monthly Meeting Pennsylvania
Amos Farquhar having requested our Certificate to be joined to your Meeting with Mary his wife...we recommend them with their six minor children viz Margaret; Charles; Phebe; Ann; Granville and Wm Henry...
Signed on behalf of Pipe Creek Monthly Meeting held the 19th of the 6th mo 1813   By Eli Elliot

#275 6th of 7th mo 1814   **BULAH KIRK**
To Redstone Monthly Meeting
Request having been made to our meeting for a Certificate for Bulah Kirk...clear of marriage engagements as far as appears as a member we recommend her
Signed on behalf of York Monthly Meeting held the 6th Day of the 7th mo 1814   By Amos Farquhar
                    Mary Updegraff clerks

#276 6th of 7th mo 1814   **SUSAN KIRK**
To Redstone Monthly Meeting
Request having been made to our meeting for certificate for Susan Kirk to be joined to yours...clear of marriage engagements as far as appears as a member we recommend her
Signed on behalf of York Monthly Meeting held the 6th Day of the 7th mo 1814   Amos Farquhar
                   Mary Updegraff clerks

#277 6th of 7th mo 1814   **TIMOTHY KIRK**
To Redstone Monthly Meeting
Timothy Kirk and Edith his wife having requested a Certificate to be joined to your Meeting...as Members we recommend them...
Signed on behalf of York Monthly Meeting held the 6th of the 7th month 1814   Amos Farquhar
                 Mary Updegraff jr clerks

#278 7th of 9th mo 1814   **SIDNEY COATS**
To Redstone Monthly Meeting
Sidney Coats a member of our Meeting having removed within the limits of yours requested our Certificate...is clear of debt and marriage engagements known to us we recommend her

REMOVALS

Signed by direction of York Monthly Meeting held the 7th of the 9th
mo 1814   Amos Farquhar
                       Mary Updegraff jr   clerks

#279 7th of 9th mo 1814   JOHN WORLEY
To Redstone Monthly Meeting
John Worley and Elizabeth his wife requested a Certificate for
themselves and six minor children: Maryann; Aaron; Jacob; Caleb; Asey
and Lydia to be joined to you...as members we recommend them Signed
in and by order of York Monthly Meeting held the 7th of the 9th mo
1814   Amos Farquhar
                       Mary Updegraff   clerks

#280 4th of 1st mo 1815   MARY GILLINGHAM
To Baltimore Monthly Meeting for the western District
Mary Gillingham a member of our meeting having removed and settled
with her husband within the compas of yours...We affectionately
recommend her...
Signed on behalf of York Monthly Meeting held 4th day of the 1st mo
1815   Amos Farquhar
                       Mary Willis   clerks

#281 7th of 6th mo 1815   MARY COATS
To Redstone Monthly Meeting
Mary Coats a member of our meeting having requested our certificate
in order to be joined to yours...We therefore recommend her
Signed in and on behalf of York Monthly Meeting
held 6th mo 7th 1815   Amos Farquhar
                           Mary Willis   clerks

#282 7th of 6th mo 1815   RACHEL COATES
To Redstone Monthly Meeting
Request having been made to our meeting for a certificate for Rachel
Coates to be joined to yours...clear of marriage engagements as far
as appears as a member we recommend her to your care. Signed in and
on behalf of York Monthly Meeting
held 6th mo 7th 1815   Amos Farquhar
                           Mary Willis   clerks

#283 6th of 9th mo 1815   FRANCIS SWAYNE
To Menallin Monthly Meeting
Francis Swayne and Sarah his wife having requested a Certificate for
themselves and their daughter Jane in order to join them to your
meeting...as members we recommend them
Signed by direction of York Monthly Meeting held the 6th of the 9th
month 1815   Amos Farquhar
                       Mary Willis Clerks

WARRINGTON MONTHLY MEETING

#284 10th of 1st mo 1816   WILLIAM HILL
To the Monthly Meeting in Baltimore for the Western District
William Hill a member of our Meeting requested our Certificate to
your meeting he having removed within your limits...We recommend him
Signed in and on behalf of York Monthly Meeting
     held the 10th day of the 1st mo 1816
                         Amos Farquhar   clerk

#285 20th of 12th mo 1815   JANE RUMMELS
To York Monthly Meeting
Jane Rummels having requested our Certificate in order to be joined
to your meeting...recommended a member...Signed in and by Direction
of Warrington Monthly Meeting held at Newbery the 20th of the 12th mo
1815   Thos McMillan
                         Ann Garretson   clerks

#286 9th of 10th mo 1816   NICHOLAS TAYLOR
To Baltimore Monthly Meeting for the Eastern District
A certificate having been requested for Nicholas Taylor a member of
our meeting who has removed within your limits...We therefore
recommend him Signed on behalf of York Monthly Meeting held the 9th
day of the 10th mo 1816   Amos Farquhar   clerk

#287 9th of 10th mo 1816   SAMUEL HARLAND
To Baltimore Monthly Meeting for the Western district
Samuel Harland having requested a Certificate to your meeting...as a
member we recommend him...
Signed on behalf and by direction of York Monthly Meeting
held the 9th day of the 10th month 1816 Amos Farquhar   clerk

#288 9th of 10th mo 1816   HERMAN LOVE
To Baltimore Monthly Meeting for the Western district
A certificate of removal to your meeting having been requested for
Herman Love...recommend...him.
Signed on behalf and by direction of York Monthly Meeting held the
9th of the 10th mo 1816   By Amos Farquhar   clerk

#289 6th of 11th mo 1816   THOMAS UNDERWOOD
To Baltimore Monthly Meeting for the Western District
A Certificate having been requested for Thomas Underwood a minor to
join him to your meeting...recommend...him a member
Signed on behalf and by direction of York Monthly Meeting
held the 6th of the 11th mo 1816   By Amos Farquhar   clerk

#290 6th of 11th mo 1816   ELI KIRK
To Baltimore Monthly Meeting for the Western district
A certificate having been Requested for Eli Kirk a minor to join him
to your meeting recommend...him a member

222

REMOVALS

Signed on behalf and by direction of York Monthly Meeting held the 6th of the 11th mo 1816 By Amos Farquhar   clerk

#291 9th of 7th mo 1817   AMOS GILBERT
To Sadsbury Monthly Meeting
Amos Gilbert having requested our Certificate we...recommend him a member...Signed on behalf and by direction of York Monthly Meeting held the 9th of the 7th mo 1817
                        Amos Farquhar clerk

#292 10th of 9th mo 1817   AMOS LEWIS
To Center Monthly Meeting
Amos Lewis having requested our Certificate We...recommend him a member...Signed by direction and on behalf of York Monthly Meeting held the 10th of the 9th month 1817
                        Amos Farquhar clerk

#293 4th of 2nd mo 1818   CHARLES FARQUHAR
To Pipe Creek Monthly Meeting
Charles Farquhar a minor and member of our meeting having removed and Settled within the limits of your meeting hath requested a certificate in order to be joined thereto we therefore recommend him...Signed in and on behalf of York Monthly Meeting held the 4th day of the 2nd month 1818
                        By Jonathan Jessop clerk at this time.

#294 9th of 9th mo 1818   ABNER THOMAS
To Sadsbury Monthly Meeting
Abner Thomas and Esther his wife Requested our Certificate of Membership for themselves and their minor Children (to wit) Ellen; George W.; Charles A; Rachel; William R; and Sarah Ann Thomas to your Meeting...we recommend them
Signed in and on behalf of York Monthly Meeting held the 9th of the 9th mo 1818   By Jonathan Jessop clerk at this time
                    and Hannah Updegraff clerk

#295 7th of 10th mo 1818   JOHN GILBERT
To Sadsbury Monthly Meeting
John Gilbert having requested our certificate to your Meeting...we recommend him...Signed by direction of York Monthly Meeting held the 7th of the 10th mo 1818
                By Amos Farquhar clerk

#296 10th of 3rd mo 1819   JAMES SPEAKMAN
To Alum Creek Monthly Meeting Delaware County State of Ohio
James Speakman having requested our certificate to your meeting, ...We recommend him   Signed by direction of York Monthly Meeting in Pennsylvania held the 10th day of 3rd mo 1819

WARRINGTON MONTHLY MEETING

Amos Farquhar   clerk

#297 5th of 5th mo 1819   ELISHA KIRK
To Short Creek Monthly Meeting in the State of Ohio
Elisha Kirk having requested a Certificate to your meeting...is clear of Marriage Engagements known to us, as a member we recommend him Signed in and on behalf of York Monthly Meeting in Pennsylvania held the 5th day of the 5th mo 1819   Amos Farquhar clerk

#298 5th of 1st mo 1820   ELISHA PLUMMER
To Pipe Creek Monthly Meeting
Elisha Plummer having requested a certificate to be joined to your meeting...is clear of debt and marriage engagements, so far as we know...we recommend him to your care.
Signed on behalf of york Monthly Meeting held the 5th of the 1st mo 1820   Amos Farquhar clerk

#299 9th of 7th mo 1823   ELIZABETH SWAIN
To Philadelphia Monthly Meeting
Elizabeth Swain having requested our certificate to your monthly meeting...we recommend her to your care   Signed on behalf of York Monthly Meeting held the 9th of 7th month 1823 by
                              Jonathan Jessop   clerk
                              Hannah Updegraff   clerk

#300 7th of 6th mo 1820   EDWARD NEEDLES
To Duck Creek Monthly Meeting State of Delaware
Edward Needles having requested a Certificate to your meeting...we recommend him...Signed on behalf   of York   Monthly Meeting in Pennsylvania held the seventh day of the 6th mo 1820
                              Jonathan Jessop
                              Clerk at this time

#301 6th of 9th mo 1820   JOSEPH U. JESSOP
To Gunpowder Monthly Meeting
Request having been made for a Certificate for Joseph U. Jessop a member of our meeting who has settled within the limits of yours, ...recommended...Signed in and on behalf of York Monthly Meeting held the 6th day of the ninth month 1820
                    Amos Farquhar clerk

#302 7th of 2nd mo 1821   SUSANNA NORBURY
To Baltimore Monthly Meeting
Susanna Norbury a member of our meeting having requested our Certificate in order to be joined to yours...is free of marriage engagements known to us, we recommend her...Signed on behalf of York Monthly Meeting held the 7th of the 2nd mo 1821 by
     Amos Farquhar clerk   Hannah Updegraff   clerk

REMOVALS

#303 5th of 9th mo 1821   **LEWIS HARRY**
To Warrington Monthly Meeting
Lewis Harry and his wife Maria having requested a certificate for themselves and their child Malinda to join them to your meeting. ...recommending them to your care. Signed by Direction of York Monthly Meeting held the 5th day of the 9th month 1821
         Jonathan Jessop clerk
         Hannah Updegraff clerk

#304 10th of 4th mo 1822   **JOHN WILSON**
To Warrington Monthly Meeting
John Wilson having removed from us for some time past and now settled within your limits being a member of our Meeting we recommend him...Signed in and on behalf of York Monthly Meeting held the 10th day of the 4th month 1822 By Amos Farquhar Clerk at this time

#305 10th of 4th mo 1822   **ERASTUS U. KIRK**
To Malborough Monthly Meeting in the State of Ohio
Request having been made for a certificate for Erastus U. Kirk...recommended...Signed in and on behalf of York Monthly Meeting held the 10th day of the 4th month 1822
         Amos Farquhar clerk at this time

#306 10th of 7th mo 1822   **HENRY BUSHONG**
To Monallin Monthly Meeting
Henry Bushong and Sarah his wife members of our meeting having requested our Certificate for themselves and their five minor children viz Lydia; John; Jesse; Jacob and Caroline to be joined to your Meeting...recommended...Signed in and on behalf of York Monthly Meeting held the 10th day of the 7th month 1822
         Jonathan Jessop   clerk
         Hannah Updegraff   clerk

#307 4th of 2nd mo 1824   **HANNAH DINGE**
To Sadsbury Monthly Meeting
Hannah Dinge a member of our meeting having removed with her husband and settled within the limits of yours...we therefore recommend her...Signed in and on behalf of York Monthly Meeting held the 4th day of the 2nd month 1824
         Jonathan Jessop clerk
         Hannah Updegraff clerk

#308 10th of 2nd mo 1824   **ORPAH GARRETSON**
To Warrington Monthly Meeting
Orpah Garretson requests our certificate to your meeting she having removed with her husband to reside within the limits thereof...we recommend her...Signed in and on behalf of York Monthly Meeting held the 4th day of the 2nd mo 1824

WARRINGTON MONTHLY MEETING

Jonathan Jessop   clerk
Hannah Updegraff   clerk

#309 10th of 3rd mo 1824   MARGARET FARQUHAR
To Indian Spring Monthly Meeting
Margaret Farquhar a member of our meeting having removed and settled within the limits of your requested our Certificate...we therefore recommend her...Signed in and on behalf of York Monthly Meeting held the 10th Day of the 3rd month 1824
    By Jonathan Jessop
        Hannah Updegraff   clerks

#310 5th of 5th mo 1824   AQUILLA M. KIRK
To Marlborough Monthly Meeting in Stark County in the State of Ohio Aquilla M. Kirk and Sarah his wife having requested a Certificate for themselves and their four children (to wit) Elmira; Lydia Ann; Elizabeth Needles and Catherine in order to be joined to your Meeting...we recommend them...Signed in and on behalf of york Monthly Meeting held the 5th day of the 5th mo 1824
    By Jonathan Jessop
        Hannah Updegraff   clerks

#311 5th of 5th mo 1824   CALEB KIRK
To Marlborough Monthly Meeting Stark County in the State of Ohio. Caleb Kirk having requested our certificate for himself and Lydia his wife...we recommend them   Signed in and on behalf of York Monthly Meeting held the 5th day of the 5th month 1824
    By Jonathan Jessop
        Hannah Updegraff   clerks

#312 5th of 5th mo 1824   AMOS FARQUHAR
To Indian Spring Monthly Meeting
Amos Farquhar and Mary His Wife Members of our Meeting having requested a Certificate for themselves and children (to wit) Ann; Granville; William Henry and Mary in order to be joined to your Meeting...we recommend them   Signed in & on behalf of York Monthly Meeting held the 5th day of the 5th mo 1824
    By Jonathan Jessop
        Hannah Updegraff   clerks

#313 5th of 5th mo 1824   PHEBE FARQUHAR
To Indian Spring Monthly Meeting
Phebe Farquhar a member of our meeting having requested our Certificate in order to be joined to yours, We therefore recommend her   Signed in and on behalf of York Monthly Meeting held the 5th day of the 5th mo 1824
    By Jonathan Jessop
        Hannah Updegraff   clerks

REMOVALS

#314 5th of 5th mo 1824   CALEB KIRK
To Marlborough Monthly Meeting in Stark County in the State of Ohio
Caleb Kirk requested a Certificate for his Son Henry C. Kirk a member
of our Meeting in order to be joined to yours we recommend him
Signed in and on behalf of York Monthly Meeting held the 5th day of
the 5th month 1824   By Jonathan Jessop clerk

#315 20th of 10th mo 1825   JACOB THOMAS
To York Monthly Meeting
Jacob Thomas and Margaret his wife requested our Certificate in order
to be joined to your Meeting we therefore Recommend them as members
of our society with their four minor children Namely Jonathan;
Esther; Ellen; and Rachel   Signed on behalf of Menalen Monthly
Meeting had the 20th of the 10th mo 1825
                             Samuel Comly
                             Hannah Garretson clerks
                                               at present

#316 4th of 10th mo 1826   JACOB WORLEY
Whereas Jacob Worley having been a member of the Society of friends
but hath so far deviated from the principles of truth as professed
by them as to leave his wife and family and is gone away in a very
disreputable manner; for which disorderly conduct we disown him the
said Jacob Worley from being any longer a member of our religious
Society untill his future good conduct shall recommend him worthy--
At York Monthly Meeting 10th mo 4th 1826
Approved and signed   By John Elgar clerk at this time

#317 10th of 6th mo 1829   JACOB THOMAS
To New Garden Monthly Meeting Ohio
Jacob Thomas and Margaret his wife requested our Certificate for
themselves and their minor children Esther, Ellen R., and Rachel to
be joined to your meeting...we recommend them...Signed on behalf of
York Monthly Meeting held the 10th of the 6th mo 1829
               By   John Love Clerk at this time
                    Elizabeth Willis clerk at this time

#318 10th of 5th mo 1829   HANNAH THOMAS
To New Garden Monthly Meeting
Hannah Thomas having requested our Certificate to your meeting we
hereby inform you that she is a member and recommend her...
Signed in and on behalf of York Monthly Meeting held the 10th of the
5th mo 1829   By John Love clerk at this time
                     Elizabeth Willis clerk at this time

#319 10th of 6th mo 1829   JONATHAN THOMAS
To New Garden Monthly Meeting in the State of Ohio

WARRINGTON MONTHLY MEETING

Jonathan Thomas requested a certificate to be joined to your meeting...recommend him...Signed in and on behalf of York Monthly Meeting held the 10th day of the 6th month 1829
By John Love clerk at this time

#320 10th of 6th mo 1829   ABEL THOMAS
To New Garden Monthly Meeting in the State of Ohio
Abel Thomas requested a Certificate to be joined to your meeting. ...we recommend him...Signed in and on behalf of York Monthly Meeting held the 10th day of the 6th month 1829
By John Love clerk at this time

#321 10th of 6th mo 1829   WILLIAM OWEN
To White Water Monthly Meeting of Friends in Wayne County, Ohio
William Owen having requested our certificate in order to be joined to your meeting...we therefore recommend him...
Signed in and on behalf of York Monthly Meeting held the 10th of 6th month 1829   By John Love clerk at this time

#322 5th of 4th mo 1832   ELIZA SMITH
To Birmingham Monthly Meeting in Chester County
Eliza Smith having moved within the limits of your meeting requested our certificate to be joined thereto...we recommend her Signed in and on behalf of York Monthly Meeting held the 5th of the 4th mo 1832 By Jonathan Jessop
Elizabeth Willis   clerks

#323 5th of 4th mo 1832   SARAH SMITH
To Birmingham Monthly Meeting in Chester County
Sarah Smith having moved within the limits of your meeting, requests our certificate to be joined thereto...we recommend her
Signed in and on behalf of York Monthly Meeting
held the 5th day of the 4th month 1832   By Jonathan Jessop
Elizabeth Willis   clerks

#324 5th of 4th mo 1832   EPHRAIM SMITH
To Birmingham Monthly Meeting in Chester County
Request being made for certificate for Ephraim and Jesse Smith minor children of Samuel deceased to join them to your Meeting, as members we recommend them...Signed in and on behalf of York Monthly Meeting held the 5th day of the 4th mo 1832
By Jonathan Jessop   clerk

#325 4th of 8th mo 1832   RICHARD RUMMEL
Richard Rummel having a right of membership among Friends has so far deviated from the path of rectitude as to be guilty of Fornication and has also accomplished his marriage contrary to the order of society and having been treated with on the [-?-] and showing no

REMOVALS

disposition to condemn his out going we therefore disown him from being any longer a member of our religious society...Signed in and by direction of York Monthly Meeting
By Jonathan Jessop clerk 11th mo 8th 1832

#326 10th of 1st mo 1833   SAMUEL SMITH
To New Garden Monthly Meeting in Chester County
Samuel Smith a member of our meeting requested our certificate to be joined to your meeting we recommend him...Signed in and on behalf of York Monthly Meeting held the 10th of 1st mo 1833
By Jonathan Jessop clerk

#327 6th of 2nd mo 1834   HANNAH UPDEGRAFF
To Baltimore Monthly Meeting for the Western District
Hannah Updegraff having removed within the limits of your meeting requests our Certificate to be joined thereto...we therefore recommend her...Signed in and by direction of York Monthly Meeting held the 6th of 2nd mo 1834   by   Elisha Vale
Elizabeth Willis   clerks

#328 12th of 4th mo 1834   MARY WETHERALD
To Baltimore Monthly Meeting
Mary Wetherald having removed within the limits of your meeting requests our certificate to be joined thereto...we recommend her
Signed on behalf of York Monthly Meeting held the 12th of the 4th mo 1834   By Elisha Vale
Elizabeth Willis   clerks

#329 10th of 4th mo 1834   ESTHER WETHERALD
To Baltimore Monthly Meeting
Esther Wetherald having removed within the limits of your meeting requests our certificate to be joined thereto...we recommend her Signed on behalf of York Monthly Meeting held the 10th of the 4th mo 1834   Elisha Vale
Elizabeth Willis   clerks

#330 9th of 7th mo 1835   HANNAH SMITH
To the Monthly Meeting of Friends held at Little Britton
Hannah Smith having removed within the limits of your meeting requests our certificate for herself and daughter Maria Smith to be joined thereto...we recommend them Signed in and on behalf of York Monthly Meeting held the 7th mon 9th 1835
By Joel Fisher
Elizabeth Willis clerks

#331 9th of 2nd mo 1836   SAMUEL A. KIRK
To Smithfield Monthly Meeting Ohio

WARRINGTON MONTHLY MEETING

Samuel A. Kirk requested our certificate to your meeting...we recommend him Signed in and on behalf of York Monthly Meeting held the ninth of the 2nd [?] month 1836
        By Jos. Fisher clerk

#332 9th of 9th mo 1836   ISRAEL UNDERWOOD
To Warrington Monthly meeting
Israel Underwood having removed within the verge of your Meeting ...we recommend him...Signed in and on behalf of York Monthly Meeting held the 9th of 9th mo 1836 [?]   by Joel Fisher clerk

#333 5th of 9th mo 1844   BARTHOLOMEW FUSSEE
To Kennet Monthly Meeting
Bartholomew Fussee and Rebecca his wife request our certificate for themselves and their five minor children (to wit) Joshua L; Morris; Susan; Lydia R; and Edward C. Fussee to be joined to your meeting...we recommend them...Signed in and on behalf of York Monthly Meeting held the 5th of the 9th mo 1844
        By Jonathan Jessop
           Mary Fisher   clerks

#334 11th of 4th mo 1844   JACOB HEWES
To Chester Monthly Meeting
Jacob Hewes a member of our meeting requested a Certificate of membership in order to be joined to your Meeting we recommend him Signed in and on behalf of York Monthly Meeting held the 11th of 4th mo 1844   By Jonathan Jessop clerk at this time

#335 13th of 6th mo 1844   WILLIAM TYSON
To Menallen Monthly Meeting
William Tyson and Mary Jane his wife Requests our certificate for themselves and two minor children (to wit) Robert and Lewis to be joined to your Meeting...we recommend them...Signed on behalf of York Monthly Meeting held 6th mo 13th 1844
        By   Jonathan Jessop clerk at this time
           Mary Fisher clerk

#336 9th of 3rd mo 1848   ELISHA VALE
To Monallen Monthly Meeting
Elisha Vale and Edith his wife requests our Certificate for themselves and 4 minor children to wit; Rebecca; Joseph; Guli Elma and Josiah to be joined to your Meeting...we Recommend them Signed on behalf of York Monthly Meeting held 3rd mo 9th 1848
        By   Edward Jessop
           Mary Ann Chalfont   clerks

REMOVALS

#337 18th of 5th mo 1848   SARAH ROBERTS
To Pipe Creek Monthly Meeting
Sarah Roberts having removed within the limits of your Meeting
Requests our Certificate to be joined thereto...we Recommend her
Signed in and on behalf of York Monthly Meeting held the 18th of the
5th mo 1848   By   Edward Jessop
                           Mary Ann Chalfont   clerks

#338 10th of 1st mo 1850   WILLIAM VALE
To Smithfield Monthly Meeting Ohio
William Vale has removed within the limits of your meeting...we
recommend him   Signed on behalf of York Monthly Meeting
held the 10th of the 1st mo 1850
               By Jonathan Jessop clerk at this time

#339 10th of 1st mo 1850   RUTHANNA REYNARD
To Smithfield Monthly Meeting
Ruthanna Reynard a Member of Meeting having Removed and settled
within the limits of yours we recommend her Signed in and on behalf
of York Monthly Meeting held the 10th of the 1st mo 1850
          By Jonathan Jessop Clerk at this time
               Mary Ann Chalfont clerk

#340 6th of 2nd mo 1851   DEBORAH FARQUER
To Pipecreek Monthly Meeting
Deborah Farquer having removed within the verge of your Meeting
requests our Certificate...we recommend her...Signed by direction of
York Monthly Meeting held the 6th of the 2nd month 1851
               By Jonathan Jessop
               Mary Ann Chalfant clerks

#341 9th of 10th mo 1851   JOEL FISHER
To Monallen Monthly Meeting
Joel Fisher and Mary his wife having removed within the limits of
your Meeting request our Certificate...we recommend them...
Signed in and on behalf of York Monthly Meeting the 9th of the 10th
month 1851   By   Jonathan Jessop
                       Mary Ann Chalfant   clerks

#342 4th of 6th 1854   AMOS GRIEST
To Menallen Monthly Meeting
Amos Griest and his wife Margaret having removed and settled within
the verge of yours requested our certificate for themselves and their
two minor children Rachel Ann and Willing Griest...we hereby
recommend them...Signed in and on behalf of York Monthly Meeting held
the 4th of the 6th mo 1854
            By Jonathan Jessop   Mary Ann Chalfant   clerks

231

WARRINGTON MONTHLY MEETING

#343 5th of 5th mo 1790   **SARAH MILLER**
To the Monthly Meeting of Friends to be held at Hossam
Sarah Miller being removed from us to live with her sister within the verge of your Meeting requested our Certificate to you...leaves us clear of Debt or marriage engagements...we recommend her...Signed in and on behalf of our Monthly Meeting held at York Town the 5th day of 5th mo 1790
         By   John Love   clerk at this time
             Hannah Yarnall   clerk

#344 23rd of 4th mo 1829   **THOMAS WETHERALD**
To York Monthly Meeting Pennsylvania
Our beloved Friends Thomas Wetherald a Minister in unity with us having requested a Certificate of removal for himself, Ann, his wife, and their five minor children viz Mary; Esther; Joseph Earnshaw; Samuel Brook; and Thomas, Jr...we therefore recommend them...Signed by direction and on behalf of Alexandria Monthly Meeting in the District of Columbia held the 23rd of the 4th mo 1829
               Geo - ? - clerk at this time
               Margaret Hallowell clerk
respected friend please to hand the above to the Monthly Meeting and the other half by Thomas Wetherald and oblidge thy friend
    S. Myers

#345 19th of 3rd mo 1829   **ELISHA VALE**
To York Monthly Meeting
Elisha Vale and Martha his wife requests our certificate for themselves and their five minor children namely:
Sarah Ann; Jane K; William E; Ruthanna and Ann...we recommend them...Signed on behalf of Warrington Monthly Meeting held at Warrington the 19th of the 3rd mo 1829
             Lewis Harry
             Ann Garretson--Clerk

#346 6th of 2nd mo 1851   **DEBORAH FARQUHAR**
To Pipe Creek Monthly Meeting
Deborah Farquhar having removed within the verges of your meeting...we recommend her...Signed by direction of York Monthly Meeting held the 6th of the 2nd month 1851
         By   Jonathan Jessop
           Mary Ann Chalfant

Appendix A

BIRTHS AND DEATHS

Sources:
1. Births and Deaths, Menallen Monthly Meeting Book B (1775-1857)
2. Births and Deaths, Warrington Monthly Meeting (1745-18--)
3. Births and Deaths, Menallen Monthly Meeting Book A

Menallen Book A appears to have been copied, in 1850, from Warrington, with some differences, such as dates of death added later, variations in spelling, omissions, etc. Where there are exact duplicates, the second occurrance is deleted.

Dates are expressed as day-month-year. It is evident on the original documents that some information, such as marriage or death notes added at a later time may have given the date as month-day-year.

Name		Born	Died	Father	Born	Died	Mother	Born	Died
Joel	Bateman	16-2-1809		John			Hannah		
Lydia	Bateman	26-1-1806		John			Hannah		
Mary Ann	Bateman	18-1-1808		John			Hannah		
Mary	Beals	c1695	3-11-1763						
	Mary Beals was the wife of Jacob Beals, Sr.								
Enoch	Bennet	23-1-1754		William			Liddie		
James	Bennet	2-5-1783	21-8-1784	Joshua			Mary		
Joseph	Bennet	15-8-1781		Joshua			Mary		
Rebekah	Bennet	4-1-1785		Joshua			Mary		
Rebekah	Bennet	6-4-1756		William			Liddie		
William	Bennet	27-11-1757		William			Liddie		
Edward	Bennett	7-5-1744	16-5-1757	Joseph			Rebecca		6-11-1757
Elizabeth	Bennett	25-12-1742	16-5-1757	Joseph			Rebecca		6-11-1757
Hannah	Bennett	19-10-1745	16-5-1757	Joseph			Rebecca		6-11-1757
Isaac	Bennett	21-7-1749	16-5-1757	Joseph			Rebecca		6-11-1757
Joseph	Bennett	10-7-1739	16-5-1757	Joseph			Rebecca		6-11-1757
Joshua	Bennett	19-8-1759		William			Liddie		
Mary	Bennett	15-2-1741	16-5-1757	Joseph			Rebecca		6-11-1757
Phebe	Bennett	19-7-1736	16-5-1757	Joseph			Rebecca		6-11-1757
Rebecca	Bennett	30-1-1738	16-5-1757	Joseph			Rebecca		6-11-1757
Sarah	Bennett	29-11-1734	16-5-1757	Joseph			Rebecca		6-11-1757
William	Bennett	29-4-1733	16-5-1757	Joseph			Rebecca		6-11-1757
	Bennett	19-12-1727		Joseph			Rebecca		
	Joseph Bennett and Rebecca Fincher were married at Kennett Meeting 3-20-1724								
Aaron	Berry	22-1-1763		John			Patience		
Joseph	Berry	11-11-1766		John			Patience		

234

Name	Surname	Date	Father	Date	Mother	Date
Thomas	Berry	10-3-1765	John		Patience	
Abigail	Blackburn	9-5-1764	John	3-8-1767	Rebecca	30-3-1766
Anthony	Blackburn	17-6-1749	John	3-8-1767	Rebecca	30-3-1766
Anthony	Blackburn	12-6-1767	Joseph		Deborah	
Elenor	Blackburn	30-3-1766	John	3-8-1767	Rebecca	30-3-1766
Elizabeth	Blackburn	2-10-1755	John	3-8-1767	Rebecca	30-3-1766
James	Blackburn	16-10-1763	Joseph		Deborah	
John	Blackburn	21-6-1753	John	3-8-1767	Rebecca	30-3-1766
John	Blackburn	8-1-1762	Joseph		Deborah	
Joseph	Blackburn	7-11-1757	John	3-8-1767	Rebecca	30-3-1766
Joseph	Blackburn	11-2-1769	Joseph		Deborah	
Margaret	Blackburn	16-10-1740	John	3-8-1767	Rebecca	30-3-1766
Mary	Blackburn	19-6-1751	John	3-8-1767	Rebecca	30-3-1766
Mary	Blackburn	3-4-1759	Joseph		Deborah	
Mosses	Blackburn	16-9-1746	John	3-8-1767	Rebecca	30-3-1766
Rachael	Blackburn	1-9-1742	John	3-8-1767	Rebecca	30-3-1766
Rebeccah	Blackburn	12-12-1760	John	3-8-1767	Rebecca	30-3-1766
Samuel	Blackburn	17-5-1762	John	3-8-1767	Rebecca	30-3-1766
Thomas	Blackburn	19-8-1744	John	3-8-1767	Rebecca	30-3-1766
Thomas	Blackburn	10-11-1765	Joseph		Deborah	
David	Bonine	10-1-1785	Daniel		Mary	
Isaac	Bonine	22-3-1790	Daniel		Mary	
Mary	Bonine	4-2-1760	Daniel		Elizabeth	c1760

Elizabeth Bonine was Daniel's first wife
Mary Bonine was Daniel's third wife

Name	Surname	Date	Father	Mother	Date
Rachael	Bonine	9-6-1782	Daniel	Mary	
Rebecah	Bonine	9-8-1787	Daniel	Mary	
Sarah	Bonine	13-12-1773	Daniel	Sarah	c1773

Name		Born	Died	Father	Born	Died	Mother	Born	Died
Jane	Bowen	1720	17-2-1813	Sarah Bonine was Daniel's second wife					
Thomas	Bowen	1720	8-1-1800						
Anna	Cadwallader	10-9-1787	20-9-1802	David		12-6-1846	Susanna		11-11-1804
Beulah	Cadwallader	22-10-1795	10-9-1802	David		12-6-1846	Susanna		11-11-1804
Caleb	Cadwallader	c1731	3-5-1798						
Edith	Cadwallader	14-10-1799	29-8-1802	David		12-6-1846	Susanna		11-11-1804
Hannah	Cadwallader	4-12-1793		David		12-6-1846	Susanna		11-11-1804
James	Cadwallader	15-10-1785	27-9-1802	David		12-6-1846	Susanna		11-11-1804
Margaret	Cadwallader	9-11-1766		James		29-4-1801	Mary		4-5-1801
Mary	Cadwallader	9-11-1766		James		29-4-1801	Mary		4-5-1801
Mary	Cadwallader	8-10-1783	6-9-1802	David		12-6-1846	Susanna		11-11-1804
Phebe	Cadwallader	23-10-1789	27-9-1802	David		12-6-1846	Susanna		11-11-1804
Sarah	Cadwallader		11-11-1839	Sarah Cadwallader was wife of William Cadwallader					
Susanna	Cadwallader	30-10-1791		David		12-6-1846	Susanna		11-11-1804
William	Cadwallader	29-3-1782		David		12-6-1846	Susanna		11-11-1804
Alice	Cleaver	11-4-1817		Isaac			Elizabeth		
Benjamin	Cleaver	2-1-1822	8-8-1823	Peter			Jane		
Eli	Cleaver	13-7-1815		Isaac			Elizabeth		
Elizabeth	Cleaver	10-6-1824		Peter			Jane		
Elizabeth	Cleaver	1-4-1757	11-2-1841	Peter		12-8-1795	Miriam		29-5-1798
	Elizabeth Cleaver married -?- Vale								
Hannah	Cleaver	20-6-1791		John	21-6-1760	3-5-1823	Susanna	c1763	6-7-1823
Isaac	Cleaver	23-6-1787		John	21-6-1760	3-5-1823	Susanna	c1763	6-7-1823

Name	Surname	Date	Parent	Date	Parent	Date	Parent	Date
Jane	Cleaver	7-7-1819	Isaac		Elizabeth			
John	Cleaver	9-3-1793	John	21-6-1760	Susanna	3-5-1823	c1763	6-7-1823
John	Cleaver	2-6-1813	Isaac		Elizabeth			
John	Cleaver	14-2-1826	Peter		Jane			
John	Cleaver	21-6-1760	Peter		Miriam	12-8-1795		29-5-1798
Mariah	Cleaver	10-11-1827	Peter		Jane			
Martha	Cleaver	24-4-1789	John	21-6-1760	Susanna	3-5-1823	c1763	6-7-1823
Martha	Cleaver	3-1-1764	9-11-1782 Peter		Miriam	12-8-1795		29-5-1795
Mary	Cleaver	26-8-1785	John	21-6-1760	Susanna	3-5-1823	c1763	6-7-1823
Miriam	Cleaver	15-8-1767	20-8-1847 Peter		Miriam	12-8-1795		29-5-1798
	Miriam Cleaver married -?- Griest							
Nathan	Cleaver	10-10-1801	John	21-6-1760	Susanna	3-5-1823	c1763	6-7-1823
Peter	Cleaver	4-5-1798	John	21-6-1760	Susanna	3-5-1823	c1763	6-7-1823
Peter	Cleaver	16-10-1758	Peter		Miriam	12-8-1795		29-5-1798
Rachel	Cleaver	22-9-1809	12-1-1811 Isaac		Elizabeth			
Samuel	Cleaver	26-12-1811	Isaac		Elizabeth			
Sarah	Cleaver	22-9-1765	Peter		Miriam	12-8-1795		29-5-1798
Susanna	Cleaver	27-11-1795	John	21-6-1760	Susanna	3-5-1823	c1763	6-7-1823
Susanna	Cleaver	13-2-1823	Peter		Jane			
Elisha	Coats	17-7-1773	7-10-1773 Aaron		Mary			
Elizabeth	Coats	19-3-1771	Aaron		Mary			
Mosses	Coats	3-10-1774	Aaron		Mary			
Samuel	Coats	21-5-1768	Aaron		Mary			
Ann	Collins	17-1-1750	10-6-1757 John		Ann			
Ann	Collins	17-2-1736	10-6-1737 John		Ann			
Caleb	Collins	16-12-1732	14-6-1737 John		Ann			

John Collins, son of Joseph Collins of Goshen and
Ann Garrett, daughter of George Garrett were married

Name		Born	Died	Father	Born	Died	Mother	Born	Died
		10 mo 9th 1731 at Goshen Meeting, Chester Co., Pa.							
George	Collins	20-5-1756	20-10-1758	John			Ann		
John	Collins	1-3-1743		John			Ann		
Joseph	Collins	31-1-1740		John			Ann		
Mary	Collins	29-3-1738	6-6-1739	John			Ann		
Mary	Collins	14-3-1734	6-6-1737	John			Ann		
Peter	Collins	20-1-1747		John			Ann		
Ruth	Collins	25-8-1745		John			Ann		
Sarah	Collins	5-9-1753		John			Ann		
Amos	Comber	10-12-1750		Robert			Rebecca		
Jesse	Comber	3-3-1757		Robert			Rebecca		
John	Comber	7-8-1738		Robert			Rebecca		
Joseph	Comber	3-2-1736		Robert			Rebecca		
Lydia	Comber	19-5-1754		Robert			Rebecca		
Mary	Comber	10-1-1747		Robert			Rebecca		
Robert	Comber	15-1-1741		Robert			Rebecca		
Tamer	Comber	3-4-1743		Robert			Rebecca		
Thomas	Comber	31-6-1745		Robert			Rebecca		
Ezra	Comly	13-5-1812		Samuel	7-10-1773		Susanna	5-9-1779	
Hannah	Comly	18-1-1814	1-5-1814	Samuel	7-10-1773		Susanna	5-9-1779	
Isaac W.	Comly	23-12-1821		Samuel	7-10-1773		Susanna	5-9-1779	
Lydia	Comly	24-11-1816		Samuel	7-10-1773		Susanna	5-9-1779	
Phebe	Comly	13-3-1815	1-5-1814	Samuel	7-10-1773		Susanna	5-9-1779	
Samuel	Comly	7-10-1773		Jacob			Sarah		
Sarah T.	Comly	18-4-1810		Samuel	7-10-1773		Susanna	5-9-1779	

Susanna Comly was the daughter of William and Hannah Wierman

Name	Surname	Birth						
William	Comly	8-7-1820	22-7-1820	Samuel	7-10-1773		Susanna	5-9-1779
Abraham	Cook	8-9-1774	20-4-1778	Jacob			Mary	
Amos G.	Cook	19-1-1845		Josiah		24-10-1880	Mary	1-6-1806
Ann	Cook	20-10-1741		Peter	10-4-1700	20-4-1779	Sarah	4-21-1706 7-6-1783
Cornelius	Cook	12-9-1813		Samuel			Sarah	
Edith Ann	Cook	7-7-1841		Josiah		24-10-1880	Mary	1-6-1806
Edwin Mode	Cook	1-11-1812		Samuel			Sarah	
Elisha	Cook	26-2-1777		Samuel		10-8-1800	Ruth	
Elisha	Cook	12-1-1816		Samuel			Sarah	
George	Cook	24-10-1743	young	Peter	10-4-1700	20-4-1779	Sarah	4-21-1706 7-6-1783
Hannah	Cook	27-4-1736		Peter	c1700	20-4-1779	Sarah	c1706 7-6-1783
Hannah	Cook	3-10-1767		Samuel		10-8-1800	Hannah	9-5-1768
Hannah Jane	Cook	8-12-1821		Samuel			Sarah	
Henry	Cook	18-3-1843		Josiah		24-10-1880	Mary	1-6-1806
Isaac	Cook	28-6-1772		Jacob			Mary	
Israel	Cook	27-8-1774		Samuel		10-8-1800	Ruth	5-4-1789
Israel	Cook	16-2-1780		Samuel		10-8-1800	Ruth	5-4-1789
Jane	Cook	10-3-1809		Henry			Mary	
Jesse	Cook	15-9-1744	18-8-1818	Peter	10-4-1700	20-4-1779	Sarah	21-4-1706 7-6-1783
Jesse	Cook	5-8-1796	9-2-1880	Isaac			Sidney	
John	Cook	9-3-1758		Joseph			Mary	c1730 15-12-1759
Joseph	Cook	12-8-1731		Peter	4-10-1700	20-4-1779	Sarah	21-4-1706 7-6-1783

Peter Cook, son of Peter Cook and Elinor Norman, born 10 mo 4th,
1700 at Warwich, Cheshire, England married
Sarah Gilpin, daughter of Joseph and Hannah (Glover) Gilpin of
Birmingham, Chester Co., Pa. on the 26th of 9th mo, 1730
Sarah Gilpin was born at Birmingham, Chester Co., Pa 4 mo 21st 1706

| Joseph | Cook | 10-22-1823 | | Samuel | | | Sarah | |

Name		Born	Died	Father	Born	Died	Mother	Born	Died
Josiah W.	Cook	c1847		Josiah		24-10-1880	Mary	1-6-1806	
Lydia	Cook	15-8-1734	15-8-1741	Peter	10-4-1700	20-4-1779	Sarah	21-4-1706	7-6-1783
Lydia	Cook	7-6-1779		Jacob			Mary		
Mariah K.	Cook	c1849		Josiah		24-10-1880	Mary	1-6-1806	
Martha Jane	Cook	18-2-1840		Josiah		24-10-1880	Mary	1-6-1806	
Josiah Cook's wife Mary was the daughter of Willing and Anne Griest									
Mary	Cook	12-5-1777		Jacob			Mary		
Peter	Cook	29-9-1747		Peter	10-4-1700	20-4-1779	Sarah	21-4-1706	7-6-1783
Rebecca	Cook	14-1-1792		Wm Harvey			Elizabeth		
Rebekah	Cook	15-8-1773		Samuel		10-8-1800	Ruth		5-4-1789
Ruth Cook was Samuel's second wife									
Robert	Cook	30-6-1765	4-7-1765	Samuel		10-8-1800	Hannah		9-5-1768
Hannah Cook was Samuel's first wife									
Ruth	Cook	24-12-1732	27-4-1733	Peter	10-4-1700	20-4-1779	Sarah	21-4-1706	7-6-1783
Ruth	Cook	27-2-1784		Samuel		10-8-1800	Ruth		5-4-1789
Ruthanna	Cook	22-1-1818		Samuel			Sarah		
Samuel	Cook	15-10-1738		Peter	10-4-1700	20-4-1779	Sarah	21-4-1706	7-6-1783
Samuel	Cook	26-6-1782		Samuel		10-8-1800	Ruth		5-4-1789
Sarah	Cook	29-9-1747	15-6-1807	Peter	10-4-1700	20-4-1779	Sarah	21-4-1706	7-6-1783
Sarah	Cook	7-7-1767		Joseph			Elizabeth		
Elizabeth Cook was Joseph's second wife									
Sarah	Cook	7-12-1775		Samuel		10-8-1800	Ruth		5-4-1789
William	Cook	24-8-1766	20-10-1766	Samuel		10-8-1800	Hannah		9-5-1768
William	Cook	27-11-1778		Samuel		10-8-1800	Ruth		5-4-1789
William	Cook	22-6-1820		Samuel			Sarah		
William H.	Cook	1-1-1829		Jesse	5-8-1796	9-2-1880	Rebecca	14-1-1792	

Jesse (b.5-8-1796) was son of Isaac and Sidney Cook
Rebecca (b.14-1-1792), his wife, was daughter of Wm. and Elizabeth Harvey

Name	Surname	Date	Father	Marriage	Mother
Daniel	Cookson	19-9-1918	Daniel		Sarah
Eli	Cookson	18-8-1806 8th mo1869	Daniel	18-8-1806 8th mo 1869	Sarah
Eli Franklin	Cookson	19-3-1829	Eli		Phebe
Elizabeth	Cookson	30-11-1795	Daniel		Sarah
Esther	Cookson	22-3-1812	Daniel		Sarah
Hannah	Cookson	20-3-1814	Daniel		Sarah
Hannah Ann	Cookson	22-7-1832 20-2-1899	Eli	18-8-1806 8th mo 1869	Phebe
	Hannah Ann Cookson married -?- Garrettson				
John	Cookson	26-12-1800	Daniel		Sarah
Mary	Cookson	6-4-1797	Daniel		Sarah
Milton V.	Cookson	15-3-1835 15-6-1898	Eli	18-8-1806 8th mo 1869	Phebe
Rachel	Cookson	6-4-1816	Daniel		Sarah
Ruth	Cookson	12-12-1808	Daniel		Sarah
Samuel	Cookson	24-11-1798 24-11-1805	Daniel		Sarah
Sarah	Cookson	11-10-1802	Daniel		Sarah
Jacob	Davis	7-7-1779	Joshua		Jane
John	Davis	9-4-1773	Joshua		Jane
Marmaduke	Davis	11-3-1775	Joshua		Jane
Ruth	Davis	4-2-1772	Joshua		Jane
William	Davis	30-7-1777	Joshua		Jane
Abigail	Delap	8-9-1757 23-8-1758	William		Ruth
George	Delap	1-11-1743	William		Ruth
John	Delap	15-9-1752	William		Ruth
Mary	Delap	8-10-1759	William		Ruth
Robert	Delap	15-8-1750	William		Ruth

Name		Born	Died	Father	Born	Died	Mother	Born	Died
Sarah	Delap	2-1-1748		William			Ruth		
William	Delap	26-2-1755		William			Ruth		
Abigail	Edmundson	7-9-1767		Thomas			Mary		
Esther	Edmundson	24-2-1771		John			Ann		
Esther	Edmundson	11-5-1810		Thomas			Elizabeth		
Hannah	Edmundson	7-10-1765		Thomas			Mary		
Hannah	Edmundson	2-10-1807		Thomas			Elizabeth		
John	Edmundson	24-12-1777		John			Ann		
John	Edmundson	3-4-1770		Thomas			Mary		
Joseph	Edmundson	11-4-1769		John			Ann		
Mary	Edmundson	11-1-1774		Thomas			Mary		
Mary	Edmundson	24-5-1804		Thomas			Elizabeth		
Rachael	Edmundson	11-11-1765	8-9-1777	John			Ann		
Rachael	Edmundson	6-3-1780		John			Ann		
Rachael	Edmundson	7-1-1806	7-1-1809	Thomas			Elizabeth		
Sarah	Edmundson	13-7-1775		John			Ann		
Thomas	Edmundson	8-3-1773		John			Ann		
Thomas	Edmundson	11-1-1774		Thomas			Mary		
William	Edmundson	17-9-1763		Thomas			Mary		
William	Edmundson	21-11-1812		Thomas			Elizabeth		
Elizabeth	Elliot	8-8-1754		Jacob			Elizabeth		
Hannah	Elliot	24-11-1756		Jacob			Elizabeth		
Israel	Elliot	28-7-1759		Jacob			Elizabeth		
Jacob	Elliot	11-11-1752		Jacob			Elizabeth		
Elizabeth	Everett	8-6-1761	4-8-1801	Isaac			Martha		

Isaac Everett married Martha Griest

Name	Surname	Birth	Death	Father	Date	Mother	Date	Spouse	Date
Elizabeth	Everett	8-4-1804		Isaac	15-11-1780			Rebecca	2-8-1777
Hamilton	Everett	18-10-1805		Isaac	15-11-1780			Rebecca	2-8-1777
Hannah	Everett	27-8-1766	19-6-1772	Isaac			4-8-1801	Martha	
Hannah	Everett	12-8-1777		Isaac			4-8-1801	Martha	
Isaac	Everett	5-11-1780		Isaac			4-8-1801	Martha	
John	Everett	3-2-1771	25-2-1855	Isaac			4-8-1801	Martha	
John	Everett	7-4-1800		Isaac	15-11-1780			Rebecca	2-8-1777
Julia Ann	Everett	14-3-1803		Isaac	15-11-1780			Rebecca	2-8-1777
Malinda	Everett	16-12-1806		Isaac	15-11-1780			Rebecca	2-8-1777
Margaret	Everett	2-2-1799		Isaac	15-11-1780			Rebecca	2-8-1777

Isaac (b.15-11-1780) Everitt was son of Isaac and Martha Everitt
Rebecca (b.2-8-1777) Everitt was daughter of John and Margaret March

Name	Surname	Birth	Death	Father	Date	Mother	Date	Spouse	Date
Martha	Everett	27-8-1773		Isaac			4-8-1801	Martha	
Martha	Everett	10-3-1800		Isaac	15-11-1780			Rebecca	2-8-1777
Mary	Everett	24-10-1769	18-3-1770	Isaac			4-8-1801	Martha	
Susannah	Everett	3-10-1763		Isaac			4-8-1801	Martha	
Elizabeth	Everett	8-6-1761		Isaac			4-8-1801	Martha	
Hannah	Everett	27-8-1766	19-6-1772	Isaac			4-8-1801	Martha	
Hannah	Everett	12-8-1777		Isaac			4-8-1801	Martha	
Isaac	Everitt	5-11-1780		Isaac			4-8-1801	Martha	
John	Everitt	3-2-1771	25-2-1855	Isaac			4-8-1801	Martha	
Martha	Everitt	27-8-1773		Isaac			4-8-1801	Martha	
Mary	Everitt	24-10-1769	18-6-1770	Isaac			4-8-1801	Martha	
Susanna	Everitt	3-7-1763		Isaac			4-8-1801	Martha	
William	Fisher	20-1-1778		Samuel Alexander			6-3-1758	Susannah	
Aaron	Fraizor	15-11-1745						Phebe	

Name		Born	Died	Father	Born	Died	Mother	Born	Died
Abraham	Fraizor	20-1-1757		Alexander		6-3-1758	Phebe		
Ezekial	Fraizor	3-12-1752		Alexander		6-3-1758	Phebe		
John	Fraizor	6-1-1778		Aaron		19-4-1778	Jane		
Miriam	Fraizor	30-1-1755		Alexander		6-3-1758	Phebe		
Mosses	Fraizor	28-11-1749		Alexander		6-3-1758	Phebe		
Aaron	Garretson	16-1-1759		William	c1716	15-12-1792	Mary	c1722	1782
Aaron	Garretson	6-2-1782		John			Tamer		
Abel	Garretson	2-4-1813	2-4-1813	John	c1782	21-1-1829	Rebecca	c1777	16-3-1861
Alfred	Garretson	13-7-1833	14-8-1847	Thomas	c1788	25-1-1862	Jane	17-2-1790	1859
Alice	Garretson	14-5-1791	25-3-1819	Samuel	c1750	31-3-1822	Alice	c1768	15-7-1823
Alice Garretson married -?- Vale									
Alice	Garretson	1-11-1823	23-1-1901	Joel	c1796	18-2-1837	Elizabeth		
Alice Garretson married -?- Wright									
Alice B.	Garretson	10-8-1841	11-11-1841	Benjamin	c1800	24-6-1864	Orpah	c1803	18-10-1841
Alice Phebe	Garretson	5-11-1865	9-12-1866	Joel V.	27-4-1801		Hannah Ann	c1832	20-2-1899
Amos	Garretson	5-11-1777	28-2-1864	John		15-12-1810	Mary		3-7-1827
Ann	Garretson	21-9-1782		Joseph			Rebecca		
Ann	Garretson	22-2-1750		William	c1716	15-12-1792	Mary	c1722	1782
Ann	Garretson	14-8-1745		John			Content		30-10-1747
Ann	Garretson	6-12-1780	21-2-1781	Samuel	c1750	31-3-1822	Jane	c1753	3-1-1783
Ann	Garretson	6-1-1798	21-3-1822	Samuel	c1750	31-3-1822	Alice	c1768	15-7-1823
Ann Garretson married -?- Vale									
Ann	Garretson	10-12-1827		John J			Ann	24-6-1784	
Ann H.	Garretson	7-1-1824		Benjamin	c1800	24-6-1864	Orpah	c1803	18-10-1841
Anna	Garretson	18-7-1775		William			Mary		3-12-1817

Name	Surname	Date		Relation	Date		Relation	Date
Annie M.	Garretson	9-5-1867		Joel V.	27-4-1801		Hannah Ann	20-2-1899
Aquilla	Garretson	26-9-1825		Josiah	25-6-1780		Elizabeth	7-6-1786
Armela	Garretson	2-10-1788		William Jr			Mary	
Armelle	Garretson	2-10-1788		William			Mary	3-12-1817
Asenath	Garretson	24-3-1832		Benjamin	c1800		Orpah	18-10-1841
Barzillai	Garretson	5-3-1811		John	c1782		Rebecca	c1777
Benjamin	Garretson	12-12-1800	24-12-1864	Samuel	21-1-1829		Alice	16-3-1861
Casparus	Garretson	17-5-1745	18-8-1746	William	c1716 15-12-1792		Mary	c1722 1782
		William Garretson and Mary A. Frazer were married 9 mo 9th 1742 at Kennett Meeting						
		Mary departed this life ye 1782 aged about 60 years						
		Mary was the daughter of Alexander and Sarah Frazer						
Casparus	Garretson	6-8-1776		William			Mary	3-12-1817
Clara E.	Garretson	28-1-1872		Joel V.			Hannah Ann	20-2-1899
Content	Garretson	26-4-1754		John			Jane	
Content	Garretson	20-10-1773	21-12-1818	John	12th 1840		Mary	3rd 1827
		Content Garretson married -?- Russell						
Cornelius	Garretson	16-2-1756		John			Jane	
Cornelius	Garretson	9-3-1790		Cornelius	29-4-1829		Margaret	11-3-1790
Daniel	Garretson	6-2-1802		Jacob	16-27-1830		Mary	11-7-1825
Eli	Garretson	20-9-1794		Cornelius	29-4-1829		Hannah	
Eli	Garretson	5-12-1817		John J.			Ann	24-6-1784
Eli B.	Garretson	2-9-1830	4th 1859	Thomas	c1788		Jane	17-2-1790 1859
Eli P.	Garretson	25-10-1859		Joel V.	4-27-1801		Hannah Ann	c1832 20-2-1899
Elijah	Garretson	11-11-1799	26-7-1873	Joseph			Rebecca	
Eliza	Garretson	27-5-1815	14-4-1816	John J.			Ann	24-6-1784
Eliza	Garretson	12-1-1813		Joel	8-10-1782		Martha	15-7-1784
Eliza Jane	Garretson	23-11-1825	4-11-1847	Thomas	c1788 25-1-1862		Jane	17-2-1790 1859
Eliza S.	Garretson	2-3-1829		Benjamin	c1800 24-6-1864		Orpah	c1803 18-10-1841

245

Name		Born	Died	Father	Born	Died	Mother	Born	Died
Elizabeth	Garretson	28-12-1861		Joel V.	27-4-1801	15-12-1792	Hannah Ann		
Elizabeth	Garretson	16-8-1764		William		c1716	Mary	c1722	1782
Elizabeth	Garretson	25-8-1763		William		1-2-1810	Lydia		21-9-1803
Elizabeth	Garretson	24-5-1785	1-7-1830	Samuel	c1750	31-3-1822	Alice	c1768	15-7-1823
		Alice was Samuel Garretson's second wife							
Elizabeth H.	Garretson	28-12-1861		Joel V.			Hannah Ann	c1832	20-2-1899
		Elizabeth Garretson married -?- Cleaver							
Ezra	Garretson	25-1-1834		Benjamin	c1800	24-6-1864	Orpah	c1803	18-10-1841
Faithfull	Garretson	22-1-1774	10-6-1808	Samuel	c1750	31-3-1822	Jane	c1753	3-1-1783
		Jane was Samuel Garretson's first wife							
Franklin Greely	Garretson	15-11-1857		Joel V.	27-4-1801		Hannah Ann	c1832	20-2-1899
Franklin	Garretson	14-1-1830	13-10-1842	Joel	c1796	18-2-1837	Elizabeth		
George	Garretson	23-1-1787		Joseph			Rebecca		
Hannah	Garretson	17-6-1775		John		Dec. 1810	Mary		Aug. 1827
Hannah	Garretson	11-11-1779		Cornelius		29-4-1829	Margaret		11-3-1790
		Margaret was Cornelius' first wife							
Hannah	Garretson	10-8-1811		John J			Ann	24-6-1784	
Hannah	Garretson	17-6-1775		John		15-12-1810	Mary		3-7-1827
Hannah Maria	Garretson	29-8-1817		Josiah	25-6-1780		Elizabeth	7-6-1786	3-7-1827
Isaac	Garretson	17-2-1765		John		15-02-1810	Mary		
Isaac	Garretson	1-8-1792		Cornelius		29-4-1829	Hannah		
		Hannah Garretson was Cornelius' second wife							
Isaac	Garretson	27-4-1810	7-5-1810	Thomas	c1788	25-1-1862	Susanna	c1790	5thmo1810
		Susanna Garretson was Thomas' first wife							
Isaac	Garretson	4-6-1814	6-4-1837	John	c1782	21-1-1829	Rebecca	c1777	16-3-1861

246

Isaac	Garretson	17-2-1765		John	15-12-1810	Mary	3-7-1827
Isaac Pearson	Garretson	15-8-1810	8-10-1782	Joel	12th 1840	Martha	15-7-1784
Israel	Garretson	17-2-1765		John		Mary	3rd 1827
	John's wife Mary was formerly Mary Griest						
Israel	Garretson	7-5-1798		Jacob	27-6-1830	Mary	11-7-1825
Israel	Garretson	25-7-1830	5-7-1798	Israel		Ruth	2-6-1880
Jacob	Garretson	20-8-1800	3-5-1801	Jacob	27-6-1830	Mary	7-11-1825
Jacob	Garretson	29-8-1767		William	1-2-1810	Lydia	21-9-1803
Jacob	Garretson	4-4-1826	5-7-1798	Israel		Ruth	2-6-1880
James	Garretson	31-5-1809	1-3-1825	Jacob	27-6-1830	Mary	11-7-1825
James	Garretson	24-4-1778	1-5-1810	Samuel	31-3-1822	Jane	c1753
Jane	Garretson	12-10-1795	c1750	Joseph		Rebecca	3-1-1783
Jane	Garretson	20-3-1781		Cornelius	29-4-1829	Margaret	11-3-1790
Jane	Garretson	8-12-1775	c1750	Samuel	31-3-1822	Jane	3-1-1783
Jesse	Garretson	23-3-1810		George		Lydia	
Jesse B.	Garretson	17-4-1838	c1800	Benjamin	24-6-1864	Orpah	18-10-1841
Joel	Garretson	26-5-1796	18-2-1837	Samuel	31-3-1822	Alice	15-7-1823
Joel	Garretson	8-10-1782		John	15-12-1810	Mary	
Joel	Garretson	8-2-1828	8-10-1782	Joel		Elizabeth	8-4-1804	3-7-1827
	Elizabeth, daughter of Isaac and Rebecca Everitt, was united						
	in Marriage with Joel (b.8-10-1782) Garretson 27-7-1806						
Joel V.	Garretson	3-1-1833	c1796	Joel	18-2-1837	Elizabeth	
John	Garretson	15-12-1810					
John	Garretson	27-4-1770		John	Dec. 1810	Mary	Aug. 1827
John	Garretson	7-1-1759	c1716	William	15-12-1792	Mary	1782
John	Garretson	23-2-1741		John		Content	30-10-1747
John	Garretson	2-8-1765	18-7-1790	William	1-2-1810	Lydia	21-9-1803
John	Garretson	12-12-1778		William		Mary	3-12-1817

247

Name		Born	Died	Father	Born	Died	Mother	Born	Died
John	Garretson	7-6-1784		Joseph			Rebecca		11-3-1790
John	Garretson	28-5-1783		Cornelius		29-4-1829	Margaret		3-1-1783
John	Garretson	5-5-1782	21-1-1829	Samuel	c1750	31-3-1822	Jane	c1753	
John	Garretson	20-1-1788		John			Tamar		
John	Garretson	27-4-1770		John		15-12-1810	Mary		3-7-1827
John Everitt	Garretson	4-9-1832		Joel	8-10-1782		Elizabeth	8-4-1804	
John J.	Garretson	23-4-1873		Joel V.			Hannah Ann	c1832	20-2-1899
Joseph	Garretson	28-7-1759	22-6-1814	John			Jane		
Joseph	Garretson	29-11-1782		William			Mary		3-12-1817
Joseph	Garretson	23-3-1789		Joseph			Rebecca		
Joseph	Garretson	23-3-1808		George			Lydia		
Josiah	Garretson	25-6-1780	5th 1853	John		12th 1810	Mary		3rd 1827
Josiah T.	Garretson	27-9-1839		Benjamin	c1800	24-6-1864	Orpah	c1803	18-10-1841
Julyann	Garretson	14-10-1818	10-10-1822	Thomas	c1788	25-1-1862	Jane	17-2-1790	27-1-1859

Jane Garretson was Thomas' second wife. She had one daughter by her former husband, William Warner, to wit: Mary Warner, b. 18-1-1816, d. 14-10-1821

| Lavinia | Garretson | 6-9-1808 | | Joel | 8-10-1782 | | Martha | 15-7-1784 | |

Joel was son of John and Mary Garretson
First wife, Martha, was daughter of Isaac and Elizabeth Pearson

Louisa	Garretson	9-11-1820	16-8-1864	Joel	c1796	18-2-1837	Elizabeth		
Lydia	Garretson	11-6-1796		Jacob		27-6-1830	Mary		11-7-1825
Lydia	Garretson	4-4-1828		Israel	5-7-1798		Ruth	25-12-1804	2-6-1880
Mahlon	Garretson	18-1-1817		John	c1782	21-1-1829	Rebecca	c1777	16-3-1861
Margaret	Garretson	19-8-1796		Cornelius		29-4-1829	Hannah		
Maria	Garretson	9-7-1819		John J			Ann	24-6-1784	

248

Name	Surname	Date		Spouse	Date		Date
Maria Martha	Garretson	24-8-1818		Joel	8-10-1782	Martha	15-7-1784
Mariah	Garretson	6-7-1845		Israel	5-7-1798	Ruth	25-12-1804	2-6-1880
Martha	Garretson	21-7-1769	3-2-1789	William		Lidia	21-9-1803
	Martha married -?- Kirk				4-2-1810		
Martha	Garretson	7-8-1839		Israel	5-7-1798	Ruth	25-12-1804	2-6-1880
Mary	Garretson		3-7-1827				
Mary	Garretson	6-11-1760		William		Mary	c1722	1782
Mary	Garretson	13-1-1781		William	c1716	15-12-1792	Mary	3-12-1817
Mary	Garretson	25-6-1786	30-4-1881	John		12th 1810	Mary	3rd 1827
	Mary Garretson married -?- Tudor						
Mary	Garretson	20-9-1825	28-3-1904	Joel	c1796		Elizabeth	18-2-1837
Mary	Garretson	1-6-1836		Israel	5-7-1798	Ruth	25-12-1804	2-6-1880
Mary Ann	Garretson	9-11-1817		Joseph			Mariah	
Millie H.	Garretson	24-3-1864	30-10-1864	Joel V.	27-4-1801		Hannah Ann	
Miriam	Garretson	25-5-1755		William	c1716	15-12-1792	Mary	c1722	1782
Naomi	Garretson	25-8-1762		William	c1716	15-12-1792	Mary	c1722	1782
Nathan	Garretson	19-4-1789		John			Tamer	
Oliver	Garretson	18-5-1814		Josiah	25-6-1780		Elizabeth	7-6-1786
Orpah Jane	Garretson	3-3-1836	11-6-189?	Benjamin	c1800	24-6-1864	Orpah	c1803	18-10-1841
	Orpah Jane married -?- Evans						
Patience	Garretson	8-5-1790		William			Mary	
Phebe	Garretson	26-2-1811	8-9-1823	Josiah	25-6-1780		Elizabeth	7-6-1786	3-12-1817
Phebe	Garretson	c1751	9-7-1814	John			Content		c1751
Phebe	Garretson	4-11-1825	20-4-1826	Joseph			Mariah	
Pierce	Garretson	14-8-1808		John J.			Ann	24-6-1784
Rachel	Garretson	8-12-1788	25-12-1824	John		Dec. 1810	Mary		Aug. 1827
Rachel	Garretson	18-12-1792	27-4-1832	Samuel	c1750	31-3-1822	Alice	c1768	15-7-1823
Rachel	Garretson	18-9-1827		Thomas	c1788	25-1-1862	Jane	17-2-1790	1859

Name		Born	Died	Father	Born	Died	Mother	Born	Died
Rachel Eliz.	Garretson	29-8-1817		Josiah	25-6-1780		Elizabeth	7-6-1786	
Rebecca	Garretson	6-8-1791	25-11-1873	Joseph			Rebecca		
Rebecca	Garretson	8-5-1823		Joseph			Mariah	24-6-1784	
Rebecca	Garretson	7-10-1810		John J.			Ann		
Rebecca F.	Garretson	5-2-1876		Joel V.			Hannah Ann	c1832	20-2-1899
Rebecca R.	Garretson	23-9-1809		Josiah	25-6-1780		Elizabeth	7-6-1786	
	Elizabeth Garretson was the daughter of Jos. & Rebecca Rakestraw								
Rebeccah	Garretson	12-9-1789	5-10-1823	Samuel	c1750	31-3-1822	Alice	c1768	15-7-1823
Reuben Thomas	Garretson	5-5-1808		John, Jr.	27-4-1776		Rebecca	7-3-1774	
Robert N.	Garretson	31-10-1842	7-4-1846	Israel	7-5-1798		Ruth	25-12-1804	6-2-1880
Ruth	Garretson	13-1-1820	29-7-1822	Joseph			Mariah		
Ruth Anna	Garretson	28-1-1833		Israel	7-5-1798		Ruth	25-12-1804	6-2-1880
Ruth Anna	Garretson	3-3-1810							
Samuel	Garretson	25-8-1750		John			Jane		
	Jane Garretson was John's second wife								
Samuel	Garretson	7-12-1786		Cornelius		29-4-1829	Margaret		11-3-1790
Samuel	Garretson	19-10-1794	26-1-1822	Samuel	c1750	31-3-1822	Alice	c1768	15-7-1823
Samuel	Garretson	18-10-1820		John	c1782	21-1-1829	Rebecca	c1777	16-3-1861
Sarah	Garretson	24-5-1797	5-12-1873	Joseph			Rebecca		
Sarah	Garretson	2-3-1753		William	c1716	15-12-1792	Mary	c1722	1782
Sarah	Garretson	10-6-1752		John			Jane		
Sarah	Garretson	7-1-1785		William			Mary		
Sarah	Garretson	2-9-1788		Cornelius		29-4-1829	Margaret		3-12-1817
Sarah	Garretson	29-9-1786	4-12-1801	Samuel	c1750	31-3-1822	Alice	c1768	11-3-1790
Sarah	Garretson	29-11-1785		John			Tamar		15-7-1823
Sarah	Garretson	21-10-1820		Thomas	c1788	25-1-1862	Jane	17-2-1790	1859

Name	Surname	Date	Spouse	Date	Other	Date
Sarah Jane	Garretson	13-1-1870	Joel V.	27-4-1801	Hannah Ann	c1832	20-2-1899
Sarah S.	Garretson	7-5-1830	23-6-1831 Benjamin	c1800	24-6-1864	Orpah	c1803	18-10-1841
Sidney	Garretson	22-5-1823	John J.		Ann	24-6-1784	
Susan	Garretson	12-12-1823	23-2-1853 Thomas		Jane	17-2-1790	27-1-1859
Susanna	Garretson	17-8-1767	Feb. 1838 John		Mary		Aug. 1827
Thomas	Garretson	20-1-1788	25-1-1862 Samuel	c1788 25-1-1862	Alice	c1768 31-3-1822	15-7-1823
Warner	Garretson	26-9-1822	7-3-1823 Thomas	c1788 25-1-1862	Jane	17-2-1790	1859
William	Garretson	11-3-1748	William	c1716 15-12-1792	Mary	c1722	1782
William	Garretson	11-12-1738	4-2-1810 John		Content		30-10-1747

John Garretson and Content Hussey were married 9 mo 5, 1736 at Hockessin Meeting

Name	Surname	Date	Spouse	Date	Other	Date
William	Garretson	23-5-1779	John		Tamar		
Willie H.	Garretson	26-3-1864 20-10-187?	Joel V.		Hannah Ann	c1832	20-2-1899
Allen	Griest	15-9-1818	Uriah	29-6-1789	Mary		

Uriah (b.29-6-1789) Griest was son of Joseph and Rebecca Griest
Mary, his wife, was daughter of William -?-

Name	Surname	Date	Spouse	Date	Other	Date
Alvina	Griest	15-7-1812	Amos		Phebe		
Amanda	Griest	12-10-1847	John		Hannah		
Amos	Griest	13-9-1798	7-9-1879 Willing	27-3-1772 2-2-1833	Anne	21-8-1766	23-2-1850
Amos	Griest	23-5-1786	Joseph		Rebecca		
Amos W.	Griest	23-8-1845	Cyrus		Mary Ann		
Amy	Griest	24-3-1807	Joseph		Mary		
Ann	Griest	22-10-1757	2-11-1757 John	c1716 4-5-1780	Susanna	c1718	15-5-1776
Ann McMillan	Griest	20-11-1832	Cyrus		Mary Ann		
Anne	Griest	16-5-1796	25-4-1863 Willing	27-3-1772 2-2-1833	Anne	21-8-1766	23-2-1850

Willing Griest's wife, Anne, was the daughter of George and Anne McMillan

Name	Surname	Date	Spouse	Date	Other	Date
Anne	Griest	21-5-1796	Joseph		Mary		
Cyrus	Griest	29-5-1803 23-11-1869	Willing	27-3-1772 2-2-1833	Anne	21-8-1766	23-2-1850
Cyrus Samuel	Griest	3-1-1835	Cyrus		Mary Ann		

Name		Born	Died	Father	Born	Died	Mother	Born	Died
Daniel	Griest	9-10-1737		John	c1716	4-5-1780	Susanna	c1718	3-7-1827
Daniel	Griest	12-2-1795		Joseph			Mary Jane		
Edith	Griest			Gideon			Anne		
Edith	Griest	9-12-1800	17-4-1868	Willing	27-3-1772	2-2-1833	Rebecca	21-8-1766	23-2-1850
Edith	Griest	15-3-1798	27-3-1798	Joseph			Rebecca		
Eli	Griest	24-12-1793		Joseph			Mary		
Elisha	Griest	21-9-1821		Uriah	29-6-1789		Hannah	2-10-1807	
Eliza	Griest	26-12-1840		John			Mary Ann	2-10-1807	
Elizabeth Mary	Griest	26-12-1843		Cyrus			Hannah		
Emily	Griest	5-9-1842		John			Mary Ann		
George M.	Griest	24-8-1828		Cyrus			Rebecca		
Gideon	Griest	23-5-1796		Joseph			Susanna	c1718	15-5-1776
Hannah	Griest	7-11-1747		John	c1716	4-5-1780	Mary Ann		
Hiram	Griest	9-12-1826		Cyrus			Mary		
Isaac	Griest	1-6-1803		Joseph			Mary Ann		
Jane Cook	Griest	9-3-1830		Cyrus			Mary Ann		
Jesse Warner	Griest	20-6-1837		Cyrus			Miriam		
John	Griest			John			Susanna	c1718	15-5-1776
John	Griest	19-6-1742	1-6-1743	John	c1716	4-5-1780	Susanna	c1718	15-5-1776
John	Griest	25-8-1744	1-9-1744	John	c1716	4-5-1780	Susanna	c1718	15-5-1776
John	Griest	8-10-1749		John	c1716	4-5-1780	Hannah		
John	Griest	9-5-1844		John			Mary		
John	Griest	20-3-1805		Joseph			Susanna	c1718	15-5-1776
Joseph	Griest	12-4-1755		John	c1716	4-5-1780	Mary		
Joseph	Griest	14-8-1800		Joseph			Anne	21-8-1766	23-2-1850
Josiah	Griest	23-9-1812		Willing	27-3-1772	2-2-1833			

Name	Surname	Birth/Date	Father	Date	Mother	Date
Leander	Griest	14-8-1849	John		Hannah	
Lewis	Griest	6-10-1837	John		Hannah	2-10-1807
Lucinda Maria	Griest	14-1-1834	Uriah	29-6-1789	Mary	
Lydia	Griest	16-12-1758	John	c1716	Susanna	c1718
Lydia A.	Griest	20-4-1820	Uriah	29-6-1789	Mary	
Mahlon	Griest	28-8-1831	Uriah	29-6-1789	Mary	
Mahlon	Griest	13-1-1801	Joseph		Rebecca	
Maria	Griest	7-3-1839	John		Hannah	
Maria Edith	Griest	3-7-1840	Cyrus		Mary Ann	
Martha	Griest	20-1-1739	John	c1716	Susanna	c1718
Mary	Griest	1-6-1806	Willing	27-3-1772	Anne	21-8-1766
Mary	Griest	14-3-1809	Joseph		Mary	
Mikejah	Griest	5-3-1812	Joseph		Mary	
Miriam	Griest	12-10-1834	John		Hannah	2-10-1807

Hannah Griest was the daughter of Thomas and Elizabeth Edmundson

Name	Surname	Birth/Date	Father	Date	Mother	Date
Nancy (Mary?)	Griest	5-8-1745	John	c1716	Susanna	c1718
Nathan	Griest	28-9-1829	Uriah	29-6-1789	Mary	
Nathan	Griest	17-9-1787	Joseph		Rebecca	
Nathan	Griest	18-11-1788	Joseph		Rebecca	
Phebe Malvina	Griest	18-6-1803	Uriah	29-6-1789	Mary	
Rachel Ann	Griest	13-5-1836	Amos		Margaret	
Rebecca	Griest	7-10-1896	John		Hannah	2-10-1807
Ruth	Griest	14-1-1835	Willing	27-3-1772	Anne	21-8-1766
Ruth	Griest	1-2-1808	Joseph		Rebecca	
Susan	Griest	29-7-1797	James	15-5-1813	Hannah	

Susan Griest was daughter of James and Hannah Swope

Name	Surname	Birth/Date	Father	Date	Mother	Date
Susannah	Griest	15-3-1754	John	c1716	Susanna	c1718
Thomas	Griest	14-2-1752	John	c1716	Susanna	c1718

Name		Born	Died	Father	Born	Died	Mother	Born	Died
Uriah	Griest	29-6-1789		Joseph			Rebecca		
William	Griest	5-6-1846		John			Hannah		
William	Griest	30-7-1798		Joseph			Mary		
William Elmer	Griest	1-8-1825		Uriah	29-6-1789		Mary		
Willing	Griest	27-3-1772	2-2-1833	Willing			Anne		
Willing	Griest	27-12-1898		Amos			Margaret		
Abraham	Griffith	1-10-1745		William		21-9-1778	Ester	c1722	18-4-1762
Abraham	Griffith	24-2-1808		David			Rebecca		
Abraham	Griffith	22-6-1812		Benjamin		11-4-1819	Mary		3-12-1817
Abraham	Griffith	9-3-1804		William		1804	Deborah		
Allen	Griffith	19-12-1789		Jacob	27-2-1757	27-2-1811	Lydia	27-3-1757	26-2-1812
Allen	Griffith	8-8-1801		Joseph			Rebecca		
Amos	Griffith	27-4-1775		William		21-9-1778	Joanna		21-4-1794
Amos	Griffith	13-8-1780	20-12-1784	Jacob	27-2-1757	27-2-1811	Lydia	27-3-1757	26-2-1812
Amos	Griffith	24-4-1819	21-7-1823	Amos			Mary		
Anne	Griffith	28-9-1794		William		1804	Deborah		
Benjamin	Griffith	22-3-1774		William		21-9-1778	Joanna		21-4-1794
Daniel	Griffith	9-10-1812		David			Rebecca		
Daniel	Griffith	13-9-1808		Benjamin		11-4-1819	Mary		3-12-1817
David	Griffith	2-6-1759		William		21-9-1778	Ester	c1722	18-4-1762
David	Griffith	2-11-1810		Benjamin		11-4-1819	Mary		3-12-1817
Deborah	Griffith	21-9-1772		William		21-9-1778	Joanna		21-4-1794
Edith	Griffith	13-3-1805		Joseph			Rebecca		
Esther	Griffith	13-1-1766	7-6-1818	William		21-9-1778	Joanna		21-4-1794
Esther	Griffith	25-10-1814		Joseph			Rebecca		
Ethan	Griffith	15-4-1801		Joseph			Rebecca		

George	Griffith	17-12-1792	William			Deborah	
Guilielma	Griffith	30-9-1812	Joseph			Rebecca	
Hannah	Griffith	4-7-1787	Jacob	27-2-1757	27-2-1811	Lydia	27-3-1757	26-2-1812
Hannah	Griffith	15-2-1795	Joseph			Rebecca	
Isaac	Griffith	5-2-1779	Jacob	27-2-1757	27-2-1811	Lydia	27-3-1757	26-2-1812
Isaac	Griffith	26-5-1754	29-12-1773 William		21-9-1778	Ester	c1722	18-4-1762
Israel	Griffith	28-12-1784	Jacob	27-2-1757	27-2-1811	Lydia	27-3-1757	26-2-1812
Jacob	Griffith	27-2-1757	William		21-9-1778	Ester	c1722	18-4-1762
Jesse	Griffith	17-12-1778	William		21-9-1778	Joanna		21-4-1794
Joanna	Griffith	3-8-1814	Amos			Mary	
John	Griffith	2-3-1767	29-2-1828 William		21-9-1778	Joanna		21-4-1794
John	Griffith	16-1-1826	19-4-1830 Amos			Mary	
Joseph	Griffith	5-10-1768	William			Joanna		21-4-1794
Julie	Griffith	20-9-1799	William		1804	Deborah	
Levi	Griffith	27-12-1797	Joseph			Rebecca	
Maria	Griffith	4-2-1796	Joseph			Rebecca	
Mary	Griffith	16-3-1771	William		21-9-1778	Joanna		21-4-1794
Mary	Griffith	8-8-1821	16-7-1823 Amos			Mary	
Mary	Griffith	11-1-1817	Benjamin		11-4-1819	Mary		3-12-1817
Mode	Griffith	26-9-1806	Joseph			Rebecca	
Nancy	Griffith	10-2-1815	Benjamin		11-4-1819	Mary		3-12-1817
Oliver	Griffith	12-10-1797	William		1804	Deborah	
Phebe	Griffith	5-12-1807	Joseph			Rebecca	
Rachel	Griffith	6-4-1817	Joseph			Rebecca	
Rebecca	Griffith	23-8-1782	Jacob	27-2-1757	27-2-1811	Lydia	27-3-1757	26-2-1812
Rebecca	Griffith	3-10-1799	Joseph			Rebecca	
Rebecca	Griffith	7-4-1814	Benjamin		11-4-1819	Mary		3-12-1817
Ruth	Griffith	22-1-1770	2-3-1829 William		21-9-1778	Joanna		21-4-1794

Name		Born	Died	Father	Born	Died	Mother	Born	Died
Ruth	Griffith	25-8-1816		Amos			Mary		
Ruth	Griffith	23-9-1793		Joseph			Rebecca		
Sarah	Griffith	21-10-1812		Joseph			Rebecca		
Stephen	Griffith	25-7-1743	22-9-1746	William		21-9-1778	Ester	c1722	18-4-1762
Susanna	Griffith	24-7-1810		Amos			Mary		
William	Griffith	2-11-1741	9-10-1746	William		21-9-1778	Esther	c1722	18-4-1762
William	Griffith	6-11-1764	21-4-1804	William		21-9-1778	Joanna		21-4-1794
Esther Griffith was William's first wife									
Joanna Griffith was William's second wife									
William	Griffith	1-2-1799		William			Deborah		
William	Griffith	6-12-1810		David			Rebecca		
William	Griffith	10-4-1812		Amos			Mary		
Ann	Grist	22-10-1757	2-11-1757	John	c1716	4-5-1780	Susannah	c1718	15-5-1776
Daniel	Grist	9-10-1737		John	c1716	4-5-1780	Susanna	c1718	15-5-1776
John (b.c1716) Griest, son of John and Martha of Bethel,									
married Susanna Pyle, daughter of Daniel and Mary of									
Bethel, 9th mo 18, 1736 at Chichester Meeting									
Hannah	Grist	7-11-1747		John	c1716	4-5-1780	Susannah	c1718	15-5-1776
John	Grist	19-6-1741	1-6-1743	John	c1716	4-5-1780	Susannah	c1718	15-5-1776
John	Grist	25-8-1744	9 mo 1744	John	c1716	4-5-1780	Susannah	c1718	15-5-1776
John	Grist	8-10-1749		John	c1716	4-5-1780	Susannah	c1718	15-5-1776
Joseph	Grist	12-4-1755		John	c1716	4-5-1780	Susannah	c1718	15-5-1776
Lydia	Grist	16-12-1758		John	c1716	4-5-1780	Susannah	c1718	15-5-1776
Martha	Grist	20-1-1739		John	c1716	4-5-1780	Susannah	c1718	15-5-1776
Mary	Grist	5-8-1745	3-7-1827	John	c1716	4-5-1780	Susannah	c1718	15-5-1776
Mary married -?- Garretson									

Name	Surname	Date 1	Date 2	Father	Date 3	Date 4	Mother	Date 5	Date 6
Susannah	Grist	15-3-1754	21-4-1754	John	c1716	4-5-1780	Susannah	c1718	15-5-1776
Thomas	Grist	14-2-1752		John	c1716	4-5-1780	Susannah	c1718	15-5-1776
Mary	Hammel	18-11-1756		James			Mary		13-4-1757
Elizabeth	Hammond	1-7-1745		John			Sarah		
Elizabeth	Hammond	1-7-1745		John			Deborah		
John	Hammond	10-10-1753		John			Sarah		
John	Hammond	10-10-1753		John			Deborah		
Mary	Hammond	18-11-1755		John			Sarah		
Mary	Hammond	18-6-1755		John			Deborah		
Nathan	Hammond	1-11-1749		John			Sarah		
Nathan	Hammond	1-11-1749		John			Deborah		
Sarah	Hammond	11-10-1743		John			Sarah		
Sarah	Hammond	11-10-1743		John			Deborah		
Tamar	Hammond	10-9-1759		John			Sarah		
Tamar	Hammond	10-9-1759		John			Deborah		
Benjamin	Harris			Benjamin			Rebecca		
Benjamin	Harris	c1827		Jacob			Mary		
Ellen	Harris	28-10-1821		Jacob			Mary		
Hiram	Harris	20-5-1836	9-3-1852	Benjamin			Jane	12-1-1881	22-9-1880
Joel	Harris	c 1823		Jacob			Mary		
John	Harris	9-10-1808		Jacob			Mary		

Jacob Harris was son of Benjamin Harris
Mary Harris was daughter of John Wright

Name	Surname	Date 1	Date 2	Father	Mother	Date 5	Date 6
Maria	Harris	20-10-1830		Benjamin	Jane	12-1-1881	22-9-1880
Martha	Harris	20-6-1826		Benjamin	Jane		
Mary Ann	Harris	31-12-1812		Jacob	Mary		
Matilda Jane	Harris	23-3-1833	28-8-1840	Benjamin	Jane		

Name		Born	Died	Father	Born	Died	Mother	Born	Died
Rach	Harris	12-5-1817		Jacob			Mary		
Rebecca	Harris	5-9-1819		Jacob			Mary		
Rebecca Ann	Harris	27-9-1828		Benjamin			Jane		
Samuel	Harris	25-11-1810		Jacob			Mary		
Samuel H.	Harris	27-7-1824	15-4-1908	Benjamin			Jane		
	Jane Harris was the daughter of Levi and Martha Hutton								
Silas	Harris	19-2-1805		Jacob			Mary		
William	Harris	c1825		Jacob			Mary		
Lewis Hicks	Harry	20-9-1825	22-12-1820	Lewis			Maria		12-11-1826
Melinda	Harry	27-2-1821		Lewis			Maria		12-11-1826
Naomi	Harry	23-3-1822		Lewis			Maria		12-11-1826
William									
Griffith	Harry	9-2-1823		Lewis			Maria		12-11-1826
Rebecca	Harvey	14-1-1792		William			Elizabeth		
Abel	Hewett	5-3-1779		Jonathan			Ann		
Joseph	Hewett	25-9-1782		Jonathan			Ann		
Samuel	Hewett	6-4-1789		Joseph			Rachel		
Sarah	Hewett	24-11-1780		Jonathan			Ann		
Thomas	Holland	7-10-1777		Thomas	c1747	7-4-1777	Mary		
Ann Pearson	Hoopes	5-3-1827	25-1-1835	Job	2-12-1795		Rhoda	13-5-1796	4-6-1857
Daniel	Hoopes	30-11-1801		William		17-9-1843	Phebe		4-6-1857
Elizabeth	Hoopes	5-2-1790		William		17-9-1843	Phebe		
Elizabeth	Hoopes	28-10-1838		Job	2-12-1795		Rhoda	13-5-1796	
Hannah	Hoopes	19-2-1836		Job	2-12-1795		Rhoda	13-5-1796	
Isaac	Hoopes	21-1-1813	1-10-1820	William		17-9-1843	Phebe		4-6-1857
Isaac A.	Hoopes	1-10-1818	11-11-1818	Job	2-12-1795		Rhoda	13-5-1796	

Name	Surname	Date	Parent	Date	Parent	Date	Date
James	Hoopes	10-12-1799	William	17-9-1843	Phebe		4-6-1857
Jane	Hoopes	28-6-1807	William	17-9-1843	Phebe		4-6-1857
Job	Hoopes	12-2-1795	William	17-9-1843	Phebe		4-6-1857
Joel							
Garretson	Hoopes	26-6-1825	Job	2-12-1795	Rhoda	13-5-1796	
Lewis	Hoopes	18-8-1819	Job	2-12-1795	Rhoda	13-5-1796	
Lydia	Hoopes	29-3-1818	William		Phebe		4-6-1857
Lydia Ann	Hoopes	15-1-1824 6-3-1824	Job	2-12-1795	Rhoda	13-5-1796	
Mary	Hoopes	24-4-1796	William		Phebe		4-6-1857
Mary A.	Hoopes	10-4-1821 11-6-1886	Job	2-12-1795	Rhoda	13-5-1796	
	Mary A. married -?- Wright						
Phebe	Hoopes	20-2-1811	William	17-9-1843	Phebe		4-6-1857
Phebe Jane	Hoopes	18-9-1831	Job	2-12-1795	Rhoda	13-5-1796	
Rebecca							
Wickersham	Hoopes	4-11-1834	Job	2-12-1795	Rhoda	13-5-1796	
Rhoda Ann	Hoopes	29-9-1829	Job	2-12-1795	Rhoda	13-5-1796	
Ruth	Hoopes	23-8-1804 3-6-1828	William	17-9-1843	Phebe		4-6-1857
Sarah	Hoopes	7-2-1824	William	17-9-1843	Phebe		4-6-1857
Waln	Hoopes	16-6-1816	William	17-9-1843	Phebe		4-6-1857
William	Hoopes	10-4-1809 4-6-1846	William	17-9-1843	Phebe		4-6-1857
Ann Pearson	Hoops	3-5-1827 25-1-1835	Job		Phebe		
Daniel	Hoops	30-11-1801	William	17-9-1843	Phebe		6-4-1851
Elizabeth	Hoops	5-2-1798	William	17-9-1843	Phebe		6-4-1851
Elizabeth							
Nebinger	Hoops	28-10-1838	Job		Rhoda		
Hannah	Hoops	19-9-1836	Job		Rhoda		
Isaac	Hoops	21-1-1813 1-10-1820	William	17-9-1843	Phebe		6-4-1851
Isaac A.	Hoops	10-1-1818 11-11-1818	Job		Rhoda		

259

Name		Born	Died	Father	Born	Died	Mother	Born	Died
James	Hoops	10-12-1799		William		17-9-1843	Phebe		6-4-1851
Jane	Hoops	28-6-1807		William		17-9-1843	Phebe		6-4-1851
Job	Hoops	12-2-1793		William		17-9-1843	Phebe		6-4-1851
Job, Jr	Hoops	12-2-1795		Job			Rhoda		
Joel Garretson	Hoops	26-6-1825		Job			Rhoda		
Lewis	Hoops	18-8-1819		Job			Rhoda		
Lydia	Hoops	29-3-1818		William		17-9-1843	Phebe		6-4-1851
Lydia Ann	Hoops	15-1-1824	3-6-1824	Job			Rhoda		
Mary	Hoops	24-4-1796		William		17-9-1843	Phebe		6-4-1851
Mary A.	Hoops	4-10-1821		Job			Rhoda		
Phebe	Hoops	20-2-1811		William		17-9-1843	Phebe		6-4-1851
Phebe Jane	Hoops	18-9-1831		Job			Rhoda		
Rebecca	Hoops	11-4-1834		Job			Rhoda		
Rhoda Ann	Hoops	29-7-1829		Job			Rhoda		
Rhoda Jr.	Hoops	13-5-1796		Job			Rhoda		
Ruth	Hoops	23-8-1804	3-6-1824	William		17-9-1843	Phebe		6-4-1851
Sarah	Hoops	7-3-1824		William		17-9-1843	Phebe		6-4-1851
Waln	Hoops	16-6-1816		William		17-9-1843	Phebe		6-4-1851
William	Hoops	10-4-1809	6-4-1846	William		17-9-1843	Phebe		6-4-1851
Amos	Hussey	15-3-1763		Riccord			Miriam		
Ann	Hussey	3-7-1744		Christophe			Ann		
Ann	Hussey	31-5-1771		Jedaiah			Jane		
Betty	Hussey	3-11-1759		John			Betty		
Christopher	Hussey	2-7-1756		Christophe			Ann		
Christopher	Hussey	28-7-1767		Jedaiah			Jane		
Edith	Hussey	25-1-1777		Riccord			Miriam		

Elizabeth	Hussey	6-7-1737		Christophe	Ann
	Christopher Hussey and Ann Garretson were married 9 mo 5th 1736 at Hockesin Meeting				
George	Hussey	9-3-1758		John	Betty
Hannah	Hussey	31-10-1759		Riccord	Miriam
Hannah	Hussey	7-4-1775		Jedaiah	Jane
Jane	Hussey	13-8-1781		Jedaiah	Jane
Jedaiah	Hussey	27-2-1777	9-10-1828	Jedaiah	Jane
Jehu	Hussey	12-11-1767	1768	Riccord	Miriam
Jesse	Hussey	4-12-1761	16-1-1762	Riccord	Miriam
John	Hussey	28-4-1769		Jedaiah	Jane
Lydia	Hussey	27-3-1757		Riccord	Miriam
Lydia	Hussey	21-10-1786		Jedaiah	Jane
Margaret	Hussey	7-1-1751		John	Betty
Mary	Hussey	6-4-1773		Riccord	Miriam
Mary	Hussey	31-3-1765		Jedaiah	Jane
Miriam	Hussey	25-12-1769		Riccord	Miriam
Naomi	Hussey	29-1-1742		Christophe	Ann
Nathan	Hussey	16-7-1755		John	Betty
Nathan	Hussey	12-8-1778	3rd 1808	Jedaiah	Jane
Rebekah	Hussey	4-5-1758		Riccord	Miriam
Ruth	Hussey	12-4-1765		Riccord	Miriam
Stephen	Hussey	10-7-1739		Christophe	Ann
Susanna	Hussey	7-8-1775	young	Riccord	Miriam
Levi	Hutton	10-10-1778		Samuel	Mary
Ann	Hutton	26-8-1761	17-5-1795	Jno	Ann
Betty	Hutton	20-2-1761		Joseph	Betty
Jane	Hutton			Levi	Martha
Joseph	Hutton	30-10-1755		Joseph	Betty

Name		Born	Died	Father	Born	Died	Mother	Born	Died
Joshua	Hutton	25-7-1748		Joseph			Betty		
Levi	Hutton	10-10-1770		Samuel			Mary		
Levi	Hutton	5-6-1752	3-10-1753	William			Deborah		
	William Hutton and Deborah Todd were married 16-9-1736 in Newgarden Meeting, Chester Co., Pa.								
Levi	Hutton	31-1-1757?		William			Deborah		
Rachel	Hutton	21-8-1750		Joseph			Betty		
Simmeon	Hutton	17-2-1765		Joseph			Betty		
Susannah	Hutton	17-12-1755		William			Deborah		
Susannah	Hutton	18-6-1758	27-4-1762	Joseph			Betty		
Tamar	Hutton	3-2-1754		William			Deborah		
Benjamin	Jennings	27-1-1766		Thomas			Susannah		
Samuel	Jennings	2-10-1764		Thomas			Susannah		
Sarah	Jennings	10-10-1768		Thomas			Susannah		
Abel	John	26-7-1793		Joseph	20-9-1756		Mary	4-2-1760	
Daniel	John	2-11-1782	10-10-1785	Joseph	20-9-1756		Mary	4-2-1760	
	Mary John was the daughter of Daniel Bonine								
Elizabeth	John	20-9-1784		Joseph	20-9-1756		Mary	4-2-1760	
Hannah	John	26-6-1786		Joseph	20-9-1756		Mary	4-2-1760	
Joseph	John	20-9-1756		Abel			Mary		
Mary	John	27-12-1875		Abel			Mary		
Rachael	John	19-11-1795		Joseph	20-9-1756		Mary	4-2-1760	
Rebecca	John	16-10-1790		Joseph	20-9-1756		Mary	4-2-1760	
Robert	John	26-3-1863		Abel			Mary		
Sarah	John	2-9-1788		Joseph	20-9-1756		Mary	4-2-1760	

Barzilla							
Anthony	Jones	6-5-1856		Thomas	28-1-1826	Martha	1-1-1884
Edwin Thomas	Jones	20-5-1860	30-11-1862	Thomas	28-1-1826	Martha	1-1-1884
Hannah	Jones	24-1-1777		Edward		Content	7-5-1781
Hiram Benjamin	Jones	8-4-1851		Thomas	28-1-1826	Martha	1-1-1884
Jane	Jones	19-2-1775		Edward		Content	7-5-1781
Jane Edna	Jones	26-3-1864		Thomas	28-1-1826	Martha	1-1-1884
John	Jones	29-11-1772	25-1-1773	Edward		Content	7-5-1781
		Content Jones was Edward's first wife					
Joshua	Jones	11-11-1788	26-3-1817	Edward		Sarah	
		Sarah was Edward Jones' second wife					
Phebe	Jones	21-3-1779		Edward		Content	7-5-1781
Rachael	Jones	27-8-1793	13-1-1844	Edward		Sarah	
		Rachael Jones married -?- Harker					
Benjamin	Kendall	31-12-1756		Thomas		Margaret	
Elizabeth	Kendall	20-3-1759		Thomas		Margaret	
Elizabeth	Kendall	20-3-1759		Thomas		Margaret	
Mary	Kendall	4-10-17??		Thomas		Sarah	c1750
		Sarah was Thomas Kendall's first wife					
William	Kendall	29-7-1754		Thomas		Margaret	
		Margaret Kendall was Thomas' second wife					
Thomas	Kettlewell	17-2-1792		John		Margaret	
Gulielma	Kightley	8-1-1780		James		Elizabeth	
James	Kightley	30-12-1775		James		Elizabeth	
Cornelius	Leech	20-9-1811	28-8-1819	Thomas		Hannah	
Eli	Leech	14-9-1822		Thomas		Hannah	

263

Name		Born	Died	Father	Born	Died	Mother	Born	Died
Jane	Leech	19-12-1805		Thomas			Hannah		
Joel	Leech	17-9-1820	8-10-1820	Thomas			Hannah		
John	Leech	6-1-1804		Thomas			Hannah		
Joseph	Leech	24-11-1802		Thomas			Hannah		
Margaret	Leech	9-4-1808	7-9-1819	Thomas			Hannah		
Samuel	Leech	2-7-1816	3-9-1819	Thomas			Hannah		
Sarah Ann	Leech	19-6-1818		Thomas			Hannah		
Thomas	Leech	23-4-1810	1-10-1811	Thomas			Hannah		
William	Leech	6-4-1814	12-3-1817	Thomas			Hannah		
Elizabeth	Lewis	28-4-1767		Samuel			Catherine		
Born within the verge of Warrington Monthly Meeting									
Elizabeth	Marsh	27-7-1762		John			Margaret		
Hannah	Marsh	c1783		John			Margaret		
Hugh	Marsh	c1781		John			Margaret		
John	Marsh	1-3-1771		John			Margaret		
Jonathan	Marsh	1-6-1760	21-3-1850	John			Margaret		
Lydia	Marsh	c1779		John			Margaret		
Margret	Marsh	28-11-1764		John			Margaret		
Mary	Marsh	16-1-1767		John			Margaret		
Rebekah	Marsh	10-3-1769	13-7-1770	John			Margaret		
Rebekah	Marsh	2-5-1777		John			Margaret		
Susanna	Marsh	17-3-1771		John			Margaret		
William	Marsh	20-7-1775		John			Margaret		
Ann	McGrew	29-4-1741		James			Mary		
Archibald	McGrew	14-4-1757		Finly			Elizabeth		

Deborah M.	McGrew	14-7-1739	James		Mary
Dinah	McGrew	9-3-1769	Finley		Dinah
Finley	McGrew	23-2-1751	Finley		Elizabeth
Finley	McGrew	13-1-1735	James		Mary
Finley	McGrew	27-3-1767	Finley		Dinah
Finley	McGrew	22-11-1783	Finley	24-4-1751	Mary
Isabel	McGrew	4-3-1752	Finley	1-8-1752	Elizabeth
James	McGrew	27-12-1744	Finly		Elizabeth
James	McGrew	1-12-1762	Finley		Dinah
James, Jr.	McGrew	25-6-1751	James		Mary
John	McGrew	13-10-1760	Finley		Dinah
Margaret	McGrew	10-8-1777	Finley		Dinah
Mary	McGrew	5-11-1748	James		Mary
Mary	McGrew	2-10-1763	Finley		Dinah
Mary	McGrew	13-3-1786	Finley	24-4-1751	Mary
Nathan	McGrew	10-3-1743	James		Mary
Nathan	McGrew	26-9-1746	Finly		Elizabeth
Nathan	McGrew	1-6-1765	Finley	24-4-1751	Dinah
Peter	McGrew	9-4-1788	Finley		Mary
Rebecca	McGrew	19-5-1755	Finley		Elizabeth
Rebekah	McGrew	16-9-1770	Finley		Dinah
Samuel	McGrew	17-8-1790	Finley	24-4-1751	Mary
Simeon	McGrew	3-12-1781	James	24-4-1751	Mary
William	McGrew	5-11-1745	Finley		Mary
William	McGrew	22-2-1796	Finley	24-4-1751	Mary
	McGrew	24-1-1748	John		Elizabeth
Abigail	McMillan	18-4-1757			Jane

10-6-1753 appears for: Deborah M., Finley (22-11-1783), Mary (13-3-1786), Nathan (1-6-1765), Rebekah, Samuel, William (22-2-1796)

Name		Born	Died	Father	Born	Died	Mother	Born	Died
Ann	McMillan	5-4-1801	19-6-1888	Jacob			Ruth		3rd 1829
	Ann McMillan was wife of Joseph Leech								
Anne	McMillan	21-8-1763	22-2-1850	George		11-7-1795	Ann		29-1-1815
	Anne married Willing Griest								
Cyrus	McMillan	22-2-1803	1872	Jacob			Ruth		3rd 1829
David	McMillan	2-3-1772		William			Deborah		4-9-1797
David	McMillan	28-8-????		William			Mary		
Deborah	McMillan	13-9-1764	24-11-1766	William			Deborah		4-9-1797
Deborah	McMillan	10-8-1778		William			Deborah		4-9-1797
Deborah	McMillan	6-12-1765		George		11-7-1795	Ann		29-1-1815
Edith	McMillan	15-7-1806	21-7-1812	Jacob			Ruth		3rd 1829
Eliza Ann	McMillan	20-5-1828		Enos			Sarah		
Enos	McMillan	9-9-1799	3-6-1890	Jacob			Ruth		3rd 1829
George	McMillan	26-5-1761	22-5-1846	George			Ann		29-1-1815
George	McMillan	26-1-1810	14-4-1853	Jacob			Ruth		3rd 1829
Henry	McMillan	20-11-1774		William			Deborah		4-9-1797
Jacob	McMillan	9-6-1812		John			Esther		7-6-1818
Jacob	McMillan	28-6-1779	1-1-1833	George		11-7-1795	Ann		29-1-1815
Jacob	McMillan	19-11-1797		Thomas			Ruth		
Jacob	McMillan	26-1-1805	31-1-1805	Jacob			Ruth		3rd 1829
Jane	McMillan	17-8-1814		John			Esther		7-6-1818
Jane	McMillan	29-9-1781	28-11-1782	George		11-7-1795	Ann		29-1-1815
John	McMillan	10-7-1786		William			Deborah		4-9-1797
Jonathan	McMillan	2-3-1772		William			Deborah		4-9-1797
Joseph	McMillan	10-10-1783	26-3-1826	George		11-7-1795	Ann		29-1-1815
Joseph	McMillan	6-9-1795		Thomas			Ruth		

Lydia	McMillan	21-9-1766	William		Deborah	4-9-1797
Mahlon	McMillan	2-2-1800	Thomas		Ruth	
Mariah	McMillan	13-4-1798	Thomas		Ruth	
Mary	McMillan	3-2-1810	John		Esther	7-6-1818
	John McMillan's wife Esther was Esther Griffith					
Mary	McMillan	20-4-1761	William		Deborah	4-9-1797
Mary	McMillan	16-2-1767 8-8-1827	George	11-7-1795	Ann	29-1-1815
	Mary married -?- Vale					
Oscar	McMillan	2-7-1818	John		Esther	7-6-1818
Rebecah	McMillan	7-7-1759 19-12-1814	George	11-7-1795	Ann	29-1-1815
	Rebecah married -?- Garretson					
Rebekah	McMillan	21-4-1813 14-8-1821	Jacob		Ruth	3rd 1829
Ruth	McMillan	4-3-1808 23-3-1887	Jacob		Ruth	3rd 1829
	Ruth McMillan was wife of Jesse Cook					
Samuel	McMillan	15-11-1816	John		Esther	7-6-1818
Samuel	McMillan	26-2-1770 10-4-1777	William		Deborah	4-9-1797
Sarah	McMillan	3-3-1760	John		Jane	
Thomas	McMillan	22-4-1763	William		Deborah	4-9-1797
Thomas	McMillan	14-5-1762	John		Jane	
Thomas	McMillan	16-10-1769	George	11-7-1795	Ann	29-1-1815
Uriah	McMillan	28-1-1826	Enos		Sarah	
William	McMillan	13-10-1767	William		Deborah	4-9-1797
Abigail	McMillen	18-4-1757	John		Jane	
Ann	McMillen	21-8-1766 23-2-1850	George	2-4-1732 11-7-1795	Ann	21-1-1815
Ann	McMillen	15-4-1801	Jacob		Ruth	2-3-1829
Anne	McMillen	21-8-1766 23-2-1850	George		Anne	
Cyrus	McMillen	22-2-1803	Jacob		Ruth	2-3-1829
David	McMillen	2-3-1772	William		Deborah	4-9-1797

267

Name		Born	Died	Father	Born	Died	Mother	Born	Died
Deborah	McMillen	13-9-1764	24-11-1766	William			Deborah		4-9-1797
Deborah	McMillen	10-8-1778		William			Deborah		4-9-1797
Deborah	McMillen	Deborah McMillen was the wife of Thomas McMillen	22-9-1764						
Deborah	McMillen	6-12-1768		George	2-4-1732	11-7-1795	Ann		21-1-1815
Edith	McMillen	15-7-1806	20-7-1812	Jacob			Ruth		2-3-1829
Eliza Ann	McMillen	20-5-1828		Enos			Sarah		
Enos	McMillen	9-9-1799		Jacob			Ruth		
George	McMillen	26-5-1763	22-5-1846	George	2-4-1732	11-7-1795	Ann		21-1-1815
George	McMillen	20-1-1810		Jacob			Ruth		2-3-1829
Henry	McMillen	20-11-1774		William			Deborah		4-9-1797
Jacob	McMillen	28-6-1777	1-1-1833	George	2-4-1732	11-7-1795	Ann		21-1-1815
Jacob	McMillen	19-11-1797		Thomas			Ruth		
Jacob	McMillen	26-1-1805	31-1-1805	Jacob			Ruth		2-3-1829
Jane	McMillen	29-9-1780	28-11-1782	George	2-4-1732	11-7-1795	Ann		21-1-1815
John	McMillen	10-7-1785		William			Deborah		4-9-1797
Jonathan	McMillen	2-3-1772		William			Deborah		4-9-1797
Joseph	McMillen	10-10-1782	26-3-1826	George	2-4-1732	11-7-1795	Ann		21-1-1815
Joseph	McMillen	6-9-1795		Thomas			Ruth		
Lydia	McMillen	21-9-1766		William			Deborah		4-9-1797
Mahlon	McMillen	2-2-1800		Thomas			Ruth		
Mariah	McMillen	13-4-1798		Thomas			Ruth		
Mary	McMillen	20-4-1761		William			Deborah		4-9-1797
Mary	McMillen	16-2-1768	8-8-1827	George	2-4-1732	11-7-1795	Ann		21-1-1815
Rebecca	McMillen	7-7-1759	19-12-1814	George	2-4-1732	11-7-1795	Ann		21-1-1815
Rebekah	McMillen	21-4-1813	15-8-1820	Jacob			Ruth		2-3-1829

Name	Surname	Date		Parent	Date	Other	Date
Ruth	McMillen	4-3-1805		Jacob		Ruth	2-3-1829
Samuel	McMillen	26-2-1770	10-4-1777	William		Deborah	4-9-1797
Sarah	McMillen	3-3-1760		John		Jane	
Thomas	McMillen	22-4-1763		William		Deborah	4-9-1797
Thomas	McMillen	14-5-1762		John		Jane	
Thomas	McMillen	16-10-1773		George	2-4-1732 11-7-1795	Ann	21-1-1815
Uriah	McMillen	28-1-1826		Enos		Sarah	
William	McMillen	13-10-1767		William		Deborah	4-9-1797
Jacob	McMiller	9-6-1812		John		Esther	7-6-1818
James	McMiller	17-8-1814		John		Esther	7-6-1818
Mary	McMiller	3-2-1810		John		Esther	7-6-1818
		John McMiller's wife was Esther Griffith					
Osker	McMiller	2-7-1818		John		Esther	7-6-1818
Samuel	McMiller	15-11-1816		John		Esther	7-6-1818
Elijah	Mickle	8-2-1740		John		Jane	
Hannah	Mickle	14-10-1745		John		Jane	
Jane	Mickle	16-1-1747		John		Jane	
John	Mickle	4-12-1753		John		Jane	
Mary	Mickle	4-10-1741		John		Jane	
Samuel	Mickle	26-2-1756		John		Jane	
Sarah	Mickle	29-10-1737		John		Jane	
Mary	Mills	3-7-1765		William	14-11-1784	Susannah	
Phebe	Mills	22-1-1769		William	14-11-1784	Susannah	
Rebecah	Mills	20-12-1766		William	14-11-1784	Susanna	
Robert	Mills	7-10-1774	28-8-1782	William	14-11-1784	Susannah	
Susanna	Mills	11-12-1770		William	14-11-1784	Susannah	
Jane	Morthland	20-9-1758	23-8-1800	William		Ruth	
	Jane Morthland married -?- Squibb						

Name		Born	Died	Father	Born	Died	Mother	Born	Died
Rebekah	Morthland	8-10-1763	Feb 1825	William			Ruth		
	Rebekah Morthland married -?- Davis (?)								
Robert	Morthland	23-1-1761	15-10-1822	William			Ruth		
Ann	Morton	16-9-1785		John			Hannah		
Benjamin	Morton	14-8-1789		John			Hannah		
Hannah	Morton	13-7-1795		John			Hannah		
John	Morton	4-4-1792		John			Hannah		
Mary	Morton	22-9-1787		John			Hannah		
Aaron	Packer	6-11-1780		Moses		9-11-1797	Jane		3-9-1788
James	Packer	30-3-1779		Moses		9-11-1797	Jane		3-9-1788
Lydia	Packer	11-9-1777		Moses		9-11-1797	Jane		3-9-1788
	Jane Packer Wife of Moses Packer Departed this life ye								
	3rd day of ye 9th mo 1788 about 2 in the afternoon								
Ann	Pearson	17-10-1790		Isaac			Elizabeth		
Ann	Pearson	38-6-1800		Isaac			Elizabeth		
Charlotte	Pearson	2-4-1819		Isaac	26-7-1792	11-7-182-	Mary W.	1-4-1797	1830
	Isaac (b.26-7-1792) was son of Isaac and Elizabeth Pearson								
	Mary W. (b.1-4-1797) Pearson was daughter of Wm. and Sarah Wierman								
Elias	Pearson	22-5-1788	9-11-1828	Isaac			Elizabeth		
Elizabeth	Pearson	15-11-1794		Isaac			Elizabeth		
Harry	Pearson	28-12-1797		Isaac			Elizabeth		
Isaac	Pearson	26-7-1792		Isaac			Elizabeth		
Isaac William	Pearson	6-6-1824		Isaac	26-7-1792	11-7-182-	Mary W.	1-4-1797	1830
Martha	Pearson	15-7-1704	25-2-1792	Isaac			Elizabeth		
Martha G.	Pearson	1-3-1821		Isaac	26-7-1792	11-7-182-	Mary W.	1-4-1797	1830

William	Pearson	5-6-1786	17-10-1796	Isaac		Elizabeth
Amos	Penrose	29-4-1776		Thomas		Abijah
Amos	Penrose	13-3-1776		Thomas		Abijah
Anna	Penrose	27-6-1781		Thomas		Abijah
Anna	Penrose	22-6-1781		Thomas		Abijah
Cyrus	Penrose	19-3-1792		Thomas		Abigail
Eliakim	Penrose	10-9-1817	12-2-1903	Josiah	28-3-1790 28-11-1860	Rachel	8-12-1788 25-12-1824
Elisha	Penrose	11-4-1816	4-3-1903	Josiah	28-3-1790 28-11-1860	Rachel	8-12-1788 25-12-1824

Josiah. (b.28-3-1790) Penrose was son of Thos. and Abigail Penrose
Rachel (b.8-12-1788) Penrose was daughter of John and Mary Garretson

Hannah	Penrose	29-4-1779		Thomas		Abijah
Hannah	Penrose	4-3-1824	21-4-1908	Josiah	28-3-1790 28-11-1860	Rachel	8-12-1788 25-12-1824
Huldah	Penrose	12-1-1820	16-5-1908	Josiah	28-3-1790 28-11-1860	Rachel	8-12-1788 25-12-1824
Josiah	Penrose	28-3-1790		Thomas		Abigail
Thomas	Penrose	3-5-1787		Thomas		Abigail
William	Penrose	9-5-1784		Thomas		Abijah
Amos	Pidgeon	21-12-1792		John		Susanna
Isaac	Pidgeon	15-4-1791		John		Susanna
Benjamin						
Walker	Pilkington	30-11-1806		Richard	31-10-1767 15-11-1819	Sarah	18-13-1771
Hepzibah	Pilkington	25-2-1804		Richard	31-10-1767 15-11-1819	Sarah	18-13-1771
Levi	Pilkington	19-7-1809		Richard	31-10-1767 15-11-1819	Sarah	18-13-1771
Matilda	Pilkington	20-5-1812		Richard	31-10-1767 15-11-1819	Sarah	18-13-1771
Rebecca	Pilkington	7-9-1801		Richard	31-10-1767 15-11-1819	Sarah	18-13-1771
Ruth	Pilkington	20-5-1797		Richard	31-10-1767 15-11-1819	Sarah	18-13-1771

Richard (b.31-10-1767) was son of Vincent and Rebecca Pilkington
Sarah, his wife, (b.18-3-1771) was daughter of Benjamin and Ruth Walker

Sarah Ann	Pilkington	9-7-1815		Richard	31-10-1767 15-11-1819	Sarah	18-13-1771

Name		Born	Died	Father	Born	Died	Mother	Born	Died
Vincent	Pilkington	16-3-1799	14-12-1819	Richard	31-10-1767	15-11-1819	Sarah	18-13-1771	
Abel Morth	Russell	18-2-1808		Jesse	17-3-1772		Content	20-9-1773	
Hannah	Russell	4-5-1806		Jesse	17-3-1772		Content	20-9-1773	
Isaac	Russell	18-8-1810		Jesse	17-3-1772		Content	20-9-1773	
Jonathan	Russell	16-11-1801		Jesse	17-3-1772		Content	20-9-1773	

Jesse (b.17-3-1772) was son of John and Hannah Russell
Content (b.20-9-1773) was daughter of John and Mary Garretson.

Name		Born	Died	Father	Born	Died	Mother	Born	Died
Mary	Russell	11-9-1813		Jesse	17-3-1772		Content	20-9-1773	
Mary Ann	Russell	2-5-1804		Jesse	17-3-1772		Content	20-9-1773	
Sarah	Russell	25-3-1816		Jesse	17-3-1772		Content	20-9-1773	
Emily	Smith	8-7-1853	17-8-1853	Nathan			Edith		
George A.	Smith	14-3-1857		Nathan			Edith		
Gideon	Smith	5-7-1842		Nathan			Edith		

Edith Smith was the daughter of Gideon and Jane Griest

Name		Born	Died	Father	Born	Died	Mother	Born	Died
Jesse	Smith	24-11-1849		Nathan			Edith		
Martha	Smith	24-7-1848		Nathan			Edith		
Nathan	Smith			Thomas					
Phebe Jane	Smith	28-8-1844	22-10-1861	Nathan			Edith		
Rebecca	Smith	14-7-1847	9-2-1847	Nathan			Edith		
William Riley	Smith	27-5-1855	13-8-1855	Nathan			Edith		
Ann	Taylor	5-11-1765		Joseph		12-6-1842	Ann		
Betty	Taylor	11-11-1761		Joseph		12-6-1842	Ann		
Esther	Taylor	7-11-1774		Joseph		12-6-1842	Ann		

John	Taylor	10-10-1763		Joseph	Ann
Joseph	Taylor	12-4-1768		Joseph	Ann
Libni	Taylor	6-10-1770		Joseph	Ann
Mary	Taylor	4-8-1777		Joseph	Ann
Rebekah	Taylor	9-2-1780		Joseph	Ann
Abel	Thomas	1-8-1802		Jacob	Margaret
Ann	Thomas	24-8-1792		John	Jane
Benjamin	Thomas	16-1-1771	19-8-1777	Jehu	Sarah
Benjamin	Thomas	14-8-1778		Jehu	Sarah
Edward	Thomas	25-6-1781		John	Jane
Elizabeth	Thomas	18-10-1787		John	Jane
Ellen R.	Thomas	23-8-1814	2-11-1791	Jacob	Margaret
Esher E.	Thomas	30-1-1812		Jacob	Margaret
Hannah	Thomas	8-4-1783		John	Jane
Hannah	Thomas	24-11-1804		Jacob	Margaret
Isaac	Thomas	11-10-1793		Jehu	Sarah
Jane	Thomas	3-3-1795		John	Jane
Jehu	Thomas	21-3-1784		Jehu	Sarah
John	Thomas	13-2-1779		John	Jane
Jonah	Thomas	19-10-1789		John	Jane
Jonathan	Thomas	14-6-1807		Jacob	Margaret
Lydia	Thomas	3-10-1777		John	Jane
Martha	Thomas	1-4-1773	11-8-1777	Jehu	Sarah
Mordecai Wm.	Thomas	10-10-1791		Jehu	Sarah
Rachael W.	Thomas	13-2-1817		Jacob	Margaret
Rachel	Thomas	11-10-1788		Jehu	Sarah
Rebecca	Thomas	4-12-1809	30-9-1823	Jacob	Margaret
Rebekah	Thomas		6-8-1791		

		12-6-1842	Joseph	Ann
		12-6-1842	Joseph	Ann
		12-6-1842	Joseph	Ann
		12-6-1842	Joseph	Ann
		12-6-1842	Jacob	Margaret

Name		Born	Died	Father	Born	Died	Mother	Born	Died
	Rebekah Thomas was the widow of John Thomas Sr.								
Rebekah	Thomas	8-1-1776	12-8-1777	Jehu			Sarah		
Rebekah	Thomas	30-7-1785		John			Jane		
Sarah	Thomas	18-3-1781		Jehu			Sarah		
Sarah	Thomas	19-10-1789		John			Jane		
Susannah	Thomas	27-5-1786		Jehu			Sarah		
Isaac	Tudor	15-12-1827	30-1-1853						
Lewis	Tudor		4-1-1903	Isaac		30-1-1853	Mary	25-6-1786	30-9-1881
	Isaac Tudor was son of John Tudor								
	Mary (b.25-6-1786), his wife, was daughter of John and Mary Garretson								
Martha Ann	Tudor	15-8-1830	15-9-1889	Isaac		30-1-1853	Mary	25-6-1786	30-9-1881
Alexander	Underwood	23-12-1761		John		1-7-1776	Mary		
Alvinia	Underwood	15-7-1812		Amos Griest			Phebe Griest		
Amanda	Underwood	26-3-1834		William	7-10-1810		Alvina	15-7-1812	
	Alvina Underwood was the daughter of Amos and Phebe Griest								
Ann	Underwood	27-4-1791		Elihu			Anne		
Asahel	Underwood	14-4-1773	2-6-1781	Benjamin		8-12-1803	Susannah		
Benjamin	Underwood	24-10-1770	6-5-1771	Benjamin		8-12-1803	Susannah		
Benjamin	Underwood	12-6-1789		Elihu			Anne		
Charles	Underwood	15-12-1795		Enoch			Mary		
Elihu	Underwood	19-9-1764		John		1-7-1776	Mary		
Elihu	Underwood	25-12-1745		William	c1722	18-5-1786	Ruth	c1723	14-11-1789
Elihu	Underwood	19-3-1784		Elihu			Anne		
Elizabeth	Underwood	19-2-1787		Elihu			Anne		
Enoch	Underwood	14-11-1758		Benjamin		8-12-1803	Susannah		

Hannah	Underwood	4-7-1761	William	c1722	18-5-1786	Ruth	c1723	14-11-1789
Isaac	Underwood	21-5-1800	Charles			Hannah		
Jacob	Underwood	25-10-1756 28-19-1784	William	c1722	18-5-1786	Ruth	c1723	14-11-1789
Jacob	Underwood	7-2-1780	Elihu			Anne		
James	Underwood	4-5-1794	Enoch			Mary		
Jane	Underwood	23-3-1752	William	c1722	18-5-1786	Ruth	c1723	14-11-1789
Jesse	Underwood	6-11-1766	William	c1722	18-5-1786	Ruth	c1723	14-11-1789
Jesse	Underwood	8-6-1794	Elihu			Anne		
Lydia	Underwood	29-10-1749	William	c1722	18-5-1786	Ruth	c1723	14-11-1789
Martha	Underwood	6-9-1756	Benjamin		8-12-1803	Susannah		
Mary	Underwood	16-7-1767	Benjamin		8-12-1803	Susannah		
Mary	Underwood	2-10-1771	Elihu			Anne		
Mary	Underwood	30-6-1797 9-8-1798	Enoch			Mary		
Mary	Underwood	6-8-1798	Charles			Hannah		
Michael	Underwood	7-6-1764	Benjamin		8-12-1803	Susannah		
	Michael Underwood was disowned							
Nehemiah	Underwood	17-12-1753	Benjamin		8-12-1803	Susannah		
Obed	Underwood	26-10-1763	William	c1722	18-5-1786	Ruth	c1723	14-11-1789
Olive	Underwood	27-3-1754 22-3-1777	William	c1722	18-5-1786	Ruth	c1723	14-11-1789
Rachel	Underwood	13-3-1769	William	c1722	18-5-1786	Ruth	c1723	14-11-1789
Rebekah	Underwood	6-10-1759	John		1-7-1776	Mary		
Ruth	Underwood	23-3-1759	William	c1722	18-5-1786	Ruth	c1723	14-11-1789
Ruth	Underwood	24-10-1775	Elihu			Anne		
Samuel	Underwood	4-12-1767	John		1-7-1776	Mary		
Sarah	Underwood	2-2-1752	Benjamin		8-12-1803	Susannah		
Sarah	Underwood	2-11-1777	Elihu			Anne		
Stephen	Underwood	13-7-1774 14-11-1774	Elihu			Anne		
Stephen	Underwood	9-11-1777	Elihu			Anne		

Name		Born	Died	Father	Born	Died	Mother	Born	Died
Susannah	Underwood	28-1-1782	21-2-1788	Elihu			Ann		
William	Underwood	7-10-1810		Zephaniah			Hannah		
William	Underwood	26-3-1744		William	c1722	18-5-1786	Ruth	c1723	14-11-1789
	William Underwood, son of Alexander of Londongrove, married Ruth Beals								
	of Londongrove (daughter Wm., deceased) 1st mo 2nd 1742/3								
William	Underwood	19-3-1773	1-4-1773	Elihu			Anne		
Willing	Underwood	30-11-1761		Benjamin		8-12-1803	Susannah		
Willing	Underwood	30-11-1761		Benjamin		8-12-1803	Susannah		
Zephaniah	Underwood	13-12-1747		William	c1722	18-5-1786	Ruth	c1723	14-11-1789
Ann	Updegraf	27-12-1760		Harman			Lydia		
Ann	Vale	22-1-1753		Robert			Sarah		
Ann	Vale	30-4-1786	1819	William			Anna		8-4-1816
	Ann Vale married Jediah Hussey								
Ann	Vale	12-5-1796		John			Deborah		
Ann	Vale	14-1-1829		Elisha			Martha		26-7-1804
Beulah	Vale	3-9-1794		John			Deborah		26-7-1804
Child	Vale	11-12-1792	11-12-1792	Joshua			Elizabeth		
Deborah	Vale	16-12-1819	13-3-1820	Robert	c1783	19-8-1820	Martha		
Eli	Vale	16-5-1789		John			Deborah		
Elisha	Vale	21-1-1788		William			Anna		8-4-1816
Eliza	Vale	15-1-1809	8-11-1820	Robert	c1783	19-8-1820	Martha		
Eliza Ann	Vale	10-10-1819		Nathan			Ann		21-3-1822
	Ann Vale was Nathan's second wife								
Elizabeth	Vale	5-3-1794	13-2-1862	Joshua			Elizabeth		
	Elizabeth married -?- Garretson								

Elizabeth	Vale	21-9-1812	Nathan		Alice	25-3-1819
		Alice Vale was Nathan's first wife				
Hannah	Vale	16-9-1783	12-7-1863	William	Anna	8-4-1816
Isaac	Vale	4-9-1781	10-9-1781	William	Anna	8-4-1816
Isaac	Vale	1-2-1813		Robert	Martha	
Jacob						
Garretson			c1783	19-8-1820		
James	Vale	7-7-1821		John	Lydia	10-9-1821
Jane H.	Vale	22-6-1784		John	Deborah	26-7-1804
John	Vale	27-8-1819		Elisha	Martha	
John	Vale	6-2-1817	7-2-1817	John	Lydia	10-9-1821
John	Vale	30-12-1760		Robert	Sarah	
John	Vale	16-7-1792	1821	William	Anna	8-4-1816
John C.	Vale	17-8-1821	20-8-1821	Elisha	Martha	
Joseph	Vale	28-7-1821	15-8-1823	Robert	Martha	
Joshua	Vale	30-7-1784	14-2-1785	William	Anna	c1783 19-8-1820
Joshua	Vale	18-2-1757		Robert	Sarah	
Lydia	Vale	27-12-1796		Joshua	Elizabeth	
Lydia	Vale	19-11-1797	1800	William	Anna	8-4-1816
Maria	Vale	28-8-1792		John	Deborah	26-7-1804
Mary	Vale	5-12-1827	22-2-1828	Elisha	Martha	
Mary	Vale	9-2-1818	17-8-1835	John	Lydia	10-9-1821
Mary	Vale	28-4-1783	21-5-1783	Joshua	Elizabeth	
Mary	Vale	5-12-1787		Joshua	Elizabeth	
Mary	Vale	2-1-1779	7-1-1779	William	Anna	8-4-1816
Nathan	Vale	5-11-1794		William	Elizabeth	8-4-1816
Peter	Vale	22-7-1784		Joshua	Elizabeth	
Phebe	Vale	17-7-1790		Joshua	Elizabeth	
	Vale	6-6-1799		John	Deborah	26-7-1804

Name	Surname	Born	Died	Father	Born	Died	Mother	Born	Died
Phebe	Vale	7-1-1801	25-12-1887	William			Anna		8-4-1816
	Phebe Vale married Eli Cookson								
Rebeccah M.	Vale	21-9-1812		Nathan			Alice		25-3-1819
Robert	Vale	13-12-1751		Robert			Sarah		
Robert	Vale	22-6-1784		John			Deborah		26-7-1804
Ruthanna	Vale	20-8-1822		Elisha			Martha		
Sarah	Vale	25-9-1799		Joshua			Elizabeth		
Sarah	Vale	17-5-1780	28-5-1780	William			Anna		8-4-1816
Sarah	Vale	5-12-1789	5-3-1863	William			Anna		8-4-1816
Sarah Ann	Vale	10-12-1814		Elisha			Martha		
Susanna	Vale	11-2-1811		Robert	c1783	19-8-1820	Martha		
William	Vale	22-11-1754		Robert			Sarah		
William	Vale	21-4-1819	20-10-1846	John		10-9-1821	Lydia		
William E.	Vale	27-1-1825		Elisha			Martha		
Abner	Vore	27-4-1787		Peter			Betty		
Benjamin	Vore	5-6-1785		Peter			Betty		
Joseph	Vore	30-8-1783		Peter			Betty		
Peter	Vore	14-10-1791		Peter			Betty		
Sarah	Vore	14-8-1789		Peter			Betty		
Abel	Walker	13-4-1792		Abel		3-4-1817	Ann		4-3-1824
Abel	Walker	14-9-1827		Joel			Mary M		
Abner	Walker	8-8-1779		Benjamin		31-12-1821	Ruth		8-5-1817
Ann	Walker	7-7-1776		Asahel			Ann		
Asahel	Walker	6-9-1786		Benjamin		31-12-1821	Ruth		8-5-1817
Benjamin	Walker	7-5-1782		Benjamin		31-12-1821	Ruth		8-5-1817

Name	Surname	Date	Father		Mother			Date
Benjamin	Walker	13-1-1797	Abel		Ann	3-4-1817		
Edward	Walker	21-1-1772 12-5-1772	Asahel		Ann				
Elias Hix	Walker	24-11-1825	Joel		Mary M			4-3-1824
Elija	Walker	23-1-1790	Abel		Ann	3-4-1817		
Eliza	Walker	29-1-1790	Abel		Ann	3-4-1817		4-3-1824
Elizabeth	Walker	9-1-1810	Asahel	c1786	Mary	14-10-1877	c1787	18-4-1827
Garretson Cook	Walker	6-5-1835	Asahel	c1786	Lydia G.	14-10-1877	c1796	22-6-1869
Hannah	Walker	1-5-1785	Abel		Ann	3-4-1817		
Hannah Anna	Walker	2-10-1833	Joel		Mary M.			4-3-1824
Hephzibah	Walker	19-10-1784	Benjamin		Ruth	31-12-1821		8-5-1817
Isaac	Walker	8-2-1792	Benjamin		Ruth	31-12-1821		8-5-1817
Isaac	Walker	22-7-1779	Asahel		Ann			
Isaac	Walker	13-7-1809	Asahel	c1786	Mary	14-10-1877	c1787	18-4-1827
	Mary Walker was Asahel's first wife							
Isaac John	Walker	12-3-1824	Joel		Mary M.			
Jeremiah	Walker	11-9-1830	Joel		Mary M.			
Jerman	Walker	22-5-1773 31-8-1782	Benjamin		Ruth	31-12-1821		8-5-1817
Joel	Walker	14-4-1794	Abel		Ann	3-4-1817		4-3-1824
John	Walker	10-8-1775	Benjamin		Ruth	31-12-1821		8-5-1817
Joseph	Walker	20-8-1787	Abel		Ann	3-4-1817		4-3-1824
Joshua V.	Walker	3-11-1822	Asahel		Mary			18-4-1827
Leah	Walker	5-4-1782	Abel		Ann	3-4-1817		4-3-1824
Lewis Pierson	Walker	25-4-1833	Asahel	c1786	Lydia G.	14-10-1877	c1796	22-6-1869
Lewis Morris	Walker	11-2-1822	Joel		Mary M.			
Louisa	Walker	14-10-1814	Asahel	c1786	Mary	14-10-1877	c1787	18-4-1827
Lydia Jane	Walker	30-1-1837	Asahel	c1786	Lydia G.	14-10-1877	c1796	22-6-1869
Mary Ann	Walker	16-3-1816	Asahel	c1786	Mary	14-10-1877	c1787	18-4-1827
Morris E.	Walker	16-2-1820	Asahel	c1786	Mary	14-10-1877	c1787	18-4-1827

Name		Born	Died	Father	Born	Died	Mother	Born	Died
Phebe	Walker	18-8-1777	30-1-1782	Benjamin		31-12-1821	Ruth		8-5-1817
Phebe Angeline	Walker	5-3-1838		Asahel	c1786	14-10-1877	Lydia G.	c1796	22-6-1869
Priscilla	Walker	10-14-1814		Asahel	c1786	14-10-1877	Mary Ann	c1787	18-4-1827
Rachel	Walker	24-3-1781	23-4-1781	Abel		3-4-1817	Ann		4-3-1824
Rachel M.	Walker	25-3-1835		Joel			Mary M.		
Rebekah	Walker	23-3-1774		Asahel			Ann		
Ruth Anna	Walker	5-11-1831		Asahel			Lydia		
		Lydia Walker, widow of John Vale, was Asahel's second wife							
Ruthanna	Walker	11-5-1831		Asahel	c1786	14-10-1877	Lydia G.	c1796	22-6-1869
Sarah	Walker	18-3-1772		Benjamin		31-12-1821	Ruth		8-5-1817
Sarah	Walker	6-9-1778	10-9-1804	Abel		3-4-1817	Ann		4-3-1824
		Sarah married -?- Fletcher							
Sarah	Walker	1-4-1827		Asahel	c1786	14-10-1877	Mary Jane	c1787	18-4-1827
Mary	Warner	18-1-1816	14-10-1821	William			Sarah		27-1-1859
Adeline	Wickersham	23-2-1839		Thomas	27-4-1801		Sarah	6-8-1804	
Edith	Wickersham	22-9-1835		Abner			Anne		
Edward	Wickersham	29-3-1803		Jesse		3 mo 1826	Phebe		
Eli	Wickersham	23-5-1818		Jesse		3 mo 1826	Phebe		
Elias Hicks	Wickersham	31-8-1828		Thomas	27-4-1801		Sarah	6-8-1804	
		This family left Newberry on the 15th of the 4th mo 1851 bound for the State of Iowa							
Eliza Mary	Wickersham	9-3-1830		Thomas	27-4-1801		Sarah	6-8-1804	
Harriet M.	Wickersham	18-1-1844		Thomas	27-4-1801		Sarah	6-8-1804	
Isaac	Wickersham	26-8-1820		Jesse		3 mo 1826	Phebe		
Israel Meredith	Wickersham	29-8-1836		Thomas			Sarah	6-8-1804	
Jane	Wickersham	19-3-1809	7-3-1811	Jesse		3 mo 1826	Phebe		

Name	Surname	Date		Parent	Date		
Jesse	Wickersham	20-4-1805		Jesse		Phebe	
Jesse	Wickersham	27-4-1833		Thomas	27-4-1801	Sarah	6-8-1804
John	Wickersham	17-9-1811	9-5-1816	Jesse		Phebe	
Joshua	Wickersham	22-5-1816		Jesse	3 mo 1826	Phebe	
Josiah	Wickersham	13-5-1825	19-2-1882	Abner	3 mo 1826	Anne	
Louis Meredith	Wickersham	4-3-1842		Thomas	27-4-1801	Sarah	8-6-1804
Lydia	Wickersham	21-3-1814		Jesse	3 mo 1826	Phebe	
Maria	Wickersham	15-3-1822		Abner		Anne	
Abner Wickersham's wife Anne was the daughter of Willing and Anne Griest
Mary Ann	Wickersham	15-5-1831		Abner		Anne	
Phebe	Wickersham	3-9-1822		Jesse	3 mo 1826	Phebe	
Sidney	Wickersham	22-3-1807		Jesse	3 mo 1826	Phebe	
Thomas	Wickersham	27-4-1801		Jesse	3 mo 1826	Phebe	
Eliza	Wierman	30-9-1807	5-11- ??	William		Sarah	
Erney	Wierman	11-10-1795		William		Sarah	
Hannah	Wierman	9-7-1787		William	8-7-1746	Hannah	10-1-1748
Hannah Mary	Wierman	19-3-1832		Joel	7-8-1784	Lydia S.	
Joel (b.7-8-1784) Wierman was son of William and Hannah Wierman
Lydia S. Wierman was daughter of Jos. and Mary Lundy
Isaac	Wierman	13-10-1781		William	8-7-1746	Hannah	10-1-1748
Joel	Wierman	7-8-1784		William	8-7-1746	Hannah	10-1-1748
John	Wierman	3-7-1773	12-10-??	William	8-7-1746	Hannah	10-1-1748
Lucretia	Wierman	19-5-1835		Joel	7-8-1784	Lydia S.	
Lydia	Wierman	7-10-1793		William	8-7-1746	Hannah	10-1-1748
Mary	Wierman	20-2-1796		William	8-7-1746	Hannah	10-1-1748
Mary	Wierman	1-4-1797		William		Sarah	
Miriam	Wierman	27-4-1803	23-12-??	William		Sarah	
Nicholas	Wierman	8-7-1771		William	8-7-1746	Hannah	10-1-1748

Name		Born	Died	Father	Born	Died	Mother	Born	Died
Peter	Wierman	15-6-1805	William (b.8-7-1746) was son of Nicholas and Sarah Wierman						
			Hannah (b.10-1-1748) was daughter of John and Susanna Griest						
Peter	Wierman	15-6-1805	5-11-??	William	8-7-1746		Sarah		
Phebe	Wierman	8-2-1790		William	8-7-1746		Hannah	10-1-1748	
Phebe	Wierman	31-1-1887		Joel	7-8-1784		Lydia S.		
Sarah	Wierman	11-6-1775		William	8-7-1746		Hannah	10-1-1748	
Sarah	Wierman	28-12-1800		William			Sarah		
Susanna	Wierman	5-9-1779		William	8-7-1746		Hannah	10-1-1748	
William C.	Wierman	21-5-1799		William			Sarah		
Elizbeth	Williams	16-9-1769		Jacob			Ruth		
Hannah	Williams	15-2-1762		Jacob			Ruth		
Israel	Williams	21-9-1759		Jacob			Ruth		
		Israel, Hannah, Sarah, Jane were born within the verge of Uchland Monthly Meeting							
		Elizabeth and Ruth were born within the verge of Warrington Monthly Meeting							
Jane	Williams	12-5-1767		Jacob			Ruth		
Ruth	Williams	1-12-1772		Jacob			Ruth		
Sarah	Williams	13-9-1764		Jacob			Ruth		
Hanah	Willis	7-9-1759		William			Betty	c1734	8-7-1769
Joel	Willis	23-8-1764		William			Betty	c1734	8-7-1769
John	Willis	26-7-1754		William			Betty	c1734	8-7-1769
Lydia	Willis	13-5-1762		William			Betty		8-7-1769
Susana	Willis	19-8-1756		William			Betty	c1734	8-7-1769
Alice	Wilson	6-12-1782		Benjamin	c1739	3-8-1813	Sarah	c1745	12-11-1815
		c1739	3-8-1813						
Benjamin	Wilson	7-8-1801		George			Sarah		
Benjamin	Wilson								
Betsy	Wilson	9-5-1809	24-7-1813	George			Sarah		

Name	Surname	Birth					
George	Wilson	10-3-1778	15-9-1785	Benjamin	c1739	3-8-1813	Sarah	c1745	12-11-1815
John	Wilson	26-9-1806		George			Sarah		
Mary	Wilson	13-9-1780		Benjamin	c1739	3-8-1813	Sarah	c1745	12-11-1815
Ruth	Wilson	1-11-1775	11-7-1784	Benjamin	c1739	3-8-1813	Sarah	c1745	12-11-1815
Ruth	Wilson	7-1-1804		George			Sarah		
Sarah	Wilson	c1745	12-11-1815					
Sarah	Wilson	29-1-1785		Benjamin	c1739	3-8-1813	Sarah	c1745	12-11-1815
William B.	Wilson	11-2-1800		George			Sarah		
Aaron	Wright	30-9-1810		Jonathan			Mary		
Abel T.	Wright	21-1-1810	11-9-1869	William			Rachael		
Alice	Wright	7-11-1771	1-7-1777	Benjamin			Jane		
Alice	Wright	16-2-1779		Benjamin			Jane		
Ann	Wright	4-3-1791		John			Ann		
Ann	Wright	25-8-1826		William	21-12-1788		Phebe	8-2-1790	
Benjamin	Wright	21-7-1783		Benjamin			Jane		
Charles Osburn	Wright	27-1-1821	16-8-1821	Thomas			Anna		
Eliza R.	Wright	26-2-1852		Charles S.	6-10-1816	16-11-1872	Hannah G.	4-3-1824	21-4-1908
Elizabeth	Wright	12-7-1776		Benjamin			Jane		
Elizabeth	Wright	5-11-1808		William			Rachael		
Ellen	Wright	7-12-1804	10-2-1883	William			Rachael		

William Wright was son of John Wright
Rachael, his wife, was daughter of Abel Thomas

Emilie	Wright	20-6-1849		Charles S.	6-10-1816	16-11-1872	Hannah G.	4-3-1824	21-4-1908
George Edwar	Wright	19-8-1855		Charles S.	6-10-1816	16-11-1872	Hannah G.	4-3-1824	21-4-1908
Hannah	Wright	24-8-1812		Jonathan			Mary		
Hannah	Wright	16-10-1818		William	21-12-1788		Phebe	8-2-1790	

William (b.21-12-1788) Wright was son of John and Ann Wright
Phebe (b.8-2-1790), his wife, was daughter of William and Hannah Wierman

283

Name	Born	Died	Father	Born	Died	Mother	Born	Died
Hanson Wright	12-9-1818		Thomas			Anna		
Harris Wright	23-2-1817		Thomas			Anna		
Henry Wright			William H.	16-3-1812		Jane	10-3-1809	
Isaac Wright	1-12-1828		William	21-12-1788		Phebe	8-2-1790	
Isaac J. Wright	9-7-1813	6-7-1892	William			Rachael		
Israel Pemberton Wright	27-8-1808		Thomas			Anna		

Thomas Wright was son of John Wright
Anna, his wife, was daughter of Benjamin Harris

Name	Born	Died	Father	Born	Died	Mother	Born	Died
Jane Wright	4-6-1790		Benjamin			Jane		
Jesse Wright	30-3-1774		Benjamin			Jane		
Jesse Wright	21-3-1829		William H.	16-3-1812		Jane	10-3-1809	
John Wright	17-9-1769		Benjamin			Jane		
John Wright	23-6-1820		William	21-12-1788		Phebe	8-2-1790	
John Wright	8-4-1793		John			Ann		
Josiah Wright	27-9-1808		Jonathan			Mary		
Leah Wright	23-2-1810		Thomas			Anna		
Lucy Wright	23-11-1814		Thomas			Anna		
Lydia Wright	16-7-1812		Thomas			Anna		
Mahlon Wright	14-1-1807		Jonathan			Mary		
Martha Wright	10-9-1767		Benjamin			Jane		
Martha H. Wright			William H.	16-3-1812		Jane	10-3-1809	
Mary Wright	5-6-1786		John			Ann		
Rachael Wright	14-3-1796		John			Ann		
Rachael Wright	9-4-1822		William	21-12-1788		Phebe	8-2-1790	
Rachel A. Wright	20-7-1847		Charles S.	6-10-1816	16-11-1872	Hannah G.	4-3-1824	21-4-1908

Charles S. (b.6-10-1816) Wright was son of John and Alice Wright

Hannah G. (b.4-3-1824), his wife, was daughter of Josiah and Rachel Penrose

Samuel	Wright		27-9-1782	John	
				Ann	
Samuel B.	Wright		4-3-1835	William H. 16-3-1812	10-3-1809
				Jane	

William H. (b.16-3-1812) Wright was son of Samuel B. and Elizabeth Wright
Jane (b.10-3-1809), his wife, was daughter of Henry and Mary Cook

Sarah	Wright		14-1-1837	William H. 16-3-1812	10-3-1809
				Jane	
Savanah	Wright		5-2-1818	William	
				Rachael	
Thomas	Wright		20-12-1785	Benjamin	
				Jane	
Thomas	Wright		6-8-1784	John	
				Ann	
Thomas Hammond	Wright	8-7-1882	30-10-1806	William	
				Rachael	
William	Wright		21-12-1788	John	
				Ann	
William	Wright		15-3-1812	William H. 16-3-1812	10-3-1809
				Jane	
William H.	Wright		27-7-1824	Samuel	
				Elizabeth	
William H.	Wright	9-1-1882	27-7-1824	William 21-12-1788	8-2-1790
				Phebe	
William W.	Wright			William 21-12-1788	8-2-1790
				Phebe	

Appendix B

Locations of other

Meetings mentioned in

Certificates of Removal

Abington MM	Montgomery Co., Pa.
Alexandria MM	Alexandria Co., Va.
Alum Creek MM	Ohio
Baltimore MM	Baltimore Co., Md
Birmingham MM	Chester Co., Pa.
Bradford MM	Chester Co., Pa.
Center MM, Va.	Frederick Co., Va
Chester MM	Delaware Co., Pa.
Concord MM, Ohio	Belmont Co., Ohio
Crooked Run MM	Frederick Co., Va.
Deep River MM.	Guilford Co., N.C.
Deer Creek MM, Md.	Harford Co., Md.
Deer Creek MM, Ohio	formerly Marlborough MM
Duck Creek MM	Delaware
Ewchlan MM	Chester Co., Pa.
Exeter MM	Berks Co., Pa.
Fairfax MM	Fairfax Co., Va
Goose Creek MM	Bedford Co., Va.
Gunpowder MM	Baltimore Co., Md.
Gwynedd MM	Montgomery Co., Pa.
Horsham MM	Montgomery Co., Pa.
Indian Springs MM	Montgomery Co., Md.
Kennet MM	Chester Co., Pa.
Little Britton MM	Lancaster Co., Pa.
London Grove MM	Chester Co., Pa
Marlborough MM, N.C.	Randolph Co., N.C.
Marlborough MM, Ohio	Ohio
Menallen MM	Adams Co. Pa.
New Garden MM, Pa.	Chester Co., Pa.
New Garden MM, N.C.	Guilford Co., N.C.
New Garden QM, Ohio	name changed to Western QM in 1851. Joined to Salem QM in 1859
New Garden MM, Ind.	Howard Co., Ind.
Nottingham MM	Cecil Co., Md.
Philadelphia MM	Philadelphia Co., Pa.
Pine St MM.,Phila	Philadelphia Co., Pa.
Pipe Creek MM	Carroll Co., Md.
Plainfield MM	Ohio
Redstone MM	Fayette Co., Pa.
Sadsbury MM	Lancaster Co., Pa.
Short Creek MM	Ohio
South River MM	Rockbridge Co., Va.
Uwchlan MM	Chester Co., Pa.
Warrington MM	York Co., Pa.
Westland MM	Washington Co., Pa.
White Water MM	Wayne Co., Ohio
Wilmington MM	New Castle Co., Del.
York MM	York Co., Pa.

Appendix C

Full text of original

Certificates

Warrington Monthly Meeting maintained a separate book for the purpose of copying the marriage certificate in full for every marriage completed under their care. York Monthly Meeting kept a separate book for all certificates of Removal.

On the following pages are the full text of a sample Certificate of Marriage and a sample Certificate of Removal. The wording has changed very little in 250 years.

Whereas John Garretson of Newbery in the County of Lanchester in the province of pencilvania and Jane Carson daughter of Patrick Carson of Newbery in the County and province aforesaid having appeared before several monthly meetings of the Christian people of God called Quakers and decleared their intention of marriage with each other according to the good order used amongst them and having Consent of parents and Relations consarned their said proposals was alowed of by the said meetings.

Now thefe are to Certifie to home it may consarn that for the full accomplishing of their said intentions they the said John Garretson and Jane Carson appeared at a publick meeting of the said people for that purpose appointed at Newbery this twenty second day of the sixth month in the year of our Lord one thousand Seven hundred and Fourty nine and then and there in the Said afsembly the said John Garretson taking the Said Jane Garretson by the hand did in a solomn manner openly declear that he took her the said Jane Carson to be his wife promifsing with the Lords afsistance to be unto her a Loving and Faithfull husband till death should seperate them and then and there in the said afsembly the said Jane Carson did in Like manner openly declear that shee took the said John Garretson to be her husband promifsing with the Lords afsistance to be unto him a Faithfull and Loving wife till death should seperate them or words to that affect and moreover they the said John Garretson and Jane Carson shee according to the custom of marriage afsuming the name of her husband did then and there to thefe prefents set their hands and for a further confirmation we whofe names are here alfo underwritten who were present at the solemnization of the said marriage and superscription have as witnefses thereunto set our hands the day and year above written

	Thomas Cox	John Garretson
Abraham Ellot	Christopher Hufsey	Jane Garretson
James Mills	John Day	Margaret Carson
William Griffiths	Joseph Garretson	Ann Hufsey
Archey Mackey	Samuel Cox	Martha Garretson
Francis Fincher	William Beals	Mary Garretson
Armol Fincher	Benjamin Underwood	Mary Garretson
Joseph Heald	William Bennett	Sarah Carson
John Day	Alexander Underwood	Sarah Farmer
Robert Mills jur	Petter Stoute	Sarah Leach
John Cefna	William Underwood	Joanna Heald
Jesper Robenet	Samuel Underwood	Ester Foulk
Sarah Mills	John Ellot	
Mary Kinwithey		
Neomie Cox		

To the Monthly Meeting of Friends at Fairfax--

>Whereas <u>Christopher Hussey</u> Requested our Certificate to be joined to your Meeting he being removed within the Verge thereof, Thefe are therefor to inform you that he is in Membership with us. Frequently attended our Religious Meetings, and do not Find but that his Life and Conversation was in a good degree orderly, and is Clear of Debt and Marriage Engagements as far as appears -- As such we recommend him to your Christian care and Remain your affectionate Friends,--
>
>Signed in and by order of ye our Monthly Meeting at York heald the 7th of the 11th mo 1787 by
>Elisha Kirk Cleark

INDEX

The index does not include the witnesses to the marriages nor the names listed in Appendix A, Births and Deaths.

The references are to Document number, not page number.

Key

M: marriage
R: removal

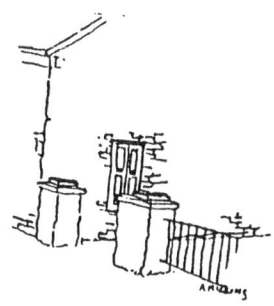

Name		Doc#
Allen	David	224 M
	Elizabeth	215 M
	Elizabeth	224 M
	James	215 M
	Sarah	215 M
	Sarah	224 M
	Thomas	224 M
Altemus	Leonard	305 M
	Sarah	305 M
Armitage	John	289 M
	Rachel	289 M
	Sarah	289 M
	William H.	289 M
Atherton	Abigail	130 M
	Ann	88 M
	Elizabeth	139 M
	Henery	88 M
	Phebe	130 M
	Richard	130 M
	Thomas	88 M
	Thomas	130 M
	Thomas	139 M
Atkinson	Alice	282 M
	Cephas	125 M
	Cephas	138 M
	Cephas	189 M
	Cephas	190 M
	Hannah	125 M
	Hannah	138 M
	Jane	125 M
	Jane	190 M
	Jane	282 M
	John	282 M
	Joseph	189 M
	Margaret	138 M
	Susanna	189 M
	Thomas	282 M
Baily	Charles	230 M
	Hannah	230 M
	Jane	230 M
Ballenger	Samuel	54 R
Ballinger	Saml	24 R
	Saml	25 R
	Saml	35 R
	Samuel	32 R
Bane	James	242 M
	Margret	242 M
Beal	Jacob	1 M
Beals	Boater	10 M
	Elizabeth	127 M
	Jacob	11 M
	Jacob	127 M
	Jacob	136 M
	Jacob, Jr.	48 M
	John	10 M
	Liddia	48 M
	Martha	127 M
	Mary	1 M
	Rachel	11 M
	Rebekah	136 M
	Sarah	10 M
	Solomon	136 M
	William	1 M
Bennet	Ann	80 R
	Ann	118 R
	Ann	245 R
Bennett	Hannah	78 M
	Joseph	19 M
	Joseph	26 M
	Joseph	78 M
	Joshua	290 M
	Joshua F.	290 M
	Mary	290 M
	Phebe	26 M
	Rebecca	78 M
	Sarah	19 M
	Sarah	290 M
Benson	Abraham	81 R
	Abraham	209 R
	Amos	81 R
	Amos	211 R
	Benjamin	81 R
	Benjamin	208 R
	Benjamin, Jr.	208 R
	Elizabeth	81 R
	Hannah	81 R
	Hannah	208 R
	Hannah, Jr.	81 R
	Hannah, Jr.	208 R
	Jesse	81 R
	Jesse	208 R
	Levi	81 R
	Levi	208 R
	Reuben	81 R
Bentley	John	84 R

Name		Doc#	Name		Doc#
Bentley	John	90 R	Boone	Joshua	265 M
(continued)			(continued)		
	Susanna	23 R	Bowen	Ann	151 M
	Susanna	84 R		Ann	134 R
	Susanna	90 R		Jane	134 M
Blackburn	Alice	151 M		Jean	121 M
	Ann	151 M		Jean	151 M
	Anthony	146 M		Jonathan	151 M
	Deborah	28 M		Mary	134 M
	Elizabeth	111 M		Sarah	121 M
	Elizabeth	91 M		Thomas	121 M
	John	28 M		Thomas	134 M
	John	58 M		Thomas	151 M
	John	82 M	Brachen	Caleb	94 R
	John	83 M	Bracken	Caleb	160 R
	John	91 M		Elisha	160 R
	John	146 M		Rachel	160 R
	Joseph	28 M		Rebecca	160 R
	Margreat	58 M		Solomon	160 R
	Mary	67 M	Bradley	Charles	167 M
	Mary	83 M		Joseph	167 M
	Mary	146 M		Mary	167 M
	Moses	83 M		Ruth	167 M
	Rachel	33 M	Braselton	John	31 M
	Rachel	82 M		Sarah	31 M
	Rebecca	146 M		William	31 M
	Rebeckah	58 M	Brinton	Susanna	252 R
	Rebeckah	82 M		Wm	252 R
	Rebeckah	83 M	Brookes	Margaret	244 R
	Rebeckah	91 M		Margaret	247 R
	Rebekah	158 M	Brooks	Margaret	246 R
	Thomas	91 M	Broomel	Isaac	244 R
	Thomas	111 M		Isaac	247 R
	Thomas	151 M	Brown	John G.	304 M
	Thomas	158 M		Sarah W.	304 M
Blair	Rebecca	79 R		Susanna	304 M
	Rebecca	177 R		Thomas	304 M
Blatchford	Elizabeth	142 M	Buller	Sarah	4 M
	Richard	142 M	Bushong	Caroline	306 R
Bonine	Daniel	164 M		Henry	306 R
	Daniel	165 M		Jacob	306 R
	Elizabeth	164 M		Jesse	306 R
	James	165 M		John	306 R
	Mary	164 M		Lydia	306 R
	Mary	165 M		Sarah	306 R
Boone	Esther	265 M			
	Isaac	265 M	Cadwalader	Abigail	128 M
	Jane	265 M		David	103 M

Name		Doc#	Name		Doc#
Cadwalader	David	116 M	Cleaver	Miriam	188 M
(continued)			(continued)		
	David	128 M		Miriam	196 M
	David	163 M		Peter	21 M
	Hannah	116 M		Peter	168 M
	Hannah	128 M		Peter	188 M
	James	163 M		Peter	196 M
	Mary	103 M		Peter, Jr.	21 M
	Mary	163 M		Petter	21 M
	Susanna	163 M		Sarah	196 M
Cadwallader	David	185 M		Susanna	236 M
	David	232 M		Susanna	239 M
	David	291 M		Susanna	240 M
	Elizabeth	232 M		Susanna	244 M
	Hannah	185 M		Susanna	249 M
	Hannah	291 M		Susanna	251 M
	James	170 M	Coates	Hannah	56 R
	James	232 M		Rachel	282 R
	Lydia	185 M		Samuel	140 R
	Mary	170 M	Coats	Aaron	9 R
	Mary	232 M		Aaron	24 R
	Sarah	170 M		Aaron	25 R
	Susanna	291 M		Aaron	35 R
Carson	Mary	15 M		Aaron	36 R
	Mary	44 M		Aron	8 R
	Mergreate	44 M		Hannah	73 R
	Patrick	3 M		Hannah	103 R
	Patrick	44 M		Mary	281 R
	Richard	44 M		Samuel	46 R
Clark	Ruth	191 R		Samuel	52 R
	Samuel	191 R		Sidney	278 R
Cleaver	Ann	249 M		Sidny	44 R
	Elizabeth	21 M	Collins	John	62 M
	Elizabeth	168 M		John	70 M
	Elizabeth	239 M		Joseph	70 M
	Hannah	244 M		Mary	62 M
	Isaac	239 M		Rebeckah	70 M
	John	236 M	Comer	Elizabeth	30 M
	John	239 M		Elizabeth	46 M
	John	240 M		John	46 M
	John	244 M		Joseph	30 M
	John	249 M		Rebecah	30 M
	John	249 M		Robert	30 M
	John	251 M		Robert	46 M
	Martha	236 M	Conard	Hannah	239 R
	Mary	240 M		Mary	239 R
	Miriam	21 M	Conard	Sarah	189 R
	Miriam	168 M		Sarah	239 R

Name		Doc#	Name		Doc#
Conard	Thomas	123 R	Cook	Ruth	287 M
(continued)			(continued)		
	Thomas	155 R		Ruth G.	295 M
	Thomas	157 R		Samuel	66 M
	Thomas	186 R		Samuel	202 M
	Thos	239 R		Samuel	204 M
	William	239 R		Samuel	277 M
Cook	Anne	286 M		Samuel	280 M
	Asahel W.	308 M		Samuel	288 M
	Elizabeth	64 M		Samuel	295 M
	Elizabeth	288 M		Sarah	10 M
	Elizabeth	308 M		Sarah	64 M
	Elizabeth	128 R		Sarah	66 M
	George W.	288 M		Sarah	80 M
	George W.	308 M		Sarah	119 M
	Hannah	12 M		Sarah	202 M
	Hannah	66 M		Sarah	255 R
	Hannah	204 M		Sidney	295 M
	Hannah	286 M		Thomas	10 M
	Hannah Carol	308 M		Thomas	98 M
	Henry	287 M		William W.	295 M
	Henry	293 M	Cookson	Daniel	205 M
	Henry	298 M		Daniel	263 M
	Jacob	98 M		Daniel	289 M
	Jacob	214 M		Mary	205 M
	Jane	277 M		Mary	263 M
	Jane	280 M		Rachel	289 M
	Jane	288 M		Samuel	176 M
	Jesse	80 M		Samuel	205 M
	Jesse	287 M		Sarah	176 M
	John	286 M		Sarah	205 M
	Joseph	64 M		Sarah	263 M
	Josiah	293 M		Sarah	289 M
	Josiah	298 M	Cooper	Andrew	129 R
	Maria Jane	277 M		Andrew	179 R
	Mary	80 M		Catrine	129 R
	Mary	98 M		Hannah	129 R
	Mary	214 M		James	129 R
	Mary	287 M		James	179 R
	Mary	293 M		James	252 R
	Mary	298 M	Cooper	Jeremiah	252 R
	Mary Ann	280 M		Mary	129 R
	Peter	12 M		Rachel	129 R
	Peter	64 M		Rebecca	129 R
	Peter	66 M		Rebecca	179 R
	Peter	80 M		Thomas	129 R
	Peter	119 M		Thomas	179 R
	Ruth	202 M	Cope	Harman	82 R

Name		Doc#	Name		Doc#
Cope (continued)	Harman U.	232 R	Craige (continued)	William	56 M
	John	82 R	Creage	John	76 M
	Lydia	82 R		Susannah	76 M
	Mary	82 R			
Copelan	David	22 M	Davies	Jane	92 M
	Rachel	22 M		John	92 M
	Richard	22 M		Joshua	92 M
Copland	David	165 M	Davis	Elizabeth	232 M
	Mary	165 M		Hannah	232 M
Cox	Alexander J.	264 R		John	232 M
	Ann	132 M	Day	John	19 M
	Arabella D.	264 R		John, Jr.	45 M
	Catherine A.	264 R		Sarah	19 M
	David			Sarah	45 M
	Hutchison	267 R	Denen	Andrew	33 M
	Eamey	14 M		Rachel	33 M
	Elenora L.	264 R	Dinge	Hannah	307 R
	Elizabeth	16 M	Ducket	Mary	115 M
	Elizabeth	46 M		Thomas	115 M
	Emey	255 M	Duckett	Mary	195 M
	Henry	264 R			
	Henry W.	264 R	Edmundson	Caleb	51 M
	Jacob	101 M		Elizabeth	199 M
	Jane Eliza	264 R		Esther	51 M
	John	14 M		Esther	200 M
	Joshua	255 M		Hannah	184 M
	Joshua			John	199 M
	Hamilton	268 R		John	200 M
	Martha	265 R		John	205 M
	Mary	14 M		Joseph	199 M
	Mary	264 R		Joseph	35 R
	Rebecca	170 R		Joseph, Jr.	48 R
	Rebekah	5 M		Mary	51 M
	Richard	5 M		Mary	184 M
	Richard	46 M		Mary	225 M
	Richard	266 R		Rebecah	23 M
	Robert	101 M		Samuel	23 M
	Ruth G.	255 M		Sarah	176 M
	Sackville H.	264 R		Sarah	199 M
	Sarah	101 M		Sarah	200 M
	Susanna	131 M		Sarah	205 M
	William	131 M		Thomas	51 M
	William	132 M		Thomas	184 M
	William	255 M		Thomas	225 M
	William J.	264 R		Thomas	37 R
Craige	Joanna	56 M		Thomas	89 R
	Mary	56 M	Elgar	John	229 R

Name		Doc#	Name		Doc#
Elgar	Joseph	102 M	Farquhar	Granville	274 R
(continued)			(continued)		
	Joseph	226 R		Granville	312 R
	Margaret	226 R		Lydia	143 R
	Margt	102 M		Margaret	274 R
	Nathan	241 R		Margaret	309 R
Elliot	Alexander	139 M		Mary	274 R
	Elizabeth	139 M		Mary	312 R
	Isaac	139 M		Phebe	274 R
Embree	James	146 R		Phebe	313 R
England	Hannah	250 M		Sarah	192 R
	John	250 M		William Henr	312 R
	Samuel	250 M		Wm. Henry	274 R
	Sarah	250 M	Faulkner	Jesse	73 M
Evans	Cadwalader	89 M	Fincher	Armel	23 M
	Cadwalader	170 M		Francis	23 M
	Eleanor	89 M		Rebeca	23 M
	Sarah	170 M	Fisher	Alice	53 M
Everit	John	69 M		Alice	125 M
	Mary	69 M		Alice	126 M
Everitt	Edward	27 M		Alice	140 M
	Isaac	36 M		Betty	214 R
	Isaac	201 M		Elihu	214 R
	Jane	27 M		Elizabeth	126 M
	John	27 M		Elizabeth	153 M
	John	36 M		Hannah	66 M
	John	201 M		Isaac	153 M
	Martha	36 M		James	53 M
	Martha	201 M		James	125 M
	Susanna	201 M		James	126 M
				James	140 M
Falkner	Jane	73 M		James	153 M
	Jesse	85 M		James	153 R
	Mary	85 M		Jane	53 M
Farquar	-?-	184 M		Jane	125 M
	Hannah	184 M		Joel	214 R
	Rachel	34 M		Joel	341 R
	Sarah	184 M		Lydia	214 R
	Thomas	184 M		Mary	341 R
	William, Jr.	34 M		Ruth	214 R
Farquhar	Amos	274 R		Saml	9 R
	Amos	312 R		Saml	24 R
	Ann	274 R		Saml	25 R
	Ann	312 R		Samuel	140 M
	Charles	274 R		Samuel	8 R
	Charles	293 R		Samuel	214 R
	Deborah	340 R		Seth	214 R
	Deborah	346 R		Susanna	140 M

Name		Doc#	Name		Doc#
Fisher	Susanna	214 R	Garretson	Anne	308 M
(continued)			(continued)		
	Thomas	165 R		Benjamin	305 M
	William	66 M		Content	104 M
Fletcher	Henry	226 M		Cornelius	138 M
	John	226 M		Cornelius	222 M
	Sarah	226 M		Cornelius	238 M
Fraizer	Alexander	123 M		Cornelius	291 M
	Elizabeth	68 M		Cornelius	184 R
	Ezekiel	123 M		Cornelius	190 R
	James	68 M		Cornelius	197 R
	Phebe	84 M		Cornelius	251 R
	Rebekah	123 M		Cornelius, Jr.	184 R
Frazer	Aaron	245 M		Daniel	286 M
	Alexander	21 M		Daniel	308 M
	Alice	245 M		Eli	184 R
	Aron	174 M		Eli	251 R
	Jane	174 M		Eliza	299 M
	Jane	245 M		Elizabeth	166 M
	Sarah	21 M		Elizabeth	239 M
Frazier	Aaron	104 R		Elizabeth	247 M
Frazor	Aaron	83 R		Elizabeth	260 M
	Miriam	21 M		Elizabeth	302 M
French	Deborah	219 R		George	233 M
Fussee	Bartholomew	333 R		Hannah	184 R
	Edward C.	333 R		Hannah	251 R
	Joshua L.	333 R		Hannah C.	291 M
	Lydia R.	333 R		Hannah Carol	308 M
	Morris	333 R		Hannah, Jr.	175 R
	Rebecca	333 R		Isaac	75 R
	Susan	333 R		Isaac	184 R
				Isaac	251 R
Gardner	Barzilla	119 R		Isaac	260 R
Garretson	Aaron	162 M		Israel	278 M
	Alice	239 M		Israel	292 M
	Alice	241 M		Israel	307 M
	Alice	243 M		Israel, Jr.	292 M
	Alice	245 M		Jacob	253 M
	Alice	251 M		Jacob	278 M
	Alice	258 M		Jacob	286 M
	Alice	260 M		James	260 R
	Alice	302 M		Jane	3 M
	Alice	305 M		Jane	110 M
	Ann	65 M		Jane	138 M
	Ann	238 M		Jane	159 M
	Ann	260 R		Jane	222 M
	Anne	94 M		Jane	247 M
	Anne	286 M		Jane	258 M

Name		Doc#	Name		Doc#
Garretson	Jane	292 M	Garretson	Mary	54 M
(continued)			(continued)		
	Jane	301 M		Mary	122 M
	Jesse	251 R		Mary	155 M
	Joel	260 M		Mary	162 M
	Joel	302 M		Mary	253 M
	John	3 M		Mary	278 M
	John	48 M		Mary	286 M
	John	54 M		Naomy	181 M
	John	65 M		Orpah	308 R
	John	84 M		Phebe	84 M
	John	104 M		Rachel	292 M
	John	110 M		Rachel	251 R
	John	138 M		Rebecca	159 M
	John	155 M		Rebecca	233 M
	John	159 M		Rebecca	237 M
	John	247 M		Rebecca	241 M
	John	299 M		Rebecca	254 M
	John	184 R		Rebecca	299 M
	Joseph	159 M		Rebekah	256 M
	Joseph	233 M		Rhoda	305 M
	Joseph	237 M		Ruth	278 M
	Joseph	254 M		Ruth	292 M
	Joseph	256 M		Ruth	307 M
	Joseph	8 R		Samuel	110 M
	Joseph	9 R		Samuel	238 M
	Joseph	24 R		Samuel	239 M
	Joseph	25 R		Samuel	241 M
	Joseph	35 R		Samuel	243 M
	Joseph	36 R		Samuel	247 M
	Joseph	147 R		Samuel	251 M
	Joseph	197 R		Samuel	258 M
	Joseph	251 R		Samuel	260 M
	Liddia	48 M		Samuel	291 M
	Lydia	186 M		Samuel	305 M
	Lydia	191 M		Samuel	184 R
	Lydia	233 M		Samuel	260 R
	Lydia	253 M		Sarah	112 M
	Lydia	307 M		Sarah	256 M
	Mahlon	299 M		Sarah	301 M
	Margaret	138 M		Sarah	184 R
	Margaret	222 M		Susanna	251 M
	Margaret	238 M		Tamar	155 M
	Margaret	291 M		Thomas	251 M
	Margaret	184 R		Thomas	258 M
	Margaret	251 R		Thomas	292 M
	Maria	254 M		Thomas	301 M
	Martha	191 M		William	48 M

Name		Doc#	Name		Doc#
Garretson	William	94 M	Griest	John	36 M
(continued)			(continued)		
	William	112 M		John	54 M
	William	122 M		John	65 M
	William	155 M		John	95 M
	William	162 M		John	131 M
	William	166 M		John	132 M
	William	181 M		John	141 M
	William	186 M		John	180 M
	William	191 M		John	188 M
Garwood	Mary	149 M		Joseph	180 M
	Obed	149 M		Joseph	257 M
	Rebekah	149 M		Josiah	178 M
Gibbons	Deborah	252 R		Lydia	141 M
	Wm	252 R		Margaret	342 R
Gilbert	Amos	234 R		Martha	9 M
	Amos	291 R		Martha	36 M
	John	295 R		Martha	285 M
Gillingham	Mary	280 R		Mary	54 M
Gray	Enoch	210 R		Mary	214 M
Green	Joseph	117 M		Mary	257 M
	Lydia	117 M		Mary	261 M
Gregg	Joseph	62 M		Mary	298 M
	Mary	62 M		Mary Ann	280 M
Griest	Amos	285 M		Maryann S.	178 M
	Amos	342 R		Miriam	188 M
	Ann	35 M		Rachel Ann	342 R
	Ann	65 M		Rebekah	180 M
	Ann	132 M		Rebekah	257 M
	Ann	188 M		Ruth	295 M
	Ann	206 M		Sarah	9 M
	Ann	214 M		Susanah	6 M
	Ann	285 M		Susanna	131 M
	Anne	206 M		Susanna	180 M
	Anne	264 M		Susannah	54 M
	Anne	280 M		Thomas	132 M
	Anne	295 M		Uriah	257 M
	Anne	298 M		Willin	206 M
	Cyrus	280 M		Willing	65 M
	Daniel	35 M		Willing	214 M
	Daniel	188 M		Willing	264 M
	Esther	261 M		Willing	280 M
	Hannah	95 M		Willing	285 M
	Isaac	214 M		Willing	295 M
	Isaac	261 M		Willing	298 M
	John	6 M		Willing	342 R
	John	9 M	Griffith	Abraham	202 M
	John	35 M		Abraham	218 M

Name		Doc#	Name		Doc#
Griffith	Amos	240 M	Griffith	William	198 M
(continued)			(continued)		
	Amos	65 R		William	202 M
	Amous	78 R		William	217 M
	Deborah	198 M		William	240 M
	Deborah	231 M		William	248 M
	Deborah	248 M	Grist	Amos	240 R
	Elizabeth	91 M		Pheby	240 R
	Elizabeth	202 M			
	Elizabeth	218 M	Hadley	Mabel	210 R
	Eve	59 M	Haines	Esther	200 M
	Eve	91 M		Nathan	200 M
	Eve	93 M		Sophia	200 M
	Eve	146 M		William	200 M
	George	248 M	Hains	Rachel	224 R
	Jacob	148 M	Hamel	James	15 M
	Joanna	56 M		Mary	15 M
	Joanna	175 M	Hammersly	Eliza	228 R
	Joanna	198 M	Hammond	Daniel	67 M
	Joanna	217 M		Deborah	79 M
	Johanna	240 M		Deborah	155 M
	John	85 M		Elizabeth	79 M
	John, Jr.	85 M		James	67 M
	Joseph	255 M		John	79 M
	Joseph	262 M		John	155 M
	Lydia	148 M		John	162 M
	Maria	262 M		Mary	67 M
	Mary	85 M		Mary	162 M
	Mary	146 M		Tamer	155 M
	Mary	240 M	Hamond	Alice	39 M
	Rebecca	255 M		Daniel	39 M
	Rebecca	262 M		Deborah	59 M
	Rebekah	109 M		James	39 M
	Ruth	217 M		John	59 M
	Ruth	255 M		Sarah	59 M
	Sarah	59 M	Harlan	Ann	61 M
	Sarah	202 M		James	61 M
	Sarah	248 M	Harland	Samuel	287 R
	Susanna	93 M	Harrey	Miriam	20 M
	Thomas	59 M	Harris	Benjamin	306 M
	Thomas	91 M		Jane	306 M
	Thomas	93 M		Julia	306 M
	Thomas	109 M		Samuel H.	306 M
	Thomas	146 M	Harry	Jesse	262 M
	William	56 M		Jesse	244 R
	William	59 M		Lewis	262 M
	William	148 M		Lewis	244 R
	William	198 M		Lewis	303 R

Name		Doc#	Name		Doc#
Harry	Malinda	303 R	Holland	Mary	107 M
(continued)			(continued)		
	Maria	262 M		Mary	117 R
	Maria	303 R		Thomas	107 M
	Mary	262 M		Thomas	70 R
	Mary	244 R	Hoopes	Job	300 M
	Mary, Jr.	246 R		Mary A.	300 M
	Orpha	247 R		Phebe	294 M
Heald	Lidia	32 M		Rhoda	300 M
	Susana	2 M		Rhoda	305 M
	Thomas	2 M		Sarah Ann	294 M
	Thomas	32 M		Waln	294 M
Hendricks	Alice	71 M		William	294 M
	Mary	120 M	Hoops	Elisha	258 M
	Mary	144 M		Mary	258 M
	Nathan	144 M	Hopkins	John Wallis	139 R
	Patience	150 M		John Wollas	93 R
	Samuel	71 M		Leaven	176 R
	Samuel	120 M		Leven	133 R
	Samuel	144 M	Hurst	David	96 R
	Samuel	150 M	Hussey	Ann	30 M
Hendrix	Lydia	156 M		Ann	213 M
	Samuel	156 M		Betty	177 M
Hewes	Jacob	334 R		Christopher	30 M
Hewit	Deborah M.	124 M		Christopher	2 R
	George	124 M		Edith	212 M
	Joseph	124 M		Elizabeth	30 M
	Sarah	124 M		Hannah	193 M
Hewitt	Ann	147 M		Hannah	211 M
	Jonathan	147 M		Hannah	228 M
Hill	William	262 R		Hannah	250 M
	William	284 R		Jane	63 M
Hinshaw	Ann	29 M		Jane	211 M
	Jacob	29 M		Jane	213 M
Hobson	Ann	88 M		Jane	228 M
	Ann	130 M		Jane	229 M
	Elizabeth	142 M		Jane	252 M
	Francis	88 M		Jane	263 M
	Francis	96 M		Jedaiah	63 M
	Francis	130 M		Jedaiah	213 M
	Francis	142 M		Jediah	211 M
	Phebe	130 M		Jediah	228 M
	Susanna	96 M		Jediah	229 M
Hodge	Francis	27 M		Jediah	252 M
	Jane	27 M		Jediah	263 M
Holland	Henry	107 M		Jediah	86 R
	Henry	117 M		Jodiah	24 R
	Lydia	117 M		Jodiah	25 R

Name		Doc#	Name		Doc#
Hussey	John	63 M	Jackson	Isaac, Jr.	210 R
(continued)			(continued)		
	John	177 M		Sarah	210 R
	Lydia	148 M	James	Amos	254 R
	Lydia	229 M		Hannah	204 M
	Mary C.	263 M		Mary	257 R
	Miriam	20 M		Sarah	204 M
	Miriam	180 M		Thomas	204 M
	Miriam	192 M	Janney	James	55 R
	Miriam	193 M		James	64 R
	Miriam	212 M	Jeffries	Lydia	237 R
	Nathan	2 M	Jenkins	Hannah	58 R
	Nathan	228 M	Jennings	Susannah	60 M
	Rebekah	180 M		Thomas	60 M
	Record	180 M	Jessop	Ann	9 R
	Record	192 M		Ann	14 R
	Record	193 M		Ann	98 R
	Record	212 M		Ann	99 R
	Riccord	20 M		Ann	163 R
	Riccord	148 M		Ann	200 R
	Ruth	192 M		Hannah	14 R
	Sarah	171 R		Jonathan	8 R
	Sarah	188 R		Jonathan	9 R
	Susana	2 M		Jonathan	24 R
Hutton	Betty	133 M		Jonathan	35 R
	Betty	42 R		Jonathan	36 R
	Betty	138 R		Joseph U.	301 R
	Deborah	135 M	Jinkins	David	16 M
	Elijah	42 R		Elizabeth	16 M
	Isaiah	42 R	John	Abel	147 M
	Joseph	13 M		Abel	164 M
	Joseph	106 M		Ann	87 M
	Joseph	133 M		Ann	147 M
	Joseph	187 M		Ann	199 R
	Joseph, Jr.	210 R		Ann	259 R
	Joshua	106 M		Hannah	108 M
	Mary	13 M		Jane	174 M
	Mary	187 M		Joseph	164 M
	Rachel	106 M		Mary	98 M
	Rachel	42 R		Mary	164 M
	Rachel	138 R		Mary	164 M
	Samuel	13 M		Rachel	196 R
	Sarah	42 R		Rachel	258 R
	Sarah	161 R		Ruth	87 M
	Simeon	187 M		Samuel	98 M
	Susanna	135 M		Samuel	108 M
	William	135 M		Samuel	174 M
Jackson	Hannah	210 R		Samuel	87 M

Name		Doc#	Name		Doc#
Johnson	Elizabeth	166 M	Kent	Maria Jane	277 M
	James	166 M	(continued)		
	Thomas	166 M	Kenworthy	Hannah	244 M
Jones	Betty	182 M		Isaac	244 M
	Betty	9 R		Joshua	69 M
	Betty	125 R		Mary	69 M
	Betty	144 R		Mary	244 M
	Content	104 M		William	69 M
	Content	203 M		William	244 M
	Content	297 M	Kersey	Eliza	51 R
	Edward	104 M		Elizabeth	78 M
	Edward	203 M		Elizabeth	102 R
	Edward	221 M		Hannah	78 M
	Edward	297 M		Hannah	102 R
	Jane	203 M		Hannah	218 R
	John	104 M		Jesse	51 R
	John	182 M		Jesse	102 R
	John	8 R		Joseph	24 R
	John	9 R		Joseph	25 R
	John	24 R		Joshua	150 R
	John	25 R		Lydia	102 R
	John	35 R		Samuel	217 R
	John	36 R		William	78 M
	John	144 R		William	218 R
	John, Jr.	144 R		Wm.	8 R
	Mary	50 M		Wm.	9 R
	Mary	145 R		Wm.	24 R
	Phebe	221 M		Wm.	25 R
	Rachel	144 R	Kettlewell	John	242 M
	Samuel	21 R		Margret	242 M
	Samuel	43 R	Kirk	Aquilla M.	310 R
	Samuel	124 R		Bulah	275 R
	Sarah	182 M		Caleb	179 M
	Susanna	96 M		Caleb	183 M
Jonston	Elizabeth	186 M		Caleb	24 R
Jordan	Josiah	24 R		Caleb	25 R
	Josiah	25 R		Caleb	35 R
	Josiah	28 R		Caleb	36 R
	Josiah	34 R		Caleb	311 R
	Lydia	34 R		Caleb	314 R
	Lydia	72 R		Catherine	310 R
	Lydia	122 R		Deborah	220 M
				Edith	183 M
Kendall	Margret	8 M		Edith	277 R
	Thomas	8 M		Eli	183 M
Kent	Daniel	277 M		Eli	24 R
	Esther	277 M		Eli	25 R
	Joseph	277 M		Eli	31 R

Name		Doc#	Name		Doc#
Kirk	Eli	35 R	Kirk	Martha	180 R
(continued)			(continued)		
	Eli	36 R		Martha	185 R
	Eli	290 R		Mary	103 M
	Elisha	8 R		Mary	9 R
	Elisha	9 R		Mary	212 R
	Elisha	35 R		Mary, Jr.	212 R
	Elisha	36 R		Nathan	203 R
	Elisha	297 R		Nathan	263 R
	Elizabeth	179 M		Priscilla	106 R
	Elizabeth	183 M		Rachel	106 M
	Elizabeth	186 M		Rachel	213 R
	Elizabeth N.	310 R		Ruth	9 R
	Elmira	310 R		Ruth	17 R
	Erastus U.	305 R		Ruth	18 R
	Ezekiel	220 M		Samuel	180 R
	Hannah	116 M		Samuel	185 R
	Hannah	191 M		Samuel A.	331 R
	Hannah	210 M		Sarah	186 M
	Hannah	220 M		Sarah	210 M
	Hannah	235 M		Sarah	248 M
	Hannah	306 M		Sarah	180 R
	Hannah	151 R		Sarah	185 R
	Henry C.	314 R		Sarah	310 R
	Isaac	191 M		Susan	276 R
	Isaac	246 M		Thomas	116 M
	Isaac	248 M		Thomas	186 M
	Isaac	180 R		Timothy	103 M
	Isaac	185 R		Timothy	106 M
	Jacob	191 M		Timothy	116 M
	Jacob	210 M		Timothy	186 M
	Jacob	235 M		Timothy	8 R
	Jacob	306 M		Timothy	9 R
	Jacob	180 R		Timothy	212 R
	Jacob	185 R		Timothy	277 R
	Jane	246 M		William	216 R
	Jane	248 M		William	273 R
	Jane	180 R			
	Jane	185 R	Leach	Hannah	198 R
	Joseph	236 R	Leech	Anne	283 M
	Joseph	270 R		Hannah	282 M
	Julia	306 M		Hannah	283 M
	Lydia	179 M		Hannah	294 M
	Lydia	311 R		Jane	222 M
	Lydia Ann	310 R		Jane	282 M
	Mahlon	212 R		Joseph	283 M
	Martha	191 M		Phebe	72 M
	Martha	246 M		Phebe	209 M

Name		Doc#	Name		Doc#
Leech (continued)	Phebe	222 M	Love (continued)	John	25 R
	Phebe	223 M		John	32 R
	Rebekah	209 M		John	35 R
	Sarah	72 M		John	269 R
	Sarah	101 M		Mary	11 R
	Sarah Ann	294 M	Low	Joshua	41 M
	Thomas	72 M		Joshua	75 M
	Thomas	101 M		Mary	41 M
	Thomas	209 M		Mary	75 M
	Thomas	222 M			
	Thomas	223 M	Machlan	John	157 M
	Thomas	282 M		Mary	157 M
	Thomas	283 M	Man	Lydia	244 R
	Thomas	294 M	Marsh	Ann	199 M
	William	222 M		Ann	212 M
Lewis	Amos	202 R		Edith	212 M
	Amos	292 R		Elizabeth	43 M
	Eli	243 R		Elizabeth	199 M
	Elizabeth	169 M		Hannah	193 M
	Hannah	173 R		James	212 M
	Hannah	227 R		John	24 M
	Rebekah	99 M		John	43 M
	Sarah	174 R		John	193 M
	Sarah	225 R		John	201 M
	William	99 M		Jonathan	43 M
	William	169 M		Jonathan	193 M
Lindley	Jacob	210 R		Jonathan	199 M
	Ruth Ann	210 R		Jonathan	212 M
Lord	Jehu	244 R		Margaret	201 M
Love	Ann	154 M		Margret	24 M
	Ann	160 M		Rebecah	193 M
	Ann	9 R		Rebecca	43 M
	Faithful	110 M		Susanna	201 M
	Faithful	160 M	Mason	Elizabeth	39 R
	Faithfull	152 M		Elizabeth	49 R
	Faithfull	154 M		Rachel	39 R
	Harman	220 R		Rachel	49 R
	Herman	288 R	Matthews	Hannah	9 R
	James	110 M		Hannah	235 R
	James	152 M		Jesse	9 R
	James	154 M		Jesse	38 R
	James	160 M		Margaret	102 M
	Jane	110 M		Mordecai	192 M
	John	154 M		Rachel	192 M
	John	8 R		Ruth	192 M
	John	9 R		Thomas	192 M
	John	24 R		William	102 M

Name		Doc#	Name		Doc#
Matthews	William	24 R	McMillan	George	206 M
(continued)				George	216 M
	William	36 R		George	217 M
	Wm	8 R		George	231 M
	Wm	9 R		George	241 M
	Wm	35 R		George	259 M
McGrail	Elizabeth	111 M		George	284 M
	James	111 M		Hannah	211 M
	Lydia	156 M		Jacob	217 M
	Mary	144 M		Jacob	276 M
	Owen	111 M		Jacob	283 M
	Owen	144 M		Jacob	287 M
	Owen	156 M		Jane	203 M
	William	156 M		Jane	216 M
McGrew	Deborah	28 M		Joanna	175 M
	Finley	120 M		John	175 M
	Finley	150 M		Jonathan	213 M
	James	82 M		Joseph	241 M
	James	83 M		Maria	254 M
	Mary	82 M		Mary	77 M
	Mary	83 M		Mary	194 M
	Mary	120 M		Mary	259 M
	Nathan	82 M		Rebecca	241 M
	Patience	150 M		Rebeckah	284 M
	Peter	150 M		Rebekah	159 M
	Rachel	82 M		Ruth	217 M
McKisson	Hannah	166 R		Ruth	254 M
McMillan	Ann	29 M		Ruth	276 M
	Ann	159 M		Ruth	283 M
	Ann	198 M		Ruth	287 M
	Ann	206 M		Sarah	276 M
	Ann	213 M		Susanna	284 M
	Ann	216 M		Thomas	29 M
	Ann	217 M		Thomas	77 M
	Ann	231 M		Thomas	203 M
	Ann	241 M		Thomas	216 M
	Ann	259 M		Thomas	254 M
	Anne	206 M		Thos	276 M
	Anne	283 M		William	194 M
	David	211 M		William	211 M
	Deborah	194 M		William	213 M
	Deborah	198 M		William	26 R
	Deborah	203 M		Wm	203 M
	Deborah	211 M	McMullin	James	53 R
	Deborah	213 M	McMun	George	3 R
	George	29 M	McMunn	Wm.	24 R
	George	159 M		Wm.	25 R
	George	198 M		Wm.	35 R

Name		Doc#	Name		Doc#
Mendenhall	Jonathan	77 R	Mills	Robert	49 M
	Jonathan	105 R	(continued)		
	Richard	164 R		Robert	105 M
Meredith	Ann	303 M		Susanah	49 M
	Ann S.	303 M		Susannah	115 R
	Elizabeth	247 M		William	49 M
	Elizabeth	281 M	Moore	Abraham	69 R
	George	303 M		Abraham	136 R
	Israel	247 M		Amy	130 R
	Israel	281 M		Andrew	215 M
	Lewis	303 M		Andrew	224 M
	Sarah	281 M		Andrew	127 R
Mickle	John, Sr.	109 M		Andrew	132 R
	John, Jr.	109 M		Anna	69 R
	Rebekah	109 M		Anna	136 R
Milhous	Jesse	33 R		Dinah	111 R
Miller	Hannah	90 M		Dinah	130 R
	James	194 M		Dinah	135 R
	Lydia	1 R		Elijah	215 M
	Lydia	29 R		Elijah	137 R
	Mary	115 M		Eliza	132 R
	Mary	194 M		Esther	136 R
	Mary	87 R		Hesther	69 R
	Robert	90 M		Isaac	130 R
	Robert	115 M		James	69 R
	Robert	194 M		James	136 R
	Robert	210 M		Jeremiah	136 R
	Samuel	90 M		Lydia	69 R
	Sarah	90 M		Lydia	113 R
	Sarah	194 M		Lydia	130 R
	Sarah	210 M		Lydia	136 R
	Sarah	41 R		Lydia, Jr.	69 R
	Sarah	343 R		Rebecca	127 R
	Solomon	8 R		Rebekah	215 M
	Solomon	9 R		Rebekah	224 M
	Solomon	24 R		Samuel	112 R
	Solomon	25 R		Sarah	215 M
	Solomon	35 R		Sarah	224 M
	Solomon	36 R		Sarah	131 R
	Solomon	58 R		Thomas	111 R
	Solomon	63 R		Thomas	135 R
	Thomas	210 M		William	71 R
Mills	Anna	219 M	More	Amy	167 R
	Anna	227 M		Andrew	158 R
	John	227 M		Dinah	167 R
	Mary	49 M		Isaac	167 R
	Phebe	105 M		Jeremiah	183 R
	Rachel	227 M		Lydia	167 R

Name		Doc#
More	Lydia	169 R
(continued)	Mary	252 R
	Moses	149 R
	Rebecca	158 R
	Samuel	167 R
	Sarah	159 R
	Sarah	167 R
Morris	Isaac	118 M
	Isaac	285 M
	John	118 M
	Martha	118 M
	Martha	285 M
Morsell	Mary	225 M
	William	225 M
Morthland	Hugh	17 M
	Hugh	25 M
	Hugh	42 M
	Hugh	43 M
	Jane	161 M
	Margreat	42 M
	Mary	25 M
	Rebecca	42 M
	Rebecca	43 M
	Ruth	17 M
	Ruth	161 M
	Samuel	42 M
	Samuel	76 M
	Susannah	76 M
	William	17 M
	William	161 M
Morton	Deborah	124 M
	Elizabeth	153 M
	John	81 M
	John	124 M
	John	153 M
	Margaret	81 M
	Mary	81 M
	Mary	124 M
Mullineux	Edward	1 M
	Mary	1 M
Musgrave	Abraham	143 M
	John	143 M
	John	171 M
	Mary	143 M
	Sarah	143 M
	Sarah	171 M

Name		Doc#
Nebinger	Elizabeth	303 M
	John	303 M
Needles	Edward	300 R
Nevet	Hannah	12 M
	Mary	74 M
	Thomas	74 M
	William	12 M
Newlan	Hannah	81 M
	Margret	81 M
	William	81 M
Norbury	Jacob	133 M
	Jacob	4 R
	Jacob	5 R
	Jacob	24 R
	Jacob	25 R
	Jacob	40 R
	Jacob	162 R
	Susanna	302 R
Oldham	Isaac	52 M
	Mary	52 M
	Rebecca	245 M
	Rebekah	158 M
	Thomas	158 M
	Thomas	245 M
	William	158 M
Owen	Sara	9 R
	Thomas	207 R
	William	321 R
Ozbun	Mathew	5 M
	Rebekah	5 M
	William	5 M
Passmore	Mary	44 M
	William	44 M
Peden	Alexander	197 M
	Isaac	149 M
	Lydia	149 M
	Lydia	197 M
	Rebekah	149 M
	Samuel	149 M
	Samuel	197 M
Pennock	Elizabeth	246 R
	Elizabeth	247 R
	Hannah	244 R
	Hannah	246 R
	John	244 R
	John	246 R

Name		Doc#	Name		Doc#
Pennock	John	247 R	Plumer	Asa	31 R
(continued)			Plummer	Asa	101 R
	Joseph	244 R		Elisha	298 R
	Joseph	246 R	Pope	Elizabeth	7 M
	Joseph	247 R		Samuel	7 M
Penrose	Abigail	128 M	Price	Ann	177 M
	An, Jr.	15 R		Betty	177 M
	Ann	51 M		Daniel	177 M
	Ann	63 M		Samuel	177 M
	Ann	72 M	Pugh	Else	87 M
	Ann	128 M		Jesse	87 M
	Ann	163 M		Job	87 M
	Ann	107 R		Ruth	87 M
	Hannah	108 M	Pusey	Caleb	246 R
	Jane	63 M		Caleb	247 R
	Mary	51 M		Hannah	244 R
	Phebe	72 M		Naomi	244 R
	Susanna	163 M		Naomi	247 R
	Thomas	128 M		Nathan	10 R
	William	51 M		Nathan	142 R
	William	63 M		Neomy	246 R
	William	72 M		Rebecca	247 R
	William	108 M			
	William	128 M	Ragen	Daniel	36 R
	William	163 M		Daniel	205 R
Philips	George	53 M		Ruth	9 R
	Jane	53 M		Ruth	205 R
	Jane	190 M	Randels	Elizabeth	126 M
	John	53 M		Mary	126 M
	John	70 M		William	126 M
	Rebeckah	70 M	Randles	Hannah	90 M
Phillips	Deborah	97 R		Mary	90 M
	Deborah	156 R		William	90 M
	Deborah	215 R	Rankin	Abigail	37 M
	Edmond	77 M		John	37 M
	Hannah	92 R	Reynard	Ruthanna	339 R
	Hannah	121 R	Richards	Catharine	297 M
	Lydia	210 R		David	297 M
	Mary	77 M		John	297 M
	Nathan	77 M		Phebe	297 M
Pierce	Ann	238 M	Richardson	Hannah	97 M
	Elizabeth	238 M		Samuel	97 M
	George	22 R	Roberts	Sarah	337 R
	Moses	238 M	Rodes	Abigail	37 M
Pilkington	Rebecca	208 M		Benjamin	37 M
	Richard	208 M	Rogers	Andrew	35 M
	Sarah	208 M		Ann	35 M
	Vincent	208 M	Rosborough	Cathrine	57 M

Name		Doc#	Name		Doc#
Rosborough (continued)	Elener	42 M	Smith (continued)	Samuel	326 R
	Elinor	57 M		Samuel, Jr.	252 R
	Margreat	42 M		Sarah	323 R
	Robert	42 M		Thomas	279 M
	Robert	57 M	Speakman	Ann	172 M
Rudduck	Margret	8 M		Hannah	172 M
Rummel	Richard	325 R		James	172 M
Rummells	James	252 M		James	296 R
	Jane	252 M		Joshua	172 M
	May	252 M		Thomas	12 R
	Richard	252 M	Spencer	Samuel	210 R
Rummels	Jane	285 R	Squibb	Jane	161 M
				Mary	9 M
Scott	Amos	20 R		Maryann	178 M
	Amos	187 R		Robert	9 M
	Elizabeth	247 M		Sarah	9 M
	Esther	187 R		Sarah	161 M
	James	247 M		William	9 M
	Levi	187 R		William	161 M
	Rachel	148 R	Stabler	Edward	8 R
	Rachel	187 R	Standly	Beulah	47 R
	William	187 R	Stanton	John	22 M
Sharpless	Rebecca	74 R		Rachel	22 M
Sheperd	Margreat	58 M	Star	Esther	265 M
	Solomon	58 M		John	265 M
Shipherd	Sarah	31 M		Phebe	265 M
	Solomon	31 M	Stebler	Edward	9 R
Smith	Eliza	252 R	Stephen	Elizabeth	169 M
	Eliza	322 R		Jonathan	169 M
	Ephraim	324 R		Mary	169 M
	Hannah	330 R		Samuel	169 M
	James	50 M	Stevenson	Elizabeth	7 M
	James	279 M	Strahl	Isaac	76 R
	Jesse	324 R	Strall	Ann	88 R
	John	11 M		Ann	91 R
	Joseph	11 M		Isaac	95 R
	Joseph	246 R		John	88 R
	Joseph	247 R	Swain	Elizabeth	299 R
	Leah	279 M		Orpha	230 R
	Lewis	252 R	Swayne	Eli	221 R
	Maria	330 R		Ely	206 R
	Mary	50 M		Francis	204 R
	Mary	279 M		Francis	283 R
	Orpha	252 R		Jane	283 R
	Rachel	11 M		Mary	244 R
	Ruth	252 R		Mary	246 R
	Samuel	252 R		Orpah	210 R

Name		Doc#	Name		Doc#
Swayne	Sarah	283 R	Thomas	Jacob	315 R
(continued)			(continued)		
Taughinbaugh	Ann S.	303 M		Jacob	317 R
	George	303 M		James	173 M
Taylor	Ann	38 M		James	181 M
	Benjamin	218 M		James	197 M
	Caleb	154 R		Jehu	86 M
	Caleb	231 R		John	86 M
	Elizabeth	218 M		John	89 M
	Jane	216 M		John	123 M
	Jane	218 M		John	256 M
	Joseph	38 M		Jonathan	315 R
	Joseph	216 M		Jonathan	319 R
	Joseph	218 M		Lydia	197 M
	Joseph	154 R		Margaret	315 R
	Nicholas	154 R		Margaret	317 R
	Nicholas	286 R		Mary	9 R
	Nicholas Way	261 R		Mary	68 R
	Sarah	171 M		Naomy	181 M
	Sarah	154 R		Nathan	234 M
	Thomas	171 M		Nathan	290 M
	Thomas	154 R		Rachel	253 R
	Thomas	261 R		Rachel	294 R
	Thomas, Jr.	154 R		Rachel	315 R
	Thos	231 R		Rachel	317 R
	William	154 R		Rebekah	123 M
	William	223 R		Sarah	86 M
Thomas	Abel	320 R		Sarah	234 M
	Abner	253 R		Sarah	256 M
	Abner	294 R		Sarah	290 M
	Charles A.	253 R		Sarah Ann	294 R
	Charles A.	294 R		William R.	294 R
	Deborah	173 M	Thompson	Mary	210 R
	Deborah	197 M	Thornbrugh	Cathrine	57 M
	Eleanor	89 M		Phebe	129 M
	Elen	253 R		Robert	57 M
	Elenor	256 M		Robert	129 M
	Ellen	294 R		Thomas	129 M
	Ellen	315 R	Todd	Hannah	40 M
	Ellen R.	317 R		John	40 M
	Esther	253 R		Robert	40 M
	Esther	294 R	Tyson	Lewis	335 R
	Esther	315 R		Mary Jane	335 R
	Esther	317 R		Robert	335 R
	George	294 R		William	335 R
	George W.	253 R			
	Hannah	318 R	Underhill	Joseph	47 M
	Isaac	256 M		Martha	47 M

Name		Doc#	Name		Doc#
Underhill (continued)	Mary	47 M	Underwood (continued)	Nehemiah	114 M
Underwood	Alexander	6 M		Rachel	114 M
	Alexander	17 M		Rebecca	230 M
	Alexander	24 M		Rebeckah	220 M
	Alexander	25 M		Rebeckah	233 R
	Alexander	47 M		Rebekah	99 M
	Alexander	141 R		Rebekah	136 M
	Alexander	172 R		Rhoda	172 R
	Alexander	193 R		Rhoda	193 R
	Alexander, Jr.	172 R		Ruth	17 M
	Alexander, Jr.	193 R		Ruth	167 M
	Ann	47 M		Samuel	47 M
	Anne	94 M		Samuel	172 R
	Benjamin	6 M		Samuel	193 R
	Benjamin	86 M		Sarah	86 M
	Benjamin	114 M		Sarah	182 M
	Benjamin	118 M		Susanah	6 M
	Benjamin	182 M		Susanna	182 M
	Benjamin	187 M		Thomas	193 R
	Benjamin	108 R		Thomas	289 R
	Benjamin	109 R		William	92 M
	Charles	233 R		William	94 M
	Deborah	220 M		William	99 M
	Elihu	24 M		William	167 M
	Elihu	94 M		William	182 M
	Enoch	8 R		William	220 M
	Enoch	9 R		Zephaniah	99 M
	Enoch	16 R		Zephaniah	220 M
	Enoch	24 R		Zephaniah	230 M
	Enoch	25 R		Zephaniah	233 R
	Enoch	27 R	Updegraf	Harman	32 M
	Hannah	230 M		Lidia	32 M
	Hannah	233 R	Updegraff	Abner	109 R
	Harman	172 R		Abner	120 R
	Harman	193 R		Ambrose	152 M
	Israel	332 R		Ambrose	8 R
	Jane	92 M		Ambrose	9 R
	Jane	207 M		Ambrose	24 R
	John	25 M		Ambrose	25 R
	John	136 M		Ambrose	35 R
	John	207 M		Ambrose	36 R
	Margret	24 M		Ambrose	249 R
	Martha	118 M		Ann	61 M
	Mary	25 M		Ann	154 M
	Mary	47 M		Ann	160 M
	Mary	187 M		Ann	61 R
	Mary	207 M		Ann Jr	61 R

Name		Doc#	Name		Doc#
Updegraff	Betty	62 R	Updegraff	Samuel	8 R
(continued)			(continued)		
	Cyrus	249 R		Samuel	248 R
	Edith	183 M		Sarah	45 M
	Edith	61 R		Sarah	194 R
	Edith	249 R		Sarah	249 R
	Eli	61 R		Susanna	152 M
	Faithfull	152 M		Susanna	160 M
	Hannah	181 R		Susanna	183 M
	Hannah	195 R		Susanna	271 R
	Hannah	327 R		Susannah	250 R
	Harman	45 M		William	45 M
	Harman	61 M			
	Harman	154 M	Vale	Alice	243 M
	Harman	24 R		Ann	113 M
	Harmon	75 M		Ann	228 M
	Herman	9 R		Ann	246 M
	Herman	25 R		Ann	249 M
	Israel	238 R		Ann	250 M
	James	100 R		Ann	253 M
	John	61 M		Ann	257 M
	Joseph	100 M		Ann	345 R
	Joseph	152 M		Anna	145 M
	Joseph	160 M		Deborah	173 M
	Joseph	183 M		Deborah	231 M
	Joseph	8 R		Deborah	236 M
	Joseph	9 R		Deborah	249 M
	Joseph	24 R		Edith	336 R
	Joseph	25 R		Elisha	246 M
	Joseph	35 R		Elisha	336 R
	Joseph	36 R		Elisha	345 R
	Josiah	178 R		Elizabeth	168 M
	Lydia	154 M		Elizabeth	243 M
	Lydia	179 M		Elizabeth	260 M
	Lydia	9 R		Elizabeth	261 M
	Mary	75 M		Elizabeth	276 M
	Mary	100 M		Esther	261 M
	Mary	179 M		Guli Elma	336 R
	Mary	9 R		Hannah	228 M
	Nathan	160 M		Isaac	296 M
	Rachel	222 R		Jane K.	345 R
	Rachel	249 R		John	173 M
	Saml	9 R		John	231 M
	Saml	24 R		John	236 M
	Saml	25 R		John	249 M
	Saml	35 R		John	253 M
	Samuel	75 M		John	293 M
	Samuel	179 M		Joseph	336 R

Name		Doc#	Name		Doc#
Vale	Joshua	168 M	Vernon	Aaron	195 M
(continued)				Mary	195 M
	Joshua	243 M	Vore	Christian	157 M
	Joshua	260 M		Christian	185 M
	Joshua	261 M		Gidion	6 R
	Joshua	276 M		Gidion	7 R
	Josiah	336 R		Hannah	13 R
	Lydia	253 M		Jacob	157 M
	Lydia	293 M		Jesse	185 M
	Martha	236 M		Jesse	6 R
	Martha	296 M		Jesse	7 R
	Martha	345 R		Jesse	13 R
	Martha	246 M		Lydia	185 M
	Mary	257 M		Lydia	6 R
	Mary	259 M		Lydia	7 R
	Mary	293 M		Lydia	13 R
	Mary Ann	296 M		Mary	157 M
	Nathan	243 M		Sarah	185 M
	Peter	261 M			
	Rebecca	336 R	Walker	Abel	113 M
	Robert	4 M		Abel	279 M
	Robert	113 M		Able	226 M
	Robert	119 M		Ann	113 M
	Robert	145 M		Ann	226 M
	Robert	168 M		Ann	279 M
	Robert	173 M		Asahel	288 M
	Robert	231 M		Asahel	296 M
	Robert	236 M		Asahel	304 M
	Robert	259 M		Benjamin	208 M
	Robert	296 M		Elizabeth	288 M
	Ruthanna	345 R		Isaac	113 M
	Sarah	4 M		John	278 M
	Sarah	119 M		Leah	279 M
	Sarah	168 M		Lydia	278 M
	Sarah	173 M		Mary	288 M
	Sarah	231 M		Mary	296 M
	Sarah	259 M		Mary	304 M
	Sarah	276 M		Mary Ann	296 M
	Sarah Ann	345 R		Ruth	208 M
	William	145 M		Ruth	278 M
	William	228 M		Sarah	208 M
	William	246 M		Sarah	226 M
	William	250 M		Sarah	304 M
	William	253 M	Wall	Absalom	209 M
	William	257 M		Azariah	209 M
	William	259 M		Margaret	209 M
	William	338 R		Rebekah	209 M
	William E.	345 R	Walmsley	Ruth	106 R

Name		Doc#	Name		Doc#
Waln	Alice	234 M	Whinnery	Robert	223 M
	Eli	234 M	(continued)		
	Sarah	234 M		Thomas	105 M
	Sarah	290 M		Thomas	229 M
	William	234 M		William	223 M
Walton	Benjamin	244 R		William	229 M
Warner	Jane	258 M	Whitson	Hannah	252 R
Warren	Susannah	60 M	Wickersham	Abner	264 M
Watson	James	134 M		Abner	307 M
	Mary	134 M		Anna	219 M
Way	Neomy	168 R		Anna	221 M
Webb	Edith	137 M		Anna	233 M
	Edith	143 M		Anna	235 M
	Hannah	137 M		Anna	237 M
	Joseph	100 M		Anne	264 M
Webb	Joseph	137 M		Anne	307 M
	Joseph	143 M		Edward	284 M
	Mary	100 M		Eliza	299 M
	Moses	114 R		Elizabeth	68 M
	Moses	152 M		Hannah	235 M
	Sarah	143 M		Isaac	68 M
Welch	Andrew	137 M		James	112 M
	Hannah	137 M		James	219 M
	Hannah	9 R		James	227 M
	Mary	137 M		James	264 M
	William	137 M		James	299 M
	Wm	8 R		Jesse	221 M
	Wm	9 R		Jesse	233 M
	Wm	36 R		Jesse	235 M
Welsh	Mary	41 M		Jesse	237 M
Wetherald	Ann	344 R		Jesse	281 M
	Esther	329 R		Jesse	284 M
	Esther	344 R		John	237 M
	Joseph E.	344 R		Josiah	307 M
	Mary	328 R		Lydia	233 M
	Mary	344 R		Lydia	307 M
	Samuel B.	344 R		Mary	74 M
	Thomas	344 R		Mary	299 M
	Thomas, Jr.	344 R		Phebe	221 M
Wethereld	Anna	145 M		Phebe	281 M
	John	122 M		Phebe	284 M
	John	145 M		Phebe	297 M
	Mary	122 M		Rachel	227 M
Whinnery	Abigail	223 M		Rebecca	237 M
	Abigail	229 M		Richard	68 M
	Lydia	229 M		Richard	74 M
	Phebe	105 M		Sarah	112 M
	Phebe	223 M		Sarah	227 M

Name		Doc#	Name		Doc#
Wickersham	Sarah	264 M	Willis	Hannah	172 M
(continued)			(continued)		
	Sarah	281 M		Hannah	9 R
	Susanna	284 M		Hannah	17 R
	Thomas	281 M		Hannah	18 R
	William	74 M		Hannah	60 R
	William	227 M		Henery	26 M
Wierman	Eamey	14 M		Henry	38 M
	Emey	196 M		Joel	8 R
	Gartrude	14 M		Joel	9 R
	Gartrude	18 M		Joel	60 R
	Hannah	40 M		John	26 M
	Hannah	95 M		Jonathan	60 R
	Hannah	207 M		Lydia	60 R
	Henery	80 M		Phebe	26 M
	Henry	40 M		Robert	189 M
	Henry	135 M		Susanna	140 M
	Jane	207 M		Susanna	189 M
	Lydia	141 M		William	97 M
	Mary	80 M		William	140 M
	Nicholas	95 M		William	172 M
	Nicholas	129 M		Wm.	8 R
	Nicholas	141 M		Wm.	9 R
	Nicholas	207 M		Wm.	24 R
	Phebe	129 M		Wm.	25 R
	Priscilla	80 M		Wm.	35 R
	Prisilla	135 M		Wm.	36 R
	Prisily	40 M	Wilson	Alice	39 M
	Sarah	196 M		Benjamin	121 M
	Susanna	135 M		David	210 R
	William	14 M		George	39 M
	William	18 M		George	121 M
	William	95 M		John	127 M
	William	196 M		John	304 R
	William	207 M		Martha	127 M
Wilkeson	Elizabeth	49 M		Rebekah	127 M
	Joseph	49 M		Ruth	121 M
	Susanah	49 M		Sarah	121 M
Wilkinson	Elizabeth	64 M		William	127 M
	Joseph	64 M	Worley	Aaron	279 R
	Joseph	107 M		Ann	9 R
	Mary	107 M		Ann	272 R
Williams	Mary	242 R		Asey	279 R
	Mary	256 R		Caleb	279 R
Willis	Ann	38 M		Elizabeth	279 R
	Bettey	140 M		Jacob	8 R
	Betty	172 M		Jacob	9 R
	Hannah	97 M		Jacob	17 R

Name		Doc#	Name		Doc#
Worley (continued)	Jacob	18 R	Wright (continued)	John	93 M
	Jacob	24 R		John Juner	79 M
	Jacob	25 R		Jonathan	93 M
	Jacob	35 R		Jonathan	50 R
	Jacob	36 R		Mary	13 M
	Jacob	279 R		Mary A.	300 M
	Jacob	316 R		Nathan	300 M
	John	59 R		Nathan	302 M
	John	116 R		Rachel	34 M
	John	126 R		Rachel	301 M
	John	201 R		Rhoda	67 R
	John	279 R		Rhoda	110 R
	Lydia	279 R		Samuel	18 M
	Maryann	279 R		Sarah G.	301 M
Wright	Alice	71 M		Susanna	93 M
	Alice G.	302 M		Thomas	50 R
	Benjamin	73 M		Thomas	66 R
	Benjamin	182 R		William	301 M
	Elijah	300 M			
	Elizabeth	71 M	Yarnal	John	114 M
	Elizabeth	79 M		Rachel	114 M
	Elizabeth	93 M	Yarnall	Hannah	57 R
	Elizabeth	300 M		Isaac	57 R
	Elizabeth	302 M		Mordecai	57 R
	Elizabeth	67 R		Peter	8 R
	Elizabeth	110 R		Peter	19 R
	Gartrude	18 M		Peter	25 R
	Hiram	302 M		Peter	30 R
	Isaac J.	301 M		Peter	35 R
	James	67 R		Peter	45 R
	James	110 R		Peter	57 R
	Jane	73 M		Peter	85 R
	John	13 M		Peter, Jr.	57 R
	John	18 M		Rebeccah	57 R
	John	71 M	Yarnel	Hannah	9 R
	John	73 M		Peter	9 R
	John	79 M	Younger	Mary	52 M

www.ingramcontent.com/pod-product-compliance
Lightning Source LLC
Chambersburg PA
CBHW060552230426
43670CB00011B/1795